LINUX

NETWORK ADMINISTRATOR'S GUIDE

LINUX

NETWORK ADMINISTRATOR'S GUIDE

OLAF KIRCH

O'REILLY®

Beijing • Cambridge • Farnham • Köln • Paris • Sebastopol • Taipei • Tokyo

Linux Network Administrator's Guide
by Olaf Kirch

Editor: Andy Oram

Production Editor: Stephen Spainhour

Printing History:

January 1995:	First Edition
March 1995:	Minor corrections

For complete copyright information, refer to Appendix C, *Copyright and Licensing Information.*

ISBN: 1-56592-087-2

For Britta

TABLE OF CONTENTS

FIGURES

FOREWORD

You are about to embark upon a fantastic adventure into the world of Linux. Put simply, Linux brings back the excitement and fervor that personal computing once had, in its days of infancy, when self-avowed "hackers" would spend sleepless nights with oscilloscope and soldering iron to assemble a system from a home-brew kit. Perhaps the tools and the times have changed (instead of a soldering iron, you'll use a debugger), but the feeling has not. Hacking is alive and well, and Linux embodies that spirit in a complete UNIX clone for the personal computer.

Despite its origins, Linux is no longer just for the nocturnal programming aficionado. Thousands of people, with backgrounds ranging from GNU gaucho to computing cowpoke, are turning to Linux as the operating system solution for business, education, and—okay, okay—just plain fun.

How did Linux become so powerful and so popular, without having been developed by a team of well-paid (or not-so-well-paid) professional programmers? Is this something that the FBI should be looking into?

Cooperation. That's what it's all about. Linux is free—meant in the sense of both costlessness and liberty—and this freedom fosters positive interaction between programmers who have the shared dream of a complete, working UNIX clone. Ask any developer why they spend hour upon hour on the self-described time-sink known as Linux, and they'll give you the same answer: hack value, pure and simple.

What you may not know is that by merely running Linux, you are supporting the growth and development of free software, worldwide. Having free access to software, with the ability to modify and distribute it with no restrictions, is held by many to be a fundamental right of all computer users. (It's up there along with the rights of life, liberty, and the pursuit of more diskspace.) Software defines how computers are used, operating systems being an extreme example. When you choose a particular operating system, you are selecting the model by which your machine will run, in all respects, from the user interface to the lowest-level device drivers.

The greatest aspect of Linux is that it is developed and supported by and for its users. The computer software market doesn't define the direction in which Linux will go—the needs of its users do. This is a much more tangible goal than striving for profit or market share. Although this means that Linux may not appeal to everyone, the audience for which it is intended can directly influence its behavior. To put it in a nutshell, Linux is our pet operating system. What can possibly beat that?

Power to the people. Linux is here.

Matt Welsh
Coordinator, Linux Documentation Project
9 November 1994

PREFACE

With the Internet becoming a buzzword recently, and otherwise serious people joyriding along the Information Superhighway, computer networking seems to be moving toward the status of TV sets and microwave ovens. The Internet is getting unusually high media coverage, and social science majors are descending on Usenet newsgroups to conduct research on the new "Internet Culture."

Of course, networking has been around for a long time. Connecting computers to form local area networks has been common practice, even at small installations, and so have long-haul links using public telephone lines. A rapidly growing conglomerate of world-wide networks has, however, made joining the global village a viable option even for small non-profit organizations of private computer users. Setting up an Internet host with mail and news capabilities offering dialup access has become affordable, and the advent of ISDN (Integrated Services Digital Network) will doubtlessly accelerate this trend.

Talking about computer networks quite frequently means talking about UNIX. Of course, UNIX is neither the only operating system with network capabilities, nor will it remain a front runner forever, but it has been in the networking business for a long time and will surely continue to be for some time to come.

What makes UNIX particularly interesting to private users is that there has been much activity to bring free UNIXoid operating systems to the PC, such as 386BSD, FreeBSD—and Linux.

Linux is a freely-distributable UNIX clone for personal computers. It currently runs on Intel 386, 486, and Pentium machines, but it is being ported to other architectures such as the Motorola 680x0, DEC Alpha, and MIPS processors.

Linux has been developed by a large team of volunteers across the Internet. The project was started in 1990 by Linus Torvalds, a Finnish college student, as an operating systems course project. Since that time, Linux has snowballed into a full-featured UNIX clone capable of running applications as diverse as Emacs, the X

Window System, TeX, and a horde of other software. A great deal of hardware is supported, and Linux contains a complete implementation of TCP/IP networking, including SLIP and PPP. Linux is powerful, fast, and free, and its popularity in the world beyond the Internet is growing rapidly.

The Linux operating system itself is covered by the GNU General Public License, the same copyright license used by software developed by the Free Software Foundation. This license allows anyone to redistribute or modify the software (free of charge or for a profit) as long as all modifications and distributions are freely distributable as well. The term "free software" refers to freedom, not just cost.

Linux can coexist with other operating systems on your machine, such as MS-DOS, OS/2, and so forth. Linux can use its own drive partitions, and therefore not interfere with other operating systems in any way. You can install a Linux boot manager to select which operating system to load when the system is booted.

Sources of Information

If you are new to the world of Linux, there are a number of resources that you should look into. Having access to the Internet is helpful, but not required.

Linux Documentation Project Manuals

The Linux Documentation Project is a group of volunteers producing a set of manuals and papers about Linux, on topics from installation to kernel programming. These manuals include:

Linux Installation and Getting Started
by Matt Welsh. This book describes how to obtain, install, and use the Linux software. It includes an introductory UNIX tutorial and information on systems administration, the X Window System, and networking, as well.

Linux Kernel Hacker's Guide
by Michael K. Johnson. This book is a guide to the internals of the Linux system, intended for UNIX systems programmers who wish to add features to the Linux kernel itself.

Other manuals, such as a User's Guide, a Programmer's Guide, and a System Administrator's Guide, are currently under development. For more information on the LDP, contact Matt Welsh, at *mdw@sunsite.unc.edu*.

INFO-SHEET and META-FAQ
These are two introductory documents about the Linux system. The *INFO-SHEET* is a technical overview of the Linux system, detailing features and available software. The *META-FAQ* is an extensive list of pointers to more information about Linux—your roadmap to the wide array of Linux documentation.

HOWTO Documents

The Linux HOWTOs are a series of papers (each averaging about a dozen pages) on various aspects of the system—such as installation and configuration of the X Window System software, or using the *term* communications package. These are generally located in the *HOWTO* subdirectory of the FTP sites listed below. See the Bibliography at the end of this book, or the file *HOWTO-INDEX* for a list of what's available.

You might want to obtain the *Installation HOWTO*, which describes how to install Linux on your system; the *Hardware Compatibility HOWTO*, which contains a list of hardware known to work with Linux; and the *Distribution HOWTO*, which lists software vendors who sell Linux on diskette and CD-ROM.

Linux Frequently Asked Questions
The *Linux Frequently Asked Questions* (FAQ) list contains a wide assortment of questions and answers about the system. It is a must-read for all newcomers.

Linux Software Map

This is a list of software and applications which are available for Linux. Although it is far from complete (literally thousands of programs can be, or have been, ported to the system), many larger applications are included in the Linux Software Map.

Linux Documentation Available via FTP

If you have access to anonymous FTP, you can obtain all Linux documentation listed above from various sites, including

```
sunsite.unc.edu:/pub/Linux/docs
```

and

```
tsx-11.mit.edu:/pub/linux/docs
```

These sites are mirrored by a number of sites all around the world.

Documentation Available via WWW

There are many Linux-based WWW sites available. The Home Site for the Linux Documentation Project can be accessed via the URL

```
http://sunsite.unc.edu/mdw/linux.html
```

It contains hypertext versions of many Linux HOWTOs and other documents, as well as pointers to other Linux WWW archives.

Documentation Available Commercially

A number of publishing companies and software vendors provide Linux software and documentation via mail order. Two such vendors are SSC, Inc. (P.O. Box 55549, Seattle, WA 98155, 206-FOR-UNIX, *sales@ssc.com*) and Linux Systems Labs (18300 Tara Drive, Clinton Twp., MI 48036, 313-954-2829, 800-432-0556, *info@lsl.com*). Both companies sell *Linux Installation and Getting Started* and the Linux HOWTO documents in printed and bound form.

O'Reilly & Associates is publishing a series of Linux books, including the *Linux Network Administrator's Guide*, from the Linux Documentation Project. Also included in the series is *Running Linux*, an installation and user guide to the system, describing how to get the most out of personal computing with Linux.

Linux Usenet Newsgroups

If you have access to Usenet news, the following Linux-related newsgroups are available:

comp.os.linux.announce
> This is a moderated newsgroup containing announcements of new software, distributions, bug reports, and goings-on in the Linux community. All Linux users should read this group. Submissions may be mailed to *linux-announce@tc.cornell.edu*.

comp.os.linux.help
> General questions and answers about installing or using Linux.

comp.os.linux.admin
> Discussions relating to systems administration under Linux.

comp.os.linux.development
> Discussions about developing the Linux kernel and system itself.

comp.os.linux.misc
> A catch-all newsgroup for miscellaneous discussions that don't fall under the above categories.

There are also several newsgroups devoted to Linux in languages other than English, such as *fr.comp.os.linux* in France and *de.comp.os.linux* in Germany.

Linux Journal

Linux Journal is a monthly magazine for the Linux community, written and published by a number of Linux activists. It contains articles ranging from novice questions-and-answers to kernel programming internals. Even if you have Usenet access, this magazine is a good way to stay in touch with the Linux community.

Linux Journal is published by SSC, Inc. (P.O. Box 55549, Seattle, WA 98155, 206-FOR-UNIX, *sales@ssc.com*).

Obtaining Linux

There is no single distribution of the Linux software; instead, there are many such distributions, such as Slackware, Debian, Yggdrasil, and so forth. Each distribution contains everything that you need to run a complete Linux system: the kernel, basic utilities, libraries, support files, and applications software.

Linux distributions may be obtained for free via a number of online sources, such as the Internet, bulletin board systems, or online services such as CompuServe and Prodigy. On the Internet, Linux may be downloaded from various FTP archive sites; the most popular are:

```
sunsite.unc.edu:/pub/Linux
tsx-11.mit.edu:/pub/linux
nic.funet.fi:/pub/OS/Linux
```

The above sources of Linux information contain details on how to obtain Linux from other places.

Linux may also be purchased on diskette, tape, or CD-ROM from a number of software vendors. The Linux *Distribution HOWTO* contains a near-complete list. Both SSC, Inc. and Linux Systems Labs, listed above, sell Linux on CD-ROM.

File System Standards

Throughout the past, one of the problems that afflicted Linux distributions as well as separate packages was that there was no single accepted file system layout. This resulted in incompatibilities between different packages, and confronted users and administrators alike with the task to locate various files and programs.

To improve this situation, in August 1993, several people formed the Linux File System Standard Group, or FSSTND Group for short, coordinated by Daniel Quinlan. After six months of discussion, the group presented a draft that presents a coherent file sytem structure and defines the location of most essential programs and configuration files.

This standard is supposed to be implemented by most major Linux distributions and packages. Throughout this book, we will therefore assume that any files discussed reside in the location specified by the standard; only where there is a long tradition that conflicts with this specification will alternative locations be mentioned.

The Linux File System Standard can be obtained from all major Linux FTP sites and their mirrors; for instance, you can find it on **sunsite.unc.edu** below

/pub/linux/docs. Daniel Quinlan, the coordinator of the FSSTND group can be reached at *quinlan@netcom.com*.

About This Book

When I joined the Linux Documentation Project in 1992, I wrote two small chapters on UUCP and *smail*, which I meant to contribute to the System Administrator's Guide. Development of TCP/IP networking was just beginning, and when those "small chapters" started to grow, I wondered aloud if it wouldn't be nice to have a Networking Guide. "Great," everyone said, "Go for it!" So I went for it and wrote the first version of the Networking Guide, which I released in September 1993.

The new Networking Guide, which you are reading right now, is a complete rewrite that features several new applications that have become available to Linux users since the first release.

The book is organized roughly in the sequence of steps you have to take to configure your system for networking. It starts by discussing basic concepts of networks, and TCP/IP-based networks in particular. We then slowly work our way up from configuring TCP/IP at the device level to the setup of common applications such as *rlogin* and friends, the Network File System, and the Network Information System. This is followed by a chapter on how to set up your machine as a UUCP node. The remainder of the book is dedicated to two major applications that run on top of both TCP/IP and UUCP: electronic mail and news.

The email part features an introduction to the more intimate parts of mail transport and routing, and the myriad of addressing schemes you may be confronted with. It describes the configuration and management of *smail*, a mail transport agent commonly used on smaller mail hubs, and *sendmail*, which is for people who have to do more complicated routing or have to handle a large volume of mail. The *sendmail* chapter has been written and contributed by Vince Skahan.

The news part gives you an overview of how Usenet news works. It covers C News, the most widely used news transport software at the moment, and the use of NNTP to provide newsreading access to a local network. The book closes with a chapter on the care and feeding of the most popular newsreaders on Linux.

Of course, a book can never exhaustively answer all questions you might have. So if you follow the instructions in this book, and something still does not work, please be patient. Some of your problems may be due to stupid mistakes on my part, but also may be caused by changes in the networking software. Therefore, you should check the listed information resources first. There's a good chance that you are not alone with your problems, so a fix or at least a proposed workaround is likely to be known. If you have the opportunity, you should also try to get the latest kernel and network release from one of the Linux FTP sites or a BBS near you. Many problems are caused by software from different stages of development, which fail to work together properly. After all, Linux is a "work in progress."

Another good place to inform yourself about current development is the Networking HOWTO. It is maintained by Terry Dawson[*] and contains the most up-to-date information. The current version can be obtained from the FTP sites listed above. For problems you can't solve in any other way, you may also contact the author of this book. However, please, refrain from asking developers for help. They are already devoting a major part of their spare time to Linux anyway, and occasionally even have a life beyond the net. :-)

The Official Printed Version

In autumn 1993, Andy Oram, who has been around the LDP mailing list from almost the very beginning, asked me about publishing my book at O'Reilly & Associates. I was excited about this; I had never imagined my book being that successful. We finally agreed that O'Reilly would produce an enhanced Official Printed Version of the Networking Guide with me, while I retained the original copyright so that the source of the book could be freely distributed. This means that you can choose freely: you can get the LaTeX source distributed on the network (or the preformatted DVI or PostScript versions, for that matter) and print it out, or you can purchase the official printed version from O'Reilly.

Why, then, would you want to pay money for something you can get for free? Is Tim O'Reilly out of his mind for publishing something everyone can print and even sell herself?[†] Or is there any difference between these versions?

The answers are "it depends," "no, definitely not," and "yes and no." O'Reilly & Associates do take a risk in publishing the Networking Guide, but I hope it will pay off for them. If it does, I believe this project can serve as an example of how the free software world and companies can cooperate to produce something both benefit from. In my view, the great service O'Reilly is doing to the Linux community (apart from the book becoming readily available in your local bookstore) is that it may help Linux be recognized as something to be taken seriously: a viable and useful alternative to commercial PC UNIX operating systems.

Why are they publishing it? The reason is that they see it as their kind of book. It's what they'd hope to produce if they contracted with an author to write about Linux. The pace, the level of detail, and the style fit in well with their other offerings.

The point of the LDP license is to make sure no one gets shut out. Other people can print out copies of this book, and no one will blame you if you get one of these copies. But if you haven't gotten a chance to see the O'Reilly version, try to get to a bookstore or look at a friend's copy. We think you'll like what you see, and will want to buy it for your own.

---

* Terry Dawson can be reached at *terryd@extro.ucc.su.oz.au.*
† Note that while you are allowed to print out the online version, you may *not* run the O'Reilly book through a photocopier, much less sell any of those (hypothetical) copies.

So what about the differences between the printed version and the online one? Andy Oram has made great efforts at transforming my early ramblings into something actually worth printing. (He has also been reviewing the other books put out by the Linux Documentation Project, contributing whatever professional skills he can to the Linux community.)

Since Andy started reviewing the Networking Guide and editing the copies I sent him, the book has improved vastly over what it was half a year ago. It would be nowhere close to where it is now without his contributions. The same is true of Stephen Spainhour, who has copyedited the book to get it into the shape you see now. All these edits have been fed back into the online version, so there is no difference in content.

Still, the O'Reilly version *is* different. The people at O'Reilly have put a lot of work into the look and feel, producing a much more pleasant layout than you could ever get out of standard LaTeX. In addition, Chris Reilley has nicely redone all the figures from the original network version and produced a couple of extra figures. He has done a great job at actually visualizing what I originally meant my amateurish XFIG drawings to convey. Chris Tong and Susan Reisler have also created a much improved index.

All his edits have been fed back into online version, as will any changes that will be made to the Networking Guide during the copy-editing phase at O'Reilly. So there will be no difference in content. Still, the O'Reilly version *will* be different: On one hand, people at O'Reilly are putting a lot of work into the look and feel, producing a much more pleasant layout than you could ever get out of standard LaTeX. On the other hand, it will feature a couple of enhancements like an improved index, and better and more figures.

Overview

Chapter 1, *Introduction to Networking*, discusses the history of Linux and covers basic networking information on UUCP, TCP/IP, various protocols, hardware, and security. The next few chapters deal with configuring Linux for TCP/IP networking and running some major applications. We examine IP a little closer in Chapter 2, *Issues of TCP/IP Networking*, before getting our hands dirty with file editing and the like. If you already know about the way IP routing works and how address resolution is performed, you might want to skip this chapter.

Chapter 3, *Configuring the Networking Hardware*, deals with very basic configuration issues, such as building a kernel and setting up your Ethernet board. The configuration of your serial ports is covered separately in Chapter 4, *Setting Up the Serial Hardware*, because the discussion does not apply to TCP/IP networking only, but is also relevant for UUCP.

Chapter 5, *Configuring TCP/IP Networking*, helps you to set up your machine for TCP/IP networking. It contains installation hints for standalone hosts with loopback enabled only, and hosts connected to an Ethernet. It also introduces you to a few useful tools you can use to test and debug your setup. Chapter 6, *Name Service and Resolver Configuration*, discusses how to configure hostname resolution and explains how to set up a name server.

Chapter 7, *Serial Line IP*, explains how to establish SLIP connections and gives a detailed reference for *dip*, a tool that allows you to automate most of the necessary steps. Chapter 8, *The Point-to-Point Protocol*, covers PPP and *pppd*, the PPP daemon.

Chapter 9, *Important Network Features*, gives a short introduction to setting up some of the most important network applications, such as *rlogin, rcp*, etc. This chapter also covers how services are managed by the *inetd* superuser, and how you may restrict certain security-relevant services to a set of trusted hosts.

Chapter 10, *The Network Information System*, and Chapter 11, *The Network File System*, discuss NIS and NFS. NIS is a useful tool to distribute administative information such as user passwords in a local area network. NFS allows you to share file systems between several hosts in your network.

Chapter 12, *Managing Taylor UUCP*, gives you an extensive introduction to the administration of Taylor UUCP, a free implementation of the UUCP suite.

The remainder of the book is taken up by a detailed tour of electronic mail and Usenet news. Chapter 13, *Electronic Mail*, introduces you to the central concepts of electronic mail, like what a mail address looks like, and how the mail handling system manages to get your message to the recipient.

Chapter 14, *Getting smail Up and Running*, and Chapter 15, *Sendmail+IDA*, cover the setup of *smail* and *sendmail*, two mail transport agents you can use for Linux. This book explains both of them, because *smail* is easier to install for the beginner, while *sendmail* is more flexible.

Chapter 16, *Netnews*, and Chapter 17, *C News*, explain the way news is managed in Usenet, and how you install and use C News, a popular software package for managing Usenet news. Chapter 18, *A Description of NNTP*, briefly covers how to set up an NNTP daemon to provide news reading access for your local network. And finally, Chapter 19, *Newsreader Configuration*, shows you how to configure and maintain various newsreaders.

Conventions Used in This Book

The following is a list of the typographical conventions used in this book.

Bold	is used for machine names, hostnames, or site names, for user names and IDs, and for occasional emphasis.
Italic	is used for file and directory names, program and command names, command-line options, email addressesand path names, and to emphasize new terms.

Constant Width	is used in examples to show the contents of files or the output from commands, and to indicate environment variables and keywords from code.
Constant Italic	is used to indicate variable options or keywords that the user is to replace with the actual value.
Constant Bold	is used in examples to show commands or other text that should be typed literally by the user.

There are also several icons located in the left margin throughout the text.

This icon indicates material that is specific to installing or operating Linux, as opposed to other UNIX systems. The bird is the storm petrel, which has become a kind of mascot for the Linux project.

This icon is for Caution: you can make a mistake here that hurts your system or is hard to recover from.

Cite

This icon indicates a reference to another part of this book or to another source of information. The cite string underneath the book may be either a key for a book, HOWTO article, or RFC cited in the Bibliography at the end of the book; a pointer to another chapter or appendix in this book; or a referral to a particular program's manual page.

Acknowledgments

The biggest thanks in this effort go to Vince Skahan, who wrote Chapter 15 on *sendmail.* Vince has been administering large numbers of UNIX systems since 1987 and currently runs IDA *sendmail* on approximately 300 UNIX workstations for over 2000 users. He admits to losing considerable sleep from editing quite a few *sendmail.cf* files "the hard way" before discovering IDA *sendmail* in 1990. He also admits to anxiously awaiting the delivery of the first *perl*-based version of *sendmail* for even more obscure fun...[*] Vince can be reached at *vince@victrola.wa.com*

This book owes very much to the numerous people who took the time to proofread it and help iron out many mistakes, both technical and grammatical (never knew that there was such a thing as a dangling participle). The most vigorous among them was Andy Oram at O'Reilly & Associates.

I also owe many thanks to the people at O'Reilly I've had the pleasure to work with: Stephen Spainhour, who copyedited and formatted the book to get it into the shape you can see now; Chris Reilley, who has done all the figures; Edie Freeman and Jennifer Niederst, who designed the cover, the internal layout, and the use of old woodcuts as a visual theme (an idea suggested by Lar Kaufman); Susan Reisler

---

[*] Don't you think we could do it with *sed*, Vince?

and Chris Tong for greatly expanding the index and making it more professional; Barbara Yoder for arranging an interview with me to go in the O'Reilly catalog; and finally, Tim O'Reilly for the courage of taking up such a project.

I am greatly indebted to Andres Sepúlveda, Wolfgang Michaelis, Michael K. Johnson, and all developers who spared the time to check the information provided in the Networking Guide. I also wish to thank all those who read the first version of the Networking Guide and sent me corrections and suggestions. You can find a hopefully complete list of contributors in the file *Thanks* in the online distribution. Finally, this book would not have been possible without the support of Holger Grothe, who provided me with the critical Internet connectivity.

I would also like to thank the following groups and companies who printed the first edition of the Networking Guide and have donated money either to me, or to the Linux Documentation Project as a whole: Linux Support Team, Erlangen, Germany; S.u.S.E. GmbH, Fuerth, Germany; and Linux System Labs, Inc., Clinton Twp., United States.

Vince says: Thanks to Neil Rickert and Paul Pomes for lots of help over the years regarding the care and feeding of Sendmail+IDA, and to Rich Braun for doing the initial port of Sendmail+IDA to Linux. The biggest thanks by far go to my wife Susan for all her support on this and other projects.

The Hall of Fame

A large number of people have contributed to the Networking Guide, besides those I have already mentioned, by reviewing it and sending me corrections and suggestions. I am very grateful to them.

Here is a list of those whose contributions left a trace in my mail folders. I apologize to all those whom I can't acknowledge because I simply failed to save their mail.

Al Longyear, Alan Cox, Andres Sepulveda, Ben Cooper, Cameron Spitzer, D.J. Roberts, Emilio Lopes, Fred N. van Kempen, Gert Doering, Greg Hankins, Heiko Eissfeldt, J.P. Szikora, Johannes Stille, Karl Eichwalder, Les Johnson, Ludger Kunz, Marc van Diest, Michael K. Johnson, Michael Nebel, Michael Wing, Mitch D'Souza, Paul Gortmaker, Peter Brouwer, Peter Eriksson, Phil Hughes, Raul Deluth Miller, Rich Braun, Rick Sladkey, Ronald Aarts, Swen Thüemmler, Terry Dawson, Thomas Quinot, Yury Shevchuk.

CHAPTER ONE
INTRODUCTION TO NETWORKING

History

The idea of networking is probably as old as telecommunications itself. Consider people living in the Stone Age, where drums may have been used to transmit messages between individuals. Suppose caveman A wants to invite caveman B over for a game of hurling rocks at each other, but they live too far apart for B to hear A banging his drum. What are A's options? He could 1) walk over to B's place, 2) get a bigger drum, or 3) ask C, who lives halfway between them, to forward the message. The last is called networking.

Of course, we have come a long way from the primitive pursuits and devices of our forebears. Nowadays, we have computers talk to each other over vast assemblages of wires, fiber optics, microwaves, and the like, to make an appointment for Saturday's soccer match.[*] In the following description, we will deal with the means and ways by which this is accomplished, but leave out the wires, as well as the soccer part.

We will describe two types of networks in this guide: those based on UUCP and those based on TCP/IP. These are protocol suites and software packages that supply means to transport data between two computers. In this chapter, we will look at both types of networks and discuss their underlying principles.

We define a network as a collection of *hosts* that are able to communicate with each other, often by relying on the services of a number of dedicated hosts that relay data between the participants. Hosts are very often computers, but need not be; one can also think of X-terminals or intelligent printers as hosts. Small agglomerations of hosts are also called *sites*.

---

* The original spirit of which (see above) still shows on some occasions in Europe.

1

Communication is impossible without some sort of language or code. In computer networks, these languages are collectively referred to as *protocols*. However, you shouldn't think of written protocols here, but rather of the highly formalized code of behavior observed when heads of state meet, for instance. In a very similar fashion, the protocols used in computer networks are nothing but very strict rules for the exchange of messages between two or more hosts.

UUCP Networks

UUCP is an abbreviation for UNIX-to-UNIX Copy. It started out as a package of programs to transfer files over serial lines, schedule those transfers, and initiate execution of programs on remote sites. It has undergone major changes since its first implementation in the late seventies, but it is still rather spartan in the services it offers. Its main application is still in wide-area networks based on dialup telephone links.

UUCP was first developed by Bell Laboratories in 1977 for communication between their UNIX development sites. In mid-1978, this network already connected over 80 sites. It was running email as an application, as well as remote printing. However, the system's central use was in distributing new software and bugfixes. Today, UUCP is not confined solely to the UNIX environment. There are both free and commercial ports available for a variety of platforms, including AmigaOS, DOS, Atari's TOS, etc.

One of the main disadvantages of UUCP networks is their low bandwidth. On one hand, telephone equipment places a tight limit on the maximum transfer rate. On the other hand, UUCP links are rarely permanent connections; instead, hosts dial up each other at regular intervals. Hence, most of the time it takes a mail message to travel a UUCP network, it sits idly on some host's disk awaiting the next time a connection is established.

Despite these limitations, there are still many UUCP networks operating all over the world, run mainly by hobbyists, which offer private users network access at reasonable prices. The main reason for the popularity of UUCP is that it is dirt cheap compared to having your computer connected to The Big Internet Cable. To make your computer a UUCP node, all you need is a modem, a working UUCP implementation, and another UUCP node that is willing to feed you mail and news.

How to Use UUCP

The idea behind UUCP is rather simple: as its name indicates, it basically copies files from one host to another, but it also allows certain actions to be performed on the remote host.

Suppose your machine is allowed to access a hypothetical host named **swim** and have it execute the *lpr* print command for you. Then you could type the following command to have this book printed on **swim**:[*]

```
$ uux -r swim!lpr !netguide.dvi
```

This makes *uux*, a command from the UUCP suite, schedule a *job* for **swim**. This job consists of the input file *netguide.dvi* and the request to feed this file to *lpr*. The *−r* flag tells *uux* not to call the remote system immediately, but to store the job away until a connection is established. This is called *spooling*.

UUCP also allows you to forward jobs and files through several hosts, provided they cooperate. Assume that **swim** has a UUCP link with **groucho**, which maintains a large archive of UNIX applications. To download the file *tripwire-1.0.tar.gz* to your site, you issue the command:

```
$ uucp -mr swim!groucho!~/security/tripwire-1.0.tar.gz trip.tgz
```

The job created will request **swim** to fetch the file from **groucho** and send it to your site, where UUCP will store it in *trip.tgz* and notify you via mail of the file's arrival. This will be done in three steps. First, your site sends the job to **swim**. When **swim** establishes contact with **groucho** the next time, it downloads the file. The final step is the actual transfer from **swim** to your host.

The most important services provided by UUCP networks these days are electronic mail and news.

Electronic mail—email for short—allows you to exchange messages with users on remote hosts without actually having to know how to access these hosts. The task of directing a message from your site to the destination site is performed entirely by the mail handling system. In a UUCP environment, mail is usually transported by executing the *rmail* command on a neighboring host, passing it the recipient address and the mail message. *rmail* will then forward the message to another host, and so on, until it reaches the destination host. We will look at this in detail in Chapter 13, *Electronic Mail*.

News can be described as a type of distributed bulletin board system. Most often, this term refers to Usenet news, which is by far the most widely known news exchange network, with an estimated number of 120,000 participating sites. The origins of Usenet date back to 1979, when, after the release of UUCP with the new UNIX V7, three graduate students had the idea of a general information exchange within the UNIX community. They put together some scripts, which became the first Netnews system. In 1980, this network connected three sites: **duke**, **unc**, and **phs**, at two universities in North Carolina. Out of this, Usenet eventually grew. Although it originated as a UUCP-based network, it is no longer confined to one single type of network.

---

[*] When using *bash*, the GNU Bourne Again Shell, you have to escape the exclamation mark, because it is a history character.

The basic unit of information is the article, which can be posted to a hierarchy of newsgroups dedicated to specific topics. Most sites receive only a selection of all newsgroups, which carry an average of 60MB worth of articles a day.

In the UUCP world, news is generally sent across a UUCP link by collecting all articles from the groups requested and packing them up in a number of *batches*. These are sent to the receiving site, where they are fed to the *rnews* command for unpacking and further processing.

Finally, UUCP is also the medium of choice for many dialup archive sites that offer public access. You can usually access them by dialing them up with UUCP and logging in as a guest user. Then, you can download files from a publicly accessible archive area. These guest accounts often have a login name and password of **uucp/nuucp** or something similar.

TCP/IP Networks

Although UUCP may be a reasonable choice for low-cost dialup network links, there are many situations in which its store-and-forward technique proves too inflexible, for example, in Local Area Networks (LANs). These are usually made up of a small number of machines located in the same building, or even on the same floor, that are interconnected to provide a homogeneous working environment. Typically, you would want to share files between these hosts or run distributed applications on different machines.

These tasks require a completely different approach to networking. Instead of forwarding entire files along with a job description, all data is broken up in smaller chunks (packets), which are forwarded immediately to the destination host, where they are reassembled. This type of network is called a *packet-switched* network. Among other things, this allows you to run interactive applications over the network. The cost of this is, of course, a greatly increased complexity in software.

The solution that UNIX systems—and many non-UNIX sites—have adopted is known as TCP/IP. In this section, we will have a look at its underlying concepts.

Introduction to TCP/IP Networks

TCP/IP traces its origins to a research project funded by the United States Defense Advanced Research Projects Agency (DARPA) in 1969. The ARPANET was an experimental network that was converted into an operational one in 1975 after it had proven to be a success.

In 1983, the new protocol suite TCP/IP was adopted as a standard, and all hosts on the network were required to use it. When ARPANET finally grew into the Internet (with ARPANET itself passing out of existence in 1990), the use of TCP/IP had spread to networks beyond the Internet itself. Most notable are UNIX local area networks, but in the advent of fast digital telephone equipment such as ISDN, it also has a promising future as a transport for dialup networks.

For something concrete to look at as we discuss TCP/IP throughout the following sections, we will consider Groucho Marx University (GMU), situated somewhere in Fredland, as an example. Most departments run their own local area networks, while some share one and others run several of them. They are all interconnected and are hooked to the Internet through a single high-speed link.

Suppose your Linux box is connected to a LAN of UNIX hosts at the Mathematics department, and its name is **erdos**. To access a host at the Physics department, say **quark**, you enter the following command:

```
$ rlogin quark.physics
Welcome to the Physics Department at GMU
(ttyq2) login:
```

At the prompt, you enter your login name, say **andres**, and your password. You are then given a shell on **quark**, to which you can type as if you were sitting at the system's console. After you exit the shell, you are returned to your own machine's prompt. You have just used one of the instantaneous, interactive applications that TCP/IP provides: remote login.

While being logged into **quark**, you might also want to run an X11-based application, like a function plotting program or a PostScript previewer. To tell this application that you want to have its windows displayed on your host's screen, you have to set the DISPLAY environment variable:

```
$ export DISPLAY=erdos.maths:0.0
```

If you now start your application, it will contact your X server instead of **quark**'s, and display all its windows on your screen. Of course, this requires that you have X11 runnning on **erdos**. The point here is that TCP/IP allows **quark** and **erdos** to send X11 packets back and forth to give you the illusion that you're on a single system. The network is almost transparent here.

Another very important application in TCP/IP networks is NFS, which stands for *Network File System*. It is another form of making the network transparent, because it basically allows you to mount directory hierarchies from other hosts so that they appear as local file systems. For example, all users' home directories can be kept on a central server machine from which all other hosts on the LAN mount the directory. The effect is that users can log into any machine and find themselves in the same home directory. Similarly, it is possible to install applications that require large amounts of disk space (such as TeX) on only one machine and export these directories to other machines. We will come back to NFS in Chapter 11, *The Network File System*.

Of course, these are only examples of what you can do over TCP/IP networks. The possibilities are almost limitless.

We will now have a closer look at the way TCP/IP works. This information will help you understand how and why you have to configure your machine. We will start by examining the hardware, and slowly work our way up.

Ethernets

The type of hardware most widely used throughout LANs is what is commonly known as *Ethernet*. It consists of a single cable with hosts attached to it through connectors, taps, or transceivers. Simple Ethernets are quite inexpensive to install, which together with a net transfer rate of 10 Megabits per second, accounts for much of its popularity.

Ethernets come in three flavors, *thick*, *thin*, and *twisted pair*. Thin and thick Ethernet each use a coaxial cable, differing in width and the way you may attach a host to this cable. Thin Ethernet uses a T-shaped "BNC" connector, which you insert into the cable and twist onto a plug on the back of your computer. Thick Ethernet requires that you drill a small hole into the cable, and attach a transceiver using a "vampire tap." One or more hosts can then be connected to the transceiver. Thin and thick Ethernet cable can run for a maximum of 200 and 500 meters, respectively, and are therefore also called 10base-2 and 10base-5. Twisted pair uses a cable made of two copper wires and usually requires additional hardware known as *active hubs*. Twisted pair is also known as 10base-T.

Although adding a host to a thick Ethernet is a little hairy, it does not bring down the network. To add a host to a thin net installation, you have to disrupt network service for at least a few minutes because you have to cut the cable to insert the connector.

Most people prefer thin Ethernet because it is very inexpensive; PC cards come for as little as US $50, and cable is in the range of a few cents per meter. However, for large-scale installations, thick Ethernet is more appropriate. For example, the Ethernet at GMU's Mathematics department uses thick Ethernet, so traffic will not be disrupted each time a host is added to the network.

One of the drawbacks of Ethernet technology is its limited cable length, which precludes any use of it other than for LANs. However, several Ethernet segments can be linked to each other using repeaters, bridges, or routers. Repeaters simply copy the signals between two or more segments so that all segments together will act as if it was one Ethernet. Due to timing requirements, there may not be more than four repeaters between any two hosts on the network. Bridges and routers are more sophisticated. They analyze incoming data and forward it only when the recipient host is not on the local Ethernet.

Ethernet works like a bus system, where a host may send packets (or *frames*) of up to 1500 bytes to another host on the same Ethernet. A host is addressed by a six-byte address hardcoded into the firmware of its Ethernet board. These addresses are usually written as a sequence of two-digit hex numbers separated by colons, as in **aa:bb:cc:dd:ee:ff**.

A frame sent by one station is seen by all attached stations, but only the destination host actually picks it up and processes it. If two stations try to send at the same time, a *collision* occurs, which is resolved by the two stations aborting the send, and reattempting it a few moments later.

Other Types of Hardware

In larger installations such as Groucho Marx University, Ethernet is usually not the only type of equipment used. At Groucho Marx University, each department's LAN is linked to the campus backbone, which is a fiber optics cable running FDDI (*Fiber Distributed Data Interface*). FDDI uses an entirely different approach to transmitting data, which basically involves sending around a number of *tokens*, with a station only being allowed to send a frame if it captures a token. The main advantage of FDDI is a speed of up to 100 Mbps, and a maximum cable length of up to 200 km.

For long-distance network links, a different type of equipment is frequently used, which is based on a standard named X.25. Many so-called Public Data Networks, like Tymnet in the U.S. or Datex-P in Germany, offer this service. X.25 requires special hardware, namely a Packet Assembler/Disassembler or *PAD*. X.25 defines a set of networking protocols of its own right, but is nevertheless frequently used to connect networks running TCP/IP and other protocols. Since IP packets cannot simply be mapped onto X.25 (and vice versa), they are simply encapsulated in X.25 packets and sent over the network.

Frequently, radio amateurs use their equipment to network their computers; this is called *packet radio* or *ham radio*. The protocol used by ham radios is called AX.25, which is derived from X.25.

Other techniques involve using slow but cheap serial lines for dialup access. These require yet another protocol for transmission of packets, such as SLIP or PPP, which will be described later.

The Internet Protocol

Of course, you wouldn't want your networking to be limited to one Ethernet. Ideally, you would want to be able to use a network regardless of what hardware it runs on and how many subunits it comprises. For example, in larger installations such as Groucho Marx University, you usually have a number of separate Ethernets that have to be connected in some way. At GMU, the Math department runs two Ethernets: one network of fast machines for professors and graduates, and another one with slow machines for students. Both are linked to the FDDI campus backbone.

This connection is handled by a dedicated host, a so-called *gateway*, which handles incoming and outgoing packets by copying them between the two Ethernets and the fiber optics cable. For example, if you are at the Math department and want to access **quark** on the Physics department's LAN from your Linux box, the networking software cannot send packets to **quark** directly because it is not on the same Ethernet. Therefore, it has to rely on the gateway to act as a forwarder. The gateway (name it **sophus**) then forwards these packets to its peer gateway **niels** at the Physics epartment, using the backbone, with **niels** delivering it to the destination machine. Data flow between **erdos** and **quark** is shown in Figure 1-1.

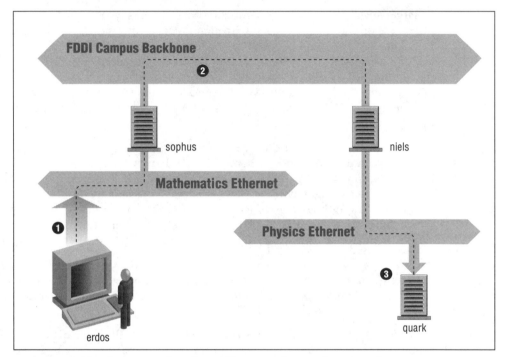

Figure 1–1. The three steps of sending a datagram from erdos to quark

This scheme of directing data to a remote host is called *routing*, and packets are often referred to as *datagrams* in this context. To facilitate things, datagram exchange is governed by a single protocol that is independent of the hardware used: IP, or *Internet Protocol*. In Chapter 2, *Issues of TCP/IP Networking*, we will cover IP and the issues of routing in greater detail.

The main benefit of IP is that it turns physically dissimilar networks into one apparently homogeneous network. This is called internetworking, and the resulting "meta-network" is called an *internet*. Note the subtle difference between *an* internet and *the* Internet here. The latter is the official name of one particular global internet.

Of course, IP also requires a hardware-independent addressing scheme. This is achieved by assigning each host a unique 32-bit number called the *IP address*. An IP address is usually written as four decimal numbers, one for each 8-bit portion, separated by dots. For example, **quark** might have an IP address of **0x954C0C04**, which would be written as **149.76.12.4**. This format is also called *dotted quad notation*.

You will notice that we now have three different types of addresses: first there is the host's name, like **quark**, then there are IP addresses, and finally, there are hardware addresses, like the 6-byte Ethernet address. All these somehow have to match so that when you type *rlogin quark*, the networking software can be given **quark**'s IP address; and when IP delivers any data to the Physics department's Ethernet, it somehow has to find out what Ethernet address corresponds to the IP address.

We will deal with these situations in Chapter 2. For now, it's enough to remember that these steps of finding addresses are called *hostname resolution*, for mapping hostnames onto IP addresses, and *address resolution*, for mapping the latter to hardware addresses.

IP Over Serial Lines

RFC 1055
RFC 1144

On serial lines, a "de facto" standard known as SLIP, or *Serial Line IP*, is frequently used. A modification of SLIP is known as CSLIP, or *Compressed SLIP*, and performs compression of IP headers to make better use of the relatively low bandwidth provided by serial links. A different serial protocol is PPP, or *Point-to-Point Protocol*. PPP has many more features than SLIP, including a link negotiation phase. Its main advantage over SLIP is that it isn't limited to transporting IP datagrams, but is designed to allow for any type of datagrams to be transmitted.

The Transmission Control Protocol

Sending datagrams from one host to another is not the whole story. If you log into **quark**, you want to have a reliable connection between your *rlogin* process on **erdos** and the shell process on **quark**. Thus, the information sent to and fro must be split up into packets by the sender and reassembled into a character stream by the receiver. Trivial as it seems, this involves a number of hairy tasks.

A very important thing to know about IP is that, by intent, it is not reliable. Assume that ten people on your Ethernet started downloading the latest release of XFree86 from GMU's FTP server. The amount of traffic generated might be too much for the gateway to handle, because it's too slow and it's tight on memory. Now if you happen to send a packet to **quark**, **sophus** might just be out of buffer space for a moment and therefore unable to forward it. IP solves this problem by simply discarding it. The packet is irrevocably lost. It is therefore the responsibility of the communicating hosts to check the integrity and completeness of the data and retransmit it in case of an error.

This is performed by yet another protocol, TCP, or *Transmission Control Protocol*, which builds a reliable service on top of IP. The essential property of TCP is that it uses IP to give you the illusion of a simple connection between the two processes on your host and the remote machine, so you don't have to care about how and along which route your data actually travels. A TCP connection works essentially like a two-way pipe that both processes may write to and read from. Think of it as a telephone conversation.

TCP identifies the end points of such a connection by the IP addresses of the two hosts involved and the number of a *port* on each host. Ports may be viewed as attachment points for network connections. If we are to strain the telephone example a little more, one might compare IP addresses to area codes (numbers map to cities), and port numbers to local codes (numbers map to individual people's telephones).

In the *rlogin* example, the client application (*rlogin*) opens a port on **erdos** and connects to port 513 on **quark**, which the *rlogind* server is known to listen to. This establishes a TCP connection. Using this connection, *rlogind* performs the authorization procedure and then spawns the shell. The shell's standard input and output are redirected to the TCP connection so that anything you type to *rlogin* on your machine will be passed through the TCP stream and be given to the shell as standard input.

The User Datagram Protocol

Of course, TCP isn't the only user protocol in TCP/IP networking. Although suitable for applications like *rlogin*, the overhead involved is prohibitive for applications like NFS, which instead uses a sibling protocol of TCP called UDP, or *User Datagram Protocol*. Just like TCP, UDP allows an application to contact a service on a certain port of the remote machine, but it doesn't establish a connection for this. Instead, you use it to send single packets to the destination service—hence its name.

Assume you have mounted the TeX directory hierarchy from the department's central NFS server **galois**, and you want to view a document describing how to use LaTeX. You start your editor, which first reads in the entire file. However, it would take too long to establish a TCP connection with **galois**, send the file, and release it again. Instead, a request is made to **galois**, which sends the file in a couple of UDP packets, which is much faster. However, UDP was not made to deal with packet loss or corruption. It is up to the application, NFS in this case, to take care of this.

More on Ports

Ports may be viewed as attachment points for network connections. If an application wants to offer a certain service, it attaches itself to a port and waits for clients (this is also called *listening* on the port). A client that wants to use this service allocates a port on its local host and connects to the server's port on the remote host.

An important property of ports is that once a connection has been established between the client and the server, another copy of the server may attach to the server port and listen for more clients. This permits, for instance, several concurrent remote logins to the same host, all using the same port 513. TCP is able to tell these connections from each other because they all come from different ports or hosts. For example, if you twice log into **quark** from **erdos**, then the first *rlogin* client will use the local port 1023, and the second one will use port 1022. Both however, will connect to the same port 513 on **quark**.

This example shows the use of ports as rendezvous points, where a client contacts a specific port to obtain a specific service. In order for a client to know the proper port number, an agreement has to be reached between the administrators of both systems on the assignment of these numbers. For services that are widely used, such as *rlogin*, these numbers have to be administered centrally. This is done by the IETF (Internet Engineering Task Force), which regularly releases an RFC titled *Assigned Numbers*. It describes, among other things, the port numbers assigned to well-known services. Linux uses a file called */etc/services* that maps service names to numbers.

RFC 1340

It is worth noting that although both TCP and UDP connections rely on ports, these numbers do not conflict. This means that TCP port 513, for example, is different from UDP port 513. In fact, these ports serve as access points for two different services, namely *rlogin* (TCP) and *rwho* (UDP).

The Socket Library

In UNIX operating systems, the software performing all the tasks and protocols described above is usually part of the kernel, and so it is in Linux. The programming interface most common in the UNIX world is the *Berkeley Socket Library*. Its name derives from a popular analogy that views ports as sockets, and connecting to a port as plugging in. It provides the *bind* call to specify a remote host, a transport protocol, and a service that a program can connect or listen to (using *connect*, *listen*, and *accept*). The socket library is somewhat more general in that it provides not only a class of TCP/IP-based sockets (the *AF_INET* sockets), but also a class that handles connections local to the machine (the *AF_UNIX* class). Some implementations can also handle other classes as well, like the XNS (*Xerox Networking System*) protocol or X.25.

In Linux, the socket library is part of the standard *libc* C library. Currently, it only supports *AF_INET* and *AF_UNIX* sockets, but efforts are being made to incorporate support for Novell's networking protocols so that eventually one or more socket classes for these will be added.

Linux Networking

As the result of a concerted effort of programmers around the world, Linux wouldn't have been possible without the global network. So it's not surprising that in the early stages of development, several people started to work on providing it with network capabilities. A UUCP implementation was running on Linux almost from the very beginning, and work on TCP/IP-based networking started around autumn 1992, when Ross Biro and others created what now has become known as Net-1.

After Ross quit active development in May 1993, Fred van Kempen began to work on a new implementation, rewriting major parts of the code. This was known as Net-2. The first public release, Net-2d, was made in Summer 1993 (as part of the 0.99.10 kernel), and has since been maintained and expanded by several people, most notably Alan Cox, as Net-2Debugged. After heavy debugging and numerous improvements to the code, he changed its name to Net-3 after Linux 1.0 was released. This is the version of the networking code currently included in the official kernel releases.

Net-3 offers device drivers for a wide variety of Ethernet boards, as well as SLIP (for sending network traffic over serial lines) and PLIP (for parallel lines). With Net-3, Linux has a TCP/IP implementation that behaves very well in local area network environments, showing uptimes that beat some of the commercial PC UNIXes. Development currently moves toward the necessary stability to reliably run it on Internet hosts.

Beside these facilities, there are several projects going on that will enhance the versatility of Linux. A driver for PPP (the point-to-point protocol, another way to send network traffic over serial lines), is at beta stage currently, and an AX.25 driver for ham radio is at alpha stage. Alan Cox has also implemented a driver for Novell's IPX protocol, but the effort for a complete networking suite compatible with Novell's has been put on hold for the moment because of Novell's unwillingness to provide the necessary documentation. Another very promising undertaking is *samba*, a free NetBIOS server for UNIX systems written by Andrew Tridgell.[*]

Different Streaks of Development

Fred continued development, going on to Net-2e, which features a much revised design of the networking layer. However, not much has been heard of Net-2e lately.

Yet another implementation of TCP/IP networking comes from Matthias Urlichs, who wrote an ISDN driver for Linux and FreeBSD. For this, he integrated some of the BSD networking code in the Linux kernel.

---

[*] NetBIOS is the protocol on which applications like *lanmanager* and Windows for Workgroups are based.

For the foreseeable future, however, Net-3 seems to be here to stay. Alan is currently working on an implementation of the AX.25 protocol used by ham radio amateurs. Doubtlessly, the yet-to-be-developed "module" code for the kernel will also bring new impetus to the networking code. Modules allow you to add drivers to the kernel at run time.

Although these different network implementations all strive to provide the same service, there are major differences between them at the kernel and device levels. Therefore, you will not be able to configure a system running a Net-2e kernel with utilities from Net-2d or Net-3, and vice versa. This only applies to commands that deal with kernel internals rather closely; applications and common networking commands such as *rlogin* or *telnet* run on either of them.

Nevertheless, all of these different network versions should not worry you. Unless you are participating in active development, you will not have to worry about which version of the TCP/IP code you run. The official kernel releases will always be accompanied by a set of networking tools that are compatible with the networking code present in the kernel.

Where to Get the Code

The latest version of the Linux network code can be obtained by anonymous FTP from various sites. The official FTP site for Net-3 is **sunacm.swan.ac.uk**, mirrored by **sunsite.unc.edu** below *system/Network/sunacm*. The latest Net-2e patch kit and binaries are available from **ftp.aris.com**. Matthias Urlichs's BSD-derived networking code can be obtained from **ftp.ira.uka.de** in */pub/system/linux/netbsd*.

The latest kernels can be found on **nic.funet.fi** in */pub/OS/Linux/PEOPLE/Linus*; **sunsite** and **tsx-11.mit.edu** mirror this directory.

Maintaining Your System

Throughout this book, we will mainly deal with installation and configuration issues. Administration is, however, much more than that—after setting up a service, you have to keep it running, too. For most services, only a little attendance will be necessary, while some, like mail and news, require that you perform routine tasks to keep your system up to date. We will discuss these tasks in later chapters.

The absolute minimum in maintenance is to check system and per-application log files regularly for error conditions and unusual events. Commonly, you will want to do this by writing a couple of administrative shell scripts and periodically running them from *cron*. The source distributions of some major applications, like *smail* or C News, contain such scripts. You only have to tailor them to suit your needs and preferences.

The output from any of your *cron* jobs should be mailed to an administrative account. By default, many applications will send error reports, usage statistics, or log file summaries to the **root** account. This makes sense only if you log in as **root** frequently; a much better idea is to forward **root**'s mail to your personal account by setting up a mail alias as described in Chapter 14, *Getting smail Up and Running*.

However carefully you have configured your site, Murphy's law guarantees that some problem *will* surface eventually. Therefore, maintaining a system also means being available for complaints. Usually, people expect that the system administrator can at least be reached via email as *root*, but there are also other addresses that are commonly used to reach the person responsible for a specific aspect of maintenance. For instance, complaints about a malfunctioning mail configuration will usually be addressed to *postmaster*, and problems with the news system may be reported to *newsmaster* or *usenet*. Mail to *hostmaster* should be redirected to the person in charge of the host's basic network services, and the DNS name service if you run a name server.

System Security

Another very important aspect of system administration in a network environment is protecting your system and users from intruders. Carelessly managed systems offer malicious people many targets. Attacks range from password guessing to Ethernet snooping, and the damage caused may range from faked mail messages to data loss or violation of your users' privacy. We will mention some particular problems when discussing the context they may occur in and some common defenses against them.

UNIX Security

This section will discuss a few examples and basic techniques in dealing with system security. Of course, the topics covered cannot treat in detail all security issues you may be faced with; they merely serve to illustrate the problems that may arise. Therefore, reading a good book on security is an absolute must, especially in a networked system.

System security starts with good system administration. This includes checking the ownership and permissions of all vital files and directories, monitoring use of privileged accounts, etc. The COPS program, for instance, will check your file system and common configuration files for unusual permissions or other anomalies. It is also wise to use a password suite that enforces certain rules on the users' passwords that make them hard to guess. The shadow password suite, for instance, requires a password to have at least five letters and contain both upper and lower case numbers and digits.

When making a service accessible to the network, make sure to give it "least privilege," meaning don't permit it to do things that aren't required for it to work as designed. For example, you should make programs setuid to **root** or some other privileged account only when necessary. Also, if you want to use a service for only a very limited application, don't hesitate to configure it as restrictively as your special application allows. For instance, if you want to allow diskless hosts to boot from your machine, you must provide TFTP (*Trivial File Transfer Protocol*) so that they can download basic configuration files from the */boot* directory. However, when used unrestricted, TFTP allows any user anywhere in the world to download any world-readable file from your system. If this is not what you want, why not restrict TFTP service to the */boot* directory?*

Along the same line of thought, you might want to restrict certain services to users from certain hosts, say from your local network. In Chapter 9, we introduce *tcpd*, which does this for a variety of network applications.

Another important point is to avoid "dangerous" software. Of course, any software you use can be dangerous, because software may have bugs that clever people might exploit to gain access to your system. Things like this happen, and there's no complete protection against it. This problem affects free software and commercial products alike.† However, programs that require special privilege are inherently more dangerous than others, because any loophole can have drastic consequences.‡ If you install a setuid program for network purposes, be doubly careful that you don't miss anything from the documentation so that you don't create a security breach by accident.

You can never rule out that your precautions might fail, regardless of how careful you have been. You should therefore make sure you detect intruders early. Checking the system log files is a good starting point, but the intruder is probably as clever and will delete any obvious traces he or she left. However, there are tools like *tripwire*, written by Gene Kim and Gene Spafford, that allow you to check vital system files to see if their contents or permissions have been changed. *tripwire* computes various strong checksums over these files and stores them in a database. During subsequent runs, the checksums are re-computed and compared to the stored ones to detect any modifications.

---

* We will come back to this in Chapter 9, *Important Network Features*.
† There have been commercial UNIX systems (that you have to pay lots of money for) that came with a setuid-**root** shell script, which allowed users to gain **root** privilege using a simple standard trick.
‡ In 1988, the RTM worm brought much of the Internet to a grinding halt, partly by exploiting a gaping hole in some *sendmail* programs. This hole has long been fixed since.

## CHAPTER TWO

ISSUES OF TCP/IP NETWORKING

W̶e will now turn to the details you'll come in touch with when connecting your Linux machine to a TCP/IP network, including dealing with IP addresses, hostnames, and sometimes routing issues. This chapter gives you the background you need in order to understand what your setup requires, while the next chapters will cover the tools you will use.

Inter-networking

To learn more about TCP/IP and the reasons behind it, refer to the three-volume set *Internetworking with TCP/IP*, by Douglas R. Comer. For a guide to managing a TCP/IP network, see *TCP/IP Network Administration* by Craig Hunt.

TCP

Networking Interfaces

To hide the diversity of equipment that may be used in a networking environment, TCP/IP defines an abstract *interface* through which the hardware is accessed. This interface offers a set of operations which is the same for all types of hardware and basically deals with sending and receiving packets.

For each peripheral device you want to use for networking, a corresponding interface has to be present in the kernel. For example, Ethernet interfaces in Linux are called *eth0* and *eth1*, and SLIP interfaces come as *sl0*, *sl1*, etc. These interface names are used for configuration purposes when you want to name a particular physical device to the kernel. They have no meaning beyond that.

To be useable for TCP/IP networking, an interface must be assigned an IP address that serves as its identification when communicating with the rest of the world. This address is different from the interface name mentioned above; if you compare an interface to a door, then the address is like the name-plate pinned on it.

Of course, there are other device parameters that may be set. One of these is the maximum size of datagrams that can be processed by that particular piece of hardware, also called *Maximum Transfer Unit* or MTU. Other attributes will be introduced later.

IP Addresses

As mentioned in the previous chapter, the addresses understood by the IP networking protocol are 32-bit numbers. Every machine must be assigned a number unique to the networking environment. If you are running a local network that does not have TCP/IP traffic with other networks, you may assign these numbers according to your personal preferences. However, for sites on the Internet, numbers are assigned by a central authority, the Network Information Center, or NIC.[*]

For easier reading, IP addresses are split up into four 8-bit numbers called *octets*. For example, **quark.physics.groucho.edu** has an IP address of **0x954C0C04**, which is written as **149.76.12.4**. This format is often referred to as the *dotted quad notation*.

Another reason for this notation is that IP addresses are split into a *network* number, which is contained in the leading octets, and a *host* number, which is the remainder. When applying to the NIC for IP addresses, you are not assigned an address for each single host you plan to use. Instead, you are given a network number and allowed to assign all valid IP addresses within this range to hosts on your network according to your preferences.

Depending on the size of the network, the host part may need to be smaller or larger. To accomodate different needs, there are several classes of networks, defining different splits of IP addresses.

Class A
> Class A comprises networks **1.0.0.0** through **127.0.0.0**. The network number is contained in the first octet. This provides for a 24-bit host part, allowing roughly 1.6 million hosts.

Class B
> Class B contains networks **128.0.0.0** through **191.255.0.0**; the network number is in the first two octets. This allows for 16320 nets with 65024 hosts each.

Class C
> Class C networks range from **192.0.0.0** through **223.255.255.0**, with the network number being contained in the first three octets. This allows for nearly 2 million networks with up to 254 hosts.

---

[*] Frequently, IP addresses will be assigned to you by the provider that you buy your IP connectivity from. However, you may also apply to NIC directly for an IP address for your network by sending a mail to *hostmaster@internic.net*.

Classes D, E, and F
 Addresses falling into the range of 224.0.0.0 through 254.0.0.0 are either experimental or are reserved for future use and don't specify any network.

If we go back to the example in the previous chapter, we find that 149.76.12.4, the address of **quark**, refers to host 12.4 on the class B network 149.76.0.0.

You may have noticed that in the above list not all possible values were allowed for each octet in the host part. This is because host numbers with octets all 0 or all **255** are reserved for special purposes. An address where all host part bits are zero refers to the network, and one where all bits of the host part are 1 is called a broadcast address. This refers to all hosts on the specified network simultaneously. Thus, 149.76.255.255 is not a valid host address, but refers to all hosts on network **149.76.0.0**.

There are also two network addresses that are reserved, 0.0.0.0 and 127.0.0.0. The first is called the *default route*, the latter the *loopback address*. The default route has something to do with the way IP routes datagrams, which will be dealt with in the next section.

Network 127.0.0.0 is reserved for IP traffic local to your host. Usually, address 127.0.0.1 will be assigned to a special interface on your host, the so-called *loopback interface*, which acts like a closed circuit. Any IP packet handed to it from TCP or UDP will be returned to them as if it had just arrived from some network. This allows you to develop and test networking software without ever using a "real" network. Another useful application is when you want to use networking software on a standalone host. This may not be as uncommon as it sounds; for instance, many UUCP sites don't have IP connectivity at all, but still want to run the INN news system nevertheless. For proper operation on Linux, INN requires the loopback interface.

Address Resolution

Now that you've seen how IP addresses are made up, you may be wondering how they are used on an Ethernet to address different hosts. After all, the Ethernet protocol identifies hosts by a six octet number that has absolutely nothing in common with an IP address, doesn't it?

Right. That's why a mechanism is needed to map IP addresses onto Ethernet addresses. This is the so-called *Address Resolution Protocol*, or ARP. In fact, ARP is not confined to Ethernets, but is used on other types of networks such as ham radio as well. The idea underlying ARP is exactly what most people do when they have to find Mr. X. Ample in a throng of 150 people: they go round calling out his name, confident that he will respond if he's there.

When ARP wants to find out the Ethernet address corresponding to a given IP address, it uses a feature of Ethernet known as "broadcasting," where a datagram is addressed to all stations on the network simultaneously. The broadcast datagram sent by ARP contains a query for the IP address. Each receiving host compares this to its own IP address and if it matches, returns an ARP reply to the inquiring host. The inquiring host can now extract the sender's Ethernet address from the reply.

You may wonder how a host can reach an Internet address that may be on a different Ethernet halfway around the world, or how the host even knows the address is on an Ethernet in the first place. These questions all involve what is called routing, namely finding out the physical location of a host in a network. This will be the topic of the following section.

Let's talk about ARP a little more. Once a host has discovered an Ethernet address, it stores it in its ARP cache so that it doesn't have to query for it again the next time it wants to send a datagram to the host in question. However, it is unwise to keep this information forever; for instance, the remote host's Ethernet card may be replaced because of technical problems, so the ARP entry becomes invalid. Therefore, entries in the ARP cache are discarded after some time to force another query for the IP address.

Sometimes, it is also necessary to find out the IP address associated with a given Ethernet address. This happens when a diskless machine wants to boot from a server on the network, which is quite a common situation on local area networks. A diskless client, however, has virtually no information about itself—except for its Ethernet address! So what it basically does is broadcast a message containing a plea for boot servers to tell it its IP address. There's another protocol for this named *Reverse Address Resolution Protocol*, or RARP. Along with the BOOTP protocol, it serves to define a procedure for bootstrapping diskless clients over the network.

IP Routing

We now take up the question of how to find the host that packets go to, based on the IP address. Different parts of the address are handled in different ways; it is your job to set up the files that indicate how to treat each part.

IP Networks

When you write a letter to someone, you usually put a complete address on the envelope specifying the country, state, zip code, etc. After you put it into the letter box, the postal service will deliver it to its destination: it will be sent to the country indicated, whose national service will dispatch it to the proper state and region, etc. The advantage of this hierarchical scheme is rather obvious: wherever you post the letter, the local postmaster will know roughly which direction to forward the letter, but doesn't have to care which way the letter will travel once it reaches its destination country.

IP networks are structured in a similar way. The whole Internet consists of a number of proper networks, called *autonomous systems*. Each system performs any routing between its member hosts internally so that the task of delivering a datagram is reduced to finding a path to the destination host's network. This means as soon as the datagram is handed to *any* host on that particular network, further processing is done exclusively by the network itself.

Subnetworks

This structure is reflected by splitting IP addresses into a host and network part, as explained above. By default, the destination network is derived from the network part of the IP address. Thus, hosts with identical IP network numbers should be found within the same network, and all the hosts within a network have the same network number.[*]

It makes sense to offer a similar scheme *inside* the network too, since it may consist of a collection of hundreds of smaller networks itself with the smallest units being physical networks like Ethernets. Therefore, IP allows you to subdivide an IP network into several *subnets*.

A subnet takes over responsibility for delivering datagrams to a certain range of IP addresses from the IP network it is part of. As with classes A, B, or C, it is identified by the network part of the IP addresses. However, the network part is now extended to include some bits from the host part. The number of bits that are interpreted as the subnet number is given by the so-called *subnet mask*, or *netmask*. This is a 32-bit number too, which specifies the bit mask for the network part of the IP address.

The campus network of Groucho Marx University is an example of such a network. It has a class B network number of 149.76.0.0, and its netmask is therefore 255.255.0.0.

Internally, GMU's campus network consists of several smaller networks, such as the LANs of various departments. So the range of IP addresses is broken up into 254 subnets, 149.76.1.0 through 149.76.254.0. For example, the department of Theoretical Physics has been assigned 149.76.12.0. The campus backbone is a network by its own right, and is given 149.76.1.0. These subnets share the same IP network number, while the third octet is used to distinguish between them. They will thus use a subnet mask of 255.255.255.0.

---

[*] Autonomous systems are slightly more general. They may comprise more than one IP network.

Figure 2-1 shows how **149.76.12.4**, the address of **quark**, is interpreted differently when the address is taken as an ordinary class B network, and when used with subnetting.

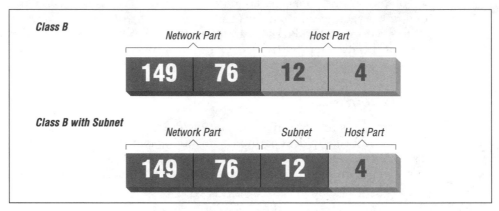

Figure 2–1. Subnetting a class B network

It is worth noting that subnetting (as the technique of generating subnets is called) is only an *internal division* of the network. Subnets are generated by the network owner (or the administrators). Frequently, subnets are created to reflect existing boundaries, be they physical (between two Ethernets), administrative (between two departments), or geographical, and authority over these subnets is delegated to some contact person. However, this structure affects only the network's internal behavior and is completely invisible to the outside world.

Gateways

Subnetting is not only an organizational benefit, it is frequently a natural consequence of hardware boundaries. The viewpoint of a host on a given physical network, such as an Ethernet, is a very limited one: the only hosts it is able to talk to directly are those of the network it is on. All other hosts can be accessed only through so-called *gateways*. A gateway is a host that is connected to two or more physical networks simultaneously and is configured to switch packets between them.

For IP to be able to easily recognize if a host is on a local physical network, different physical networks have to belong to different IP networks. For example the network number **149.76.4.0** is reserved for hosts on the mathematics LAN. When sending a datagram to **quark**, the network software on **erdos** immediately sees from the IP address **149.76.12.4** that the destination host is on a different physical network, and therefore can be reached only through a gateway (**sophus** by default).

sophus itself is connected to two distinct subnets: the Mathematics department and the campus backbone. It accesses each through a different interface, *eth0* and *fddi0*, respectively. Now, what IP address do we assign it? Should we give it one on subnet 149.76.1.0, or on 149.76.4.0?

The answer is: both. When talking to a host on the Math LAN, **sophus** should use an IP address of 149.76.4.1, and when talking to a host on the backbone, it should use 149.76.1.4.

Thus, a gateway is assigned one IP address per network it is on. These addresses—along with the corresponding netmask—are tied to the interface that the subnet is accessed through. Thus, the mapping of interfaces and addresses for **sophus** would look like this:

Interface	Address	Netmask
eth0	149.76.4.1	255.255.255.0
fddi0	149.76.1.4	255.255.255.0
lo	127.0.0.1	255.0.0.0

The last entry describes the loopback interface *lo*, which was introduced earlier.

Figure 2-2 shows a part of the network topology at Groucho Marx University (GMU). Hosts that are on two subnets at the same time are shown with both addresses.

Generally, you can ignore the subtle difference between attaching an address to a host or its interface. For hosts that are on one network only, like **erdos**, you would generally refer to the host as having this-and-that IP address, although strictly speaking, it's the Ethernet interface that has this IP address. However, this distinction is only really important when you refer to a gateway.

The Routing Table

We are now focusing our attention on how IP chooses a gateway to use when delivering a datagram to a remote network.

We have seen before that **erdos**, when given a datagram for **quark**, checks the destination address and finds that it is not on the local network. **erdos** therefore sends the datagram to the default gateway **sophus**, which is now basically faced with the same task. **sophus** recognizes that **quark** is not on any of the networks it is connected to directly, so it has to find yet another gateway to forward it through. The correct choice would be **niels**, the gateway to the Physics department. **sophus** therefore needs some information to associate a destination network with a suitable gateway.

The routing information IP uses for this is basically a table linking networks to gateways that reach them. A catch-all entry (the *default route*) must generally be supplied, too; this is the gateway associated with network 0.0.0.0. All packets to

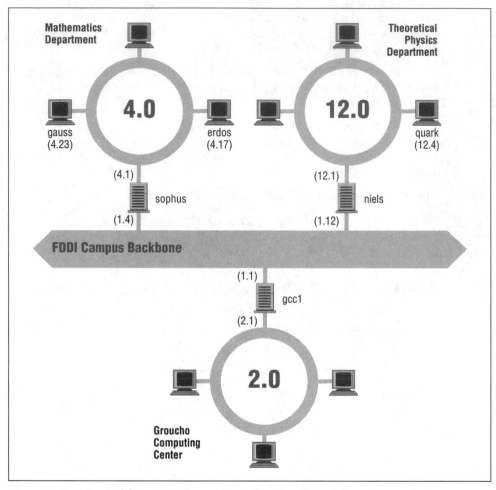

Figure 2-2. A part of the net topology at Groucho Marx University

an unknown network are sent through the default route. On **sophus**, the table might look like this:

Network	Gateway	Interface
149.76.1.0	–	*fddi0*
149.76.2.0	149.76.1.2	*fddi0*
149.76.3.0	149.76.1.3	*fddi0*
149.76.4.0	–	*eth0*
149.76.5.0	149.76.1.5	*fddi0*

Network	Gateway	Interface
...	...	...
0.0.0.0	149.76.1.2	*fddi0*

Routes to a network that **sophus** is directly connected to don't require a gateway; the gateway column here contains a hyphen.

Routing tables may be built by various means. For small LANs, it is usually most efficient to construct them by hand and feed them to IP using the *route* command at boot time (see Chapter 5, *Configuring TCP/IP Networking*). For larger networks, they are built and adjusted at run time by *routing daemons*; these run on central hosts of the network and exchange routing information to compute "optimal" routes between the member networks.

Depending on the size of the network, different routing protocols will be used. For routing inside autonomous systems (such as Groucho Marx campus), the *internal routing protocols* are used. The most prominent one is RIP, the *Routing Information Protocol*, which is implemented by the BSD *routed* daemon. For routing between autonomous systems, *external routing protocols* like EGP (*External Gateway Protocol*), or BGP (*Border Gateway Protocol*) have to be used; these (as well as RIP) have been implemented in the University of Cornell's *gated* daemon.[*]

Metric Values

Dynamic routing based on RIP chooses the best route to some destination host or network based on the number of "hops," that is, the gateways a datagram has to pass before reaching it. The shorter a route is, the better RIP rates it. Very long routes with 16 or more hops are regarded as unusable and are discarded.

To use RIP to manage routing information internal to your local network, you have to run *gated* on all hosts. At boot time, *gated* checks for all active network interfaces. If there is more than one active interface (not counting the loopback interface), it assumes the host is switching packets between several networks and will actively exchange and broadcast routing information. Otherwise, it will only passively receive any RIP updates and update the local routing table.

When broadcasting the information from the local routing table, *gated* computes the length of the route from the so-called *metric value* associated with the routing table entry. This metric value is set by the system administrator when configuring the route and should reflect the actual cost of using this route. Therefore, the metric of a route to a subnet that the host is directly connected to should always be zero, while a route going through two gateways should have a metric of two.

---

[*] *routed* is considered broken by many people. Since *gated* supports RIP as well, it is better to use that instead.

However, note that you don't have to bother about metrics when you don't use *RIP* or *gated*.

The Internet Control Message Protocol

IP has a companion protocol that we haven't talked about yet. This is the *Internet Control Message Protocol* (ICMP) and is used by the kernel networking code to communicate error messages and the like to other hosts. For instance, assume that you are on **erdos** again and want to *telnet* to port 12345 on **quark**, but there's no process listening on that port. When the first TCP packet for this port arrives on **quark**, the networking layer will recognize this and immediately return an ICMP message to **erdos** stating "Port Unreachable".

There are quite a number of messages ICMP understands, many of which deal with error conditions. However, there is one very interesting message called the Redirect message. It is generated by the routing module when it detects that another host is using it as a gateway, although there is a much shorter route. For example, after booting, the routing table of **sophus** may be incomplete. It might contain the routes to the Mathematics network, to the FDDI backbone, and the default route pointing at the Groucho Computing Center's gateway (**gcc1**). Therefore, any packets for **quark** would be sent to **gcc1** rather than to **niels**, the gateway to the Physics department. When receiving such a datagram, **gcc1** will notice that this is a poor choice of route and will forward the packet to **niels**, at the same time returning an ICMP Redirect message to **sophus** telling it of the superior route.

Now, this seems a very clever way to avoid having to set up any but the most basic routes manually. However, be warned that relying on dynamic routing schemes, be it RIP or ICMP Redirect messages, is not always a good idea. ICMP Redirect and RIP offer you little or no choice in verifying that some routing information is indeed authentic. This allows malicious good-for-nothings to disrupt your entire network traffic or do even worse things. For this reason, there are some versions of the Linux networking code that treat Redirect messages that affect network routes as if they were only Redirects for host routes.

The Domain Name System

Hostname Resolution

As described above, addressing in TCP/IP networking revolves around 32-bit numbers. However, you will have a hard time remembering more than a few of these. Therefore, hosts are generally known by "ordinary" names such as **gauss** or

strange. It is then the application's duty to find the IP address corresponding to this name. This process is called *hostname resolution.*

When an application needs to find the IP address of a given host, it relies on the library functions *gethostbyname(3)* and *gethostbyaddr(3)*. Traditionally, these and a number of related procedures were grouped in a separate library called the resolver library; on Linux, these are part of the standard *libc*. Colloquially, this collection of functions is therefore referred to as "the resolver."

Now, on a small network like an Ethernet or even a cluster of them, it is not very difficult to maintain tables mapping hostnames to addresses. This information is usually kept in a file named */etc/hosts*. When adding or removing hosts, or reassigning addresses, all you have to do is update the *hosts* on all hosts. Quite obviously, this will become burdensome with networks that comprise more than a handful of machines.

One solution to this problem is NIS, the *Network Information System,* developed by Sun Microsystems, colloquially called YP or *Yellow Pages.* NIS stores the *hosts* file (and other information) in a database on a master host from which clients may retrieve it as needed. Still, this approach is only suitable for medium-sized networks such as LANs, because it involves maintaining the entire *hosts* database centrally and distributing it to all servers.

On the Internet, address information was initially stored in a single *HOSTS.TXT* database, too. This file was maintained at the Network Information Center, or NIC, and had to be downloaded and installed by all participating sites. When the network grew, several problems with this scheme arose. Besides the administrative overhead involved in installing *HOSTS.TXT* regularly, the load on the servers that distributed it became too high. Even more severe was the problem that all names had to be registered with the NIC, which had to make sure that no name was issued twice.

This is why, in 1984, a new name resolution scheme was adopted, the *Domain Name System.* DNS was designed by Paul Mockapetris and addresses both problems simultaneously. It is thoroughly explained in *DNS and BIND* by Paul Albitz and Cricket Liu. The RFCs defining it are 1033, 1034, and 1035.

DNS

RFC 1033
RFC 1034
RFC 1035

Enter DNS

DNS organizes hostnames in a hierarchy of domains. A domain is a collection of sites that are related in some sense—be it because they form a proper network (e.g., all machines on a campus, or all hosts on BITNET), because they all belong to a certain organization (like the U.S. government), or because they're simply geographically close. For instance, universities are grouped in the **edu** domain, with each university or college using a separate *subdomain* below which their hosts are subsumed. Groucho Marx University might be given the **groucho.edu** domain, with the LAN of the Mathematics department being assigned **maths.groucho.edu**. Hosts on the departmental network would have this domain name tacked onto their hostname, so **erdos** would be known as **erdos.maths.groucho.edu**. This is called the *fully qualified domain name,* or FQDN, which uniquely identifies this host world-wide.

Figure 2-3 shows a section of the name space. The entry at the root of this tree, which is denoted by a single dot, is quite appropriately called the *root domain* and encompasses all other domains. To indicate that a hostname is a fully qualified domain name, rather than a name relative to some (implicit) local domain, it is sometimes written with a trailing dot. This signifies that the name's last component is the root domain.

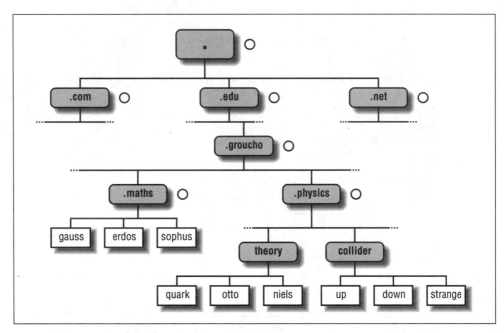

Figure 2-3. A part of the domain name space

Depending on its location in the name hierarchy, a domain may be called top-level, second-level, or third-level. More levels of subdivision occur, but they are rare. These are several top-level domains you may see frequently:

edu
(Mostly U.S.) educational institutions like universities, etc.

com
Commercial organizations, companies.

org
Non-commercial organizations. Often private UUCP networks are in this domain.

net

Gateways and other administrative hosts on a network.

mil

U.S. military institutions.

gov

U.S. government institutions.

uucp

Officially, all site names formerly used as UUCP names without domains have been moved to this domain.

Technically, the first four of these belong to the U.S. part of the Internet, but you may also see non-U.S. sites in these domains. This is especially true of the **net** domain. However, **mil** and **gov** are used exclusively in the U.S.

Outside the U.S., each country generally uses a top-level domain of its own named after the two-letter country code defined in ISO-3166. Finland, for instance, uses the **fi** domain; **fr** is used by France, **de** by Germany, and **au** by Australia. Below this top-level domain, each country's NIC is free to organize hostnames in whatever way they want. Australia, for example, has second-level domains similar to the international top-level domains, named **com.au**, **edu.au**, and so on. Others, like Germany, don't use this extra level, but rather have slightly longish names that refer directly to the organizations running a particular domain. For example, it's not uncommon to see hostnames like **ftp.informatik.uni-erlangen.de**. Chalk that up to German efficiency.

Of course, these national domains do not imply that a host below that domain is actually located in that country; it only signals that the host has been registered with that country's NIC. A Swedish manufacturer might have a branch in Australia and still have all its hosts registered with the **se** top-level domain.

Now, organizing the name space in a hierarchy of domain names nicely solves the problem of name uniqueness; with DNS, a hostname has to be unique only within its domain to give it a name different from all other hosts world-wide. Furthermore, fully qualified names are quite easy to remember. Taken by themselves, these are already very good reasons to split up a large domain into several subdomains.

But DNS does even more for you than than this. It also allows you to delegate authority over a subdomain to its administrators. For example, the maintainers at the Groucho Computing Center might create a subdomain for each department; we already encountered the **math** and **physics** subdomains above. When they find the network at the Physics department too large and chaotic to manage from outside (after all, physicists are known to be an unruly bunch of people), they may simply pass control over the **physics.groucho.edu** domain to the administrators of this network. These administrators are free to use whatever hostnames they like and assign them IP addresses from their network in whatever fashion they like, without outside interference.

To this end, the name space is split up into *zones*, each rooted at a domain. Note the subtle difference between a *zone* and a *domain*: the domain **groucho.edu** encompasses all hosts at the Groucho Marx University, while the zone **groucho.edu** includes only the hosts that are managed by the Computing Center directly, those at the Mathematics department for example. The hosts at the Physics department belong to a different zone, namely **physics.groucho.edu**. In Figure 2-3, the start of a zone is marked by a small circle to the right of the domain name.

Name Lookups with DNS

At first glance, all this domain and zone fuss seems to make name resolution an awfully complicated business. After all, if no central authority controls what names are assigned to which hosts, then how is a humble application supposed to know?!

Now comes the really ingenious part about DNS. If you want to find out the IP address of **erdos**, DNS says go ask the people that manage it, and they will tell you.

In fact, DNS is a giant distributed database. It is implemented by means of so-called name servers that supply information on a given domain or set of domains. For each zone, there are at least two, at most a few name servers that hold all authoritative information on hosts in that zone. To obtain the IP address of **erdos**, all you have to do is contact the name server for the **groucho.edu** zone, which will then return the desired data.

Easier said than done, you might think. So how do I know how to reach the name server at Groucho Marx University? In case your computer isn't equipped with an address-resolving oracle, DNS provides for this, too. When your application wants to look up information on **erdos**, it contacts a local name server, which conducts a so-called iterative query for it. It starts off by sending a query to a name server for the root domain, asking for the address of **erdos.maths.groucho.edu**. The root name server recognizes that this name does not belong to its zone of authority, but rather to one below the **edu** domain. Thus, it tells you to contact an **edu** zone name server for more information and encloses a list of all **edu** name servers along with their addresses. Your local name server will then go on and query one of those, for instance, **a.isi.edu**. In a manner similar to the root name server, **a.isi.edu** knows that the **groucho.edu** people run a zone of their own and points you to their servers. The local name server will then present its query for **erdos** to one of these, which will finally recognize the name as belonging to its zone and return the corresponding IP address.

Now, this looks like a lot of traffic being generated for looking up a measly IP address, but it's really only miniscule compared to the amount of data that would have to be transferred if we were still stuck with *HOSTS.TXT*. There's still room for improvement with this scheme, however.

To improve response time during future queries, the name server will store the information obtained in its local *cache*. So the next time anyone on your local network wants to look up the address of a host in the **groucho.edu** domain, your name server will not have to go through the whole process again but will go to the **groucho.edu** name server directly.[*]

Of course, the name server will not keep this information forever, but rather discard it after some period. This expiration interval is called the *time to live*, or TTL. Each datum in the DNS database is assigned such a TTL by administrators of the responsible zone.

Domain Name Servers

Name servers that hold all information on hosts within a zone are called *authoritative* for this zone and sometimes are referred to as *master name servers*. Any query for a host within this zone will finally wind down at one of these master name servers.

To provide a coherent picture of a zone, its master servers must be fairly well synchronized. This is achieved by making one of them the *primary* server, which loads its zone information from data files, and making the others *secondary* servers who transfer the zone data from the primary server at regular intervals.

One reason to have several name servers is to distribute work load; another is redundance. When one name server machine fails in a benign way, like crashing or losing its network connection, all queries will fall back to the other servers. Of course, this scheme doesn't protect you from server malfunctions that produce wrong replies to all DNS requests, e.g., from software bugs in the server program itself.

Of course, you can also think of running a name server that is not authoritative for any domain.[†] This type of server is useful nevertheless, as it is still able to conduct DNS queries for the applications running on the local network and cache the information. It is therefore called a *caching-only* server.

---

[*] If information weren't cached, then DNS would be about as bad as any other method, because each query would involve the root name servers.

[†] Well, almost. A name server at least has to provide name service for **localhost** and reverse lookups of **127.0.0.1**.

The DNS Database

We have seen that DNS not only deals with IP addresses of hosts, but it also exchanges information on name servers. There are, in fact, a whole bunch of different types of entries the DNS database may have.

A single piece of information from the DNS database is called a *resource record*, or RR for short. Each record has a type associated with it describing the sort of data it represents, and a class specifying the type of network it applies to. The latter accommodates the needs of different addressing schemes, like IP addresses (the IN class) or Hesiod addresses (used by MIT's Kerberos system) and a few more. The prototypical resource record type is the A record, which associates a fully qualified domain name with an IP address.

Of course, a host may have more than one name. However, one of these names must be identified as the official or *canonical hostname*, while the others are simply aliases referring to the former. The difference is that the canonical hostname is the one with an associated A record, while the others only have a record of type CNAME which points to the canonical hostname.

We will not go through all record types here, but save them for a later chapter, and give you a brief example here. Example 2-1 shows a part of the domain database that is loaded into the name servers for the **physics.groucho.edu** zone.

Example 2-1: An Excerpt from the named.hosts File for the Physics Department

```
; Authoritative Information on physics.groucho.edu.
@            IN    SOA niels.physics.groucho.edu. janet.niels.physics.groucho.edu. {
                    940902           ; serial no
                    360000           ; refresh
                    3600             ; retry
                    3600000          ; expire
                    3600             ; default ttl
                   }
;
; Name servers
             IN    NS      niels
             IN    NS      gauss.maths.groucho.edu.
gauss.maths.groucho.edu. IN A 149.76.4.23
;
; Theoretical Physics (subnet 12)
niels        IN    A       149.76.12.1
             IN    A       149.76.1.12
nameserver   IN    CNAME   niels
otto         IN    A       149.76.12.2
quark        IN    A       149.76.12.4
down         IN    A       149.76.12.5
strange      IN    A       149.76.12.6
. . .
; Collider Lab. (subnet 14)
```

Example 2–1: An Excerpt from the named.hosts File for the Physics Department (continued)

```
boson        IN    A      149.76.14.1
muon         IN    A      149.76.14.7
bogon        IN    A      149.76.14.12
  . . .
```

Apart from the A and CNAME records, you can see a special record at the top of the file, stretching several lines. This is the SOA resource record signalling the *Start Of Authority*, which holds general information on the zone the server is authoritative for. This comprises, for instance, the default time to live for all records.

Note that all names in the sample file that do not end with a dot should be interpreted relative to the **groucho.edu** domain. The special name "@" used in the SOA record refers to the domain name by itself.

We have seen above that the name servers for the **groucho.edu** domain somehow have to know about the **physics** zone so that they can point queries to their name servers. This is usually achieved by a pair of records: the NS record that gives the server's FQDN, and an A record that associates an address with that name. Since these records are what holds the name space together, they are frequently called the *glue records*. They are the only instances of records where a parent zone actually holds information on hosts in the subordinate zone. The glue records pointing to the name servers for **physics.groucho.edu** are shown in Example 2-2.

Example 2–2: An Excerpt from the named.hosts File for GMU

```
; Zone data for the groucho.edu zone.
@               IN    SOA vax12.gcc.groucho.edu. joe.vax12.gcc.groucho.edu. {
                      940701          ; serial no
                      360000          ; refresh
                      3600            ; retry
                      3600000         ; expire
                      3600            ; default ttl
                }
  . . . .
;
; Glue records for the physics.groucho.edu zone
physics         IN    NS       niels.physics.groucho.edu.
                IN    NS       gauss.maths.groucho.edu.
niels.physics   IN    A        149.76.12.1
gauss.maths     IN    A        149.76.4.23
  . . .
```

Reverse Lookups

Besides looking up the IP address belonging to a host, it is sometimes desirable to find out the canonical hostname corresponding to an address. This is called *reverse mapping* and is used by several network services to verify a client's identity. When using a single *hosts* file, reverse lookups simply involve searching the file for a host that owns the IP address in question. With DNS, an exhaustive search of the name space is out of the question of course. Instead, a special domain, **in-addr.arpa**, has been created which contains the IP addresses of all hosts in a reverted dotted-quad notation. For instance, an IP address of **149.76.12.4** corresponds to the name **4.12.76.149.in-addr.arpa**. The resource-record type linking these names to their canonical hostnames is PTR.

Creating a zone of authority usually means that its administrators are given full control over how they assign addresses to names. Since they usually have one or more IP networks or subnets at their hands, there's a one-to-many mapping between DNS zones and IP networks. The Physics department, for instance, comprises the subnets **149.76.8.0**, **149.76.12.0**, and **149.76.14.0**.

As a consequence, new zones in the **in-addr.arpa** domain have to be created along with the **physics** zone and delegated to the network administrators at the department: **8.76.149.in-addr.arpa**, **12.76.149.in-addr.arpa**, and **14.76.149.in-addr.arpa**. Otherwise, installing a new host at the Collider Lab would require them to contact their parent domain to have the new address entered into their **in-addr.arpa** zone file.

The zone database for subnet 12 is shown in Example 2-3. The corresponding glue records in the database of their parent zone are shown in Example 2-4.

Example 2-3: An Excerpt from the named.rev File for Subnet 12

```
; the 12.76.149.in-addr.arpa domain.
@         IN     SOA   niels.physics.groucho.edu. janet.niels.physics.groucho.edu. {
                        940902 360000 3600 3600000 3600
          }
2         IN     PTR         otto.physics.groucho.edu.
4         IN     PTR         quark.physics.groucho.edu.
5         IN     PTR         down.physics.groucho.edu.
6         IN     PTR         strange.physics.groucho.edu.
```

Example 2-4: An Excerpt from the named.rev File for Network 149.76

```
; the 76.149.in-addr.arpa domain.
@         IN     SOA vax12.gcc.groucho.edu. joe.vax12.gcc.groucho.edu. {
                        940701 360000 3600 3600000 3600
          }
...
; subnet 4: Mathematics Dept.
1.4       IN     PTR         sophus.maths.groucho.edu.
```

Example 2-4: An Excerpt from the named.rev File for Network 149.76 (continued)

```
17.4        IN     PTR       erdos.maths.groucho.edu.
23.4        IN     PTR       gauss.maths.groucho.edu.
. . .
; subnet 12: Physics Dept, separate zone
12          IN     NS        niels.physics.groucho.edu.
            IN     NS        gauss.maths.groucho.edu.
niels.physics.groucho.edu. IN  A 149.76.12.1
gauss.maths.groucho.edu. IN  A   149.76.4.23
. . .
```

One important consequence of the **in-addr.arpa** system is that zones can only be created as supersets of IP networks, and even more severe, that these network's netmasks have to be on byte boundaries. All subnets at Groucho Marx University have a netmask of **255.255.255.0**, hence an **in-addr.arpa** zone could be created for each subnet. However, if the netmask was **255.255.255.128** instead, creating zones for the subnet **149.76.12.128** would be impossible, because there's no way to tell DNS that the **12.76.149.in-addr.arpa** domain has been split in two zones of authority, with hostnames ranging from **1** through **127**, and **128** through **255**, respectively.

## CHAPTER THREE

CONFIGURING THE NETWORKING HARDWARE

Devices, Drivers, and All That

Up to now, we've been talking quite a bit about network interfaces and general TCP/IP issues, but we haven't really covered exactly what happens when "the networking code" in the kernel accesses a piece of hardware. For this, we have to talk a little about the concept of interfaces and drivers.

First, of course, there's the hardware itself, for example an Ethernet board: this is a slice of Epoxy cluttered with lots of tiny chips with silly numbers on them, sitting in a slot of your PC. This is what we generally call a device.

For you to be able to use the Ethernet board, special functions have to be present in your Linux kernel that understand the particular way this device is accessed. These are the so-called device drivers. For example, Linux has device drivers for several brands of Ethernet boards that are very similar in function. They are known as the "Becker Series Drivers," named after their author Donald Becker. A different example is the D-Link driver that handles a D-Link pocket adaptor attached to a parallel port.

But what do we mean when we say a driver "handles" a device? Let's go back to that Ethernet board we examined above. The driver has to be able to communicate with the peripheral's on-board logic somehow: it has to send commands and data to the board, while the board should deliver any data received to the driver.

In PCs, this communication takes place through an area of I/O memory that is mapped to on-board registers and the like. All commands and data the kernel sends to the board have to go through these registers. I/O memory is generally described by giving its starting or *base address*. Typical base addresses for Ethernet boards are 0x300 or 0x360.

Usually, you don't have to worry about any hardware issues such as the base address, because the kernel makes an attempt at boot time to detect a board's location. This called autoprobing, which means that the kernel reads several memory locations and compares the data read with what it should see if a certain Ethernet board were installed. However, there may be Ethernet boards it cannot detect automatically; this is sometimes the case with cheap Ethernet cards that are not-quite clones of standard boards from other manufacturers. Also, the kernel will attempt to detect only one Ethernet device when booting. If you're using more than one board, you have to tell the kernel about this board explicitly.

Another such parameter that you might have to tell the kernel about is the interrupt request channel. Hardware components usually interrupt the kernel when they need taken care of, for example, when data has arrived or a special condition occurs. In a PC, interrupts may occur on one of 15 interrupt channels numbered 0, 1, and 3 through 15. The interrupt number assigned to a hardware component is called its *interrupt request number* or IRQ.[*]

As described in Chapter 2, *Issues of TCP/IP Networking*, the kernel accesses a device through a so-called interface. Interfaces offer an abstract set of functions that is the same across all types of hardware, such as sending or receiving a datagram.

Interfaces are identified by means of names. These are names defined internally in the kernel and are not device files in the */dev* directory. Typical names are *eth0*, *eth1*, etc., for Ethernet interfaces. The assignment of interfaces to devices usually depends on the order in which devices are configured. For instance, the first Ethernet board installed will become *eth0*, the next will be *eth1*, and so on. SLIP interfaces are handled differently from others, because they are assigned dynamically. Whenever a SLIP connection is established, an interface is assigned to the serial port.

The picture given in Figure 3-1 illustrates the relationship between the hardware, device drivers, and interfaces.

When booting, the kernel displays what devices it detects and what interfaces it installs. The following is an excerpt of a typical boot screen:

```
    .
    .
This processor honours the WP bit even when in supervisor mode. Good.
Floppy drive(s): fd0 is 1.44M
Swansea University Computer Society NET3.010
IP Protocols: ICMP, UDP, TCP
PPP: version 0.2.1 (4 channels) OPTIMIZE_FLAGS
```

---

[*] IRQs 2 and 9 are the same because the PC has two cascaded interrupt processors with eight IRQs each; the secondary processor is connected to IRQ 2 of the primary one.

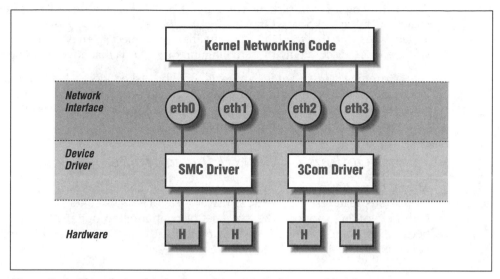

Figure 3-1. The relationship between drivers, interfaces, and hardware

```
TCP compression code copyright 1989 Regents of the University of California
PPP line discipline registered.
SLIP: version 0.7.5 (4 channels)
CSLIP: code copyright 1989 Regents of the University of California
dl0: D-Link DE-600 pocket adapter, Ethernet Address: 00:80:C8:71:76:95
Checking 386/387 coupling... Ok, fpu using exception 16 error reporting.
Linux version 1.1.11 (okir@monad) #3 Sat May 7 14:57:18 MET DST 1994
```

This shows that the kernel has been compiled with TCP/IP enabled and that it includes drivers for SLIP, CSLIP, and PPP. The third line from the bottom says that a D-Link pocket adaptor was detected and installed as interface *dl0*. If you have a different type of Ethernet card, the kernel will usually print a line starting with *eth0*, followed by the type of card detected. If you have an Ethernet card installed but don't see any such message, the kernel is unable to detect your board properly. This situation wil be discussed later in this chapter.

Kernel Configuration

Most Linux distributions come along with boot disks that work for all common types of PC hardware. This means that the kernel on those disks has all sorts of preconfigured drivers that you will never need, but which waste precious system memory because parts of the kernel cannot be swapped out. Therefore, you will generally roll your own kernel, including only those drivers you actually need or want.

Installation

When running a Linux system, you should be familiar with building a kernel. The basics of this are explained in Matt Welsh's *Installation and Getting Started Guide*, which is also part of the Linux Documentation Project's series. In this section, we will therefore discuss only those configuration options that affect networking.

When running *make config*, you will first be asked general configurations, for instance whether you want kernel math emulation or not. One of these queries asks you whether you want TCP/IP networking support. You must answer this with y to get a kernel capable of networking.

Kernel Options in Linux 1.0 and Higher

After the general option part is complete, the configuration will go on to ask you for various features such as SCSI drivers, etc. The subsequent list questions deal with networking support. The exact set of configuration options is in constant flux because of ongoing development. A typical list of options offered by most kernel versions around 1.0 and 1.1 looks like this:

```
*
* Network device support
*
Network device support? (CONFIG_ETHERCARDS) [y]
```

Despite the macro name displayed in brackets, you must answer this question with y if you want to use *any* type of networking devices, regardless of whether this is Ethernet, SLIP, or PPP. When answering this question with y, support for Ethernet-type devices is enabled automatically. Support for other types of network drivers must be enabled separately.

```
SLIP (serial line) support? (CONFIG_SLIP) [y]
  SLIP compressed headers (SL_COMPRESSED) [y]
PPP (point-to-point) support (CONFIG_PPP) [y]
PLIP (parallel port) support (CONFIG_PLIP) [n]
```

These questions concern the various link layer protocols supported by Linux. SLIP allows you to transport IP datagrams across serial lines. The compressed header option provides support for CSLIP, a technique that compresses TCP/IP headers to as little as three bytes. Note that this kernel option does not turn on CSLIP automatically, it merely provides the necessary kernel functions for it.

PPP is another protocol used to send network traffic across serial lines. It is much more flexible than SLIP and is not limited to IP, but will also support IPX once it is implemented. As PPP support has been completed only lately, this option may not be present in your kernel.

PLIP provides for a way to send IP datagrams across a parallel port connection. It is mostly used to communicate with PCs running DOS.

The following questions deal with Ethernet boards from various vendors. As more drivers are being developed, you are likely to see questions added to this section.

If you want to build a kernel you can use on a number of different machines, you can enable more than one driver.

```
NE2000/NE1000 support (CONFIG_NE2000) [y]
WD80*3 support (CONFIG_WD80x3) [n]
SMC Ultra support (CONFIG_ULTRA) [n]
3c501 support (CONFIG_EL1) [n]
3c503 support (CONFIG_EL2) [n]
3c509/3c579 support (CONFIG_EL3) [n]
HP PCLAN support (CONFIG_HPLAN) [n]
AT1500 and NE2100 (LANCE and PCnet-ISA) support (CONFIG_LANCE) [n]
AT1700 support (CONFIG_AT1700) [n]
DEPCA support (CONFIG_DEPCA) [n]
D-Link DE600 pocket adaptor support (CONFIG_DE600) [y]
AT-LAN-TEC/RealTek pocket adaptor support (CONFIG_ATP) [n]
*
* CD-ROM drivers
*
...
```

Finally, in the file system section, the configuration script will ask you whether you want support for NFS, the networking file system. NFS lets you export file systems to several hosts, which makes the files appear as if they were on an ordinary hard disk attached to the host.

```
NFS file system support (CONFIG_NFS_FS) [y]
```

Kernel Options in Linux 1.1.14 and Higher

Starting with Linux 1.1.14, which added alpha support for IPX, the configuration procedure changed slightly. The general options section now asks whether you want networking support in general. It is immediately followed by a couple of questions on miscellaneous networking options.

```
*
* Networking options
*
TCP/IP networking (CONFIG_INET) [y]
```

To use TCP/IP networking, you must answer this question with y. If you answer with n, however, you will still be able to compile the kernel with IPX support.

```
IP forwarding/gatewaying (CONFIG_IP_FORWARD) [n]
```

You have to enable this option if your system acts as a gateway between two Ethernets or between an Ethernet and a SLIP link, etc. Although it doesn't hurt to enable this by default, you may want to disable it to configure a host as a so-called *firewall*. Firewalls are hosts that are connected to two or more networks but don't route traffic between them. They are commonly used to provide users Internet access at minimal risk to the internal network. Users are allowed to log into the firewall and use Internet services, but the company's machines are protected from outside attacks because any incoming connections can't cross the firewall.

```
*
* (it is safe to leave these untouched)
*
PC/TCP compatibility mode (CONFIG_INET_PCTCP) [n]
```

This option works around an incompatibility with some versions of PC/TCP, a commercial TCP/IP implementation for DOS-based PCs. If you enable this option, you will still be able to communicate with normal UNIX machines, but performance may be hurt over slow links.

```
Reverse ARP (CONFIG_INET_RARP) [n]
```

This function enables RARP (*Reverse Address Resolution Protocol*). RARP is used by diskless clients and X terminals to inquire their IP address when booting. You should enable RARP only when you plan to serve this sort of client. The latest package of network utilities (*net-0.32d*) contains a small utility named *rarp* that allows you to add systems to the RARP cache.

```
Assume subnets are local (CONFIG_INET_SNARL) [y]
```

When sending data over TCP, the kernel has to break up the stream into several packets before giving it to IP. For hosts that can be reached over a local network such as an Ethernet, larger packets will be used than for hosts where data has to go through long-distance links.[*] If you don't enable SNARL, the kernel will assume that a network is local only if it has an interface to that network. However, if you look at the class B network at Groucho Marx University, the whole class B network is local, but most hosts interface to only one or two subnets. If you enable SNARL, the kernel will assume *all* subnets are local and use large packets when talking to all hosts on campus.

If you do want to use smaller packet sizes for data sent to specific hosts (because, for example, the data goes through a SLIP link), you can do so using the *mtu* option of *route*, which is briefly discussed at the end of this chapter.

```
Disable NAGLE algorithm (normally enabled) (CONFIG_TCP_NAGLE_OFF) [n]
```

Nagle's rule is a heuristic to avoid sending particularly small IP packets, also called *tinygrams*. Tinygrams are usually created by interactive networking tools that transmit single keystrokes, such as *telnet* or *rsh*. Tinygrams can become particularly wasteful on low-bandwidth links like SLIP. The Nagle algorithm attempts to avoid them by holding back transmission of TCP data briefly under some circum-

---

[*] This is done to avoid fragmentation by links that have a very small maximum packet size.

stances. You might only want to disable Nagle's algorithm if you have severe problems with packets getting dropped.

```
The IPX protocol (CONFIG_IPX) [n]
```

This enables support for IPX, the transport protocol used by Novell Networking. It is still under development and isn't really useful yet. One benefit will be that you can exchange data with IPX-based DOS utilities one day and route traffic between your Novell-based networks through a PPP link. Support for the high-level protocols of Novell Networking is not in sight, however, as the specifications for these are available only at horrendous cost and under a non-disclosure agreement.

Starting in the 1.1.16 kernel, Linux supports another driver type, the dummy driver. The following question appears toward the start of the device driver section.

```
Dummy net driver support (CONFIG_DUMMY) [y]
```

The dummy driver doesn't really do much, but it is quite useful on standalone or SLIP hosts. It is basically a masqueraded loopback interface. The reason to have this sort of interface is that on hosts that do SLIP but have no Ethernet, you want to have an interface that bears your IP address all the time. This is discussed in a little more detail in the section "The Dummy Interface" in Chapter 5, *Configuring TCP/IP Networking.*

A Tour of Linux Network Devices

The Linux kernel supports a number of hardware drivers for various types of equipment. This section gives a short overview of the driver families available, and the interface names used for them.

There are a number of standard names for interfaces in Linux, which are listed below. Most drivers support more than one interface, in which case the interfaces are numbered, as in *eth0, eth1*, etc.

lo　The local loopback interface. It is used for testing purposes, as well as a couple of network applications. It works like a closed circuit in that any datagram written to it will immediately be returned to the host's networking layer. There's always one loopback device present in the kernel, and there's little sense in having more.

eth0, eth1, ...
　　Ethernet cards. This is the generic interface name for most Ethernet boards.

dl0, dl1, ...
　　These interfaces access a D-Link DE-600 pocket adapter, another Ethernet device. It is a little special in that the DE-600 is driven through a parallel port.

Kernels later than 1.1.22 don't use a special interface name anymore, but give the DE-600 interface from the *eth* family, too.

sl0, sl1, ...
SLIP interfaces. SLIP interfaces are associated with serial lines in the order in which they are allocated for SLIP. The kernel supports up to four SLIP interfaces.

ppp0, ppp1, ...
PPP interfaces. Just like SLIP interfaces, a PPP interface is associated with a serial line once it is converted to PPP mode. At the moment, up to four interfaces are supported.

plip0, plip1, ...
PLIP interfaces. PLIP transports IP datagrams over parallel lines. Up to three PLIP interfaces are supported. They are allocated by the PLIP driver at system boot time and are mapped onto parallel ports.

For other interface drivers that may be added in the future, like ISDN or AX.25, other names will be introduced. Drivers for IPX and AX.25 are under development, but they are still at alpha stage.

During the following sections, we will discuss the details of using the drivers described above.

Ethernet Installation

The current Linux network code supports various brands of Ethernet cards. Most drivers were written by Donald Becker (*becker@cesdis.gsfc.nasa.gov*), who authored a family of drivers for cards based on the National Semiconductor 8390 chip; these have become known as the Becker Series Drivers. There are also drivers for a couple of products from D-Link, among them the D-Link pocket adaptor that allows you to access an Ethernet through a parallel port. The driver for this was written by Bjørn Ekwall (*bj0rn@blox.se*). The DEPCA driver was written by David C. Davies (*davies@wanton.lkg.dec.com*).

Ethernet Cabling

If you're installing an Ethernet for the first time in your life, a few words about the cabling may be in order here. Ethernet is very picky about proper cabling. The cable must be terminated on both ends with a 50 Ohm resistor, and you must not have any branches (i.e., three cables connected in a star-shape). If you are using a thin co-ax cable with T-shaped BNC junctions, these junctions must be twisted on the board's connector directly; you should not insert a cable segment.

If you connect to a thicknet installation, you have to attach your host through a transceiver (sometimes called Ethernet Attachment Unit). You can plug the transceiver into the 15-pin AUI port on your board directly, but may also use a shielded cable.

Supported Boards

Ethernet HOWTO

A complete list of supported boards is available in the Ethernet HOWTOs posted monthly to *comp.os.linux.announce* by Paul Gortmaker.[*]

Here's a list of the more widely-known boards supported by Linux. The actual list in the HOWTO is about three times longer. However, even if you find your board in this list, check the HOWTO first; there are sometimes important details about operating these cards. A case in point is the behavior of some DMA-based Ethernet boards that use the same DMA channel as the Adaptec 1542 SCSI controller by default. Unless you move one of them to a different DMA channel, you will wind up with the Ethernet board writing packet data to arbitrary locations on your hard disk.

3Com EtherLink
> Both 3c503 and 3c503/16 are supported, as are 3c507 and 3c509. The 3c501 is supported too, but is too slow to be worth buying.

Novell Eagle
> NE1000 and NE2000, and a variety of clones. NE1500 and NE2100 are supported, too.

Western Digital/SMC
> WD8003 and WD8013 (same as SMC Elite and SMC Elite Plus) are supported, and also the newer SMC Elite 16 Ultra.

Hewlett Packard
> HP 27252, HP 27247B, and HP J2405A.

D-Link
> DE-600 pocket adaptor, DE-100, DE-200, and DE-220-T. There's also a patch kit for the DE-650-T, which is a PCMCIA card.[†]

DEC
> DE200 (32K/64K), DE202, DE100, and DEPCA rev E.

---

* Paul can be reached at *gpg109@rsphysse.anu.edu.au.*

† It can be obtained, along with other Laptop-related stuff, from **tsx-11.mit.edu** in *packages/laptops.*

Allied Teliesis
    AT1500 and AT1700.

To use one of these cards with Linux, you may use a precompiled kernel from one of the major Linux distributions. These generally have drivers for all of them built in. In the long term, however, it's better to roll your own kernel and compile in only those drivers you actually need.

Ethernet Autoprobing

At boot time, the Ethernet code will try to locate your board and determine its type. The following table shows the order in which the kernel probes for cards (first one at the top) and the addresses that it checks.

Board	Addresses probed for
WD/SMC	0x300, 0x280, 0x380, 0x240
SMC 16 Ultra	0x300, 0x280
3c501	0x280
3c503	0x300, 0x310, 0x330, 0x350, 0x250, 0x280, 0x2a0, 0x2e0
NEx000	0x300, 0x280, 0x320, 0x340, 0x360
HP	0x300, 0x320, 0x340, 0x280, 0x2C0, 0x200, 0x240
DEPCA	0x300, 0x320, 0x340, 0x360

There are two limitations to the autoprobing code. For one, it may not recognize all boards properly. This is especially true for some of the cheaper clones of common boards and for some WD80x3 boards. The second problem is that the kernel will not auto-probe for more than one board at the moment. This is a feature because it is assumed you want to have control over which board is assigned which interface.

If you are using more than one board, or if the autoprobe should fail to detect your board, you have to tell the kernel explicitly about the card's base address and name.

In Net-3, you have can use two different schemes to accomplish this. One way is to change or add information in the *drivers/net/Space.c* file in the kernel source code that contains all information about drivers. This is recommended only if you are familiar with the networking code. A much better way is to provide the kernel with this information at boot time. If you use *lilo* to boot your system, you can pass parameters to the kernel by specifying them through the append option in *lilo.conf*. To inform the kernel about an Ethernet device, you can pass the following parameter:

```
ether=irq,base_addr,param1,param2,name
```

The first four parameters are numerical, while the last is the device name. All numerical values are optional; if they are omitted or set to zero, the kernel will try to detect the value by probing for it or use a default value.

The first parameter sets the IRQ assigned to the device. By default, the kernel will try to auto-detect the device's IRQ channel. The 3c503 driver has a special feature that selects a free IRQ from the list 5, 9, 3, 4, and configures the board to use this line.

The *base_addr* parameter gives the I/O base address of the board; a value of zero tells the kernel to probe the addresses listed above.

The remaining two parameters may be used differently by different drivers. For shared-memory boards such as the WD80x3, they specify start and end addresses of the shared memory area. Other cards commonly use *param1* to set the level of debugging information that is being displayed. Values of 1 through 7 denote increasing levels of verbosity, while 8 turns them off altogether; 0 denotes the default. The 3c503 driver uses *param2* to select the internal transceiver (default) or an external transceiver (a value of 1). The former uses the board's BNC connector; the latter uses its AUI port.

If you have two Ethernet boards, you can have Linux auto-detect one board and pass the second board's parameters with *lilo*. However, you must make sure the driver doesn't accidentally find the second board first or else the other one won't be registered at all. You do this by passing *lilo* a reserve option, which explicitly tells the kernel to avoid probing the I/O space taken up by the second board.

For instance, to make Linux install a second Ethernet board at 0x300 as *eth1*, you would pass the following parameters to the kernel:

```
reserve=0x300,32 ether=0,0x300,eth1
```

The **reserve** option makes sure no driver accesses the board's I/O space when probing for some device. You may also use the kernel parameters to override autoprobing for *eth0*:

```
reserve=0x340,32 ether=0,0x340,eth0
```

To turn off autoprobing altogether, you can specify a *base_addr* argument of -1:

```
ether=0,-1,eth0
```

The PLIP Driver

PLIP stands for *Parallel Line IP* and is a cheap way to network when you want to connect only two machines. It uses a parallel port and a special cable, achieving speeds of 10kBps to 20kBps.

PLIP was originally developed by Crynwr, Inc. Its design is rather ingenious (or, if you prefer, hackish): for a long time, the parallel ports on PCs used to be only uni-directional printer ports; the eight data lines could only be used to send from the PC to the peripheral device, but not the other way round. PLIP works around this by using the port's five status lines for input, which limits it to transferring all data as nibbles (half bytes) only. This mode of operation is called mode 0 PLIP. Today, these uni-directional ports don't seem to be used much anymore. Therefore, there is also a PLIP extension called mode 1 that uses the full 8-bit interface.

Currently, Linux only supports mode 0. Unlike earlier versions of the PLIP code, it now attempts to be compatible with the PLIP implementations from Crynwr, as well as the PLIP driver in NCSA *telnet*.[*] To connect two machines using PLIP, you need a special cable sold at some shops as "Null Printer" or "Turbo Laplink" cable. You can, however, make one yourself fairly easily. Appendix A, *A Null Printer Cable for PLIP*, shows you how.

The PLIP driver for Linux is the work of almost countless persons. It is currently maintained by Niibe Yutaka. If compiled into the kernel, it sets up a network interface for each of the possible printer ports, with *plip0* corresponding to parallel port *lp0*, *plip1* corresponding to *lp1*, etc. The mapping of interface to ports is currently this:

Interface	I/O Port	IRQ
plip0	0x3BC	7
plip1	0x378	7
plip2	0x278	5

If you have configured your printer port in a different way, you have to change these values in *drivers/net/Space.c* in the Linux kernel source and build a new kernel.

This mapping does not mean, however, that you cannot use these parallel ports as usual. They are accessed by the PLIP driver only when the corresponding interface is configured up.

---

[*] NCSA *telnet* is a popular program for DOS that runs TCP/IP over Ethernet or PLIP, and supports *telnet* and FTP.

The SLIP and PPP Drivers

SLIP (Serial Line IP) and PPP (Point-to-Point Protocol) are widely used protocols for sending IP packets over a serial link. A number of institutions offer dialup SLIP and PPP access to machines that are on the Internet, thus providing IP connectivity to private persons (something that's otherwise hardly affordable).

To run SLIP or PPP, no hardware modifications are necessary; you can use any serial port. Since serial port configuration is not specific to TCP/IP networking, a separate chapter has been devoted to this. Please refer to Chapter 4, *Setting Up the Serial Hardware*, for more information.

## CHAPTER FOUR

SETTING UP THE SERIAL HARDWARE

Serial HOWTO

There are rumors that there are some people out there in netland who only own one PC and don't have the money to spend on a T1 Internet link. To get their daily dose of news and mail nevertheless, they are said to rely on SLIP links, UUCP networks, and bulletin board systems (BBSs) that utilize public telephone networks.

This chapter is intended to help all those people who rely on modems to maintain their link. However, there are many details that this chapter cannot go into, for instance how to configure your modem for dialup. All these topics are covered in the Serial HOWTO by Greg Hankins,* which is posted to *comp.os.linux.announce* on a regular basis.

Communications Software for Modem Links

There are a number of communications packages available for Linux. Many of them are *terminal programs*, which allow a user to dial into another computer as if she was sitting in front of a simple terminal. The traditional terminal program for UNIXes is *kermit*. It is, however, somewhat Spartan. There are more comfortable programs available that support a dictionary of telephone numbers, script languages for calling and logging into remote computer systems, etc. One of them is *minicom*, which is close to some terminal programs former DOS users might be accustomed to. There are also X-based communications packages such as *seyon*.

---

* To be reached at *gregh@cc.gatech.edu*.

Also, a number of Linux-based BBS packages are available for people who want to run a bulletin board system. Some of these packages can be found at **sunsite.unc.edu** in */pub/Linux/system/Network.*

Apart from terminal programs, there is also software that uses a serial link non-interactively to transport data to or from your computer. The advantage of this technique is that it takes much less time to download a few dozen kilobytes automatically than it might take you to read your mail online in some mailbox and browse a bulletin board for interesting articles. On the other hand, this requires more disk storage because of the loads of useless information you usually get.

The epitome of this sort of communications software is UUCP. It is a program suite that copies files from one host to another, executes programs on a remote host, etc. It is frequently used to transport mail or news in private networks. Ian Taylor's UUCP package, which also runs under Linux, is described in the following chapter. Other non-interactive communications software is, for example, used throughout Fidonet. Ports of Fidonet applications like *ifmail* are also available.

SLIP is somewhat inbetween, allowing both interactive and non-interactive use. Many people use SLIP to dial up their campus network or some other sort of public SLIP server to run FTP sessions, etc. SLIP may however also be used over permanent or semi-permanent connections for LAN-to-LAN coupling, although this is really only interesting with ISDN.

Introduction to Serial Devices

The devices a UNIX kernel provides for accessing serial devices are typically called *ttys*. This is an abbreviation for *Teletype,*™ which used to be one of the major manufacturers of terminals in the early days of UNIX. The term is used nowadays for any character-based data terminal. Throughout this chapter, we will use the term exclusively to refer to kernel devices.

Linux distinguishes three classes of ttys: (virtual) consoles, pseudo-terminals (similar to a two-way pipe, used by applications such as X11), and serial devices. The latter are also counted as ttys, because they permit interactive sessions over a serial connection, be it from a hard-wired terminal or a remote computer over a telephone line.

Ttys have a number of configurable parameters which can be set using the *ioctl(2)* system call. Many of them apply only to serial devices since they need a great deal more flexibility to handle varying types of connections.

Among the most prominent line parameters are the line speed and parity. But there are also flags for the conversion between upper and lower case characters, of carriage return into line feed, etc. The tty driver may also support various *line disciplines* which make the device driver behave completely different. For example, the SLIP driver for Linux is implemented by means of a special line discipline.

There is a bit of ambiguity about how to measure a line's speed. The correct term is *bit rate*, which is related to the line's transfer speed measured in bits per second (or bps for short). Sometimes, you hear people refer to it as the *Baud rate*, which is not quite correct. These two terms are not interchangeable. The Baud rate refers to a physical characteristic of some serial device, namely the clock rate at which pulses are transmitted. The bit rate denotes a characteristic of an existing serial connection between two points, namely the average number of bits transferred per second. It is important to know that these two values are usually different, as most devices encode more than one bit per electrical pulse.

Accessing Serial Devices

Like all devices in a UNIX system, serial ports are accessed through device special files, located in the */dev* directory. There are two varieties of device files related to serial drivers, and for each port, there is one device file from each of them. Depending on the file it is accessed by, the device will behave differently.

The first variety is used whenever the port is used for dialing in; it has a major number of 4, and the files are named *ttyS0*, *ttyS1*, etc. The second variety is used when dialing out through a port; the files are called *cua0*, *cua1*, etc., and have a major number of 5.

Minor numbers are identical for both types. If you have your modem on one of the ports *COM1* through *COM4*, its minor number will be the *COM* port number plus 63. If your setup is different from that, for example when using a board supporting multiple serial lines, please refer to the Serial HOWTO.

Assume your modem is on *COM2*. Thus its minor number will be 65, and its major number will be 5 for dialing out. There should be a device *cua1* which has these numbers. List the serial ttys in the */dev* directory. Columns 5 and 6 should show major and minor numbers, respectively:

```
$ ls -l /dev/cua*
crw-rw-rw-  1 root     root       5,  64 Nov 30 19:31 /dev/cua0
crw-rw-rw-  1 root     root       5,  65 Nov 30 22:08 /dev/cua1
crw-rw-rw-  1 root     root       5,  66 Oct 28 11:56 /dev/cua2
crw-rw-rw-  1 root     root       5,  67 Mar 19  1992 /dev/cua3
```

If there is no such device, you will have to create one: become superuser and type

```
# mknod -m 666 /dev/cua1 c 5 65
# chown root.root /dev/cua1
```

Some people suggest making */dev/modem* a symbolic link to your modem device so that casual users don't have to remember the somewhat unintuitive *cua1*. However, you cannot use *modem* in one program and the real device file name in another. This is because these programs use *lock files* to signal that the device is being used. By convention, the lock file name for *cua1*, for instance, is *LCK..cua1*. Using different device files for the same port means that different programs will fail to recognize each other's lock files and will use the device at the same time. As a result, the applications will not work at all.

Serial Hardware

Linux currently supports a wide variety of serial boards which use the RS-232 standard. RS-232 is currently the most common standard for serial communications in the PC world. It uses a number of circuits for transmitting single bits as well as for synchronization. Additional lines may be used for signaling the presence of a carrier (used by modems) and handshake.

Although hardware handshake is optional, it is very useful. It allows either of the two stations to signal whether it is ready to receive more data, or if the other station should pause until the receiver is done processing the incoming data. The lines used for this are called "Clear to Send" (CTS) and "Ready to Send" (RTS), respectively, which accounts for the colloquial name of hardware handshake "RTS/CTS."

In PCs, the RS-232 interface is usually driven by a UART chip derived from the National Semiconductor 16450 chip, or a newer version thereof, the NSC 16550A.[*] Some brands (most notably internal modems equipped with the Rockwell chip set) also use completely different chips that have been programmed to behave as if they were 16550's.

The main difference between 16450's and 16550's is that the latter have a FIFO buffer of 16 bytes, while the former only have a 1-byte buffer. This makes 16450's suitable for speeds up to 9600 Baud, while higher speeds require a 16550-compatible chip. Besides these chips, Linux also supports the 8250 chip, which was the original UART for the PC-AT.

In the default configuration, the kernel checks the four standard serial ports *COM1* through *COM4*. These will be assigned device minor numbers 64 through 67, as described above.

If you want to configure your serial ports properly, you should install Ted Tso's *setserial* command along with the *rc.serial* script. This script should be invoked from */etc/rc* at system boot time. It uses *setserial* to configure the kernel serial devices. A typical *rc.serial* script looks like this:

setserial(8)

```
# /etc/rc.serial - serial line configuration script.
#
# Do wild interrupt detection
/sbin/setserial -W /dev/cua*
# Configure serial devices
/sbin/setserial /dev/cua0 auto_irq skip_test autoconfig
/sbin/setserial /dev/cua1 auto_irq skip_test autoconfig
/sbin/setserial /dev/cua2 auto_irq skip_test autoconfig
```

---

* There was also a NSC 16550, but its FIFO never really worked.

```
/sbin/setserial /dev/cua3 auto_irq skip_test autoconfig
# Display serial device configuration
/sbin/setserial -bg /dev/cua*
```

If your serial card is not detected, or the *setserial -bg* command shows an incorrect setting, you will have to force the configuration by explicitly supplying the correct values. Users with internal modems equipped with the Rockwell chipset are reported to experience this problem. If, for example, the UART chip is reported to be a NSC 16450, while in fact it is NSC 16550-compatible, you have to change the configuration command for the offending port to:

```
/sbin/setserial /dev/cua1 auto_irq skip_test autoconfig uart 16550
```

Similar options exist to force *COM* port, base address, and IRQ setting. Please refer to the *setserial(8)* manual page.

If your modem supports hardware handshake, you should make sure to enable it. Surprising as it is, most communication programs do not attempt to enable this by default; you have to set it manually. This is best performed in the *rc.serial* script using the *stty* command:

```
$ stty crtscts < /dev/cua1
```

To check if hardware handshake is in effect, use:

```
$ stty -a < /dev/cua1
```

This command gives you the status of all flags for that device; a flag shown with a preceding minus as in *–crtscts* means that the flag has been turned off.

CHAPTER FIVE

CONFIGURING TCP/IP NETWORKING

I n this chapter, we will go through all the steps necessary to set up TCP/IP networking on your machine. Starting with the assignment of IP addresses, we will slowly work our way through the configuration of TCP/IP network interfaces and introduce a few tools that come in quite handy when hunting down problems with your network installation.

Most of the tasks covered in this chapter you will generally have to do only once. Afterwards, you have to touch most configuration files only when adding a new system to your network or when you reconfigure your system entirely. Some of the commands used to configure TCP/IP, however, have to be executed each time the system is booted. This is usually done by invoking them from the system /etc/rc scripts.

Commonly, the network-specific part of this procedure is contained in a script called *rc.net* or *rc.inet*. Sometimes, you will also see two scripts named *rc.inet1* and *rc.inet2*, where the former initializes the kernel part of networking, while the latter starts basic networking services and applications. I will use the two-script concept of *rc.inet1* and *rc.inet2*, and their separate functionalities.

Below, I will discuss the actions performed by *rc.inet1*, while applications will be covered in later chapters. After finishing this chapter, you should have established a sequence of commands that properly configure TCP/IP networking on your computer. You should then replace any sample commands in *rc.inet1* with your commands, make sure *rc.inet1* is executed at startup time, and reboot your machine. The networking *rc* scripts that come along with your favorite Linux distribution should give you a good example.

Setting Up the proc Filesystem

Some of the configuration tools of the Net-2 release rely on the *proc* file system for communicating with the kernel. This is an interface that permits access to kernel run-time information through a file system-like mechanism. When mounted, you can list its files like any other file system, or display their contents. Typical items include the *loadavg* file, which contains the system load average, and *meminfo*, which shows current core memory and swap usage.

To this, the networking code adds the *net* directory. It contains a number of files that show things like the kernel ARP tables, the state of TCP connections, and the routing tables. Most network administration tools get their information from these files.

The *proc* file system (or *procfs* as it is also known) is usually mounted on */proc* at system boot time. The best method is to add the following line to */etc/fstab*:

```
# procfs mount point:
none              /proc           proc    defaults
```

Then execute *mount /proc* from your */etc/rc* script.

The *procfs* is nowadays configured into most kernels by default. If the *procfs* is not in your kernel, you will get a message like "mount: fs type procfs not supported by kernel." You will then have to recompile the kernel and answer "yes" when asked for *procfs* support.

Installing the Binaries

If you are using one of the pre-packaged Linux distributions, it will probably contain the major networking applications and utilities along with a coherent set of sample files. The only case where you might have to obtain and install new utilities is when you install a new kernel release. As they occasionally involve changes in the kernel networking layer, you will need to update the basic configuration tools. This at least involves recompiling, but sometimes you may also be required to obtain the latest set of binaries. These are usually distributed along with the kernel, packaged in an archive called *net-XXX.tar.gz*, where *XXX* is the version number. The release matching Linux 1.0 is 0.32b. Starting with kernel revision 1.1.27, the filename was changed to *net-tools-XXX.tar.gz*, and the version numbers now reflect the revision number of the kernel they apply to.

If you want to compile and install the standard TCP/IP network applications yourself, you can obtain the sources from most Linux FTP servers. These are more or less heavily patched versions of programs from Net-BSD or other sources. Other applications, such as Mosaic and Archie, or Gopher and IRC clients must be obtained separately. Most of them compile out of the box if you follow the instructions.

The official FTP site for Net-3 is **sunacm.swan.ac.uk**, mirrored by **sunsite.unc.edu** below *system/Network/sunacm*. The latest Net-2e patch kit and binaries are available from **ftp.aris.com**. Matthias Urlichs's BSD-derived networking code can be obtained from **ftp.ira.uka.de** in */pub/system/linux/netbsd*.

Another Example

For the remainder of this book, let me introduce a new example that is less complex than Groucho Marx University and may be closer to the tasks you will actually encounter. Consider the Virtual Brewery, a small company that brews, as the name indicates, virtual beer. To manage their business more efficiently, the virtual brewers want to network their computers, which all happen to be PCs running a bright and shiny Linux 1.0.

On the same floor, just across the hall, there's the Virtual Winery, which works closely with the brewery. The vintners run an Ethernet of their own. Quite naturally, the two companies want to link their networks once they are operational. As a first step, they want to set up a gateway host that forwards datagrams between the two subnets. Later, they also want to have a UUCP link to the outside world, through which they exchange mail and news. In the long run, they also want to set up a SLIP connection to connect to the Internet occasionally.

Setting the Hostname

Most, if not all, network applications rely on the local host's name having been set to some reasonable value. This is usually done during the boot procedure by executing the *hostname* command. To set the hostname to **name**, it is invoked as:

```
# hostname name
```

It is common practice to use the unqualified hostname without specifying the domain name. For instance, hosts at the Virtual Brewery might be called **vale.vbrew.com**, **vlager.vbrew.com**, etc. These are their official, fully qualified domain names. Their local hostnames would be only the first component of the name, such as **vale**. However, as the local hostname is frequently used to look up the host's IP address, you have to make sure that the resolver library is able to look up the host's IP address. This usually means that you have to enter the name in */etc/hosts*.

Some people suggest using the *domainname* command to set the kernel's idea of a domain name to the remaining part of the FQDN. This way you could combine the output from *hostname* and *domainname* to get the FQDN again. However, this is at best only half correct. *domainname* is generally used to set the host's NIS domain, which may be entirely different from the DNS domain your host belongs to.

Assigning IP Addresses

If you configure the networking software on your host for standalone operation (for instance, to be able to run the INN Netnews software), you can safely skip this section, because the only IP address you will need is for the loopback interface, which is always 127.0.0.1.

Things are a little more complicated with real networks like Ethernets. If you want to connect your host to an existing network, you have to ask its administrators to give you an IP address on this network. When setting up a network all by yourself, you have to assign IP addresses yourself.

Hosts within a local network should usually share addresses from the same logical IP network. Hence you have to assign an IP network address. If you have several physical networks, you either have to assign them different network numbers, or use subnetting to split your IP address range into several subnetworks. Subnetting will be revisited in the next section.

When picking an IP network number, much depends on whether you intend to get on the Internet in the near future. If so, you should obtain an official IP address *now*. The best way to proceed is to ask your network service provider to help you. If you want to obtain a network number just in case you might get on the Internet someday, request a Network Address Application Form from *hostmaster@internic.net*, or your country's own Network Information Center if there is one.[*]

If your network is not connected to the Internet and won't be in the near future, you are free to choose any legal network address. Just make sure no packets from your internal network escape to the real Internet. To make sure no harm can be done, even if packets *did* escape, you should use one of the network numbers reserved for private use. The Internet Assigned Numbers Authority (IANA) has set aside several network numbers from classes A, B, and C that you can use without registering. These addresses are only valid within your private network and are not routed between real Internet sites. The numbers are:

RFC 1597

Class	Networks
A	10.0.0.0
B	172.16.0.0 through 172.31.0.0
C	192.168.0.0 through 192.168.255.0

Note that the second and third blocks contain 16 and 256 networks, respectively.

Picking your addresses from one of these network numbers is not only useful for networks completely unconnected to the Internet; you can still implement a

---

[*] You can explore your options for getting on the Internet in the book *Connecting to the Internet: An O'Reilly Buyer's Guide* by Susan Estrada.

slightly more restricted access using a single host as a gateway. To your local network, the gateway is accessible by its internal IP address, while the outside world knows it by an officially registered address (assigned to you by your IP provider). We come back to this concept in connection with using SLIP in Chapter 7, *Serial Line IP*.

Throughout the remainder of the book, we will assume that the brewery's network manager uses a class B network number, say **172.16.0.0**. Of course, a class C network number would definitely suffice to accomodate both the Brewery's and the Winery's networks. I use a class B network here for the sake of simplicity only, as it will make the subnetting examples in the next section of this chapter more intuitive.

Creating Subnets

To operate several Ethernets (or other networks, once a driver is available), you have to split your network into subnets. Note that subnetting is required only if you have more than one *broadcast network*—point-to-point links don't count. For instance, if you have one Ethernet, and one or more SLIP links to the outside world, you don't need to subnet your network. The reason for this will be explained in Chapter 7.

To accommodate the two Ethernets, the Brewery's network manager decides to use eight bits of the host part as additional subnet bits. This leaves another eight bits for the host part, allowing for 254 hosts on each of the subnets. She then assigns subnet number 1 to the brewery, and gives the winery number 2. Their respective network addresses are thus **172.16.1.0** and **172.16.2.0**. The subnet mask is **255.255.255.0**.

vlager, which is the gateway between the two networks, is assigned a host number of 1 on both of them, which gives it the IP addresses **172.16.1.1** and **172.16.2.1**, respectively. Figure 5-1 shows the two subnets and the gateway.

Note that in this example I am using a class B network to keep things simple; a class C network would be more realistic. With the new networking code, subnetting is not limited to byte boundaries, so even a class C network may be split into several subnets. For instance, you could use two bits of the host part for the netmask, giving you four possible subnets with 64 hosts on each.[*]

---

[*] The last number on each subnet is reserved as the broadcast address, so it's in fact 63 hosts per subnet.

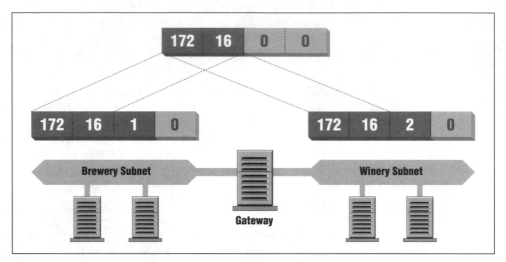

Figure 5-1. The Virtual Brewery and Virtual Winery subnets

Writing hosts and networks Files

After you have subnetted your network, you should prepare for some simple sort of hostname resolution using the */etc/hosts* file. If you are not going to use DNS or NIS for address resolution, you have to put all hosts in the *hosts* file.

Even if you want to run DNS or NIS during normal operation, you want to have some subset of all hostnames in */etc/hosts* nevertheless. For one, you want to have some sort of name resolution even when no network interfaces are running, for example, during boot time. This is not only a matter of convenience, but also allows you to use symbolic hostnames in your *rc.inet* scripts. Thus, when changing IP addresses, you only have to copy an updated *hosts* file to all machines and reboot, rather than edit a large number of *rc* files separately. Usually, you will put all local hostnames and addresses in *hosts*, adding those of any gateways and NIS servers if used.[*]

Also, during intial testing, you should make sure your resolver only uses information from the *hosts* file. Your DNS or NIS software may come with sample files that may produce strange results when being used. To make all applications use */etc/hosts* exclusively when looking up the IP address of a host, you have to edit the */etc/host.conf* file. Comment out any lines that begin with the keyword `order` by preceding them with a hash sign, and insert the line

```
order hosts
```

---

[*] You will need the address of any NIS servers only if you use Peter Eriksson's NYS. Other NIS implementations locate their servers only at run-time by using *ypbind*.

The configuration of the resolver library will be covered in detail in Chapter 6, *Name Service and Resolver Configuration.*

The *hosts* file contains one entry per line, consisting of an IP address, a hostname, and an optional list of aliases for the hostname. The fields are separated by spaces or tabs, and the address field must begin in column one. Anything following a hash sign (#) is regarded as a comment and is ignored.

Hostnames can be either fully qualified or relative to the local domain. For **vale**, you would usually enter the the fully qualified name, **vale.vbrew.com**, and **vale** by itself in the *hosts* file so that it is known by both its official name and the shorter local name.

This is an example how a *hosts* file at the Virtual Brewery might look. Two special names are included, **vlager-if1** and **vlager-if2**, which give the addresses for both interfaces used on **vlager**

```
#
# Hosts file for Virtual Brewery/Virtual Winery
#
# IP            FQDN                 aliases
#
127.0.0.1       localhost
#
172.16.1.1      vlager.vbrew.com     vlager vlager-if1
172.16.1.2      vstout.vbrew.com     vstout
172.16.1.3      vale.vbrew.com       vale
#
172.16.2.1      vlager-if2
172.16.2.2      vbeaujolais.vbrew.com vbeaujolais
172.16.2.3      vbardolino.vbrew.com  vbardolino
172.16.2.4      vchianti.vbrew.com    vchianti
```

Just as with a host's IP address, you sometimes would like to use a symbolic name for network numbers, too. Therefore, the *hosts* file has a companion called */etc/networks* that maps network names to network numbers and vice versa. At the Virtual Brewery, we might install a *networks* file like this:[*]

```
# /etc/networks for the Virtual Brewery
brew-net        172.16.1.0
wine-net        172.16.2.0
```

---

* Note that names in *networks* must not collide with hostnames from the *hosts* file, or else some programs may produce strange results.

Interface Configuration for IP

After setting up your hardware as explained in the previous chapter, you have to make these devices known to the kernel networking software. A couple of commands are used to configure the network interfaces and initialize the routing table. These tasks are usually performed from the *rc.inet1* script each time the system is booted. The basic tools for this are called *ifconfig* (where "if" stands for interface) and *route*.

ifconfig is used to make an interface accessible to the kernel networking layer. This involves the assignment of an IP address and other parameters, and activating the interface, also known as "taking up." Being active here means that the kernel will send and receive IP datagrams through the interface. The simplest way to invoke it is with:

```
ifconfig interface ip-address
```

which assigns *ip-address* to *interface* and activates it. All other parameters are set to default values. For instance, the default subnet mask is derived from the network class of the IP address, such as **255.255.0.0** for a class B address. *ifconfig* is described in detail at the end of this chapter.

route allows you to add or remove routes from the kernel routing table. It can be invoked as:

```
route [add|del] target
```

The *add* and *del* arguments determine whether to add or delete the route to *target*.

The Loopback Interface

The very first interface to be activated is the loopback interface:

```
# ifconfig lo 127.0.0.1
```

Occasionally, you will also see the dummy hostname **localhost** being used instead of the IP address. *ifconfig* will look up the name in the *hosts* file where an entry should declare it as the hostname for **127.0.0.1**:

```
# Sample /etc/hosts entry for localhost
localhost     127.0.0.1
```

To view the configuration of an interface, you invoke *ifconfig* giving it the interface name as argument:

```
$ ifconfig lo
lo        Link encap Local Loopback
          inet addr 127.0.0.1  Bcast [NONE SET]  Mask 255.0.0.0
          UP BROADCAST LOOPBACK RUNNING  MTU 2000  Metric 1
```

```
RX packets 0 errors 0 dropped 0 overrun 0
TX packets 0 errors 0 dropped 0 overrun 0
```

As you can see, the loopback interface has been assigned a netmask of **255.0.0.0**, since **127.0.0.1** is a class A address. No broadcast address is set, and there isn't much need for one anyway when you're dealing with the loopback interface. However, if you run the *rwhod* daemon on your host, you may have to set the loopback device's broadcast address in order for *rwho* to function properly. You can find out how to set the broadcast address in the section "All About ifconfig," later in this chapter.

Now, you can almost start playing with your mini-"network." What is still missing is an entry in the routing table that tells IP that it may use this interface as a route to destination **127.0.0.1**. This is accomplished by typing:

```
# route add 127.0.0.1
```

Again, you can use **localhost** instead of the IP address.

Next, you should check that everything works fine, for example by using *ping*. *ping* is the networking equivalent of a sonar device.[*] The command is used to verify that a given address is actually reachable, and to measure the delay that occurs when sending a datagram to it and back again. The time required for this is often referred to as the round-trip time.

```
# ping localhost
PING localhost (127.0.0.1): 56 data bytes
64 bytes from 127.0.0.1: icmp_seq=0 ttl=32 time=1 ms
64 bytes from 127.0.0.1: icmp_seq=1 ttl=32 time=0 ms
64 bytes from 127.0.0.1: icmp_seq=2 ttl=32 time=0 ms
^C
--- localhost ping statistics ---
3 packets transmitted, 3 packets received, 0
round-trip min/avg/max = 0/0/1 ms
```

When invoking *ping* as shown here, it will go on emitting packets forever unless interrupted by the user. The ^C above marks the place where we pressed Ctrl-C.

The above example shows that packets for **127.0.0.1** are properly delivered and a reply is returned to *ping* almost instantaneously. This shows you have succeeded in setting up your first network interface.

If the output you get from *ping* does not resemble that shown above, you are in trouble. Check any error if they indicate that some file hasn't been installed properly. Check that the *ifconfig* and *route* binaries you use are compatible with the kernel release you run and above all, that the kernel has been compiled with networking enabled (you see this from the presence of the */proc/net* directory). If you get an error message saying "Network unreachable," then you probably got the *route* command wrong. Make sure you use the same address you gave to *ifconfig*.

---

* Anyone remember Pink Floyd's "Echoes"?

The steps described above are enough to use networking applications on a stand-alone host. After adding the above lines to *rc.inet1* and making sure both *rc.inet* scripts are executed from */etc/rc*, you may reboot your machine and try out various applications. For instance, *telnet localhost* should establish a *telnet* connection to your host, giving you a login prompt.

However, the loopback interface is useful not only as an example in networking books, or as a testbed during development, but is actually used by some applications during normal operation.* Therefore, you always have to configure it, regardless of whether your machine is attached to a network or not.

Ethernet Interfaces

Configuring an Ethernet interface is pretty much the same as with the loopback interface, it just requires a few more parameters when you are using subnetting.

At the Virtual Brewery, we have subnetted the IP network, which was originally a class B network, into class C subnetworks. To make the interface recognize this, the *ifconfig* incantation would look like this:

```
# ifconfig eth0 vstout netmask 255.255.255.0
```

This command assigns the *eth0* interface the IP address of **vstout** (**172.16.1.2**). If we had omitted the netmask, *ifconfig* would have deduced the netmask from the IP network class, which would have resulted in a netmask of **255.255.0.0**. Now a quick check shows:

```
# ifconfig eth0
eth0     Link encap 10Mps Ethernet HWaddr  00:00:C0:90:B3:42
         inet addr 172.16.1.2 Bcast 172.16.1.255 Mask 255.255.255.0
         UP BROADCAST RUNNING  MTU 1500  Metric 1
         RX packets 0 errors 0 dropped 0 overrun 0
         TX packets 0 errors 0 dropped 0 overrun 0
```

You can see that *ifconfig* automatically sets the broadcast address (the Bcast field above) to the usual value, which is the host's network number with all the host bits set. Also, the message transfer unit (the maximum size of Ethernet frames the kernel will generate for this interface) has been set to the maximum value of 1500 bytes. All these values can be overidden with special options that will be described later.

Quite similar to the loopback case, you now have to install a routing entry that informs the kernel about the network that can be reached through *eth0*. For the Virtual Brewery, you would invoke *route* as

```
# route add -net 172.16.1.0
```

---

* For instance, all applications based on RPC use the loopback interface to register themselves with the *portmapper* daemon at startup.

At first, this looks a little like magic, because it's not really clear how *route* detects which interface to route through. However, the trick is rather simple: the kernel checks all interfaces that have been configured so far and compares the destination address (**172.16.1.0** in this case) to the network part of the interface address (that is, the bitwise AND of the interface address and the netmask). The only interface that matches is *eth0*.

Now, what's that *–net* option for? This is used because *route* can handle both routes to networks and routes to single hosts (as you saw above with **localhost**). When being given an address in dotted quad notation, *route* attempts to guess whether it is a network or a hostname by looking at the host part bits. If the address's host part is zero, *route* assumes it denotes a network; otherwise *route* takes it as a host address. Therefore, *route* would think that **172.16.1.0** is a host address rather than a network number, because it cannot know that we use subnetting. We therefore have to tell it explicitly that it denotes a network, giving it the *–net* flag.

Of course, the above *route* command is a little tedious to type, and it's prone to spelling mistakes. A more convenient approach is to use the network names we defined in */etc/networks*. This makes the command much more readable; even the *–net* flag can now be omitted because *route* now knows that **172.16.1.0** denotes a network.

```
# route add brew-net
```

Now that you've finished the basic configuration steps, we want to make sure your Ethernet interface is indeed running happily. Choose a host from your Ethernet, for instance **vlager**, and type:

```
# ping vlager
PING vlager: 64 byte packets
64 bytes from 172.16.1.1: icmp_seq=0. time=11. ms
64 bytes from 172.16.1.1: icmp_seq=1. time=7. ms
64 bytes from 172.16.1.1: icmp_seq=2. time=12. ms
64 bytes from 172.16.1.1: icmp_seq=3. time=3. ms
^C
----vstout.vbrew.com PING Statistics----
4 packets transmitted, 4 packets received, 0
round-trip (ms)  min/avg/max = 3/8/12
```

If you don't see any output similar to this, then something is broken, obviously. If you encounter unusual packet loss rates, this hints at a hardware problem, like bad or missing terminators, etc. If you don't receive any packets at all, you should check the interface configuration with *netstat*. The packet statistics displayed by *ifconfig* should tell you whether any packets have been sent out on the interface at all. If you have access to the remote host too, you should go over to that machine and check the interface statistics. This way you can determine exactly where the packets got dropped. In addition, you should display the routing information with *route* to see if both hosts have the correct routing entry. *route* prints out the complete kernel routing table when invoked without any arguments (*−n* only makes it print addresses as dotted quad instead of using the hostname):

```
# route -n
Kernel routing table
Destination     Gateway         Genmask         Flags Metric Ref Use    Iface
127.0.0.1       *          -    255.255.255.255 UH    1      0   112 lo
172.16.1.0      *               255.255.255.0   U     1      0    10 eth0
```

The detailed meaning of these fields is explained below in the section "Checking with netstat." The `Flags` column contains a list of flags set for each interface. `U` is always set for active interfaces, and `H` says the destination address denotes a host. If the `H` flag is set for a route that you meant to be a network route, then you have to reissue the *route* command with the *−net* option. To check whether a route you have entered is used at all, check if the `Use` field in the second to last column increases between two invocations of *ping*.

Routing Through a Gateway

In the previous section, I covered only the case of setting up a host on a single Ethernet. Quite frequently, however, one encounters networks connected to one another by gateways. These gateways may simply link two or more Ethernets, but may provide a link to the outside world, the Internet, as well. In order to use the service of a gateway, you have to provide additional routing information to the networking layer.

For instance, the Ethernets of the Virtual Brewery and the Virtual Winery are linked through such a gateway, namely the host **vlager**. Assuming that **vlager** has already been configured, we only have to add another entry to **vstout**'s routing table that tells the kernel it can reach all hosts on the Winery's network through **vlager**. The appropriate incantation of *route* is shown below; the **gw** keyword tells it that the next argument denotes a gateway.

```
# route add wine-net gw vlager
```

Of course, any host on the Winery network you wish to talk to must have a corresponding routing entry for the Brewery's network. Otherwise you would only be able to send data from **vstout** to **vbardolino**, but any response returned by the latter would go into the great bit bucket.

This example describes only a gateway that switches packets between two isolated Ethernets. Now assume that **vlager** also has a connection to the Internet (say, through an additional SLIP link). Then we would want datagrams to *any* destination network other than the Brewery to be handed to **vlager**. This can be accomplished by making it the default gateway for **vstout**:

```
# route add default gw vlager
```

The network name **default** is a shorthand for 0.0.0.0, which denotes the default route. You do not have to add this name to */etc/networks*, because it is built into *route*.

If you see high packet loss rates when pinging a host behind one or more gateways, this may hint at a very congested network. Packet loss is not so much due to technical deficiencies as due to temporary excess loads on forwarding hosts, which makes them delay or even drop incoming datagrams.

Configuring a Gateway

Configuring a machine to switch packets between two Ethernets is pretty straightforward. Assume we're back at **vlager**, which is equipped with two Ethernet boards, each being connected to one of the two networks. All you have to do is configure both interfaces separately, giving them their respective IP addresses, and that's it.

It is quite useful to add information on the two interfaces to the *hosts* file as shown below, so we have handy names for them, too:

```
172.16.1.1      vlager.vbrew.com    vlager vlager-if1
172.16.2.1      vlager-if2
```

The sequence of commands to set up the two interfaces is then:

```
# ifconfig eth0 vlager-if1
# ifconfig eth1 vlager-if2
# route add brew-net
# route add wine-net
```

The PLIP Interface

When using a PLIP link to connect two machines, things are a little different from what you have to do when using an Ethernet. The former are so-called *point-to-point* links, because they involve only two hosts ("points"), as opposed to broadcast networks.

As an example, we consider the laptop computer of some employee at the Virtual Brewery that is connected to **vlager** via PLIP. The laptop itself is called **vlite** and has only one parallel port. At boot time, this port will be registered as *plip1*. To activate the link, you have to configure the *plip1* interface using the following commands:[*]

```
# ifconfig plip1 vlite pointopoint vlager
# route add default gw vlager
```

---

[*] Note that *pointopoint* is not a typo. It's really spelled like this.

The first command configures the interface, telling the kernel that this is a point-to-point link, with the remote side having the address of **vlager**. The second installs the default route, using **vlager** as gateway. On **vlager**, a similar *ifconfig* command is necessary to activate the link (a *route* invocation is not needed):

```
# ifconfig plip1 vlager pointopoint vlite
```

The interesting point is that the *plip1* interface on **vlager** does not have to have a separate IP address, but may also be given the address **172.16.1.1**.*

Now, we have configured routing from the laptop to the Brewery's network; what's still missing is a way to route from any of the Brewery's hosts to **vlite**. One particularly cumbersome way is to add a specific route to every host's routing table that names **vlager** as a gateway to **vlite**:

```
# route add vlite gw vlager
```

A much better option when faced with temporary routes is to use dynamic routing. One way to do so is to use *gated*, a routing daemon, which you would have to install on each host in the network in order to distribute routing information dynamically. The easiest way, however, is to use *proxy ARP* (Address Resolution Protocol). With proxy ARP, **vlager** will respond to any ARP query for **vlite** by sending its own Ethernet address. The effect of this is that all packets for **vlite** will wind up at **vlager**, which then forwards them to the laptop. We will come back to proxy ARP in the section "Checking the ARP Tables."

Future Net-3 releases will contain a tool called *plipconfig*, which will allow you to set the IRQ to be used for the printer port. Later, this may even be replaced by a more general *ifconfig* command.

The SLIP and PPP Interface

Chapter 7
Chapter 8

Although SLIP and PPP links are only simple point-to-point links like PLIP connections, there is much more to be said about them. Usually, establishing a SLIP connection involves dialing up a remote site through your modem and setting the serial line to SLIP mode. PPP is used in a similar fashion.

The Dummy Interface

The dummy interface is a little exotic, but rather useful nevertheless. Its main benefit is with stand-alone hosts and machines whose only IP network connection is a dialup link. In fact, the latter are standalone hosts most of the time, too.

The dilemma with standalone hosts is that they only have a single network device active, the loopback device, which is usually assigned the address **127.0.0.1**. On

---

* Just as a matter of caution, you should however configure a PLIP or SLIP link only after you have completely set up the routing table entries for your Ethernets. With some older kernels, your network route might otherwise end up pointing at the point-to-point link.

some occasions, however, you need to send data to the "official" IP address of the local host. For instance, consider the laptop **vlite**, which has been disconnected from any network for the duration of this example. An application on **vlite** may now want to send some data to another application on the same host. Looking up **vlite** in */etc/hosts* yields an IP address of **172.16.1.65**, so the application tries to send to this address. As the loopback interface is currently the only active interface on the machine, the kernel has no idea that this address actually refers to itself! As a consequence, the kernel discards the datagram and returns an error to the application.

This is where the dummy device steps in. It solves the dilemma by simply serving as the alter ego of the loopback interface. In the case of **vlite**, you would simply give it the address **172.16.1.65** and add a host route pointing to it. Every datagram for **172.16.1.65** would then be delivered locally. The proper invocation is:

```
# ifconfig dummy vlite
# route add vlite
```

All About ifconfig

There are a lot more parameters to *ifconfig* than we have described so far. Its normal invocation is this:

```
ifconfig interface [address [parameters]]
```

interface is the interface name, and *address* is the IP address to be assigned to the interface. This may be either an IP address in dotted quad notation or a name that *ifconfig* will look up in */etc/hosts*.

If *ifconfig* is invoked with only the interface name, it displays that interface's configuration. When invoked without any parameters, it displays all interfaces you have configured so far; an option of *−a* forces it to show the inactive ones as well. A sample invocation for the Ethernet interface *eth0* may look like this:

```
# ifconfig eth0
eth0      Link encap 10Mbps Ethernet  HWaddr 00:00:C0:90:B3:42
          inet addr 172.16.1.2 Bcast 172.16.1.255 Mask 255.255.255.0
          UP BROADCAST RUNNING  MTU 1500  Metric 0
          RX packets 3136 errors 217 dropped 7 overrun 26
          TX packets 1752 errors 25 dropped 0 overrun 0
```

The MTU and Metric fields show the current MTU and metric value for that interface. The metric value is traditionally used by some operating systems to compute the cost of a route. Linux doesn't use this value yet, but defines it for compatibility nevertheless.

The RX and TX lines show how many packets have been received or transmitted error free, how many errors occurred, how many packets were dropped (probably because of low memory), and how many were lost because of an overrun.

Receiver overruns usually happen when packets come in faster than the kernel can service the last interrupt. The flag values printed by *ifconfig* correspond more or less to the names of its command-line options; they will be explained below.

The following is a list of parameters recognized by *ifconfig* with the corresponding flag names. Options that simply turn on a feature also allow it to be turned off again by preceding the option name by a dash (–).

up This makes an interface accessible to the IP layer. This option is implied when an *address* is given on the command line. It may also be used to re-eenable an interface that has been taken down temporarily using the down option.

(This option corresponds to the flags *UP* and *RUNNING.*)

down
This marks an interface as inaccessible to the IP layer. This effectively disables any IP traffic through the interface. Note that this does not delete all routing entries that use this interface automatically. If you take the interface down permanently, you should to delete these routing entries and supply alternative routes if possible.

netmask *mask*
This assigns a subnet mask to be used by the interface. It may be given as either a 32-bit hexadecimal number preceded by 0x, or as a dotted quad of decimal numbers.

pointopoint *address*
This option is used for point-to-point IP links that involve only two hosts. This option is needed to configure, for example, SLIP or PLIP interfaces.

(If a point-to-point address has been set, *ifconfig* displays the POINTOPOINT flag.)

broadcast *address*
The broadcast address is usually made up from the network number by setting all bits of the host part. Some IP implementations (systems derived from BSD 4.2, for instance) use a different scheme where all host part bits are cleared instead. The broadcast option is there to adapt to these strange environments.

(If a broadcast address has been set, *ifconfig* displays the BROADCAST flag.)

metric *number*
This option may be used to assign a metric value to the routing table entry created for the interface. This metric is used by the Routing Information Protocol (RIP) to build routing tables for the network.[*] The default metric used by

---

* RIP chooses the optimal route to a given host based on the "length" of the path. It is computed by summing up the individual metric values of each host-to-host link. By default, a hop has length 1, but this may be any positive integer less than 16. (A route length of 16 is equal to infinity. Such routes are considered unusable.) The *metric* parameter sets this hop cost, which is then broadcast by the routing daemon.

ifconfig is a value of zero. If you don't run a RIP daemon, you don't need this option at all; if you do, you will rarely need to change the metric value.

mtu *bytes*

This sets the Maximum Transmission Unit, which is the maximum number of octets the interface is able to handle in one transaction. For Ethernets, the MTU defaults to 1500; for SLIP interfaces it is 296.

arp

This is an option specific to broadcast networks such as Ethernets or packet radio. It enables the use of ARP, the Address Resolution Protocol, to detect the physical addresses of hosts attached to the network. For broadcast networks, it is on by default.

(If ARP is disabled, *ifconfig* displays the flag NOARP.)

-arp

Disables the use of ARP on this interface.

promisc

Puts the interface in promiscuous mode. On a broadcast network, this makes the interface receive all packets, regardless of whether they were destined for another host or not. This allows an analysis of network traffic using packet filters and such, also called *Ethernet snooping*. Usually, this is a good technique of hunting down network problems that are otherwise hard to detect.

On the other hand, this allows attackers to skim the traffic of your network for passwords and do other nasty things. One protection against this type of attack is to not let anyone just plug their computers into your Ethernet. Another option is to use secure authentication protocols, such as Kerberos or the SRA login suite.[*]

(This option corresponds to the flag *PROMISC.*)

-promisc

Turns off promiscuous mode.

allmulti

Multicast addresses are some sort of broadcast to a group of hosts who don't necessarily have to be on the same subnet. Multicast addresses are not yet supported by the kernel.

(This option corresponds to the flag *ALLMULTI.*)

-allmulti

Turns off multicast addresses.

---

[*] SRA can be obtained from **ftp.tamu.edu** in */pub/sec/TAMU*.

Checking with netstat

Now, I will turn to a useful tool for checking your network configuration and activity. It is called *netstat* and is in fact a collection of several tools lumped together. We will discuss each of its functions in the following sections.

Displaying the Routing Table

When invoking *netstat* with the *−r* flag, it displays the kernel routing table in the way we've been doing with *route*. On **vstout**, it produces:

```
# netstat -nr
Kernel routing table
Destination     Gateway         Genmask         Flags Metric Ref Use     Iface
127.0.0.1       *               255.255.255.255 UH    1      0        50 lo
172.16.1.0      *               255.255.255.0   U     1      0       478 eth0
172.16.2.0      172.16.1.1      255.255.255.0   UGN   1      0       250 eth0
```

The *−n* option makes *netstat* print addresses as dotted quad IP numbers rather than the symbolic host and network names. This is especially useful when you want to avoid address lookups over the network (e.g., to a DNS or NIS server).

The second column of *netstat*'s output shows the gateway the routing entry points to. If no gateway is used, an asterisk is printed instead. Column three shows the "generality" of the route. When given an IP address to find a suitable route for, the kernel goes through all routing table entries, taking the bitwise AND of the address and the genmask before comparing it to the target of the route.

The fourth column displays various flags that describe the route:

G   The route uses a gateway.

U   The interface to be used is up.

H   Only a single host can be reached through the route. For example, this is the case for the loopback entry **127.0.0.1**.

D   This is set if the table entry has been generated by an ICMP redirect message (see the section "The Internet Control Message Protocol").

M   This is set if the table entry was modified by an ICMP redirect message.

The Ref column of *netstat*'s output shows the number of references to this route, that is, how many other routes (e.g., through gateways) rely on the presence of this route. The last two columns show the number of times the routing entry has been used and the interface that datagrams are passed to for delivery.

Displaying Interface Statistics

When invoked with the *−i* flag, *netstat* will display statistics for the network interfaces currently configured. If the *−a* option is given in addition, it will print *all* interfaces present in the kernel, not only those that have been configured currently. On **vstout**, the output from *netstat* will look like this:

```
# netstat -i
Kernel Interface table
Iface    MTU Met  RX-OK RX-ERR RX-DRP RX-OVR  TX-OK TX-ERR TX-DRP TX-OVR Flags
lo         0   0   3185      0      0      0   3185      0      0      0 BLRU
eth0    1500   0 972633     17     20    120 628711    217      0      0 BRU
```

The MTU and Met fields show the current MTU and metric values for that interface. The RX and TX columns show how many packets have been received or transmitted. error-free (RX-OK/TX OK); damaged (RX-ERR/TX-ERR); how many were dropped (RX-DRP/TX-DRP); and how many were lost because of an overrun (RX-OVR/TX-OVR).

The last column shows the flags that have been set for this interface. These are one-character versions of the long flag names that are printed when you display the interface configuration with *ifconfig*:

B   A broadcast address has been set.

L   This interface is a loopback device

M   All packets are received (promiscuous mode).

N   Trailers are avoided.

O   ARP is turned off for this interface.

P   This is a point-to-point connection.

R   Interface is running.

U   Interface is up.

Displaying Connections

netstat supports a set of options to display active or passive sockets. The options *−t*, *−u*, *−w*, and *−x* show active TCP, UDP, RAW, or UNIX socket connections. If you provide the *−a* flag in addition, sockets that are waiting for a connection (i.e., listening) are displayed as well. This will give you a list of all servers that are currently running on your system.

Invoking *netstat -ta* on **vlager** produces this output:

```
$ netstat -ta
Active Internet connections
Proto Recv-Q Send-Q Local Address    Foreign Address    (State)
tcp        0      0 *:domain         *:*                LISTEN
```

tcp	0	0 *:time	*:*	LISTEN
tcp	0	0 *:smtp	*:*	LISTEN
tcp	0	0 vlager:smtp	vstout:1040	ESTABLISHED
tcp	0	0 *:telnet	*:*	LISTEN
tcp	0	0 localhost:1046	vbardolino:telnet	ESTABLISHED
tcp	0	0 *:chargen	*:*	LISTEN
tcp	0	0 *:daytime	*:*	LISTEN
tcp	0	0 *:discard	*:*	LISTEN
tcp	0	0 *:echo	*:*	LISTEN
tcp	0	0 *:shell	*:*	LISTEN
tcp	0	0 *:login	*:*	LISTEN

This shows most servers simply waiting for an incoming connection. However, the fourth line shows an incoming SMTP connection from **vstout**, and the sixth line tells you there is an outgoing *telnet* connection to **vbardolino**.[*]

Using the *−a* flag all by itself will display all sockets from all families.

Checking the ARP Tables

On some occasions, it is useful to view or even alter the contents of the kernel's ARP tables, for example when you suspect a duplicate Internet address is the cause for some intermittent network problem. The *arp* tool was made for situations like this. Its command-line options are

```
arp [-v] [-t hwtype] -a [hostname]
arp [-v] [-t hwtype] -s hostname hwaddr
arp [-v] -d hostname [hostname...]
```

All *hostname* arguments may be either symbolic hostnames or IP addresses in dotted quad notation.

The first invocation displays the ARP entry for the IP address or host specified, or all hosts known if no *hostname* is given. For example, invoking *arp* on **vlager** may yield

```
# arp -a
IP address      HW type           HW address
172.16.1.3      10Mbps Ethernet   00:00:C0:5A:42:C1
172.16.1.2      10Mbps Ethernet   00:00:C0:90:B3:42
172.16.2.4      10Mbps Ethernet   00:00:C0:04:69:AA
```

which shows the Ethernet addresses of **vlager**, **vstout** and **vale**.

Using the *−t* option you can limit the display to the hardware type specified. This may be `ether`, `ax25`, or `pronet`, standing for 10Mbps Ethernet, AMPR AX.25, and IEEE 802.5 token ring equipment, respectively.

---

[*] You can tell whether a connection is outgoing or not from the port numbers involved. The port number shown for the *calling* host will always be a simple integer, while on the host being called, a well-known service port will be in use, for which *netstat* uses the symbolic name found in */etc/services*.

The *-s* option is used to permanently add *hostname*'s Ethernet address to the ARP tables. The *hwaddr* argument specifies the hardware address, which is by default expected to be an Ethernet address specified as six hexadecimal bytes separated by colons. You may also set the hardware address for other types of hardware too, using the *-t* option.

One problem that may require you to manually add an IP address to the ARP table is when for some reason ARP queries for the remote host fail, for instance when its ARP driver is buggy or there is another host in the network that erroneously identifies itself with that host's IP address. Hard-wiring IP addresses in the ARP table is also a (very drastic) measure to protect yourself from hosts on your Ethernet that pose as someone else.

Invoking *arp* using the *-d* switch deletes all ARP entries relating to the given host. This may be used to force the interface to re-attempt to obtain the Ethernet address for the IP address in question. This is useful when a misconfigured system has broadcast wrong ARP information (of course, you have to reconfigure the broken host before).

The *-s* option may also be used to implement *proxy* ARP. This is a special technique where a host, say **gate**, acts as a gateway to another host named **fnord** by pretending that both addresses refer to the same host, namely **gate**. It does so by publishing an ARP entry for **fnord** that points to its own Ethernet interface. Now when a host sends out an ARP query for **fnord**, **gate** will return a reply containing its own Ethernet address. The querying host will then send all datagrams to **gate**, which dutifully forwards them to **fnord**.

These contortions may be necessary, for instance, when you want to access **fnord** from a DOS machine with a broken TCP implementation that doesn't understand routing too well. When you use proxy ARP, it will appear to the DOS machine as if **fnord** was on the local subnet, so it doesn't have to know about how to route through a gateway.

Another very useful application of proxy ARP is when one of your hosts acts as a gateway to some other host only temporarily, for instance through a dialup link. In a previous example, we encountered the laptop **vlite**, which was connected to **vlager** through a PLIP link only from time to time. Of course, this will work only if the address of the host you want to provide proxy ARP for is on the same IP subnet as your gateway. For instance, **vstout** could proxy ARP for any host on the Brewery subnet (172.16.1.0), but never for a host on the Winery subnet (172.16.2.0).

The proper invocation to provide proxy ARP for **fnord** is given below; of course, the Ethernet address given must be that of **gate**.

```
# arp -s fnord 00:00:c0:a1:42:e0 pub
```

The proxy ARP entry may be removed again by invoking:

```
# arp -d fnord
```

The Future

Linux networking is still evolving. Major changes at the kernel layer will bring a very flexible configuration scheme that will allow you to configure the network devices at run time. For instance, the *ifconfig* command will take arguments that set the IRQ line and DMA channel.

Another change to come soon is the additional *mtu* flag to the *route* command, which will set the Maximum Transmission Unit for a particular route. This route-specific MTU overrides the MTU specified for the interface. You will typically use this option for routes through a gateway, where the link between the gateway and the destination host requires a very low MTU.

For instance, assume host **wanderer** is connected to **vlager** through a SLIP link. When sending data from **vstout** to **wanderer**, the networking layer on **wanderer** would use packets of up to 1500 bytes because packets are sent across the Ethernet. The SLIP link, on the other hand, is operated with an MTU of 296, so the network layer on **vlager** would have to break up the IP packets into smaller fragments that fit into 296 bytes. If instead, you would have configured the route on **vstout** to use an MTU of 296 right from the start, this relatively expensive fragmentation could be avoided:

```
# route add wanderer gw vlager mtu 296
```

Note that the *mtu* option also allows you to selectively undo the effects of the "Subnets Are Local" Policy (SNARL). This policy is a kernel configuration option and is described in Chapter 3, *Configuring the Networking Hardware*.

CHAPTER SIX

NAME SERVICE AND RESOLVER CONFIGURATION

As discussed in Chapter 2, *Issues of TCP/IP Networking*, TCP/IP networking may rely on different schemes to convert names into addresses. The simplest way, which takes no advantage of the way the name space has been split up into zones, is a host table stored in */etc/hosts*. This is useful only for small LANs that are run by one single administrator and otherwise have no IP traffic with the outside world. The format of the *hosts* file has already been described in Chapter 5, *Configuring TCP/IP Networking*.

Alternatively, you can use BIND, the *Berkeley Internet Name Domain service*, for resolving hostnames to IP addresses. Configuring BIND can be a real chore, but once you've done it, changes in the network topology are easily made. On Linux, as on many other UNIXish systems, name service is provided through a program called *named*. At startup, it loads a set of master files into its internal cache and waits for queries from remote or local user processes. There are different ways to set up BIND, and not all require you to run a name server on every host.

This chapter can do little more but give a rough sketch of how to operate a name server. It should be sufficient if you have just a small LAN and an Internet uplink. For current information, you may want to check the documentation contained in the BIND sources. Apart from manpages and release notes, it contains the BIND Operator's Guide, or BOG for short. Don't let this name scare you off; it's actually a very useful document. There's also a newsgroup for DNS questions called *comp.protocols.tcp-ip.domains*.

DNS

The Resolver Library

The term "resolver" refers not to a special application but to the resolver library. This is a collection of functions that can be found in the standard C library. The central routines are *gethostbyname(2)* and *gethostbyaddr(2)*, which look up all IP addresses belonging to a host, and vice versa. They may be configured to simply look up the information in *hosts*, query a number of name servers, or use the *hosts* database of NIS (Network Information Service). Other applications, like *smail*, may include different drivers for any of these and need special care.

The parts of the resolver library that deal with DNS originally come from the BIND source, which also contains the *named* name server covered in a later section of this chapter. The upcoming version 4.6.8 of the Linux C library will contain the code from the latest BIND code (release 4.9). BIND-4.9 has changed a major feature in the resolver library, the so-called search list, which is also described below. In all other aspects, the different versions of the libraries should behave identically.

The host.conf File

The central file that controls your resolver setup is *host.conf*. It resides in */etc* and tells the resolver which services to use, and in what order.

Options in *host.conf* must occur on separate lines. Fields may be separated by white space (spaces or tabs). A hash sign (#) introduces a comment that extends to the next newline. The following options are available:

order
> This determines the order in which the resolving services are tried. Valid options are bind for querying the name server, *hosts* for lookups in */etc/hosts*, and nis for NIS lookups. Any or all of them may be specified. The order in which they appear on the line determines the order in which the respective services are tried.

multi
> Takes on or off as options. This determines if a host in */etc/hosts* is allowed to have several IP addresses, which is usually referred to as being "multi-homed." This flag has no effect on DNS or NIS queries.

nospoof
> As explained in the previous chapter, DNS allows you to find the hostname belonging to an IP address by using the **in-addr.arpa** domain. Attempts by name servers to supply a false hostname are called "*spoofing*." To guard against this, the resolver can be configured to check whether the original IP address is in fact associated with the hostname obtained. If not, the name is rejected and an error returned. This behavior is turned on by setting nospoof on.

alert
> This option takes **on** or **off** as arguments. If it is turned on, any spoof attempts will cause the resolver to log a message to the *syslog* facility.

trim
> This option takes a domain name as an argument, which will be removed from hostnames before lookup. This is useful for *hosts* entries, where you might only want to specify hostnames without local domain. A lookup of a host with the local domain name appended will have this removed, thus allowing the lookup in */etc/hosts* to succeed.
>
> trim options accumulate, making it possible to consider your host as being local to several domains.

A sample file for **vlager** is shown in Example 6-1.

Example 6-1: Sample host.conf File

```
# /etc/host.conf
# We have named running, but no NIS (yet)
order    bind hosts
# Allow multiple addrs
multi    on
# Guard against spoof attempts
nospoof on
# Trim local domain (not really necessary).
trim     vbrew.com.
```

Resolver Environment Variables

The settings from *host.conf* may be overridden using a number of environment variables:

RESOLV_HOST_CONF
> This specifies a file to be read instead of */etc/host.conf.*

RESOLV_SERV_ORDER
> Overrides the **order** option given in *host.conf.* Services are given as **hosts**, **bind**, and **nis**, separated by a space, comma, colon, or semicolon.

RESOLV_SPOOF_CHECK
> Determines the measures taken against spoofing. It is completely disabled by **off**. The values **warn** and **warn off** enable spoof checking, but turn logging on and off, respectively. A value of * turns on spoof checks, but leaves the logging facility as defined in *host.conf.*

RESOLV_MULTI
> A value of **on** or **off** may be used to override the **multi** options from *host.conf.*

RESOLV_OVERRIDE_TRIM_DOMAINS

This environment specifies a list of trim domains which override those given in *host.conf*. Trim domains were explained earlier where I discussed the `trim` keyword.

RESOLV_ADD_TRIM_DOMAINS

This environment specifies a list of trim domains which are added to those given in *host.conf*.

Configuring Name Server Lookups—resolv.conf

When configuring the resolver library to use the BIND name service for host lookups, you also have to tell it which name servers to use. There is a separate file for this called *resolv.conf*. If this file does not exist or is empty, the resolver assumes the name server is on your local host.

To run a name server on your local host, you have to set it up separately, as will be explained in the following section. If you are on a local network and have the opportunity to use an existing name server, this should always be preferred.

The most important option in *resolv.conf* is `nameserver`, which gives the IP address of a name server to use. If you specify several name servers by giving the `nameserver` option several times, they are tried in the order given. You should therefore put the most reliable server first. The current implementation allows you to have up to three `nameserver` statements in *resolv.conf*. If no `nameserver` option is given, the resolver attempts to connect to the name server on the local host.

Two other options, `domain` and `search`, let you use shortcut names for hosts in your local domain. Usually, when just telnetting to another host in your local domain, you don't want to type in the fully qualified hostname, but simply use a name like **gauss** on the command line, and have the resolver tack on the **mathematics.groucho.edu** part.

This is just what the `domain` statement is for. It lets you specify a default domain name to be appended when DNS fails to look up a hostname. For instance, when given the name **gauss**, the resolver would fail to find **gauss.** in DNS, because there is no such top-level domain. When given **mathematics.groucho.edu** as a default domain, it would then repeat the query for **gauss** with the default domain appended, this time succeeding.

That's just fine, you may think, but as soon you get out of the Math department's domain, you're back to those fully qualified domain names. Of course, you would also want to have shorthands like **quark.physics** for hosts in the Physics department's domain.

This is where the search list comes in. A search list can be specified using the `search` option, which is a generalization of the `domain` statement. Where the latter gives a single default domain, the former specifies a whole list of them, each to be tried in turn until a lookup succeeds. This list must be separated by blanks or tabs.

The **search** and **domain** statements are mutually exclusive and may not appear more than once. If neither option is given, the resolver will try to guess the default domain from the local hostname using the *getdomainname(2)* system call. If the local hostname doesn't have a domain part, the default domain will be assumed to be the root domain.

If you decide to put a **search** statement into *resolv.conf,* you should be careful about what domains you add to this list. Resolver libraries prior to BIND-4.9 used to construct a default search list from the domain name when no search list was given. This default list was made up of the default domain itself, plus all of its parent domains up to the root. This caused some problems because DNS requests wound up at name servers that were never meant to see them.

Assume you're at the Virtual Brewery and want to log into **foot.groucho.edu**. By an unfortunate slip of your fingers, you mistype **foot** as **foo**, which doesn't exist. GMU's name server will therefore tell you that it knows no such host. With the old-style search list, the resolver would now go on trying the name with **vbrew.com** and **com** appended. The latter is problematic because **groucho.edu.com** might actually be a valid domain name. Their name server might then even find **foo** in their domain, pointing you to one of their hosts—which clearly was not intended.

For some applications, these bogus host lookups can be a security problem. Therefore, you should usually limit the domains on your search list to your local organization, or something comparable. At the mathematics department of Groucho Marx University, the search list would commonly be set to **maths.groucho.edu** and **groucho.edu**.

RFC 1535

If default domains sound confusing to you, consider this sample *resolv.conf* file for the Virtual Brewery:

```
# /etc/resolv.conf
# Our domain
domain          vbrew.com
#
# We use vlager as central nameserver:
nameserver      172.16.1.1
```

When resolving the name **vale**, the resolver would look up **vale**, and failing this, **vale.vbrew.com**.

Resolver Robustness

If you are running a LAN inside a larger network, you definitely should use central name servers if they are available. The advantage is that the name servers will develop rich caches, since all queries are forwarded to them. However, this scheme has a drawback: when a fire recently destroyed the backbone cable at our university, no more work was possible on our department's LAN because the resolver couldn't reach any of the name servers anymore. There was no logging in on X terminals, no printing, etc.

Although it is not very common for campus backbones to go down in flames, one might want to take precautions against cases like this.

One option is to set up a local name server that resolves hostnames from your local domain and forwards all queries for other hostnames to the main servers. Of course, this is applicable only if you are running your own domain.

Alternatively, you can maintain a backup host table for your domain or LAN in */etc/hosts*. In */etc/host.conf* you would then include "order bind hosts" to make the resolver fall back to the hosts file if the central name server is down.

Running named

The program that provides domain name service on most UNIX machines is usually called *named* (pronounced *name-dee*). This is a server program originally developed for BSD providing name service to clients, and possibly to other name servers. The version currently used on most Linux installations seems to be BIND-4.8.3. The new version, BIND-4.9.3, is being Beta-tested at the moment and should be available on Linux soon.[*] It has many new features, such as secure zones that restrict zone transfers to certain hosts or networks. Please check the documentation contained in the source distribution for details.

This section requires some understanding of the way DNS works. If the following discussion is all Greek to you, you may want to re-read Chapter 2, which has some more information on the basics of DNS.

named is usually started at system boot time and runs until the machine goes down again. It takes its information from a configuration file called */etc/named.boot* and various files that map domain names to addresses and the like. The latter are called *zone files*. The formats and semantics of these files will be explained in the following section.

To run *named*, at the prompt simply enter

```
# /usr/sbin/named
```

named will come up and read the *named.boot* file and any zone files specified therein. It writes its process ID to */var/run/named.pid* in ASCII, downloads any zone files from primary servers if necessary, and starts listening on port 53 for DNS queries.[†]

---

* BIND-4.9 is developed by Paul Vixie, *paul@vix.com*.
† There are various *named* binaries floating around Linux FTP sites, each configured a little differently. Some have their pid file in */etc*; some store it in */tmp* or */var/tmp*.

The named.boot File

The *named.boot* file is generally very small and contains little else but pointers to master files containing zone information and pointers to other name servers. Comments in the boot file start with a semicolon and extend to the next newline. Before we discuss the format of *named.boot* in more detail, we will take a look at the sample file for **vlager** given in Example 6-2.[*]

Example 6–2: The named.boot File for vlager

```
;
; /etc/named.boot file for vlager.vbrew.com
;
directory       /var/named
;
;               domain                  file
;------------------
cache           .                       named.ca
primary         vbrew.com               named.hosts
primary         0.0.127.in-addr.arpa    named.local
primary         72.191.in-addr.arpa     named.rev
```

The **cache** and **primary** commands shown in this example load information into *named*. This information is taken from the master files specified in the second argument. They represent DNS resource records, which we will look at below.

In this example we configured *named* as the primary name server for three domains, as indicated by the **primary** statements at the end of the file. The first of these lines, for instance, instructs *named* to act as a primary server for **vbrew.com**, taking the zone data from the file *named.hosts*. The **directory** keyword tells it that all zone files are located in */var/named*.

The **cache** entry is very special and should be present on virtually all machines running a name server. Its function is two-fold: it instructs *named* to enable its cache and to load the *root name server hints* from the cache file specified (*named.ca* in our example). We will come back to the name server hints below.

Here's a list of the most important options you can use in *named.boot*:

directory

> This specifies a directory in which zone files reside. Names of files may be given relative to this directory. Several directories may be specified by repeatedly using **directory**. According to the Linux file system standard, this should be */var/named*.

---

[*] Note that the domain names in this example are given *without* the trailing dot. Earlier versions of *named* seem to treat trailing dots in *named.boot* as an error, and silently discard the line. BIND-4.9.3 is said to fix this.

primary

This takes a domain name and a filename as an argument, declaring the local server authoritative for the named domain. As a primary server, *named* loads the zone information from the given master file.

Generally, there will always be at least one `primary` entry in every boot file, namely for reverse mapping of network **127.0.0.0**, which is the local loopback network.

secondary

This statement takes a domain name, an address list, and a filename as an argument. It declares the local server a secondary master server for the domain specified.

A secondary server holds authoritative data on the domain too, but it doesn't gather it from files; instead, it tries to download it from the primary server. The IP address of at least one primary server must thus be given to *named* in the address list. The local server will contact each of them in turn until it successfully transfers the zone database, which is then stored in the backup file given as the third argument. If none of the primary servers responds, the zone data is retrieved from the backup file instead.

named will then attempt to refresh the zone data at regular intervals. This is explained later in connection with the SOA resource record type.

cache

This takes a domain name and a filename as arguments. This file contains the root server hints, which is a list of records pointing to the root name servers. Only NS and A records will be recognized. The *domain* should be the root domain name, a simple period (.).

This information is absolutely crucial to *named*; if the `cache` statement does not occur in the boot file, *named* will not develop a local cache at all. This will severely degrade performance and increase network load if the next server queried is not on the local net. Moreover, *named* will not be able to reach any root name servers, and thus it won't resolve any addresses except those it is authoritative for. An exception from this rule involves forwarding servers (see the `forwarders` option that follows).

forwarders

This statement takes an address list as an argument. The IP addresses in this list specify a list of name servers that *named* may query if it fails to resolve a query from its local cache. They are tried in order until one of them responds to the query.

slave

This statement makes the name server a *slave* server. That is, it will never perform recursive queries itself, but only forward them to servers specified with the `forwarders` statement.

There are two options that we will not describe here: `sortlist` and `domain`. Additionally, there are two directives that may be used inside these database files. These are `$INCLUDE` and `$ORIGIN`. Since they are rarely needed, we will not describe them here, either.

The DNS Database Files

Master files included by *named*, like *named.hosts*, always have a domain associated with them, which is called the *origin*. This is the domain name specified with the `cache` and `primary` commands. Within a master file, you are allowed to specify domain and host names relative to this domain. A name given in a configuration file is considered *absolute* if it ends in a single dot, otherwise it is considered relative to the origin. The origin all by itself may be referred to using "@".

The data contained in a master file is split up in *resource records*, or RRs for short. They make up the smallest unit of information available through DNS. Each resource record has a type. A records, for instance, map a hostname to an IP address, and a CNAME record associates an alias for a host with its official hostname. As an example, take a look at Example 6-4, which shows the *named.hosts* master file for the Virtual Brewery.

Resource record representations in master files share a common format:

```
[domain] [ttl] [class] type rdata
```

Fields are separated by spaces or tabs. An entry may be continued across several lines if an opening parenthesis occurs before the first newline, and the last field is followed by a closing parenthesis. Anything between a semicolon and a newline is ignored.

domain

This is the domain name to which the entry applies. If no domain name is given, the RR is assumed to apply to the domain of the previous RR.

ttl

In order to force resolvers to discard information after a certain time, each RR is associated a time to live, or *ttl* for short. The *ttl* field specifies the time in seconds that the information is valid after it has been retrieved from the server. It is a decimal number with at most eight digits.

If no *ttl* value is given, it defaults to the value of the *minimum* field of the preceding SOA record.

class

This is an address class, like IN for IP addresses, or HS for objects in the Hesiod class. For TCP/IP networking, you have to make this IN.

If no class field is given, the class of the preceding RR is assumed.

type

   This describes the type of the RR. The most common types are A, SOA, PTR, and NS. The following sections describe the various types of RRs.

rdata

   This holds the data associated with the RR. The format of this field depends on the type of the RR. Below, it will be described for each RR separately.

The following is partial list of RRs to be used in DNS master files. There are a couple more of them, which we will not explain. They are experimental, and of little use generally.

SOA

   This describes a zone of authority (SOA means "Start of Authority"). It signals that the records following the SOA RR contain authoritative information for the domain. Every master file included by a **primary** statement must contain an SOA record for this zone. The resource data contains the following fields:

   origin

      This is the canonical hostname of the primary name server for this domain. It is usually given as an absolute name.

   contact

      This is the email address of the person responsible for maintaining the domain, with the "@" sign replaced by a dot. For instance, if the responsible person at the Virtual Brewery is **janet**, then this field would contain **janet.vbrew.com**.

   serial

      This is the version number of the zone file, expressed as a single decimal number. Whenever data is changed in the zone file, this number should be incremented.

      The serial number is used by secondary name servers to recognize when zone information has changed. To stay up to date, secondary servers request the primary server's SOA record at certain intervals and compare the serial number to that of the cached SOA record. If the number has changed, the secondary servers transfer the whole zone database from the primary server.

   refresh

      This specifies the interval in seconds that the secondary servers should wait between checking the SOA record of the primary server. Again, this is a decimal number with at most eight digits.

      Generally, the network topology doesn't change too often, so this number should specify an interval of roughly a day for larger networks, and even more for smaller ones.

retry

> This number determines the intervals at which a secondary server should retry contacting the primary server if a request or a zone refresh fails. It must not be too low, or else a temporary failure of the server or a network problem could cause the secondary server to waste network resources. One hour, or perhaps one-half hour, might be a good choice.

expire

> This specifies the time in seconds after which a secondary server should finally discard all zone data if it hasn't been able to contact the primary server. You should normally set this to at least a week (604800 seconds), but increasing it to a month or more is still reasonable.

minimum

> This is the default *ttl* value for resource records that do not explicitly contain one. The *ttl* value specifies the maximum amount of time other name servers may keep the RR in their cache. This applies only to normal lookups, and has nothing to do with the time after which a secondary server should try to update the zone information.

> If the topology of your network does not change frequently, a week or even more is probably a good choice. If single RRs change more frequently, you can still assign them smaller *ttl*s individually. If, on the other hand, your network changes rather frequently, you may want to set *minimum* to around one day (86400 seconds).

A   This record associates an IP address with a hostname. The resource data field contains the address in dotted quad notation.

For each host, there must be only one A record. The hostname used in this A record is considered the official or *canonical* hostname. All other hostnames are aliases and must be mapped onto the canonical hostname using a CNAME record.

NS NS records are used to specify a zone's primary server and all its secondary servers. An NS record points to a master name server of the given zone, with the resource data field containing the hostname of the name server.

You will meet NS records in two situations. The first one is when you delegate authority to a subordinate zone; the second is within the master zone database of the subordinate zone itself. The sets of servers specified in both the parent and the delegated zone should match.

To resolve the hostname the NS record points to, an additional A record may be needed, the so-called *glue record* which gives the name server's IP address. Glue records are necessary in the parent domain's zone file whenever the server pointed to is in the delegated domain.

CNAME

> This record associates an alias for a host with its *canonical hostname*. The canonical hostname is the one the master file provides an A record for; aliases are simply linked to that name by a CNAME record, but don't have any other records of their own.

PTR

> This type of record is used to associate names in the **in-addr.arpa** domain with hostnames. It is used for reverse mapping of IP addresses to hostnames. The hostname given must be the canonical hostname.

MX

> This RR announces a *mail exchanger* for a domain. Mail exchangers are discussed in the section "Mail Routing on the Internet," in Chapter 13, *Electronic Mail.* The syntax of an MX record is

> ```
> [domain] [ttl] [class] MX preference host
> ```

> *host* names the mail exchanger for *domain.* Every mail exchanger has an integer *preference* associated with it. A mail transport agent that desires to deliver mail to *domain* will try all hosts who have an MX record for this domain until it succeeds. The one with the lowest preference value is tried first, then the others in order of increasing preference value.

HINFO

> This record provides information on the system's hardware and software. Its syntax is

> ```
> [domain] [ttl] [class] HINFO hardware software
> ```

RFC 1340

The *hardware* field identifies the hardware used by this host. There are special conventions to specify this. A list of valid names is given in the Assigned Numbers RFC. If the field contains any blanks, it must be enclosed in double quotes. The *software* field names the operating system software used by the system. Again, a valid name from the Assigned Numbers RFC should be chosen.

Writing the Master Files

Example 6-3, Example 6-4, Example 6-5, and Example 6-6 give sample files for a name server at the brewery, located on **vlager**. Due to the nature of the network discussed (a single LAN), the example is pretty straightforward.

DNS

The *named.ca* cache file shown in Example 6-3 shows sample hint records for a root name server. A typical cache file usually describes about a dozen or so name servers. You can obtain the current list of name servers for the root domain using the *nslookup* tool described in the next section.[*]

Example 6–3: The named.ca File

```
;
; /var/named/named.ca          Cache file for the brewery.
;                    We're not on the Internet, so we don't need
;                    any root servers. To activate these
;                    records, remove the semicolons.
;
; .               99999999    IN    NS  NS.NIC.DDN.MIL
; NS.NIC.DDN.MIL  99999999    IN    A   26.3.0.103
; .               99999999    IN    NS  NS.NASA.GOV
; NS.NASA.GOV     99999999    IN    A   128.102.16.10
```

Example 6–4: The named.hosts File

```
;
; /var/named/named.hosts      Local hosts at the brewery
;                             Origin is vbrew.com
;
@            IN   SOA   vlager.vbrew.com. janet.vbrew.com. (
                        16          ; serial
                        86400       ; refresh: once per day
                        3600        ; retry:   one hour
                        3600000     ; expire:  42 days
                        604800      ; minimum: 1 week
                        )
             IN   NS    vlager.vbrew.com.
;
; local mail is distributed on vlager
             IN   MX    10 vlager
;
; loopback address
localhost.   IN   A     127.0.0.1
; brewery Ethernet
vlager       IN   A     172.16.1.1
vlager-if1   IN   CNAME vlager
; vlager is also news server
news         IN   CNAME vlager
vstout       IN   A     172.16.1.2
vale         IN   A     172.16.1.3
; winery Ethernet
vlager-if2   IN   A     172.16.2.1
```

---

[*] Note that you can't query your name server for the root servers if you don't have any root server hints installed. To escape this dilemma, you can either make *nslookup* use a different name server, or you can use the sample file in Example 6-3 as a starting point, and then obtain the full list of valid servers.

Example 6-4: The named.hosts File (continued)

```
vbardolino      IN  A    172.16.2.2
vchianti        IN  A    172.16.2.3
vbeaujolais     IN  A    172.16.2.4
```

Example 6-5: The named.local File

```
;
; /var/named/named.local      Reverse mapping of 127.0.0
;                             Origin is 0.0.127.in-addr.arpa.
;
@           IN  SOA  vlager.vbrew.com. joe.vbrew.com. (
                     1          ; serial
                     360000     ; refresh: 100 hrs
                     3600       ; retry:   one hour
                     3600000    ; expire:  42 days
                     360000     ; minimum: 100 hrs
                     )
            IN  NS   vlager.vbrew.com.
1           IN  PTR  localhost.
```

Example 6-6: The named.rev File

```
;
; /var/named/named.rev        Reverse mapping of our IP addresses
;                             Origin is 72.191.in-addr.arpa.
;
@           IN  SOA  vlager.vbrew.com. joe.vbrew.com. (
                     16         ; serial
                     86400      ; refresh: once per day
                     3600       ; retry:   one hour
                     3600000    ; expire:  42 days
                     604800     ; minimum: 1 week
                     )
            IN  NS   vlager.vbrew.com.
; brewery
1.1         IN  PTR  vlager.vbrew.com.
2.1         IN  PTR  vstout.vbrew.com.
3.1         IN  PTR  vale.vbrew.com.
; winery
1.2         IN  PTR  vlager-if1.vbrew.com.
2.2         IN  PTR  vbardolino.vbrew.com.
3.2         IN  PTR  vchianti.vbrew.com.
4.2         IN  PTR  vbeaujolais.vbrew.com.
```

Verifying the Name Server Setup

There's a fine tool for checking the operation of your name server setup. It is called *nslookup* and can be used both interactively and from the command line. In the latter case, you simply invoke it as

```
$ nslookup hostname
```

nslookup queries the name server specified in *resolv.conf* for *hostname*. (If this file names more than one server, *nslookup* chooses one at random.)

The interactive mode, however, is much more exciting. Besides looking up individual hosts, you may query for any type of DNS record and transfer the entire zone information for a domain.

When invoked without argument, *nslookup* displays the name server it uses and enters interactive mode. At the > prompt, you may type any domain name you want to query. By default, it asks for class A records, those containing the IP address relating to the domain name.

You can change this by issuing

```
> set type=type
```

where *type* is one of the resource record names described earlier, or ANY.

For example, you might have the following *nslookup* session:

```
$ nslookup
Default Name Server:  rs10.hrz.th-darmstadt.de
Address:  130.83.56.60
> sunsite.unc.edu
Name Server:  rs10.hrz.th-darmstadt.de
Address:  130.83.56.60
Non-authoritative answer:
Name:    sunsite.unc.edu
Address:  152.2.22.81
```

If you try to query for a name that has no IP address associated with it, but other records were found in the DNS database, *nslookup* will come back with an error message saying "No type A records found." However, you can make it query for records other than type A by issuing the *set type* command. For example, to get the SOA record of **unc.edu**, you would issue:

```
> unc.edu
*** No address (A) records available for unc.edu
Name Server:  rs10.hrz.th-darmstadt.de
Address:  130.83.56.60
> set type=SOA
> unc.edu
Name Server:  rs10.hrz.th-darmstadt.de
```

```
Address:   130.83.56.60
Non-authoritative answer:
unc.edu
        origin = ns.unc.edu
        mail addr = shava.ns.unc.edu
        serial = 930408
        refresh = 28800 (8 hours)
        retry  = 3600 (1 hour)
        expire = 1209600 (14 days)
        minimum ttl = 86400 (1 day)
Authoritative answers can be found from:
UNC.EDU nameserver = SAMBA.ACS.UNC.EDU
SAMBA.ACS.UNC.EDU       internet address = 128.109.157.30
```

In a similar fashion you can query for MX records, etc.

```
> set type=MX
> unc.edu
Non-authoritative answer:
unc.edu preference = 10, mail exchanger = lambada.oit.unc.edu
lambada.oit.unc.edu     internet address = 152.2.22.80
Authoritative answers can be found from:
UNC.EDU nameserver = SAMBA.ACS.UNC.EDU
SAMBA.ACS.UNC.EDU       internet address = 128.109.157.30
```

Using a type of ANY returns all resource records associated with a given name.

A practical application of *nslookup* besides debugging is to obtain the current list of root name servers. You can do this by querying for all NS records associated with the root domain:

```
> set typ=NS
> .
Name Server:  fb0430.mathematik.th-darmstadt.de
Address:   130.83.2.30
Non-authoritative answer:
(root)   nameserver = NS.INTERNIC.NET
(root)   nameserver = AOS.ARL.ARMY.MIL
(root)   nameserver = C.NYSER.NET
(root)   nameserver = TERP.UMD.EDU
(root)   nameserver = NS.NASA.GOV
(root)   nameserver = NIC.NORDU.NET
(root)   nameserver = NS.NIC.DDN.MIL
Authoritative answers can be found from:
(root)   nameserver = NS.INTERNIC.NET
(root)   nameserver = AOS.ARL.ARMY.MIL
(root)   nameserver = C.NYSER.NET
(root)   nameserver = TERP.UMD.EDU
(root)   nameserver = NS.NASA.GOV
(root)   nameserver = NIC.NORDU.NET
(root)   nameserver = NS.NIC.DDN.MIL
NS.INTERNIC.NET internet address = 198.41.0.4
```

```
AOS.ARL.ARMY.MIL              internet address = 128.63.4.82
AOS.ARL.ARMY.MIL              internet address = 192.5.25.82
AOS.ARL.ARMY.MIL              internet address = 26.3.0.29
C.NYSER.NET     internet address = 192.33.4.12
TERP.UMD.EDU    internet address = 128.8.10.90
NS.NASA.GOV     internet address = 128.102.16.10
NS.NASA.GOV     internet address = 192.52.195.10
NS.NASA.GOV     internet address = 45.13.10.121
NIC.NORDU.NET   internet address = 192.36.148.17
NS.NIC.DDN.MIL  internet address = 192.112.36.4
```

To see the complete set of available commands, use the *help* command within *nslookup*.

Other Useful Tools

There are a few tools that can help you with your tasks as a BIND administrator. I will briefly describe two of them here. Please refer to the documentation that comes with these tools for more information on how to use them.

hostcvt is a tool that helps you with your initial BIND configuration by converting your */etc/hosts* file into master files for *named*. It generates both the forward (A) and reverse mapping (PTR) entries, and takes care of aliases and the like. Of course, it won't do the whole job for you, as you may still want to tune the time-out values in the SOA record, for instance, or add MX records and the like. Still, it may help you save a few aspirins. *hostcvt* is part of the BIND source, but can also be found as a standalone package on a few Linux FTP servers.

After setting up your name server, you may want to test your configuration. The ideal (and, to my knowledge) only tool for this is *dnswalk*, a *perl*-based package that walks your DNS database looking for common mistakes and verifying that the information is consistent. *dnswalk* has been released on *comp.sources.misc* recently and should be available on all FTP sites that archive this group (**ftp.uu.net** should be a safe bet if you don't know of any such site near you).

## CHAPTER SEVEN

SERIAL LINE IP

The serial line protocols, SLIP and PPP, provide Internet connectivity for the poor. Apart from a modem and a serial board equipped with a FIFO buffer, no hardware is needed. Using it is not much more complicated than a mailbox, and an increasing number of private organizations offer dialup IP at an affordable cost to everyone.

Chapter 8

There are both SLIP and PPP drivers available for Linux. SLIP has been around for quite a while and is fairly reliable. A PPP driver has been developed recently by Michael Callahan and Al Longyear.

General Requirements

To use SLIP or PPP, you have to configure some basic networking features as described in the previous chapters. At the least, you have to set up the loopback interface and provide for name resolution. When connecting to the Internet, you will of course want to use DNS. The simplest option is to put the address of some name server into your *resolv.conf* file; this server will be queried as soon as the SLIP link is activated. The closer (network-wise) this name server is to the point where you dial in, the better your response may be.

However, this solution is not optimal, because all name lookups will still go through your SLIP/PPP link. If you worry about the bandwidth this consumes, you can also set up a *caching-only* name server. It doesn't really serve a domain, but only acts as a relay for all DNS queries produced on your host. The advantage of this scheme is that it builds up a cache so that most queries have to be sent over the serial line only once. A *named.boot* file for a caching-only server looks like this:

```
; named.boot file for caching-only server
directory                                /var/named
primary        0.0.127.in-addr.arpa      db.127.0.0 ; loopback net
cache          .                         db.cache   ; root servers
```

In addition to this *name.boot* file, you also have to set up the *db.cache* file with a valid list of root name servers. This is described toward the end of Chapter 6, *Name Service and Resolver Configuration.*

SLIP Operation

Dialup IP servers frequently offer SLIP service through special user accounts. After logging into such an account, you are not dropped into the common shell; instead, a program or shell script is executed that enables the server's SLIP driver for the serial line and configures the appropriate network interface. Then you have to do the same at your end of the link.

On some operating systems, the SLIP driver is a user-space program; under Linux, it is part of the kernel, which makes it a lot faster. This requires, however, that the serial line be converted to SLIP mode explicitly. This is done by means of a special tty line discipline, SLIPDISC. While the tty is in normal line discipline (DISC0), it will exchange data only with user processes, using the normal *read(2)* and *write(2)* calls, and the SLIP driver is unable to write to or read from the tty. In SLIPDISC, the roles are reversed: now any user-space processes are blocked from writing to or reading from the tty, while all data coming in on the serial port will be passed directly to the SLIP driver.

RFC 1144

The SLIP driver itself understands a number of variations on the SLIP protocol. Apart from ordinary SLIP, it also understands CSLIP, which performs the so-called Van Jacobson header compression on outgoing IP packets. This improves throughput for interactive sessions noticeably. Additionally, there are six-bit versions for each of these protocols.

A simple way to convert a serial line to SLIP mode is by using the *slattach* tool. Assume you have your modem on */dev/cua3* and have logged into the SLIP server successfully. You will then execute:

```
# slattach /dev/cua3 &
```

This will switch the line discipline of *cua3* to SLIPDISC and attach it to one of the SLIP network interfaces. If this is your first active SLIP link, the line will be attached to *sl0*; the second would be attached to *sl1*, and so on. The current kernels support up to eight simultaneous SLIP links.

The default encapsulation chosen by *slattach* is CSLIP. You may choose any other mode using the *–p* switch. To use normal SLIP (no compression), you would use

```
# slattach -p slip /dev/cua3 &
```

Other modes are *cslip*, *slip6*, *cslip6* (for the six-bit version of SLIP), and *adaptive* for adaptive SLIP. The latter leaves it to the kernel to find out which type of SLIP encapsulation the remote end uses.

Note that you must use the same encapsulation as your peer does. For example, if **cowslip** uses CSLIP, you have to do so too. The symptoms of a mismatch will be that a *ping* to the remote host will not receive any packets back. If the other host *ping*s you, you may also see messages like "Can't build ICMP header" on your console. One way to avoid these difficulties is to use adaptive SLIP.

slattach lets you enable not only SLIP, but other protocols that use the serial line as well, like PPP or KISS (another protocol used by ham radio people). For details, please refer to the *slattach(8)* manual page.

After turning over the line to the SLIP driver, you have to configure the network interface. Again, you do this using the standard *ifconfig* and *route* commands. Assume that from **vlager**, we have dialed up a server named **cowslip**. You would then execute

```
# ifconfig sl0 vlager-slip pointopoint cowslip
# route add cowslip
# route add default gw cowslip
```

The first command configures the interface as a point-to-point link to **cowslip**, while the second and third add the route to **cowslip** and the default route using **cowslip** as a gateway.

Two things are worth noting about the *ifconfig* invocation here. The first is the pointopoint option that specifies the address of the remote end of a point-to-point link. The second is our use of **vlager-slip** as the address of the local SLIP interface.

We have discussed before that you can use the same address you assigned to **vlager**'s Ethernet interface for your SLIP link as well. In this case, **vlager-slip** might just be another alias for address **172.16.1.1**. However, it is also possible that you have to use an entirely different address for your SLIP link. One such case is when your network uses an unregistered IP network address, as the Brewery does. We will return to this in greater detail in the next section.

For the remainder of this chapter we will always use **vlager-slip** to refer to the address of the local SLIP interface.

When taking down the SLIP link, you first have to remove all routes through **cowslip** using *route* with the *del* option, take the interface down, and send *slattach* the hangup signal. Afterwards you have to hang up the modem using your terminal program again:

```
# route del default
# route del cowslip
# ifconfig sl0 down
# kill -HUP 516
```

Dealing with Private IP Networks

You will remember from Chapter 5, *Configuring TCP/IP Networking* that the Vitrual Brewery uses unregistered network numbers that are reserved for internal use only. Packets from or to one of these networks are not routed on the Internet. This means that hosts within the Brewery's network cannot talk to real Internet hosts, because their packets would be dropped silently by the first major router.

To work around this dilemma, we will configure **vlager** to act as a kind of launch pad for accessing Internet services. To the outside world, it will present itself as a normal Internet host with a registered IP address (probably assigned by the network provider). To access an Internet host, for instance an FTP server, users have to log into **vlager**, and invoke the FTP client there, so that the connection appears to come from a valid address. For other applications, there may be solutions that avoid having to log into **vlager**. For WWW users, for example, we could run a so-called *proxy server* on **vlager**, which would relay all requests from your users to the respective servers.

Of course this is a little clumsy. But apart from eliminating the paperwork of registering an IP network, it has the added benefit of going along very well with a firewall setup. Firewalls are dedicated hosts used to provide limited Internet access to users on your local network without exposing the internal hosts to network attacks from the outside world.

Assume the Brewery has been assigned IP address **192.168.5.74** for SLIP access. All you have to do to realize the setup discussed above is to enter this address into your */etc/hosts* file, naming it **vlager-slip**. The procedure of bringing up the SLIP link itself remains unchanged.

Using dip

Now, that was rather simple. Nevertheless, you might want to automate the above steps so that you only have to invoke a simple command that performs all steps shown above. This is what *dip* is for.

dip means *Dialup IP*. It was written by Fred van Kempen. The current release as of this writing is version 3.3.7. It has been patched very heavily by a number of people, so you can't speak of a single *dip* program anymore. These different strains of development will hopefully be merged in a future release.

dip provides an interpreter for a simple scripting language that can handle the modem for you, convert the line to SLIP mode, and configure the interfaces. This is rather primitive and restrictive, but sufficient for most cases. A new release of *dip* may feature a more versatile language one day.

To be able to configure the SLIP interface, *dip* requires root privilege. It would now be tempting to make *dip* setuid to **root** so that all users can dial up some SLIP server without having to give them root access. This is very dangerous, because setting up bogus interfaces and default routes with *dip* may disrupt routing on your network. Even worse, this will give your users the power to connect to *any* SLIP server and launch dangerous attacks on your network. So if you want to allow your users to fire up a SLIP connection, write small wrapper programs for each prospective SLIP server and have these wrappers invoke *dip* with the specific script that establishes the connection. These programs can then safely be made setuid to **root**.*

A Sample Script

Assume that the host to which we make our SLIP connection is **cowslip**, and that we have written a script for *dip* to run called *cowslip.dip*, which makes our connection. We invoke *dip* with the script name as argument:

```
# dip cowslip.dip
DIP: Dialup IP Protocol Driver version 3.3.7 (12/13/93)
Written by Fred N. van Kempen, MicroWalt Corporation.
connected to cowslip.moo.com with addr 192.168.5.74
#
```

The script itself is shown in Example 7-1.

Example 7–1: A Sample dip Script

```
# Sample dip script for dialing up cowslip
# Set local and remote name and address
get $local vlager-slip
get $remote cowslip
port cua3                # choose a serial port
speed 38400              # set speed to max
modem HAYES              # set modem type
reset                    # reset modem and tty
flush                    # flush out modem response
# Prepare for dialing.
send ATQ0V1E1X1\r
wait OK 2
```

---

* *diplogin* can (and must) be run as setuid to **root**, too. See the section at the end of this chapter.

Example 7–1: A Sample dip Script (continued)

```
if $errlvl != 0 goto error
dial 41988
if $errlvl != 0 goto error
wait CONNECT 60
if $errlvl != 0 goto error
# Okay, we're connected now
sleep 3
send \r\n\r\n
wait ogin: 10
if $errlvl != 0 goto error
send Svlager\n
wait ssword: 5
if $errlvl != 0 goto error
send hey-jude\n
wait running 30
if $errlvl != 0 goto error
# We have logged in, and the remote side is firing up SLIP.
print Connected to $remote with address $rmtip
default                    # Make this link our default route
mode SLIP                  # We go to SLIP mode, too
# fall through in case of error
error:
print SLIP to $remote failed.
```

After connecting to **cowslip** and enabling SLIP, *dip* will detach from the terminal and go to the background. You can then start using the normal networking services on the SLIP link. To terminate the connection, simply invoke *dip* with the *−k* option. This sends a hangup signal to *dip*, using the process ID *dip* records in */etc/dip.pid*:

```
# dip -k
```

In *dip*'s scripting language, keywords prefixed with a dollar symbol denote variable names. *dip* has a predefined set of variables which will be listed below. $remote and $local, for instance, contain the hostnames of the remote and local hosts involved in the SLIP link.

The first two statements in the sample script are *get* commands, which is *dip*'s way to set a variable. Here, the local and remote hostnames are set to **vlager** and **cowslip**, respectively.

The next five statements set up the terminal line and the modem. reset sends a reset string to the modem; for Hayes-compatible modems, this is the ATZ command. The next statement flushes out the modem response so that the login chat in the next few lines will work properly. This chat is pretty straight-forward: it simply dials 41988, the phone number of **cowslip**, and logs into the account Svlager using the password hey-jude. The wait command makes *dip* wait for the string given as its first argument; the number given as second argument makes the wait time out after that many seconds if no such string is received. The if commands interspersed in the login procedure check that no error has occurred while executing the command.

The final commands executed after logging in are default, which makes the SLIP link the default route to all hosts, and mode, which enables SLIP mode on the line and configures the interface and routing table for you.

A *dip* Reference

Although widely used, *dip* hasn't been very well documented yet. In this section, we will therefore give a reference for most of *dip*'s commands. You can get an overview of all the commands it provides by invoking *dip* in test mode and entering the *help* command. To find out about the syntax of a command, you may enter it without any arguments; of course, this does not work with commands that take no arguments.

```
$ dip -t
DIP: Dialup IP Protocol Driver version 3.3.7 (12/13/93)
Written by Fred N. van Kempen, MicroWalt Corporation.
DIP> help
DIP knows about the following commands:
        databits default  dial      echo      flush
        get      goto     help      if        init
        mode     modem    parity    print     port
        reset    send     sleep     speed     stopbits
        term     wait
DIP> echo
Usage: echo on|off
DIP> _
```

Throughout the following section, examples that display the *DIP>* prompt show how to enter a command in test mode and what output it produces. Examples lacking this prompt should be taken as script excerpts.

The modem commands

dip provides a number of commands to configure your serial line and modem. Some of these are obvious, such as port, which selects a serial port, and speed, databits, stopbits, and parity, which set the common line parameters. The modem command selects a modem type. Currently, the only type supported is HAYES (capitalization required). You have to provide *dip* with a modem type, or else it will refuse to execute the dial and reset commands. The reset command sends a reset string to the modem; the string used depends on the modem type selected. For Hayes-compatible modems, this string is ATZ.

The flush code can be used to flush out all responses the modem has sent so far. Otherwise a chat script following reset might be confused because it reads the OK responses from earlier commands.

The `init` command selects an initialization string to be passed to the modem before dialing. The default for Hayes modems is "ATE0 Q0 V1 X1", which turns on echoing of commands and long result codes, and selects blind dialing (no checking of dial tone).

The `dial` command finally sends the initialization string to the modem and dials up the remote system. The default dial command for Hayes modems is `ATD`.

echo and term

The `echo` command serves as a debugging aid. Using `echo on` makes *dip* echo to the console everything it sends to the serial device. This can be turned off again by calling `echo off`.

dip also allows you to leave script mode temporarily and enter terminal mode. In this mode, you can use *dip* just like any ordinary terminal program, writing to the serial line and reading from it. To leave this mode, enter Ctrl-].

The get command

The `get` command is *dip*'s way of setting a variable. The simplest form is to set a variable to a constant, as we did in *cowslip.dip*. You may, however, also prompt the user for input by specifying the keyword `ask` instead of a value:

```
DIP> get $local ask
Enter the value for $local: _
```

A third method is to try to obtain the value from the remote host. Bizarre as it seems at first, this is very useful in some cases. Some SLIP servers will not allow you to use your own IP address on the SLIP link, but will rather assign you one from a pool of addresses whenever you dial in, printing some message that informs you about the address you have been assigned. If the message looks something like "Your address: 192.168.5.74," then the following piece of *dip* code would let you pick up the address:

```
# finish login
wait address: 10
get $locip remote
```

The print command

This is the command used to echo text to the console that *dip* was started from. Any of *dip*'s variables may be used in print commands, such as

```
DIP> print Using port $port at speed $speed
Using port cua3 at speed 38400
```

Variable names

dip understands only a predefined set of variables. A variable name always begins with a dollar symbol and must be written in lower-case letters.

The $local and $locip variables contain the local host's name and IP address. Setting the hostname makes *dip* store the canonical hostname in $local, at the same time assigning $locip the corresponding IP address. The analogous thing happens when setting the $locip.

The $remote and $rmtip variables do the same for the remote host's name and address. $mtu contains the MTU value for the connection.

These five variables are the only ones that may be assigned values directly using the get command. A host of other variables can only be set through corresponding commands, but may be used in print statements; these are $modcm, $port, and $speed.

$errlvl is the variable through which you can access the result of the last command executed. An error level of 0 indicates success, while a non-zero value denotes an error.

The if and goto commands

The if command is a conditional branch rather than a full-featured programming *if* statement. Its syntax is

```
if var op number goto label
```

The expression must be a simple comparison between one of the variables $errlvl, $locip, and $rmtip. *var* must be an integer number; the operator *op* may be one of ==, !=, <, >, <=, and >=.

The goto command makes the execution of the script continue at the line following that bearing the *label*. A label must be the first word on the line and must be followed immediately by a colon.

send, wait, and sleep

These commands help implement simple chat scripts in *dip*. send outputs its arguments to the serial line. It does not support variables, but understands all C-style backslash character sequences such as \n and \b. The tilde character (~) is used as an abbreviation for carriage return/newline.

wait takes a word as an argument and scans all input on the serial line until it recognizes this word. The word itself may not contain any blanks. Optionally, you may give wait a timeout value as second argument; if the expected word is not received within that many seconds, the command will return with an $errlvl value of one.

The `sleep` statement may be used to wait for a certain amount of time, for instance to patiently wait for any login sequence to complete. Again, the interval is specified in seconds.

mode and default

These commands are used to flip the serial line to SLIP mode and configure the interface.

The `mode` command is the last command executed by *dip* before gong into daemon mode. Unless an error occurs, the command does not return.

`mode` takes a protocol name as argument. *dip* currently recognizes `SLIP` and `CSLIP` as valid names. The current version of *dip* does not understand adaptive SLIP, however. After enabling SLIP mode on the serial line, *dip* executes *ifconfig* to configure the interface as a point-to-point link, and invokes *route* to set the route to the remote host.

If, in addition, the script executes the `default` command before `mode`, *dip* will also make the default route point to the SLIP link.

Running in Server Mode

Setting up your SLIP client was the hard part. Doing the opposite, namely configuring your host to act as a SLIP server, is much easier.

One way to do this is to to use *dip* in server mode, which can be achieved by invoking it as *diplogin*. Its main configuration file is */etc/diphosts*, which associates login names with the address this host is assigned. Alternatively, you can also use *sliplogin*, a BSD-derived tool that features a more flexible configuration scheme that lets you execute shell scripts whenever a host connects and disconnects. It is currently in beta testing.

Both programs require that you set up one login account per SLIP client. For instance, assume you provide SLIP service to Arthur Dent at **dent.beta.com**, you might create an account named **dent** by adding the following line to your *passwd* file:

```
dent:*:501:60:Arthur Dent's SLIP account:/tmp:/usr/sbin/diplogin
```

Afterwards, you would set **dent**'s password using the *passwd* utility.

Now, when **dent** logs in, *dip* will start up as a server. To find out if he is indeed permitted to use SLIP, it will look up the username in */etc/diphosts*. This file details the access rights and connection parameter for each SLIP user. A sample entry for **dent** could look like this:

```
dent::dent.beta.com:Arthur Dent:SLIP,296
```

The first of the colon-separated fields is the name the user must log in as. The second field may contain an additional password (see below). The third is the hostname or IP address of the calling host. Next comes an informational field without any special meaning (yet). The last field describes the connection parameters. This is a comma-separated list specifying the protocol (currently one of SLIP or CSLIP), followed by the MTU.

When **dent** logs in, *diplogin* extracts the information on him from the *diphosts* file, and if the second field is not empty, prompts for an "external security password." The string entered by the user is compared to the (unencrypted) password from *diphosts*. If they do not match, the login attempt is rejected.

Otherwise, *diplogin* proceeds by flipping the serial line to CSLIP or SLIP mode and sets up the interface and route. This connection remains established until the user disconnects and the modem drops the line. *diplogin* will then return the line to normal line discipline and exit.

diplogin requires superuser privilege. If you don't have *dip* running setuid **root**, you should make *diplogin* a separate copy of *dip* instead of a simple link. *diplogin* can then safely be made setuid without affecting the status of *dip* itself.

CHAPTER EIGHT

THE POINT-TO-POINT PROTOCOL

Untangling the P's

Just like SLIP, PPP is a protocol to send datagrams across a serial connection; however, it addresses a couple of the deficiencies of SLIP. It lets the communicating sides negotiate options such as the IP address and the maximum datagram size at startup time, and it provides for client authorization. For each of these capabilities, PPP has a separate protocol. In this chapter, we will briefly cover these basic building blocks of PPP. This discussion is far from complete; if you want to know more about PPP, you are urged to read its RFC specification, as well as the dozen or so companion RFCs.[*]

RFC 1548

At the very bottom of PPP is the *High-Level Data Link Control* protocol, abbreviated HDLC,[†] which defines the boundaries around the individual PPP frames and provides a 16-bit checksum. As opposed to the more primitive SLIP encapsulation, a PPP frame is capable of holding packets from other protocols than IP, such as Novell's IPX or Appletalk. PPP achieves this by adding a protocol field to the basic HDLC frame that identifies the type of packet carried by the frame.

LCP, the *Link Control Protocol*, is used on top of HDLC to negotiate options pertaining to the data link, such as the *Maximum Receive Unit* (MRU), which states the maximum datagram size one side of the link agrees to receive.

An important step at the configuration stage of a PPP link is client authorization. Although it is not mandatory, it is really a must for dialup lines. Usually, the called host (the server) asks the client to authorize itself by proving it knows some secret key. If the caller fails to produce the correct secret, the connection is terminated. With PPP, authorization works both ways; that is, the caller may also ask the server to authenticate itself. These authentication procedures are totally independent of each other. There are two protocols for different types of authorization, which we

---

* The relevant RFCs are listed in the Bibiliography at the end of this book.
† In fact, HDLC is a much more general protocol devised by the International Standards Organization (ISO).

109

will discuss further below. They are named *Password Authentication Protocol* (PAP), and *Challenge Handshake Authentication Protocol* (CHAP).

Each network protocol that is routed across the data link, like IP, AppleTalk, etc., is configured dynamically using a corresponding *Network Control Protocol* (NCP). For instance, to send IP datagrams across the link, both PPPs must first negotiate which IP address each of them uses. The control protocol used for this is IPCP, the *Internet Protocol Control Protocol*.

Besides sending standard IP datagrams across the link, PPP also supports Van Jacobson header compression of IP datagrams. This is a technique to shrink the headers of TCP packets to as little as three bytes. It is also used in CSLIP and is more colloquially referred to as VJ header compression. The use of compression may be negotiated at startup time through IPCP as well.

PPP on Linux

On Linux, PPP functionality is split up in two parts, a low-level HDLC driver located in the kernel, and the user space *pppd* daemon that handles the various control protocols. The current release of PPP for Linux is *linux-ppp-2.1.2*, and it contains the kernel PPP module *pppd* and a program named *chat* used to dial up the remote system.

The PPP kernel driver was written by Michael Callahan. *pppd* was derived from a free PPP implementation for Sun and 386BSD machines that was written by Drew Perkins and others, and is maintained by Paul Mackerras. It was ported to Linux by Al Longyear.[*] *chat* was written by Karl Fox.[†]

Just like SLIP, PPP is implemented by means of a special line discipline. To use some serial line as a PPP link, you first establish the connection over your modem as usual, and subsequently convert the line to PPP mode. In this mode, all incoming data is passed to the PPP driver, which checks the incoming HDLC frames for validity (each HDLC frame carries a 16-bit checksum), and unwraps and dispatches them. Currently, it is able to handle IP datagrams, optionally using Van Jacobson header compression. As soon as Linux supports IPX, the PPP driver will be extended to handle IPX packets, too.

The kernel driver is aided by *pppd*, the PPP daemon, which performs the entire initialization and authentication phase that is necessary before actual network traffic can be sent across the link. *pppd*'s behavior may be fine-tuned using a number of options. As PPP is rather complex, it is impossible to explain all of them in a single chapter. This book therefore cannot cover all aspects of *pppd*, but only give

---

[*] Both authors have said they will be very busy for some time to come. If you have any questions on PPP in general, you'd best ask the people on the NET channel of the Linux activists mailing list.

[†] *karl@morningstar.com*.

pppd(8)

you an introduction. For more information, refer to the manual pages and *READMEs* in the *pppd* source distribution, which should help you sort out most questions this chapter fails to discuss. If your problems persist even after reading all documentation, you should turn to the newsgroup *comp.protocols.ppp* for help, which is the place where you will reach most of the people involved in the development of *pppd*.

Running pppd

When you want to connect to the Internet through a PPP link, you have to set up basic networking capabilities such as the loopback device, and the resolver. Both have been covered in the previous chapters. There are extra considerations about using DNS over a serial link; please refer to the Chapter 7, *Serial Line IP*, for a discussion of this.

As an introductory example of how to establish a PPP connection with *pppd*, assume you are at **vlager** again. You have already dialed up the PPP server **c3po** and logged into the **ppp** account. **c3po** has already fired up its PPP driver. After exiting the communications program you used for dialing, you execute the following command:

```
# pppd /dev/cua3 38400 crtscts defaultroute
```

This will flip the serial line *cua3* to PPP mode and establish an IP link to **c3po**. The transfer speed used on the serial port will be 38400 bps. The `crtscts` option turns on hardware handshake on the port, which is an absolute must at speeds above 9600 bps.

The first thing *pppd* does after starting up is negotiate several link characteristics with the remote end using LCP. Usually, the default set of options *pppd* tries to negotiate will work, so we won't go into this here.

For the time being, we also assume that **c3po** doesn't require any authentication from us, so the configuration phase is completed successfully.

pppd will then negotiate the IP parameters with its peer using IPCP, the IP control protocol. Since we didn't specify any particular IP address to *pppd* above, it will try to use the address obtained by having the resolver look up the local hostname. Both will then announce their addresses to each other.

Usually, there's nothing wrong with these defaults. Even if your machine is on an Ethernet, you can use the same IP address for both the Ethernet and the PPP interface. Nevertheless, *pppd* allows you to use a different address, or even to ask your peer to use some specific address. These options are discussed in the section "IP Configuration Options."

After going through the IPCP setup phase, *pppd* will prepare your host's networking layer to use the PPP link. It first configures the PPP network interface as a point-to-point link, using *ppp0* for the first PPP link that is active, *ppp1* for the second, and so on. Next, it will set up a routing table entry that points to the host at the other end of the link. In the example above, *pppd* will make the default network route point to **c3po**, because we gave it the `defaultroute` option.[*] This causes all datagrams to hosts not on your local network to be sent to **c3po**. There are a number of different routing schemes *pppd* supports, which we will cover in detail later in this chapter.

Using Options Files

Before *pppd* parses its command-line arguments, it scans several files for default options. These files may contain any valid command-line arguments spread out across an arbitrary number of lines. Comments are introduced by hash signs.

The first options file is */etc/ppp/options*, which is always scanned when *pppd* starts up. Using it to set some global defaults is a good idea, because it allows you to keep your users from doing several things that may compromise security. For instance, to make *pppd* require some kind of authentication (either PAP or CHAP) from the peer, you would add the *auth* option to this file. This option cannot be overridden by the user, so it becomes impossible to establish a PPP connection with any system that is not in your authentication databases.

The other options file, which is read after */etc/ppp/options*, is *.ppprc* in the user's home directory. It allows each user to specify her own set of default options.

A sample */etc/ppp/options* file might look like this:

```
# Global options for pppd running on vlager.vbrew.com
auth                 # require authentication
usehostname          # use local hostname for CHAP
lock                 # use UUCP-style device locking
domain vbrew.com     # our domain name
```

The first two options apply to authentication and will be explained below. The `lock` keyword makes *pppd* comply to the standard UUCP method of device locking. With this convention, each process that accesses a serial device, say */dev/cua3*, creates a lock file named *LCK..cua3* in the UUCP spool directory to signal that the device is in use. This is necessary to prevent any other programs such as *minicom* or *uucico* from opening the serial device while it is used by PPP.

The reason to provide these options in the global configuration file is that options such as those shown above cannot be overridden, and so provide for a reasonable level of security. Note however, that some options can be overridden later; one such example is the `connect` string.

---

[*] The default network route is installed only if none is present yet.

Dialing Out with chat

One of the things that may have struck you as inconvenient in the above example is that you had to establish the connection manually before you could fire up *pppd*. Unlike *dip*, *pppd* does not have its own scripting language for dialing the remote system and logging in, but rather relies on some external program or shell script to do this. The command to be executed can be given to *pppd* with the **connect** command-line option. *pppd* will redirect the command's standard input and output to the serial line. One useful program for doing this is *expect*, written by Don Libes. It has a very powerful language based on Tcl and was designed exactly for this sort of application.

Expect

The *pppd* package comes with a similar program called *chat*, which lets you specify a UUCP-style chat script. Basically, a chat script consists of an alternating sequence of strings that we expect to receive from the remote system, and the answers we are to send. We will call them *expect* and *send* strings, respectively. This is a typical excerpt from a chat script:

```
ogin: b1ff ssword: s3kr3t
```

This tells *chat* to wait for the remote system to send the login prompt and return the login name **b1ff**. We only wait for **ogin:** so that it doesn't matter if the login prompt starts with an uppercase or lowercase l, or if it arrives garbled. The following string is another expect string that makes *chat* wait for the password prompt and send our password in response.

This is basically all that chat scripts are about. A complete script to dial up a PPP server would, of course, also have to include the appropriate modem commands. Assume your modem understands the Hayes command set, and the server's telephone number is 318714. The complete *chat* invocation to establish a connection with **c3po** would then be

```
$ chat -v '' ATZ OK ATDT318714 CONNECT '' ogin: ppp word: GaGariN
```

By definition, the first string must be an expect string, but as the modem won't say anything before we have kicked it, we make *chat* skip the first expect by specifying an empty string. We go on and send ATZ, the reset command for Hayes-compatible modems, and wait for its response (OK). The next string sends the dial command along with the phone number to *chat*, and expects the CONNECT message in response. This is followed by an empty string again, because we don't want to send anything now, but rather wait for the login prompt. The remainder of the chat script works exactly as described above.

The *–v* option makes *chat* log all activities to the *syslog* daemon's local2 facility.[*]

---

[*] If you edit *syslog.conf* to redirect these log messages to a file, make sure this file isn't world readable, as *chat* also logs the entire chat script by default—including passwords and all.

Specifying the chat script on the command line bears a certain risk because users can view a process's command line with the *ps* command. You can avoid this by putting the chat script in a file, say *dial-c3po*. You make *chat* read the script from the file instead of the command line by giving it the *–f* option, followed by the filename. The complete *pppd* incantation would now look like this:

```
# pppd connect "chat -f dial-c3po" /dev/cua3 38400 -detach \
        crtscts modem defaultroute
```

Besides the *connect* option that specifies the dialup script, we have added two more options to the command line: *-detach*, which tells *pppd* not to detach from the console and become a background process, and the modem keyword, which makes it perform some modem-specific actions on the serial device, like disconnecting the line before and after the call. If you don't use this keyword, *pppd* will not monitor the port's DCD line and will therefore not detect if the remote end hangs up unexpectedly.

The examples shown above were rather simple; *chat* allows for much more complex scripts. One very useful feature is the ability to specify strings on which to abort the chat with an error. Typical abort strings are messages like BUSY or NO CARRIER that your modem usually generates when the called number is busy or doesn't answer. To make *chat* recognize these messages immediately rather than timing out, you can specify them at the beginning of the script using the ABORT keyword:

```
$ chat -v ABORT BUSY ABORT 'NO CARRIER' '' ATZ OK ...
```

chat(8)

In a similar fashion, you can change the timeout value for parts of the chat scripts by inserting *TIMEOUT* options.

Sometimes you also want to have some sort of conditional execution of parts of the chat script. For instance, when you don't receive the remote end's login prompt, you might want to send a BREAK, or a carriage return. You can achieve this by appending a sub-script to an expect string. It consists of a sequence of send and expect strings, just like the overall script itself, which are separated by hyphens. The sub-script is executed whenever the expected string it is appended to is not received in time. In the example above, we would modify the chat script as follows:

```
ogin:-BREAK-ogin: ppp ssword: GaGariN
```

Now, when *chat* doesn't see the remote system send the login prompt, the sub-script is executed by first sending a BREAK, and then waiting for the login prompt again. If the prompt now appears, the script continues as usual; otherwise it will terminate with an error.

Debugging Your PPP Setup

By default, *pppd* will log any warnings and error messages to *syslog*'s `daemon` facility. You have to add an entry to *syslog.conf* that redirects these messages to a file or even the console; otherwise *syslog* simply discards them. The following entry sends all messages to */var/log/ppp-log*:

```
daemon.*                 /var/log/ppp-log
```

If your PPP setup doesn't work at once, looking into this log file should give you a first hint of what goes wrong. If this doesn't help, you can also turn on extra debugging output using the *debug* option. This makes *pppd* log the contents of all control packets sent or received to *syslog*. All messages will go to the `daemon` facility.

Finally, the most drastic feature is to enable kernel-level debugging by invoking *pppd* with the *kdebug* option. It is followed by a numeric argument that is the bitwise OR of the following values: 1 for general debug messages, 2 for printing the contents of all incoming HDLC frames, and 4 to make the driver print all outgoing HDLC frames. To capture kernel debugging messages, you must either run a *syslogd* daemon that reads the */proc/kmsg* file, or the *klogd* daemon. Either of them directs kernel debugging to *syslog*'s `kernel` facility.

IP Configuration Options

IPCP is used to negotiate a couple of IP parameters at link configuration time. Usually, each peer sends an IPCP Configuration Request packet, indicating which values it wants to change from the defaults and to what value. Upon receipt, the remote end inspects each option in turn and either acknowledges or rejects it.

pppd gives you a lot of control about which IPCP options it will try to negotiate. You can tune this through various command-line options we will discuss below.

Choosing IP Addresses

In the example above, we had *pppd* dial up **c3po** and establish an IP link. No provisions were taken to choose a particular IP address on either end of the link. Instead, we picked **vlager**'s address as the local IP address, and let **c3po** provide its own. Sometimes, however, it is useful to have control over what address is used on one or the other end of the link. *pppd* supports several options for doing this.

To ask for particular addresses, you generally provide *pppd* with the following option:

```
local_addr:remote_addr
```

pppd(8)

`local_addr` and `remote_addr` may be specified either in dotted quad notation or as hostnames.* This option makes *pppd* attempt to use the first address as its own IP address, and the second as the peer's. If the peer rejects either of them during IPCP negotiation, no IP link will be established.†

If you want to set only the local address but accept any address the peer uses, you simply leave out the `remote_addr` part. For instance, to make **vlager** use the IP address **130.83.4.27** instead of its own, you would give it *130.83.4.27:* on the command line. Similarly, to set the remote address only, you would leave the `local_addr` field blank. By default, *pppd* will then use the address associated with your hostname.

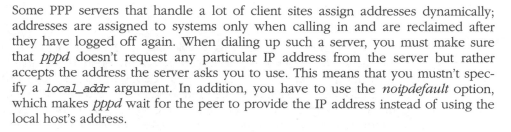

Some PPP servers that handle a lot of client sites assign addresses dynamically; addresses are assigned to systems only when calling in and are reclaimed after they have logged off again. When dialing up such a server, you must make sure that *pppd* doesn't request any particular IP address from the server but rather accepts the address the server asks you to use. This means that you mustn't specify a `local_addr` argument. In addition, you have to use the *noipdefault* option, which makes *pppd* wait for the peer to provide the IP address instead of using the local host's address.

Routing Through a PPP Link

After setting up the network interface, *pppd* will usually set up a host route to its peer only. If the remote host is on a LAN, you certainly want to be able to connect to hosts "behind" your peer as well; that is, a network route must be set up.

We have already seen above that *pppd* can be asked to set the default route using the *defaultroute* option. This option is very useful if the PPP server you dialed up will act as your Internet gateway.

The reverse case, where your system acts as a gateway for a single host, is also relatively easy to accomplish. For example, take some employee at the Virtual Brewery whose home machine is called **loner**. When connecting to **vlager** through PPP, he uses an address on the Brewery's subnet. At **vlager**, we can now give *pppd* the *proxyarp* option, which will install a proxy ARP entry for **loner**. This will automatically make **loner** accessible from all hosts at the Brewery and the Winery.

However, things aren't always as easy as that. For instance, linking two local area networks usually requires adding a specific network route, because these networks may have their own default routes. Besides, having both peers use the PPP link as the default route would generate a loop, where packets to unknown destinations would ping-pong between the peers until their time to live expired.

---

* Using hostnames in this option has consequences for CHAP authentication. Please refer to the section on CHAP in this chapter.
† You can allow the peer PPP to override your ideas of IP addresses by giving *pppd* the *ipcp-accept-local* and *ipcp-accept-remote* options.

As an example, suppose the Virtual Brewery opens a branch in some other city. The subsidiary runs an Ethernet of its own using the IP network number **172.16.3.0**, which is subnet 3 of the Brewery's class B network. The subsidiary wants to connect to the Brewery's main Ethernet via PPP to update customer databases, etc. Again, **vlager** acts as the gateway; its peer is called **sub-etha** and has an IP address of **172.16.3.1**.

When **sub-etha** connects to **vlager**, it makes the default route point to **vlager** as usual. On **vlager**, however, we will have to install a network route for subnet 3 that goes through **sub-etha**. For this, we use a feature of *pppd* not discussed so far—the *ip-up* command. This is a shell script or program located in */etc/ppp* that is executed after the PPP interface has been configured. When present, it is invoked with the following parameters:

```
ip-up iface device speed local_addr remote_addr
```

iface names the network interface used, *device* is the pathname of the serial device file used (*/dev/tty* if stdin/stdout are used), and *speed* is the device's speed. *local_addr* and *remote_addr* give the IP addresses used at both ends of the link in dotted quad notation. In our case, the *ip-up* script may contain the following code fragment:

```
#!/bin/sh
case $5 in
172.16.3.1)              # this is sub-etha
       route add -net 172.16.3.0 gw 172.16.3.1;;
...
esac
exit 0
```

In a similar fashion, */etc/ppp/ip-down* is used to undo all actions of *ip-up* after the PPP link has been taken down again.

However, the routing scheme is not yet complete. We have set up routing table entries on both PPP hosts, but so far none of the hosts on either network knows anything about the PPP link. This is not a big problem if all hosts at the subsidiary have their default route pointing at **sub-etha**, and all Brewery hosts route to **vlager** by default. If this is not the case, your only option will usually be to use a routing daemon like *gated*. After creating the network route on **vlager**, the routing daemon would broadcast the new route to all hosts on the attached subnets.

Link Control Options

We already encountered LCP, the Link Control Protocol, which is used to negotiate link characteristics and test the link.

RFC 1548

The two most important options negotiated by LCP are the Maximum Receive Unit, and the Asynchronous Control Character Map. There are a number of other LCP configuration options, but they are far too specialized to discuss here.

The Asynchronous Control Character Map, colloquially called the *async map*, is used on asynchronous links such as telephone lines to identify control characters that must be escaped (replaced by a specific two-character sequence). For instance, you may want to avoid the XON and XOFF characters used for software handshake because some misconfigured modem might choke upon receipt of an XOFF. Other candidates include Ctrl-] (the *telnet* escape character). PPP allows you to escape any of the characters with ASCII codes 0 through 31 by specifying them in the async map.

The async map is a bitmap 32 bits wide, with the least significant bit corresponding to the ASCII NUL character, and the most significant bit corrsponding to ASCII 31. If a bit is set, it signals that the corresponding character must be escaped before sending it across the link. Initially, the async map is set to *0xffffffff*, that is, all control characters will be esaped.

To tell your peer that it doesn't have to escape all control characters but only a few of them, you can specify a new async map to *pppd* using the *asyncmap* option. For instance, if only ^S and ^Q (ASCII 17 and 19, commonly used for XON and XOFF) must be escaped, use the following option:

```
asyncmap 0x000A0000
```

The Maximum Receive Unit, or MRU, signals to the peer the maximum size of HDLC frames we want to receive. Although this may remind you of the MTU value (Maximum Transfer Unit), these two have little in common. The MTU is a parameter of the kernel networking device and describes the maximum frame size the interface is able to handle. The MRU is more of an advice to the remote end not to generate any frames larger than the MRU; the interface must nevertheless be able to receive frames of up to 1500 bytes.

Choosing an MRU is therefore not so much a question of what the link is capable of transferring, but of what gives you the best throughput. If you intend to run interactive applications over the link, setting the MRU to values as low as 296 is a good idea, so that an occasional larger packet (say, from an FTP session) doesn't make your cursor "jump." To tell *pppd* to request an MRU of 296, you would give it the option *mru 296*. Small MRUs, however, only make sense if you don't have VJ header compression disabled (it is enabled by default).

pppd also understands a couple of LCP options that configure the overall behavior of the negotiation process, such as the maximum number of configuration requests that may be exchanged before the link is terminated. Unless you know exactly what you are doing, you should leave these alone.

Finally, there are two options that apply to LCP echo messages. PPP defines two messages, Echo Request and Echo Response. *pppd* uses this feature to check if a link is still operating. You can enable this by using the *lcp-echo-interval* option together with a time in seconds. If no frames are received from the remote host within this interval, *pppd* generates an Echo Request and expects the peer to return an Echo Response. If the peer does not produce a response, the link is terminated after a certain number of requests are sent. This number can be set using the *lcp-echo-failure* option. By default, this feature is disabled altogether.

General Security Considerations

A misconfigured PPP daemon can be a devastating security breach. It can be as bad as letting anyone plug their machine into your Ethernet (and that is very bad). In this section, we will discuss a few measures that should make your PPP configuration safe.

One problem with *pppd* is that to configure the network device and the routing table, it requires **root** privilege. You will usually solve this by running it setuid **root**. However, *pppd* allows users to set various security-relevant options. To protect against any attacks a user may launch by manipulating these options, it is suggested you set a couple of default values in the global */etc/ppp/options* file, like those shown in the sample file in the section "Using Options Files." Some of them, such as the authentication options, cannot be overridden by the user, and so provide a reasonable protection against manipulations.

Of course, you have to protect yourself from the systems you speak PPP with, too. To fend off hosts posing as someone else, you should always require some sort of authentication from your peer. Additionally, you should not allow foreign hosts to use any IP address they choose, but restrict them to at least a few. The following section will deal with these topics.

Authentication with PPP

CHAP Versus PAP

With PPP, each system may require its peer to authenticate itself using one of two authentication protocols. These are the Password Authentication Protocol (PAP), and the Challenge Handshake Authentication Protocol (CHAP). When a connection is established, each end can request the other to authenticate itself, regardless of whether it is the caller or the callee. Below I will loosely talk of "client" and "server" when I want to distinguish between the authenticating system and the authenticator. A PPP daemon can ask its peer for authentication by sending yet another LCP configuration request identifying the desired authentication protocol.

PAP works basically the same way as the normal login procedure. The client authenticates itself by sending a username and an (optionally encrypted) password to the server, which the server compares to its secrets database. This technique is vulnerable to eavesdroppers who may try to obtain the password by listening in on the serial line, and to repeated trial and error attacks.

CHAP does not have these deficiencies. With CHAP, the authenticator (i.e., the server) sends a randomly generated "challenge" string to the client, along with its hostname. The client uses the hostname to look up the appropriate secret, combines it with the challenge, and encrypts the string using a one-way hashing function. The result is returned to the server along with the client's hostname. The server now performs the same computation, and acknowledges the client if it arrives at the same result.

Another feature of CHAP is that it doesn't only require the client to authenticate itself at startup time, but sends challenges at regular intervals to make sure the client hasn't been replaced by an intruder, for instance by just switching phone lines.

pppd keeps the secret keys for CHAP and PAP in two separate files, called */etc/ppp/chap-secrets* and *pap-secrets*, respectively. By entering a remote host in one or the other file, you have a fine control over whether CHAP or PAP is used to authenticate ourselves with our peer, and vice versa.

By default, *pppd* doesn't require authentication from the remote, but will agree to authenticate itself when requested by the remote. As CHAP is so much stronger than PAP, *pppd* tries to use the former whenever possible. If the peer does not support it, or if *pppd* can't find a CHAP secret for the remote system in its *chap-secrets* file, it reverts to PAP. If it doesn't have a PAP secret for its peer either, it will refuse to authenticate altogether. As a consequence, the connection is closed down.

pppd(8)

This behavior can be modified in several ways. For instance, when given the *auth* keyword, *pppd* will require the peer to authenticate itself. *pppd* will agree to use either CHAP or PAP for this, as long as it has a secret for the peer in its CHAP or PAP database. There are other options to turn a particular authentication protocol on or off, but I won't describe them here.

If all systems you talk PPP with agree to authenticate themselves with you, you should put the *auth* option in the global */etc/ppp/options* file and define passwords for each system in the *chap-secrets* file. If a system doesn't support CHAP, add an entry for it to the *pap-secrets* file. This way you can make sure no unauthenticated system connects to your host.

The next two sections discuss the two PPP secrets files, *pap-secrets* and *chap-secrets*. They are located in */etc/ppp* and contain triplets of clients, servers, and passwords, optionally followed by a list of IP addresses. The interpretation of the client and server fields is different for CHAP and PAP, and also depends on whether we authenticate ourselves with the peer, or whether we require the server to authenticate itself with us.

The CHAP Secrets File

When it has to authenticate itself with some server using CHAP, *pppd* searches the *chap-secrets* file for an entry with the client field equal to the local hostname, and the server field equal to the remote hostname sent in the CHAP challenge. When requiring the peer to authenticate itself, the roles are simply reversed: *pppd* will then look for an entry with the client field equal to the remote hostname (sent in the client's CHAP response), and the server field equal to the local hostname.

The following is a sample *chap-secrets* file for **vlager**:[*]

```
# CHAP secrets for vlager.vbrew.com
#
# client            server            secret                addrs
#-----------------------------------------------------------------
vlager.vbrew.com    c3po.lucas.com    "Use The Source Luke" vlager.vbrew.com
c3po.lucas.com      vlager.vbrew.com  "riverrun, pasteve"   c3po.lucas.com
*                   vlager.vbrew.com  "VeryStupidPassword"  pub.vbrew.com
```

When establishing a PPP connection with **c3po**, **c3po** asks **vlager** to authenticate itself by sending a CHAP challenge. *pppd* then scans *chap-secrets* for an entry with the client field equal to **vlager.vbrew.com** and the server field equal to **c3po.lucas.com**,[†] and finds the first line shown above. It then produces the CHAP response from the challenge string and the secret (Use The Source Luke), and sends it off to **c3po**.

At the same time, *pppd* composes a CHAP challenge for **c3po** containing a unique challenge string and its fully qualified hostname **vlager.vbrew.com**. **c3po** constructs a CHAP response in the manner we just discussed, and returns it to **vlager**. *pppd* now extracts the client hostname (**c3po.vbrew.com**) from the response and searches the *chap-secrets* file for a line matching **c3po** as a client and **vlager** as the server. The second line does this, so *pppd* combines the CHAP challenge and the secret riverrun, pasteve, encrypts them, and compares the result to **c3po**'s CHAP response.

The optional fourth field lists the IP addresses that are acceptable for the clients named in the first field. The addresses can be given in dotted quad notation or as hostnames that are looked up with the resolver. For instance, if **c3po** requests to use an IP address during IPCP negotiation that is not in this list, the request will be rejected, and IPCP will be shut down. In the sample file shown above, **c3po** is therefore limited to using its own IP address. If the address field is empty, any addresses will be allowed; a value of "–" prevents the use of IP with that client altogether.

The third line of the sample *chap-secrets* file allows any host to establish a PPP link with **vlager** because a client or server field of * is a wildcard matching any

---

[*] The double quotes are not part of the password; they merely serve to protect the white space within the password.

[†] This hostname is taken from the CHAP challenge.

hostname. The only requirement is that it knows the secret and uses the address of **pub.vbrew.com**. Entries with wildcard hostnames may appear anywhere in the secrets file, since *pppd* will always use the most specific entry that applies to a server/client pair.

pppd may need some help forming hostnames. As explained before, the remote hostname is always provided by the peer in the CHAP challenge or response packet. The local hostname will be derived by calling the *gethostname(2)* function by default. If you have set the system name to your unqualified hostname, you have to provide *pppd* with the domain name in addition using the *domain* option:

```
# pppd ... domain vbrew.com
```

This will append the Brewery's domain name to **vlager** for all authentication-related activities. Other options that modify *pppd*'s idea of the local hostname are *usehostname* and *name*. When you give the local IP address on the command line using *local:remote*, and *local* is a name instead of a dotted quad, *pppd* will use this as the local hostname.

pppd(8)

The PAP Secrets File

The PAP secrets file is very similar to that used by CHAP. The first two fields always contain a username and a server name; the third holds the PAP secret. When the remote sends an authenticate request, *pppd* uses the entry that has a server field equal to the local hostname, and a user field equal to the username sent in the request. When authenticating itself with the peer, *pppd* picks the secret to be sent from the line with the user field equal to the local username, and the server field equal to the remote hostname.

A sample PAP secrets file might look like this:

```
# /etc/ppp/pap-secrets
#
# user          server      secret          addrs
vlager-pap      c3po        cresspahl       vlager.vbrew.com
c3po            vlager      DonaldGNUth     c3po.lucas.com
```

The first line is used to authenticate ourselves when talking to **c3po**. The second line describes how a user named **c3po** has to authenticate itself with us.

The name **vlager-pap** in column one is the username we send to **c3po**. By default, *pppd* will pick the local hostname as the username, but you can also specify a different name by giving the *user* option followed by that name.

When picking an entry from the *pap-secrets* file for authentication with the peer, *pppd* has to know the remote host's name. As it has no way of finding that out, you have to specify it on the command line using the *remotename* keyword followed by the peer's hostname. For instance, to use the above entry for authentication with **c3po**, we have to add the following option to *pppd*'s command line:

```
# pppd ... remotename c3po user vlager-pap
```

In the fourth field (and all fields following), you can specify what IP addresses are allowed for that particular host, just as in the CHAP secrets file. The peer may then only request addresses from that list. In the sample file, we require **c3po** to use its real IP address.

Note that PAP is a rather weak authentication method, and it is suggested you use CHAP instead whenever possible. We will therefore not cover PAP in greater detail here; if you are interested in using PAP, you will find some more PAP features in the *pppd(8)* manual page.

Configuring a PPP Server

Running *pppd* as a server is just a matter of adding the appropriate options to the command line. Ideally, you would create a special account, say **ppp**, and give it a script or program as a login shell that invokes *pppd* with these options. For instance, you would add the following line to */etc/passwd*:

```
ppp:*:500:200:Public PPP Account.:/tmp:/etc/ppp/ppplogin
```

Of course, you may want to use different uids and gids than those shown above. You would also have to set the password for the above account using the *passwd* command.

The *ppplogin* script might then look like this:

```
#!/bin/sh
# ppplogin - script to fire up pppd on login
mesg n
stty -echo
exec pppd -detach silent modem crtscts
```

The *mesg* command disables other users from writing to the tty by using, for instance, the *write* command. The *stty* command turns off character echoing. This is necessary because otherwise everything the peer sends would be echoed back to it. The most important *pppd* option given above is *–detach*, because it prevents *pppd* from detaching from the controlling tty. If we didn't specify this option, it would go to the background, making the shell script exit. This in turn would cause the serial line to be hung up and the connection to be dropped. The *silent* option causes *pppd* to wait until it receives a packet from the calling system before it starts sending. This prevents transmit timeouts from occurring when the calling system is slow in firing up its PPP client. The modem option makes *pppd* drive the modem control lines of the serial port. You should always turn this option on when using *pppd* with a modem. The *crtscts* option turns on hardware handshake.

Besides these options, you might want to force some sort of authentication, for example, by specifying *auth* on *pppd*'s command line or in the global options file. The manual page also discusses more specific options for turning individual authentication protocols on and off.

CHAPTER NINE

IMPORTANT
NETWORK FEATURES

After successfully setting up IP and the resolver, you have to turn to the services you want to provide over the network. This chapter covers the configuration of a few simple network applications, including the *inetd* server and the programs from the *rlogin* family. The Remote Procedure Call interface, which services like the Network File System (NFS) and the Network Information System (NIS) are based upon will be dealt with briefly, too. The configuration of NFS and NIS, however, takes up more room and will be described in separate chapters. This applies to electronic mail and Netnews as well.

Of course, we can't cover all network applications in this book. If you want to install one that's not discussed here, like *talk*, *gopher*, or *Mosaic*, please refer to its manual pages for details.

The inetd Super Server

Frequently, services are performed by so-called *daemons*. A daemon is a program that opens a certain port and waits for incoming connections. If one occurs, the daemon creates a child process which accepts the connection, while the parent continues to listen for further requests. This concept has the drawback that for every service offered, a daemon has to run that listens on the port for a connection to occur, which generally means a waste of system resources like swap space.

Thus, almost all UNIX installations run a "super server" that creates sockets for a number of services and listens on all of them simultaneously using the *select(2)* system call. When a remote host requests one of the services, the super server notices this and spawns the server specified for this port.

The super server commonly used is *inetd*, the Internet Daemon. It is started at system boot time and takes the list of services it is to manage from a startup file named */etc/inetd.conf*. In addition to those servers invoked, there are a number of trivial services performed by *inetd* itself called *internal services*. They include *chargen*, which simply generates a string of characters, and *daytime*, which returns the system's idea of the time of day.

An entry in this file consists of a single line made up of the following fields:

```
service type protocol wait user server cmdline
```

The meaning of each field is as follows:

service

> Gives the service name. The service name has to be translated to a port number by looking it up in the */etc/services* file. This file will be described in the section "The services and protocols Files."

type

> Specifies a socket type, either `stream` (for connection-oriented protocols) or `dgram` (for datagram protocols). TCP-based services should therefore always use `stream`, while UDP-based services should always use `dgram`.

protocol

> Names the transport protocol used by the service. This must be a valid protocol name found in the *protocols* file, explained below.

wait

> This option applies only to `dgram` sockets. It can be either `wait` or `nowait`. If `wait` is specified, *inetd* will execute only one server for the specified port at any time. Otherwise, it will immediately continue to listen on the port after executing the server.

> This is useful for "single-threaded" servers that read all incoming datagrams until no more arrive, and then exit. Most RPC servers are of this type and should therefore specify `wait`. The opposite type, "multi-threaded" servers, allow an unlimited number of instances to run concurrently; this is only rarely used. These servers should specify `nowait`.

> `stream` sockets should always use `nowait`.

user

> This is the login ID of the user the process is executed under. This will frequently be the **root** user, but some services may use different accounts. It is a very good idea to apply the principle of least privilege here, which states that you shouldn't run a command under a privileged account if the program doesn't require this for proper functioning. For example, the NNTP news server will run as **news**, while services that may pose a security risk (such as *tftp* or *finger*) are often run as **nobody**.

server

> Gives the full pathname of the server program to be executed. Internal services are marked by the keyword `internal`.

cmdline

This is the command line to be passed to the server. This includes argument 0, the command name. Usually, this will be the program name of the server, unless the program behaves differently when invoked by a different name.

This field is empty for internal services.

A sample *inetd.conf* file is shown in Example 9-1. The *finger* service is commented out so that it is not available. This is often done for security reasons, because it can be used by attackers to obtain names of users on your system.

Example 9-1: A Sample /etc/inetd.conf File

```
#
# inetd services
ftp        stream tcp nowait root    /usr/sbin/ftpd     in.ftpd -l
telnet     stream tcp nowait root    /usr/sbin/telnetd in.telnetd -b/etc/issue
#finger     stream tcp nowait bin     /usr/sbin/fingerd in.fingerd
#tftp       dgram  udp wait   nobody /usr/sbin/tftpd    in.tftpd
#tftp       dgram  udp wait   nobody /usr/sbin/tftpd    in.tftpd /boot/diskless
login      stream tcp nowait root    /usr/sbin/rlogind in.rlogind
shell      stream tcp nowait root    /usr/sbin/rshd    in.rshd
exec       stream tcp nowait root    /usr/sbin/rexecd  in.rexecd
#
#          inetd internal services
#
daytime    stream tcp nowait root internal
daytime    dgram  udp nowait root internal
time       stream tcp nowait root internal
time       dgram  udp nowait root internal
echo       stream tcp nowait root internal
echo       dgram  udp nowait root internal
discard    stream tcp nowait root internal
discard    dgram  udp nowait root internal
chargen    stream tcp nowait root internal
chargen    dgram  udp nowait root internal
```

The *tftp* is shown commented out as well. *tftp* implements the *Trivial File Transfer Protocol* (TFTP), which allows someone to transfer any world-readable files from your system without password checking, etc. This is especially harmful with the */etc/passwd* file, even more so when you don't use shadow passwords.

TFTP is commonly used by diskless clients and X terminals to download their code from a boot server. If you need to run *tftpd* for this reason, make sure to limit its scope to those directories clients will retrieve files from by adding those directory names to *tftpd*'s command line. This is shown in the second *tftp* line in the example.

The tcpd Access Control Facility

Since opening a computer to network access involves many security risks, applications are designed to guard against several types of attacks. Some security features, however, may be flawed (most drastically demonstrated by the RTM Internet worm), or do not distinguish between secure hosts from which requests for a particular service will be accepted, and insecure hosts whose requests should be rejected. We already briefly discussed the *finger* and *tftp* services above. One would want to limit access to these services to "trusted hosts" only, which is impossible with the usual setup, where *inetd* either provides this service to all clients, or not at all.

A useful tool for this is *tcpd*,[*] a so-called daemon wrapper. For TCP services you want to monitor or protect, it is invoked instead of the server program. *tcpd* logs the request to the *syslog* daemon, checks if the remote host is allowed to use that service, and only if this succeeds will it execute the real server program. Note that this does not work with UDP-based services.

For example, to wrap the *finger* daemon, you have to change the corresponding line in *inetd.conf* to this:

```
# wrap finger daemon
finger  stream  tcp     nowait  root    /usr/sbin/tcpd  in.fingerd
```

Without adding any access control, this will appear to the client just as a usual *finger* setup, except that any requests are logged to *syslog*'s auth facility.

Access control is implemented by means of two files called */etc/hosts.allow* and */etc/hosts.deny*. They contain entries allowing and denying access, respectively, to certain services and hosts. When *tcpd* handles a request for a service such as *finger* from a client host named **biff.foobar.com**, it scans *hosts.allow* and *hosts.deny* (in this order) for an entry matching both the service and client host. If a matching entry is found in *hosts.allow*, access is granted, regardless of any entry in *hosts.deny*. If a match is found in *hosts.deny*, the request is rejected by closing down the connection. If no match is found at all, the request is accepted.

Entries in the access files look like this:

```
servicelist: hostlist [:shellcmd]
```

servicelist is a list of service names from */etc/services*, or the keyword ALL. To match all services except *finger* and *tftp*, use "ALL EXCEPT finger, tftp."

hostlist is a list of hostnames or IP addresses, or the keywords ALL, LOCAL, or UNKNOWN. ALL matches any host, while LOCAL matches hostnames not containing a dot.[†] UNKNOWN matches any hosts whose name or address lookup failed. A name starting with a dot matches all hosts whose domain is equal to this name. For

---

[*] Written by Wietse Venema, *wietse@wzv.win.tue.nl*.

[†] Usually only local hostnames obtained from lookups in */etc/hosts* contain no dots.

example, .foobar.com matches biff.foobar.com. There are also provisions for IP network addresses and subnet numbers.

To deny access to the *finger* and *tftp* services to all but the local hosts, put the following in */etc/hosts.deny*, and leave */etc/hosts.allow* empty:

```
in.tftpd, in.fingerd: ALL EXCEPT LOCAL, .your.domain
```

The optional *shellcmd* field may contain a shell command to be invoked when the entry is matched. This is useful to set up traps that may expose potential attackers:

```
in.ftpd: ALL EXCEPT LOCAL, .vbrew.com : \
    echo "request from %d@%h: >> /var/log/finger.log; \
    if [ %h != "vlager.vbrew.com:" ]; then \
        finger -l @%h >> /var/log/finger.log \
    fi
```

The %h and %d arguments are expanded by *tcpd* to the client hostname and service name, respectively. Please refer to the *hosts access(5)* manual page for details.

hosts_access(5)

The services and protocols Files

RFC 1340

The port numbers on which certain "standard" services are offered are defined in the Assigned Numbers RFC. To enable server and client programs to convert service names to these numbers, at least part of the list is kept on each host; it is stored in a file called */etc/services*. An entry is made up like this:

```
service port/protocol    [aliases]
```

Here, *service* specifies the service name, *port* defines the port the service is offered on, and *protocol* defines which transport protocol is used. Commonly, this is either udp or tcp. It is possible for a service to be offered for more than one protocol as well as offering different services on the same port, as long as the protocols are different. The *aliases* field allows you to specify alternative names for the same service.

Usually, you don't have to change the services file that comes along with the network software on your Linux system. Nevertheless, we give a small excerpt from that file in Example 9-2.

Example 9-2: A Sample /etc/services File

```
# The services file:
#
# well-known services
echo            7/tcp                   # Echo
echo            7/udp                   #
discard         9/tcp   sink null       # Discard
discard         9/udp   sink null       #
daytime         13/tcp                  # Daytime
```

Example 9–2: A Sample /etc/services File (continued)

```
daytime      13/udp                     #
chargen      19/tcp  ttytst source  # Character Generator
chargen      19/udp  ttytst source  #
ftp-data     20/tcp                     # File Transfer Protocol (Data)
ftp          21/tcp                     # File Transfer Protocol (Control)
telnet       23/tcp                     # Virtual Terminal Protocol
smtp         25/tcp                     # Simple Mail Transfer Protocol
nntp         119/tcp readnews       # Network News Transfer Protocol
#
# UNIX services
exec         512/tcp                    # BSD rexecd
biff         512/udp comsat         # mail notification
login        513/tcp                    # remote login
who          513/udp whod           # remote who and uptime
shell        514/tcp cmd            # remote command, no passwd used
syslog       514/udp                    # remote system logging
printer      515/tcp spooler        # remote print spooling
route        520/udp router routed  # routing information protocol
```

For example, note that the *echo* service is offered on port 7 for both TCP and UDP, and that port 512 is used for two different services: remote execution (*rexec*) using TCP, and the COMSAT daemon, which notifies users of newly arrived mail, over UDP (see *xbiff(1x)*).

Like the services file, the networking library needs a way to translate protocol names—for example, those used in the services file—to protocol numbers understood by the IP layer on other hosts. This is done by looking up the name in the */etc/protocols* file. It contains one entry per line, each containing a protocol name, and the associated number. Having to touch this file is even more unlikely than having to meddle with */etc/services*. A sample file is given in Example 9-3.

Example 9–3: A Sample /etc/protocols File

```
#
# Internet (IP) protocols
#
ip    0     IP      # internet protocol, pseudo protocol number
icmp  1     ICMP    # internet control message protocol
igmp  2     IGMP    # internet group multicast protocol
tcp   6     TCP     # transmission control protocol
udp   17    UDP     # user datagram protocol
raw   255   RAW     # RAW IP interface
```

Remote Procedure Call

Chapter 10
Chapter 11

A very general mechanism for client-server applications is provided by RPC, the *Remote Procedure Call* package. RPC was developed by Sun Microsystems and is a collection of tools and library functions. Important applications built on top of RPC are NFS, the Network File System, and NIS, the Network Information System.

An RPC server consists of a collection of procedures that a client can call by sending an RPC request to the server along with the procedure parameters. The server will invoke the indicated procedure on behalf of the client, handing back the return value if there is any. In order to be machine-independent, all data exchanged between client and server is converted to a so-called *External Data Representation* format (XDR) by the sender, and converted back to the machine-local representation by the receiver. Sun has graciously placed RPC in the public domain; it is described in a series of RFCs.

RFC 1057

Sometimes, improvements to an RPC application introduce incompatible changes in the procedure call interface. Of course, simply changing the server would crash all applications that still expect the original behavior. Therefore, RPC programs have version numbers assigned to them, usually starting with 1, and with each new version of the RPC interface this counter will be bumped. Often, a server may offer several versions simultaneously; clients then indicate by the version number in their requests which implementation of the service they want to use.

The network communication between RPC servers and clients is somewhat peculiar. An RPC server offers one or more collections of procedures; each set is being called a *program* and is uniquely identified by a *program number*. A list that maps service names to program numbers is usually kept in */etc/rpc*, an excerpt of which is shown in Example 9-4.

Example 9-4: A Sample /etc/rpc File

```
#
# /etc/rpc - miscellaenous RPC-based services
#
portmapper      100000  portmap sunrpc
rstatd          100001  rstat rstat_svc rup perfmeter
rusersd         100002  rusers
nfs             100003  nfsprog
ypserv          100004  ypprog
mountd          100005  mount showmount
ypbind          100007
walld           100008  rwall shutdown
yppasswdd       100009  yppasswd
bootparam       100026
ypupdated       100028  ypupdate
```

In TCP/IP networks, the authors of RPC were faced with the problem of mapping program numbers to generic network services. They chose to have each server provide both a TCP and a UDP port for each program and each version. Generally, RPC applications will use UDP when sending data, and only fall back to TCP when the data to be transferred doesn't fit into a single UDP datagram.

Of course, client programs have to have a way to find out which port a program number maps to. Using a configuration file for this would be too unflexible; since RPC applications don't use reserved ports, there's no guarantee that a port originally meant to be used by our database application hasn't been taken by some other process. Therefore, RPC applications pick any port they can get and register it with the so-called *portmapper daemon*. The portmapper acts as a service broker for all RPC servers running on its machine. A client that wishes to contact a service with a given program number will first query the portmapper on the server's host, which returns the TCP and UDP port numbers the service can be reached at.

This method has the particular drawback that it introduces a single point of failure, much like the *inetd* daemon does for the standard Berkeley services. However, this case is even a little worse, because when the portmapper dies, all RPC port information is lost; this usually means you have to restart all RPC servers manually, or reboot the entire machine.

 On Linux, the portmapper is called *rpc.portmap* and resides in */usr/sbin*. Other than making sure it is started from *rc.inet2*, the portmapper doesn't require any configuration work.

Configuring the r Commands

There are a number of commands for executing commands on remote hosts. These are *rlogin*, *rsh*, *rcp*, and *rcmd*. They all spawn a shell on the remote host and allow the user to execute commands. Of course, the client needs to have an account on the host where the command is to be executed. Thus, all these commands perform an authorization procedure. Usually, the client will tell the user's login name to the server, which in turn requests a password that is validated in the usual way.

Sometimes, however, it is desirable to relax authorization checks for certain users. For instance, if you frequently have to log in to other machines on your LAN, you might want to be admitted without having to type your password every time.

Disabling authorization is advisable only on a small number of hosts whose password databases are synchronized, or for a small number of privileged users who need to access many machines for administrative reasons. Whenever you want to allow people to log in to your host without having to specify a login ID or password, make sure that you don't accidentally grant access to anybody else.

There are two ways to disable authorization checks for the *r* commands. One is for the superuser to allow certain or all users on certain or all hosts (the latter definitely being a bad idea) to log in without being asked for a password. This access is controlled by a file called */etc/hosts.equiv.* It contains a list of host and user names that are considered equivalent to users on the local host. An alternative option is for a user to grant other users on certain hosts access to her account. These may be listed in the file *.rhosts* in the user's home directory. For security reasons, this file must be owned by the user or the superuser and must not be a symbolic link; otherwise it will be ignored.[*]

When a client requests an *r* service, her hostname and username are searched in the */etc/hosts.equiv* file, and then in the *.rhosts* file of the user she wants to log in as. As an example, assume **janet** is working on **gauss** and tries to log into **joe**'s account on **euler**. Throughout the following example, we will refer to Janet as the *client* user, and Joe as the *local* user. Janet types this command on **gauss**:

```
$ rlogin -l joe euler
```

The server will first check *hosts.equiv*[†] to see if Janet should be granted free access, and if this fails, it will try to look her up in *.rhosts* in **joe**'s home directory.

The *hosts.equiv* file on **euler** looks like this:

```
gauss
euler
-public
quark.physics.groucho.edu     andres
```

An entry consists of a hostname, optionally followed by a username. If a hostname appears all by itself, all users from that host will be admitted to their local accounts without any checks. In the above example, Janet would be allowed to log into her account **janet** when coming from **gauss**, and the same applies to any other user except **root**. However, if Janet wants to log in as **joe**, she will be prompted for a password as usual.

If a hostname is followed by a username, as in the last line of the above sample file, this user is given password-free access to *all* accounts except the **root** account.

The hostname may also be preceded by a minus sign, as in the entry **-public**. This requires authorization for all accounts on **public**, regardless of what rights individual users grant in their *.rhosts* file.

The format of the *.rhosts* file is identical to that of *hosts.equiv*, but its meaning is a little different. Consider Joe's *.rhosts* file on **euler**:

```
chomp.cs.groucho.edu
gauss        janet
```

---

[*] In an NFS environment, you may need to give it a protection of 444 because the superuser is often very restricted in accessing files on disks mounted via NFS.

[†] Note that the *hosts.equiv* file is *not* searched when someone attempts to log in as **root**.

The first entry grants **joe** free acess when logging in from **chomp.cs.groucho.edu**, but does not affect the rights of any other account on **euler** or **chomp**. The second entry is a slight variation of this, in that it grants **janet** free access to Joe's account when logging in from **gauss**.

Note that the client's hostname is obtained by reverse mapping the caller's address to a name so that this feature will fail with hosts unknown to the resolver. The client's hostname is considered to match the name in the hosts files in one of the following cases:

1. The client's canonical hostname (not an alias) literally matches the hostname in the file.

2. If the client's hostname is a fully qualified domain name (such as returned by the resolver when you have DNS running), and it doesn't literally match the hostname in the hosts file, it is compared to that hostname expanded with the local domain name.

## CHAPTER TEN

THE NETWORK INFORMATION SYSTEM

W hen running a local area network, your overall goal is usually to provide an environment for your users that makes the network transparent. An important steppingstone to this end is to keep vital data such as user account information synchronized among all hosts. We have seen before that for hostname resolution, a powerful and sophisticated service exists—DNS. For other tasks, there is no such specialized service. Moreover, if you manage only a small LAN with no Internet connectivity, setting up DNS may not seem to be worth the trouble.

This is why Sun developed NIS, the *Network Information System*. NIS provides generic database access facilities that can be used to distribute information such as that contained in the *passwd* and *groups* files to all hosts on your network. This makes the network appear as a single system, with the same accounts on all hosts. In a similar fashion, you can use NIS to distribute the hostname information from */etc/hosts* to all machines on the network.

NIS is based on RPC, and comprises a server, a client-side library, and several administrative tools. Originally, NIS was called *Yellow Pages*, or YP, which is still used to refer to it. On the other hand, Yellow Pages is a trademark of British Telecom, which required Sun to drop that name. As things go, some names stick with people, and so YP lives on as a prefix to the names of most NIS-related commands such as *ypserv*, *ypbind*, etc.

Today, NIS is available for virtually all UNIXes, and there are even free implementations of it. One is from the BSD Net-2 release and has been derived from a public domain reference implementation donated by Sun. The library client code from this release has been in the GNU *libc* for a long time, while the administrative programs have only recently been ported to Linux by Swen Thümmler.[*] An NIS server is missing from the reference implementation. Tobias Reber has written another NIS package including all tools and a server; it is called *yps*.[†]

Currently, a complete rewrite of the NIS code called NYS is being done by Peter Eriksson,[‡] which supports both plain NIS and Sun's much revised NIS+. NYS not only provides a set of NIS tools and a server, but also adds a whole new set of library functions that will probably make it into the standard *libc* eventually. This includes a new configuration scheme for hostname resolution that replaces the current scheme using *host.conf.* The features of these functions will be discussed below.

NFS and NIS

This chapter focuses on NYS rather than the other two packages, which I will refer to as the "traditional" NIS code. If you do want to run any of these packages, the instructions in this chapter may or may not be enough. For additional information, refer to a book on NIS.

NIS HOWTO

For the time being, NYS is still under development, and therefore standard Linux utilities such as the network programs or the *login* program are not yet aware of the NYS configuration scheme. However, NYS has been integrated into the mainstream *libc* (as of version 4.6), so you can easily build your own C library with NYS support instead of the traditional NIS code. The default, however, is to use the traditional NIS code. The GNU project also seems to be interested in including NYS in their official GNU *libc*, from which the Linux library is derived. (Instructions on creating a C library with NYS support can be found in the file *README.nys* in the library source distribution.)

Getting Acquainted with NIS

NIS keeps database information in so-called *maps* containing key-value pairs. Maps are stored on a central host running the NIS server, from which clients may

---

* Swen can be reached at *swen@uni-paderborn.de.* The NIS clients are available as *yp-linux.tar.gz* from **sunsite.unc.edu** in *system/Network.*
† The current version (as of this writing) is *yps-0.21* and can be obtained from **ftp.lysator.liu.se** in the */pub/NYS* directory.
‡ To be reached at *pen@lysator.liu.se.*

retrieve the information through various RPC calls. Quite frequently, maps are stored in DBM files.[*]

The maps themselves are usually generated from master text files such as */etc/hosts* or */etc/passwd*. For some files, several maps are created, one for each search key type. For instance, you may search the *hosts* file for a hostname as well as for an IP address. Accordingly, two NIS maps are derived from it, called *hosts.byname* and *hosts.byaddr*. Table 10-1 lists common maps and the files from which they are generated.

Table 10-1: Some Standard NIS Maps and Corresponding Files

Master File	Map(s)
/etc/hosts	*hosts.byname, hosts.byaddr*
/etc/networks	*networks.byname, networks.byaddr*
/etc/passwd	*passwd.byname, passwd.byuid*
/etc/group	*group.byname, group.bygid*
/etc/services	*services.byname, services.bynumber*
/etc/rpc	*rpc.byname, rpc.bynumber*
/etc/protocols	*protocols.byname, protocols.bynumber*
/usr/lib/aliases	*mail.aliases*

You may find support for other files and maps in some NIS package or other. These usually contain information for applications not discussed in this book, such as the *bootparams* map that is used by Sun's *bootparamd* server.

For some maps, people commonly use *nicknames*, which are shorter and therefore easier to type. Note that these nicknames are understood only by *ypcat* and *ypmatch*, two tools for checking your NIS configuration. To obtain a full list of nicknames understood by them, run the following command:

```
$ ypcat -x
NIS map nickname translation table:
        "passwd" -> "passwd.byname"
        "group" -> "group.byname"
        "networks" -> "networks.byaddr"
        "hosts" -> "hosts.byname"
        "protocols" -> "protocols.bynumber"
        "services" -> "services.byname"
        "aliases" -> "mail.aliases"
        "ethers" -> "ethers.byname"
        "rpc" -> "rpc.bynumber"
        "netmasks" -> "netmasks.byaddr"
        "publickey" -> "publickey.byname"
        "netid" -> "netid.byname"
```

* DBM is a simple database management library that uses hashing techniques to speed up search operations. There's a free DBM implementation from the GNU project called *gdbm*, which is part of most Linux distributions.

```
"passwd.adjunct" -> "passwd.adjunct.byname"
"group.adjunct" -> "group.adjunct.byname"
"timezone" -> "timezone.byname"
```

The NIS server program is traditionally called *ypserv*. For an average network, a single server usually suffices; large networks may choose to run several of these on different machines and different segments of the network to relieve the load on the server machines and routers. These servers are synchronized by making one of them the *master server*, and the others *slave servers*. Maps are created only on the master server's host. From there, they are distributed to all slaves.

We have been talking very vaguely about "networks." Of course there's a distinctive concept in NIS that refers to a network as the collection of all hosts that share part of their system configuration data through NIS: the *NIS domain*. Unfortunately, NIS domains have absolutely nothing in common with the domains we encountered in DNS. To avoid any ambiguity throughout this chapter, I will therefore always specify which type of domain I mean.

NIS domains have a purely administrative function only. They are mostly invisible to users, except for the sharing of passwords between all machines in the domain. Therefore, the name given to an NIS domain is relevant only to the administrators. Usually, any name will do, as long as it is different from any other NIS domain name on your local network. For instance, the administrator at the Virtual Brewery may choose to create two NIS domains, one for the Brewery itself, and one for the Winery, which she names **brewery** and **winery**, respectively. Another quite common scheme is to simply use the DNS domain name for NIS as well. To set and display the NIS domain name of your host, you can use the *domainname* command. When invoked without any argument, it prints the current NIS domain name; to set the domain name, you must become the superuser and type:

```
# domainname brewery
```

NIS domains determine which NIS server an application will query. For instance, the *login* program on a host at the Winery should, of course, only query the Winery's NIS server (or one of them, if there are several) for a user's password information, while an application on a Brewery host should stick with the Brewery's server.

One mystery now remains to be solved, namely how a client finds out which server to connect to. The simplest approach would be to have a configuration file that names the host on which to find the server. However, this approach is rather inflexible because it doesn't allow clients to use different servers (from the same domain, of course) depending on their availability. Therefore, traditional NIS implementations rely on a special daemon called *ypbind* to detect a suitable NIS server in their NIS domain. Before being able to perform any NIS queries, an application first finds out from *ypbind* which server to use.

ypbind probes for servers by broadcasting to the local IP network; the first to respond is assumed to be the fastest one and is used in all subsequent NIS queries. After a certain interval has elapsed, or if the server becomes unavailable, *ypbind* probes for active servers again.

Now the arguable point about dynamic binding is that you rarely need it, and that it introduces a security problem: *ypbind* blindly believes whoever answers, which could be a humble NIS server as well as a malicious intruder. Needless to say this becomes especially troublesome if you manage your password databases over NIS. To guard against this, the Linux NIS library does *not* use *ypbind* by default, but rather picks up the server hostname from a configuration file.

NIS Versus NIS+

NIS and NIS+ share little more than their name and a common goal. NIS+ is structured in an entirely different way. Instead of a flat name space with disjoint NIS domains, it uses a hierarchical name space similar to that of DNS. Instead of maps, so-called *tables* are used that are made up of rows and columns, where each row represents an object in the NIS+ database and the columns cover those properties of the objects that NIS+ knows and cares about. Each table for a given NIS+ domain comprises those of its parent domains. In addition, an entry in a table may contain a link to another table. These features make it possible to structure information in many ways.

Traditional NIS has an RPC version number of 2, while NIS+ is version 3. NIS+ does not seem to be very widely used yet, and I don't really know that much about it. (Well, almost nothing.) For this reason, we will not deal with it here.

The Client Side of NIS

If you are familiar with writing or porting network applications, you will notice that most of the NIS maps listed above correspond to library functions in the C library. For instance, to obtain *passwd* information, you generally use the *getpwnam* and *getpwuid* functions, which return the account information associated with the given username or numerical user ID, respectively. Under normal circumstances, these functions will perform the requested lookup on the standard file, such as */etc/passwd*.

An NIS-aware implementation of these functions, however, will modify this behavior and place an RPC call to have the NIS server look up the user name or ID. This happens transparently to the application. The function may either "append" the NIS map to the original file or entirely "replace" it. Of course, this does not refer to a real modification of the file, it only means that it *appears* to the application as if the file has been replaced or appended.

For traditional NIS implementations, there used to be certain conventions as to which maps replaced and which were appended to the original information. Some, like the *passwd* maps, required kludgy modifications of the *passwd* file

which, when done incorrectly, would open up security holes. To avoid these pit-
falls, NYS uses a general configuration scheme that determines whether a particular set of client functions uses the original files, NIS, or NIS+, and in which order.
This will be described later in this chapter.

Running an NIS Server

After so much theoretical techno-babble, it's time to get our hands dirty with
actual configuration work. In this section, we will cover the configuration of an
NIS server. If an NIS server is running on your network, you won't have to set up
your own; in this case, you may safely skip this section.

Note that if you are just going to experiment with the server, make sure you don't
set it up for an NIS domain name that is already in use on your network. This may
disrupt the entire network service and make a lot of people very unhappy and
very angry.

There are currently two NIS servers freely available for Linux, one contained in
Tobias Reber's *yps* package, and the other in Peter Eriksson's *ypserv* package. It
shouldn't matter which one you run, regardless of whether you use NYS or the
standard NIS client code that is in *libc* currently. At the time of this writing, the
code for the handling of NIS slave servers seems to be more complete in *yps*. On
the other hand, *ypserv* fixes a common security problem with NIS (described later
in this chapter), which *yps* does not. So, your choice depends entirely on what
you need.

After installing the server program (*ypserv*) in */usr/sbin*, you should create the
directory that is going to hold the map files your server is to distribute. When setting up an NIS domain for the **brewery** domain, the maps would go to
/var/yp/brewery. The server determines if it is serving a particular NIS domain by
checking whether the map directory is present. If you are disabling service for
some NIS domain, make sure to remove the directory as well.

Maps are usually stored in DBM files to speed up lookups. They are created from
the master files using a program called *makedbm* (for Tobias's server) or *dbmload*
(for Peter's server). These may not be interchangeable. Transforming a master file
into a form parseable by *dbmload* usually requires some *awk* or *sed* magic, which
tends to be a little tedious to type and hard to remember. Therefore, Peter Eriksson's *ypserv* package contains a Makefile (called *ypMakefile*) that does all these
jobs for you. You should install it as *Makefile* in your map directory and edit it to
reflect the maps you want to distribute. Towards the top of the file, you find the
all target that lists the services *ypserv* is to offer. By default, the line looks something like this:

```
all: ethers hosts networks protocols rpc services passwd group netid
```

If you don't want to produce the *ethers.byname* and *ethers.byaddr* maps, for example, simply remove the `ethers` prerequisite from this rule. To test your setup, you can start with just one or two maps, like the *services.** maps.

After editing the *Makefile*, while in the map directory, type *make*. This will automatically generate and install the maps. You have to make sure to update the maps whenever you change the master files, otherwise the changes will remain invisible to the network.

The next section explains how to configure the NIS client code. If your setup doesn't work, you should try to find out whether any requests arrive at your server or not. If you specify the *–debug* command-line flag to *ypserv*, it prints debugging messages to the console about all incoming NIS queries and the results returned. These should give you a hint as to where the problem lies. Tobias's server has no such option.

NIS Server Security

NIS used to have a major security flaw: it left your password file readable by virtually anyone in the entire Internet, which made for quite a number of possible intruders. As long as an intruder knew your NIS domain name and the address of your server, he could simply send it a request for the *passwd.byname* map and instantly receive all your system passwords. With a fast password-cracking program like *crack* and a good dictionary, guessing at least a few of your users' passwords is rarely a problem.

This is what the so-called *securenets* option is all about. It simply restricts access to your NIS server to certain hosts, based on their IP address or network number. The latest version of *ypserv* implements this feature in a rather convenient way, using the *etc/hosts.allow* and */etc/hosts.deny* files we already encountered in Chapter 9, *Important Network Features*.* For instance, to restrict access to hosts from within the Brewery, their network manager would add the following line to *hosts.allow*.

```
ypserv: 172.16.2.
```

This would let all hosts from IP network **172.16.2.0** access the NIS server. To shut out all other hosts, a corresponding entry in *hosts.deny* would have to read:

```
ypserv: ALL
```

---

* To enable this option, you may have to recompile the server. Please read the instructions in the *README* included in the distribution.

IP numbers are not the only way you can specify hosts or networks in *hosts.allow* and *hosts.deny*. Please refer to the *hosts_access(5)* manual page on your system for details. However, be warned that you *cannot* use host or domain names for the ypserv entry. If you specify a hostname, the server tries to resolve this hostname—but the resolver in turn calls *ypserv*, and you fall into an endless loop.

You can also use the secure portmapper instead of the securenets option in *ypserv*. The secure portmapper (*portmap-3.0*)[*] uses the *hosts.allow* scheme as well, but offers this for all RPC servers, not just *ypserv*. However, you should not use both the securenets option and the secure portmapper at the same time because of the overhead this authorization incurs.

Setting Up an NIS Client with NYS

Throughout the remainder of this chapter, we will cover the configuration of an NIS client.

Your first step should be to tell NYS which server to use for NIS service. You can set the server name in the */etc/yp.conf* configuration file. A very simple file for a host on the Winery's network may look like this:

```
# yp.conf - YP configuration for NYS library.
#
domainname winery
server     vbardolino
```

The first statement tells your host that it belongs to the **winery** NIS domain. If you omit this line, NYS will use the domain name you assigned your system through the *domainname* command. The **server** statement names the NIS server to use. Of course, the IP address corresponding to **vbardolino** must be set in the *hosts* file; alternatively, you may use the IP address itself with the **server** statement.

In the form shown above, the **server** command tells NYS to use the named server whatever the current NIS domain may be. If, however, you are moving your machine between different NIS domains frequently, you may want to keep information for several domains in the *yp.conf* file. You can have information on the servers for various NIS domains in *yp.conf* by adding the NIS domain name to the **server** statement. For instance, you might change the above sample file for a laptop to look like this:

```
# yp.conf - YP configuration for NYS library.
#
server vbardolino winery
server vstout     brewery
```

---

[*] Available via anonymous FTP from **sunsite.unc.edu** below the *Linux/systems/Network* directory.

This lets you bring up the laptop in any of the two domains by simply setting the desired NIS domain at boot time through the *domainname* command.

After creating this basic configuration file and making sure it is world-readable, you should run your first test to check if you can connect to your server. Make sure to choose any map your server distributes, like *hosts.byname*, and try to retrieve it by using the *ypcat* utility. *ypcat*, like all other administrative NIS tools, should live in */usr/sbin*.

```
# ypcat hosts.byname
172.16.2.2      vbeaujolais.vbrew.com      vbeaujolais
172.16.2.3      vbardolino.vbrew.com       vbardolino
172.16.1.1      vlager.vbrew.com           vlager
172.16.2.1      vlager.vbrew.com           vlager
172.16.1.2      vstout.vbrew.com           vstout
172.16.1.3      vale.vbrew.com             vale
172.16.2.4      vchianti.vbrew.com         vchianti
```

The output you get should resemble that just shown. If you get an error message instead that says "Can't bind to server which serves domain," then either the NIS domain name you've set doesn't have a matching server defined in *yp.conf*, or the server is unreachable for some reason. In the latter case, make sure that a *ping* to the host yields a positive result, and that it is indeed running an NIS server. You can verify the latter by using *rpcinfo*, which should produce the following output:

```
# rpcinfo -u serverhost ypserv
program 100004 version 2 ready and waiting
```

Choosing the Right Maps

Having made sure you can reach the NIS server, you have to decide which configuration files to replace or augment with NIS maps. Commonly, you will want to use NIS maps for the host and password lookup functions. The former is especially useful if you do not have BIND name service. The password lookup lets all users log into their account from any system in the NIS domain; this usually goes along with sharing a central */home* directory between all hosts via NFS. The password map is explained detail in the next section.

Other maps, like *services.byname*, don't provide such dramatic gains, but do save you some editing work. The *services.byname* map is valuable if you install any network applications that use a service name not in the standard *services* file.

Generally, you want to have some choice of when a lookup function uses the local files and when it queries the NIS server. NYS allows you to configure the order in which a function accesses these services. This is controlled through the */etc/nsswitch.conf* file, which stands for *Name Service Switch*, but of course isn't limited to the name service. For any of the data lookup functions supported by NYS, it contains a line naming the services to use.

The right order of services depends on the type of data. It is unlikely that the *services.byname* map will contain entries differing from those in the local *services* file; it may only contain additional entries. So it appears reasonable to query the local files first, and check NIS only if the service name isn't found. Hostname information, on the other hand, may change very frequently, so DNS or the NIS server should always have the most accurate account, while the local *hosts* file is only kept as a backup if DNS and NIS should fail. In this case, you would want to check the local file last.

The following example shows how to force *gethostbyname*, *gethostbyaddr*, and *getservbyname* to look in NIS and DNS before the *hosts* file. They will try each of the listed services in turn; if a lookup succeeds, the result is returned; otherwise the next service is tried.

```
# small sample /etc/nsswitch.conf
#
hosts:     nis dns files
services:  files nis
```

The complete list of services that may be used with an entry in the *nsswitch.conf* file is shown below. The actual maps, files, servers, and objects being queried depend on the entry name.

nisplus or nis+
:   Use the NIS+ server for this domain. The location of the server is obtained from the */etc/nis.conf* file.

nis
:   Use the current NIS server of this domain. The location of the server queried is configured in the *yp.conf* file as shown in the previous section. For the hosts entry, the maps *hosts.byname* and *hosts.byaddr* are queried.

dns
:   Use the DNS name server. This service type is only useful with the hosts entry. The name servers queried are still determined by the standard *resolv.conf* file.

files
:   Use the local file, such as the */etc/hosts* file for the hosts entry.

dbm
:   Look up the information from DBM files located in */var/dbm*. The name used for the file is that of the corresponding NIS map.

Currently, NYS supports the following *nsswitch.conf* entries: hosts, networks, passwd, group, shadow, gshadow, services, protocols, rpc, and ethers. More entries are likely to be added.

Example 10-1 shows a more complete example which introduces another feature of *nsswitch.conf*. The [NOTFOUND=return] keyword in the hosts entry tells NYS to return if the desired item couldn't be found in the NIS or DNS database. That is, NYS will continue and search the local files *only* if calls to the NIS and DNS servers fail for some other reason. The local files will then be used only at boot time and as a backup when the NIS server is down.

Example 10–1: Sample nsswitch.conf File

```
# /etc/nsswitch.conf
#
hosts:      nis dns [NOTFOUND=return] files
networks:   nis [NOTFOUND=return] files
services:   files nis
protocols:  files nis
rpc:        files nis
```

Using the passwd and group Maps

One of the major applications of NIS is synchronizing user and account information on all hosts in an NIS domain. To this end, you usually keep only a small local */etc/passwd* file, to which the site-wide information from the NIS maps is appended. However, simply enabling NIS lookups for this service in *nsswitch.conf* is not nearly enough.

When relying on the password information distributed by NIS, you first have to make sure that the numeric user IDs of any users you have in your local *passwd* file match the NIS server's idea of user IDs. You will want this for other purposes as well, like mounting NFS volumes from other hosts in your network.

If any of the numeric IDs in */etc/passwd* or */etc/group* differ from those in the maps, you have to adjust file ownerships for all files that belong to that user. First, you should change all uids and gids in *passwd* and *group* to the new values, then find all files that belong to the users just changed, and finally change their ownership. Assume **news** used to have a user ID of 9, and **okir** had a user ID of 103, which were changed to some other value; you could then issue the following commands:

```
# find / -uid   9 -print >/tmp/uid.9
# find / -uid 103 -print >/tmp/uid.103
# cat /tmp/uid.9   | xargs chown news
# cat /tmp/uid.103 | xargs chown okir
```

It is important that you execute these commands with the new *passwd* file installed, and that you collect all filenames before you change the ownership of any of them. To update the group ownerships of files, you use a similar command.

Having done this, the numerical uids and gids on your system will agree with those on all other hosts in your NIS domain. The next step will be to add configuration lines to *nsswitch.conf* that enable NIS lookups for user and group information:

```
# /etc/nsswitch.conf - passwd and group treatment
passwd: nis files
group:  nis files
```

This affects where the *login* command and all its friends look for user information. When a user tries to log in, *login* queries the NIS maps first, and if this lookup fails, falls back to the local files. Usually, you will remove almost all users from your local files, and leave entries only for **root** and generic accounts like **mail** in it. This is because some vital system tasks may have to map uids to usernames or vice versa. For example, administrative *cron* jobs may execute the *su* command to temporarily become **news**, or the UUCP subsystem may mail a status report. If **news** and **uucp** don't have entries in the local *passwd* file, these jobs will fail miserably during an NIS brownout.

There are two big caveats in order here. On the one hand, the setup as described up to here works only for login suites that don't use shadow passwords, like those included in the *util-linux* package. The intricacies of using shadow passwords with NIS will be covered below. On the other hand, the login commands are not the only ones that access the *passwd* file—look at the *ls* command which most people use almost constantly. Whenever doing a long listing, *ls* will display the symbolic names for user and group owners of a file; that is, for each uid and gid it encounters, it will have to query the NIS server once. This will slow things down rather badly if your local network is clogged, or even worse, when the NIS server is not on the same physical network, so that datagrams have to pass through a router.

Still, this is not the whole story. Imagine what happens if a user wants to change her password. Usually, she will invoke *passwd*, which reads the new password and updates the local *passwd* file. This is impossible with NIS, since that file isn't available locally anymore, but having users log into the NIS server whenever they want to change their password is not an option either. Therefore, NIS provides a drop-in replacement for *passwd* called *yppasswd*, which does the analoguous thing in the presence of NIS. To change the password on the server host, it contacts the *yppasswdd* daemon on that host via RPC, and provides it with the updated password information. Usually, you install *yppasswd* over the normal program by doing something like this:

```
# cd /bin
# mv passwd passwd.old
# ln yppasswd passwd
```

At the same time, you have to install *rpc.yppasswdd* on the server and start it from *rc.inet2*. This will effectively hide any of the contortions of NIS from your users.

Using NIS with Shadow Support

Using NIS in conjunction with shadow password files is a somewhat tricky issue. Shadow passwords were invented to keep normal users from reading other users' passwords, even in their encrypted state. On the other hand, NIS requires you to make these passwords available network-wide, which defeats the original purpose of having shadow passwords at all.

Currently, there is no real solution to this dilemma. The only way to distribute password and user information by NIS is through the standard *passwd.** maps. If you do have shadow passwords installed, the easiest way to share them is to generate a proper *passwd* file from */etc/shadow* using tools like *pwuncov*, and create the NIS maps from that file.

Of course, there are some hacks necessary to use NIS and shadow passwords at the same time, for instance, by installing an */etc/shadow* file on each host in the network, while distributing user IDs, etc. through NIS. Needless to say, this hack is really crude and defies the goal of NIS, which is to ease the task of system administration. In my opinion, a policy to enforce users to choose "good" passwords is much better than hiding the passwords away in an additional file that creates incompatibilities.

Using the Traditional NIS Code

If you are using the client code that is currently in the standard *libc*, configuring an NIS client is a little different. First off, the traditional code supports maps only for *hosts*, *passwd*, and *group* lookups. Also, the way it combines information from local files with that from NIS maps is very different from the way NYS does it.

For instance, to use the NIS password maps, you have to include the following line somewhere in your */etc/passwd* map:

```
+:*:0:0:::
```

This marks the place where the password lookup functions "insert" the NIS maps. Inserting a similar line (minus the last two colons) into */etc/group* does the same for the *group.** maps.

To use the *hosts.** maps offered by your YP server, change the order line in the *host.conf* file. For instance, if you want to use NIS, DNS, and the */etc/hosts* file (in that order), you need to change the line to this:

```
order yp bind hosts
```

Unlike NYS, the traditional YP code relies on a *ypbind* daemon to locate an active server for the YP clients. *ypbind* must be invoked at boot time after the NIS domain has been set and the RPC portmapper has been started.

Until recently, *ypbind* went searching for servers by sending out RPC broadcasts. As discussed earlier, this is inherently insecure. Therefore, the latest version of YP tools (from the *yp-linux* distributuion) now has a *ypbind* daemon that supports the */etc/yp.conf* configuration file, too. If this file exists, it will scan the file for one or more lines that look like this:

```
# yp.conf - name YP server for ypbind.
ypserver      vbardolino
```

ypbind then checks the named hosts for active servers.[*] If *ypbind* does not find a *yp.conf* file, or if none of the named servers respond, it will revert to the old method of sending RPC broadcasts.

Recently, there have been numerous bug reports that NIS fails with an error message saying:

```
clntudp_create: RPC: portmapper failure - RPC: unable to receive
```

These are due to an incompatible change in the way *ypbind* communicates the binding information to the library functions. Obtaining the latest sources for the NIS utilities and recompiling them should cure this problem.[†]

---

[*] Note that the keyword is different from what you have to use to tell NYS about the server's name.

[†] The source for *yp-linux* can be obtained from site **ftp.uni-paderborn.de** in the directory */pub/Linux/LOCAL.*

## CHAPTER ELEVEN

THE NETWORK FILE SYSTEM

N FS, the Network File System, is probably the most prominent network service using RPC. It allows you to access files on remote hosts in exactly the same way you would access local files. This is made possible by a mixture of kernel functionality on the client side and an NFS server on the server side. This file access is completely transparent to the client and works across a variety of server and host architectures.

NFS and NIS

NFS offers a number of useful features:

- Data accessed by all users can be kept on a central host, with clients mounting this directory at boot time. For example, you can keep all user accounts on one host and have all hosts on your network mount /home from that host. If installed alongside NIS, users can log into any system and still work on one set of files.

- Data consuming large amounts of disk space can be kept on a single host. For example, all files and programs relating to LaTeX and METAFONT can be kept and maintained in one place.

- Administrative data can be kept on a single host. There is no need to use *rcp* to install the same stupid file on 20 different machines.

RFC 1094
NIS HOWTO

It's not too hard to set up basic NFS operation on both the client and server; this chapter tells you how.

Linux NFS is largely the work of Rick Sladkey,* who wrote the NFS kernel code and large parts of the NFS server. The latter is derived from the *unfsd* user space NFS server, originally written by Mark Shand, and the *hnfs* Harris NFS server, written by Donald Becker.

Let's have a look at how NFS works. A client tries to mount a directory from a remote host on a local directory just the same way it does a physical device. However, the syntax used to specify the remote directory is different. For example, to mount */home* from host **vlager** to */users* on **vale**, the administrator issues the following command on **vale**:†

```
# mount -t nfs vlager:/home /users
```

mount will try to connect to the *mountd* mount daemon on **vlager** via RPC. The server will check if **vale** is permitted to mount the directory in question, and if so, return it a file handle. This file handle will be used in all subsequent requests to files below */users*.

When someone accesses a file over NFS, the kernel places an RPC call to *nfsd* (the NFS daemon) on the server machine. This call takes the file handle, the name of the file to be accessed, and the user's user and group IDs as parameters. These are used in determining access rights to the specified file. In order to prevent unauthorized users from reading or modifying files, user and group IDs must be the same on both hosts.

On most UNIX implementations, the NFS functionality of both client and server is implemented as kernel-level daemons that are started from user space at system boot. These are the NFS daemon (*nfsd*) on the server host, and the *Block I/O Daemon* (*biod*) on the client host. To improve throughput, *biod* performs asynchronous I/O using read-ahead and write-behind; also, several *nfsd* daemons are usually run concurrently.

The NFS implementation of Linux is a little different in that the client code is tightly integrated in the virtual file system (VFS) layer of the kernel and doesn't require additional control through *biod*. On the other hand, the server code runs entirely in user space, so running several copies of the server at the same time is almost impossible because of the synchronization issues it would involve. Linux NFS currently also lacks read-ahead and write-behind, but Rick Sladkey plans to add this someday.‡

The biggest problem with the Linux NFS code is that the Linux kernel as of version 1.0 is not able to allocate memory in chunks bigger than 4K. As a consequence, the networking code cannot handle datagrams bigger than roughly 3500

---

* Rick can be reached at *jrs@world.std.com.*
† Note that you can omit the *–t nfs* argument, because *mount* sees from the colon that this specifies an NFS volume.
‡ The problem with write-behind is that the kernel buffer cache is indexed by device/inode pairs, and therefore can't be used for NFS-mounted file systems.

bytes after subtracting header sizes, etc. This means that transfers to and from NFS daemons running on systems that use large UDP datagrams by default (e.g., 8K on SunOS) need to be downsized artificially. This hurts performance badly under some circumstances.[*] This limit is gone in late Linux-1.1 kernels, and the client code has been modified to take advantage of this.

Preparing NFS

Before you can use NFS, be it as server or client, you must make sure your kernel has NFS support compiled in. Newer kernels have a simple interface on the *proc* file system for this, the */proc/filesystems* file, which you can display using *cat*:

```
$ cat /proc/file systems
        minix
        ext2
        msdos
nodev   proc
nodev   nfs
```

If nfs is missing from this list, you have to compile your own kernel with NFS enabled. Configuring the kernel network options is explained in the section "Kernel Configuration" in Chapter 3, *Configuring the Networking Hardware.*

For older kernels prior to Linux 1.1, the easiest way to find out whether your kernel has NFS support enabled is to actually try to mount an NFS file system. For this, you could create a test directory below */tmp*, and try to mount a local directory on it:

```
# mkdir /tmp/test
# mount localhost:/etc /tmp/test
```

If this mount attempt fails with an error message saying "fs type nfs not supported by kernel," you must make a new kernel with NFS enabled. Any other error messages are completely harmless, as you haven't configured the NFS daemons on your host yet.

Mounting an NFS Volume

NFS volumes[†] are mounted very nearly the way usual file systems are mounted. You invoke *mount* using the following syntax:

```
# mount -t nfs nfs_volume local_dir options
```

---

[*] As explained to me by Alan Cox: The NFS specification requires the server to flush each block of data written to disk before it returns an acknowledgment. As BSD kernels are only capable of page-sized writes (4K), writing four chunks of 1K each to a BSD-based NFS server results in four write operations of 4K each.
[†] One doesn't say file system, because these are not proper file systems.

nfs_volume is given as *remote_host:remote_dir*. Since this notation is unique to NFS file systems, you can leave out the *–t nfs* option.

There are a number of additional options that you can specify to *mount* upon mounting an NFS volume. These may either be given following the *–o* switch on the command line or in the options field of the */etc/fstab* entry for the volume. In both cases, multiple options are separated from each other by commas. Options specified on the command line always override those given in the *fstab* file.

Here is a sample entry from */etc/fstab*:

```
# volume                mount point        type  options
news:/usr/spool/news    /usr/spool/news    nfs   timeo=14,intr
```

This volume can then be mounted using this command:

```
# mount news:/usr/spool/news
```

In the absence of an *fstab* entry, NFS *mount* invocations look a lot uglier. For instance, suppose you mount your users' home directories from a machine named **moonshot**, which uses a default block size of 4K for read/write operations. You might decrease block size to 2K to suit Linux's datagram size limit by issuing the command:

```
# mount moonshot:/home /home -o rsize=2048,wsize=2048
```

nfs(5)

The list of all valid options is described in its entirety in the *nfs(5)* manual page that comes with Rick Sladkey's NFS-aware *mount* tool (which can be found in Rik Faith's *util-linux* package). The following is a partial list of options you would probably want to use:

rsize=*n* and wsize=*n*
> These specify the datagram size used by the NFS clients on read and write requests, respectively. They currently default to 1024 bytes due to the limit on UDP datagram size described above.

timeo=*n*
> This sets the time (in tenths of a second) the NFS client will wait for a request to complete. The default value is 7 (0.7 seconds).

hard
> Explicitly mark this volume as hard-mounted. This is on by default.

soft
> Soft-mount the driver (as opposed to hard-mount).

intr
> Allow signals to interrupt an NFS call. Useful for aborting when the server doesn't respond.

Except for rsize and wsize, all of these options apply to the client's behavior if the server should become temporarily inaccessible. They play together in the following way: Whenever the client sends a request to the NFS server, it expects the operation to have finished after a given interval (specified in the timeout option). If no confirmation is received within this time, a so-called *minor timeout* occurs, and the operation is retried with the timeout interval doubled. After reaching a maximum timeout of 60 seconds, a *major timeout* occurs.

By default, a major timeout will cause the client to print a message to the console and start all over again, this time with an initial timeout interval twice that of the previous cascade. Potentially, this may go on forever. Volumes that stubbornly retry an operation until the server becomes available again are called *hard-mounted*. The opposite variety, called *soft-mounted*, generate an I/O error for the calling process whenever a major timeout occurs. Because of the write-behind introduced by the buffer cache, this error condition is not propagated to the process itself before it calls the *write* function the next time, so a program can never be sure that a write operation to a soft-mounted volume has succeded at all.

Whether you hard or soft-mount a volume depends partly on taste but also on the type of information you want to access from a volume. For example, if you mount your X programs by NFS, you certainly would not want your X session to go berserk just because someone brought the network to a grinding halt by firing up seven copies of *xv* at the same time or by pulling the Ethernet plug for a moment. By hard-mounting these programs, you make sure that your computer will wait until it is able to re-establish contact with your NFS server. On the other hand, non-critical data such as NFS-mounted news partitions or FTP archives may as well be soft-mounted, so if the remote machine is temporarily unreachable or down, it doesn't hang your session. If your network connection to the server is flaky or goes through a loaded router, you may either increase the initial timeout using the timeo option or hard-mount the volumes, but allow for signals interrupting the NFS call so that you may still abort any hanging file access.

Usually, the *mountd* daemon will in some way or other keep track of which directories have been mounted by what hosts. This information can be displayed using the *showmount* program, which is also included in the NFS server package. The Linux *mountd*, however, does not do this yet.

The NFS Daemons

If you want to provide NFS service to other hosts, you have to run the *nfsd* and *mountd* daemons on your machine. As RPC-based programs, they are not managed by *inetd*, but are started up at boot time and register themselves with the portmapper. Therefore, you have to make sure to start them only after *rpc.portmap* is running. Usually, you include the following lines in your *rc.inet2* script:

```
if [ -x /usr/sbin/rpc.mountd ]; then
        /usr/sbin/rpc.mountd; echo -n " mountd"
fi
if [ -x /usr/sbin/rpc.nfsd ]; then
```

```
                          /usr/sbin/rpc.nfsd; echo -n " nfsd"
        fi
```

The ownership information of the files an NFS daemon provides to its clients usually contains only numerical user and group IDs. If both client and server associate the same user and group names with these numerical IDs, they are said to share the same uid/gid space. For example, this is the case when you use NIS to distribute the *passwd* information to all hosts on your LAN.

On some occasions, however, they do not match. Rather than updating the uids and gids of the client to match those of the server, you can use the *ugidd* mapping daemon to work around this. Using the `map_daemon` option explained below, you can tell *nfsd* to map the server's uid/gid space to the client's uid/gid space with the aid of the *ugidd* on the client.

ugidd is an RPC-based server that is started from *rc.inet2*, just like *nfsd* and *mountd*:

```
        if [ -x /usr/sbin/rpc.ugidd ]; then
                /usr/sbin/rpc.ugidd; echo -n " ugidd"
        fi
```

The exports File

For each client, a server determines the type of access that is allowed to the server's files. This access is specified in the */etc/exports* file that lists shared files.

By default, *mountd* will not allow anyone to mount directories from the local host, which is a rather sensible attitude. To permit one or more hosts to NFS-mount a directory, it must *exported*, that is, must be specified in the *exports* file. A sample file may look like this:

```
        # exports file for vlager
        /home           vale(rw) vstout(rw) vlight(rw)
        /usr/X386       vale(ro) vstout(ro) vlight(ro)
        /usr/TeX        vale(ro) vstout(ro) vlight(ro)
        /               vale(rw,no_root_squash)
        /home/ftp           (ro)
```

Each line defines a directory and the hosts that are allowed to mount it. A hostname is usually a fully qualified domain name but may additionally contain the *** and **?** wildcards, which act the way they do with the Bourne shell. For instance, `lab*.foo.com` matches **lab01.foo.com** as well as **laber.foo.com**. If no hostname is given, as with the */home/ftp* directory in the example above, any host is allowed to mount this directory.

When checking a client host against the *exports* file, *mountd* will look up the client's hostname using the *gethostbyaddr* call. With DNS, this call returns the client's canonical hostname, so you must make sure not to use aliases in *exports*.

Without using DNS, the returned name is the first hostname found in the *hosts* file that matches the client's address.

The hostname is followed by an optional comma-separated list of flags, enclosed in brackets. These flags may take the following values:

insecure
> Permit non-authenticated access from this machine.

unix-rpc
> Require UNIX-domain RPC authentication from this machine. This simply requires that requests originate from a reserved Internet port (i.e., the port number has to be less than 1024). This option is on by default.

secure-rpc
> Require secure RPC authentication from this machine. This has not been implemented yet. See Sun's documentation on Secure RPC.

kerberos
> Require Kerberos authentication on accesses from this machine. This has not been implemented yet. See the MIT documentation on the Kerberos authentication system.

root_squash
> This is a security feature that denies the superusers on the specified hosts any special access rights by mapping requests from uid 0 on the client to uid 65534 (-2) on the server. This uid should be associated with the user **nobody**.

no_root_squash
> Don't map requests from uid 0. This option is on by default.

ro   Mount file hierarchy read-only. This option is on by default.

rw   Mount file hierarchy read-write.

link_relative
> Convert absolute symbolic links (where the link contents start with a slash) into relative links by prepending ../ as many times as necessary to get from the directory containing the link to the root on the server. This option only makes sense when a host's entire file system is mounted; otherwise, some of the links might point to nowhere, or even worse, to files they were never meant to point to. This option is on by default.

link_absolute
> Leave all symbolic links as they are (the normal behavior for Sun-supplied NFS servers).

map_identity
> The map_identity option tells the server to assume that the client uses the same uids and gids as the server. This option is on by default.

map_daemon
> This option tells the NFS server to assume that client and server do not share the same uid/gid space. *nfsd* will then build a list mapping IDs between client and server by querying the client's *ugidd* daemon.

An error parsing the *exports* file is reported to *syslogd*'s daemon facility at level notice whenever *nfsd* or *mountd* is started up.

Note that hostnames are obtained from the client's IP address by reverse mapping, so you have to have the resolver configured properly. If you use BIND and are very security-conscious, you should enable spoof checking in your *host.conf* file.

The Linux Automounter

Sometimes, it is wasteful to mount all NFS volumes users might possibly want to access, either because of the sheer number of volumes to be mounted, or because of the time this would take at startup. A viable alternative to this is a so-called *automounter*. This is a daemon that automatically and transparently mounts any NFS volume as needed, and unmounts them after they have not been used for some time. One of the clever things about an automounter is that it is able to mount a certain volume from alternative places. For instance, you may keep copies of your X programs and support files on two or three hosts and have all other hosts mount them via NFS. Using an automounter, you may specify all three of them to be mounted on */usr/X386*; the automounter will then try to mount any of these until one of the mount attempts succeeds.

The automounter commonly used with Linux is called *amd*. It was originally written by Jan-Simon Pendry and has been ported to Linux by Mitch D'Souza. The current version is *amd-5.3*.

Explaining *amd* is beyond the scope of this chapter. For a good manual, refer to the sources; they contain a Texinfo file with very detailed information.

CHAPTER TWELVE

MANAGING TAYLOR UUCP

UUCP was designed in the late seventies by Mike Lesk at AT&T Bell Laboratories to provide a simple dialup network over public telephone lines. Since most people who want to have email and Usenet News on their home machine still communicate through modems, UUCP has remained very popular. Although there are many implementations of UUCP running on a wide variety of hardware platforms and operating systems, they are compatible to a high degree.

However, as with most software that has somehow become "standard" over the years, there is no UUCP which one would call *the* UUCP. It has undergone a steady evolution since the first version was implemented in 1976. Currently, there are two major species which differ mainly in their support of hardware and their configuration. Of these two, various implementations exist, each varying slightly from its siblings.

One species is the so-called Version 2 UUCP, which dates back to a 1977 implementation by Mike Lesk, David A. Novitz, and Greg Chesson. Although it is fairly old, it is still in frequent use. Recent implementations of Version 2 provide much of the comfort of the newer UUCP species.

The second species was developed in 1983 and is commonly referred to as BNU (Basic Networking Utilities), HoneyDanBer UUCP, or HDB for short. The name is derived from the authors' names—P. Honeyman, D. A. Novitz, and B. E. Redman. HDB was conceived to eliminate some of Version 2 UUCP's deficiencies. For example, new transfer protocols were added, and the spool directory was split so that now there is one directory for each site you have UUCP traffic with.

The implementation of UUCP currently distributed with Linux is Taylor UUCP 1.04,[*] which is the version this chapter is based upon. Taylor UUCP Version 1.04 was released in February 1993. Apart from traditional configuration files, Taylor UUCP can also be compiled to understand the new-style—a.k.a. Taylor—configuration files.

Version 1.05 has been released recently and will soon make its way into most distributions. The differences between these versions mostly affect features you will never use, so you should be able to configure Taylor UUCP 1.05 using the information from this book.

As included in most Linux distributions, Taylor UUCP is usually compiled for BNU compatibility, or the Taylor configuration scheme, or both. The Taylor scheme is much more flexible and probably easier to understand than the often rather obscure BNU configuration files, so I will describe the Taylor scheme below.

The purpose of this chapter is not to give you an exhaustive description of what the command-line options for the UUCP commands are and what they do, but to give you an introduction on how to set up a working UUCP node. The first section gives a gentle introduction about how UUCP implements remote execution and file transfers. If you are not entirely new to UUCP, you might want to skip to the section "UUCP Configuration Files," which explains the various files used to set up UUCP.

We will, however, assume that you are familiar with the user programs of the UUCP suite. These are *uucp* and *uux*. For a description, refer to the online manual pages.

Besides the publicly accessible programs *uux* and *uucp*, the UUCP suite contains a number of commands used for administrative purposes only. They are used to monitor UUCP traffic across your node, remove old log files, or compile statistics. None of these will be described here because they are peripheral to the main tasks of UUCP. Besides, they're well documented and fairly easy to understand. However, there is a third category, which comprises the actual UUCP "work horses." They are called *uucico* (where *cico* stands for copy-in copy-out), and *uuxqt*, which executes jobs sent from remote systems. These are the subjects of this chapter.

Those who don't find everything they need in this chapter should read the documentation that comes with the UUCP package. This is a set of Texinfo files that describe the setup using the Taylor configuration scheme.

Managing
UUCP

UUCP HOWTO

If you want to use BNU or even (shudder!) Version 2 configuration files, there is a very good book called *Managing UUCP and Usenet*, from O'Reilly & Associates. I have found it very useful. Another good source for information about UUCP on Linux is Vince Skahan's UUCP-HOWTO, which is posted regularly to *comp.os.linux.announce*.

---

[*] Written and copyrighted by Ian Taylor, 1993.

There's also a newsgroup for the discussion of UUCP called *comp.mail.uucp*. If you have questions specific to Taylor UUCP, you may be better off asking them there, rather than on the *comp.os.linux* groups.

UUCP Transfers and Remote Execution

The concept of *jobs* is vital to the understanding of UUCP. Every transfer that a user initiates with *uucp* or *uux* is called a job. It is made up of a command to be executed on a remote system, and a collection of files to be transferred between sites. One of these parts can be excluded.

As an example, assume you issued the following command on your host, which makes UUCP copy the file *netguide.ps* to host **pablo**, and makes it execute the *lpr* command to print the file.

```
$ uux -r pablo!lpr !netguide.ps
```

UUCP does not generally call the remote system immediately to execute a job (or else you could make do with *kermit*). Instead, it temporarily stores the job description away. This is called *spooling*. The directory tree under which jobs are stored is therefore called the *spool directory* and is generally located in */var/spool/uucp*. In our example, the job description would contain information about the remote command to be executed (*lpr*), the user who requested the execution, and a couple of other items. In addition to the job description, UUCP has to store the input file *netguide.ps*.

The exact location and naming of spool files may vary, depending on some compile-time options. HDB-compatible UUCPs generally store spool files in a */var/spool/uucp* subdirectory with the name of the remote site. When compiled for Taylor configuration, UUCP will create subdirectories below the site-specific spool directory for different types of spool files.

At regular intervals, UUCP dials up the remote system. When a connection to the remote machine is established, UUCP transfers the files describing the job, plus any input files. The incoming jobs will not be executed immediately, but only after the connection terminates. This is done by *uuxqt*, which also takes care of forwarding any jobs that are designated for another site.

To distinguish between important and less important jobs, UUCP associates a *grade* with each job. This is a single letter, ranging from 0 through 9, A through Z, and a through z, in decreasing precedence. Mail is customarily spooled with grade B or C, while news is spooled with grade N. Jobs with higher grade are transferred earlier. Grades may be assigned using the –g flag when invoking *uucp* or *uux*.

You can also disallow the transfer of jobs below a given grade at certain times. This is also called the *maximum spool grade* allowed during a conversation and defaults to z. Note the terminological ambiguity here: a file is transferred only if it is *equal or above* the maximum spool grade.

The Inner Workings of uucico

To understand why *uucico* needs to know certain things, a quick description of how it actually connects to a remote system is helpful.

When you execute *uucico* *-s* `system` from the command line, *uucico* first has to connect physically. The actions taken depend on the type of connection to open—e.g., when using a telephone line, it has to find a modem and dial out. Over TCP, it has to call *gethostbyname* to convert the name to a network address, find out which port to open, and bind the address to the corresponding socket.

After this connection has been established, an authorization procedure has to be passed. This procedure generally consists of the remote system asking for a login name and possibly a password. This is commonly called the *login chat*. The authorization procedure is performed either by the usual *getty/login* suite, or on TCP sockets, by *uucico* itself. If authorization succeeds, the remote end fires up *uucico*. The local copy of *uucico* that initiated the connection is referred to as *master*, and the remote copy as *slave*.

Next follows the *handshake phase*: the master now sends its hostname plus several flags. The slave checks this hostname for permission to log in, send and receive files, etc. The flags describe (among other things) the maximum grade of spool files to transfer. If enabled, a conversation count or *call sequence number* check takes place here. With this feature, both sites maintain a count of successful connections, which are compared. If they do not match, the handshake fails. This is useful to protect yourself against impostors.

Finally, the two *uucico*'s try to agree on a common *transfer protocol*. This protocol governs the way data is transferred, checked for consistency, and retransmitted in case of an error. There is a need for different protocols because of the differing types of connections supported. For example, telephone lines require a "safe" protocol, which is pessimistic about errors, while TCP transmission is inherently reliable and can use a more efficient protocol that foregoes most extra error checking.

After the handshake is complete, the actual transmission phase begins. Both ends turn on the selected protocol driver. At this point the drivers possibly perform a protocol-specific initialization sequence.

The master then sends all files queued for the remote system whose spool grade is high enough. When it has finished, it informs the slave that it is done and that the slave may now hang up. The slave now can either agree to hang up or take over the conversation. This is a change of roles: now the remote system becomes master, and the local one becomes slave. The new master now sends its files. When done, both *uucico*s exchange termination messages and close the connection.

We will not go into this in greater detail: please refer to either the sources or any good book on UUCP for this. There is also a really antique article floating around the net, written by David A. Novitz, which gives a detailed description of the UUCP protocol.* The Taylor UUCP FAQ also discusses some details of the way UUCP is implemented. It is posted to *comp.mail.uucp* regularly.

uucico Command-line Options

uucico(1)

This section describes the most important command-line options for *uucico*.

−s system

Call the named *system* unless prohibited by call time restrictions.

−S system

Call the named *system* unconditionally.

−r1

Start *uucico* in master mode. This is the default when *−s* or *−S* is given. All by itself, the *−r1* option causes *uucico* to try to call all systems in *sys*, unless prohibited by call or retry time restrictions.

−r0

Start *uucico* in slave mode. This is the default when no *−s* or *−S* is given. In slave mode, either standard input/output are assumed to be connected to a serial port, or the TCP port specified by the *−p* option is used.

−x type, −X type

Turn on debugging of the specified type. Several types can be given as a comma-separated list. The following types are valid: abnormal, chat, handshake, uucp-proto, proto, port, config, spooldir, execute, incoming, and outgoing. Using all turns on all options. For compatibility with other UUCP implementations, a number may be specified instead, which turns on debugging for the first *n* items from the above list.

Debugging messages will be logged to the file *Debug* below */var/spool/uucp*.

UUCP Configuration Files

In contrast to simpler file transfer programs, UUCP was designed to be able to handle all transfers automatically. Once it is set up properly, interference by the administrator should not be necessary on a day-to-day basis. The information required for this automated transfer is kept in a couple of configuration files that reside in the directory */usr/lib/uucp*. Most of these files are used only when dialing out.

---

* It's also included in the 4.4BSD *System Manager's Manual*.

A Gentle Introduction to Taylor UUCP

To say that UUCP configuration is hard would be an understatement. It is really a hairy subject, and the sometimes terse format of the configuration files doesn't make things easier (although the Taylor format is almost easy reading compared to the older formats in HDB or Version 2).

To give you a feel for how all the configuration files interact, we will introduce you to the most important ones and have a look at sample entries from these files. We won't explain everything in detail now; a more accurate account is given in separate sections below. If you want to set up your machine for UUCP, you had best start with some sample files and adapt them gradually. You can pick either those shown below or those included in your favorite Linux distribution.

All files described in this section are kept in */usr/lib/uucp* or a subdirectory thereof. Some Linux distributions contain UUCP binaries that have support for both HDB and Taylor configuration enabled, and use different subdirectories for each configuration file set. There will usually be a *README* file in */usr/lib/uucp*.

For UUCP to work properly, these files must be owned by the **uucp** user. Some of them contain passwords and telephone numbers, and therefore should have permissions of 600.*

The central UUCP configuration file is */usr/lib/uucp/config*, which is used to set general parameters. The most important of them (and for now, the only one) is your host's UUCP name. At the Virtual Brewery, they use **vstout** as their UUCP gateway:

```
# /usr/lib/uucp/config - UUCP main configuration file
hostname          vstout
```

The next important configuration file is the *sys* file. It contains all the system-specific information of sites you are linked to. This includes the site's name and information on the link itself, such as the telephone number when using a modem link. A typical entry for a modem-connected site called **pablo** would look like this:

```
# /usr/lib/uucp/sys - name UUCP neighbors
# system: pablo
system            pablo
time              Any
phone             123-456
port              serial1
speed             38400
chat              ogin: vstout ssword: lorca
```

The **port** names a port to be used, and **time** specifies the times at which it can be called. **chat** describes the login chat scripts—the sequence of strings that must be

---

* Note that although most UUCP commands must be setuid to **uucp**, you must make sure the *uuchk* program is *not*. Otherwise, users will be able to display system passwords even though the files have mode 600.

exchanged to allow *uucico* to log into **pablo**. We will get back to chat scripts later. The **port** command simply names an entry in the *port* file. (Refer to Figure 12-1.) You can assign whatever name you like as long as it refers to a valid entry in *port*.

The *port* file holds information specific to the link itself. For modem links, it describes the device special file to be used, the range of speeds supported, and the type of dialing equipment connected to the port. The entry below describes */dev/cua1* (a.k.a. COM 2), to which a NakWell modem is connected that is capable of running at speeds up to 38400 bps. The port's name is chosen to match the port name given in the *sys* file.

```
# /usr/lib/uucp/port - UUCP ports
# /dev/cua1 (COM2)
port            serial1
type            modem
device          /dev/cua1
speed           38400
dialer          nakwell
```

The information pertaining to the dialers is kept in yet another file called—you guessed it—*dial*. For each dialer type, it basically contains the sequence of commands to be issued to dial up a remote site, given the telephone number. Again, this is specified as a chat script. For example, the entry for NakWell might look like this:

```
# /usr/lib/uucp/dial - per-dialer information
# NakWell modems
dialer          nakwell
chat            "" ATZ OK ATDT\T CONNECT
```

The line starting with **chat** specifies the modem chat, which is the sequence of commands sent to and received from the modem to initialize it and make it dial the desired number. The \T sequence will be replaced with the phone number by *uucico*.

To give you a rough idea how *uucico* deals with these configuration files, assume you issue the following command:

```
$ uucico -s pablo
```

The first thing *uucico* does is look up **pablo** in the *sys* file. From the *sys* file entry for **pablo** it sees that it should use the **serial1** port to establish the connection. The *port* file tells it that this is a modem port, and that it has a NakWell modem attached.

uucico now searches *dial* for the entry describing the NakWell modem, and having found one, opens the serial port */dev/cua1* and executes the dialer chat. That is, it sends *ATZ*, waits for the *OK* response, etc. When encountering the string \T, it substitutes the phone number (123-456) extracted from the *sys* file.

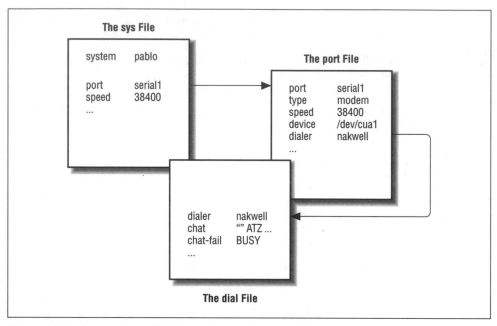

Figure 12–1. Interaction of Taylor UUCP configuration files

After the modem returns *CONNECT*, the connection has been established, and the modem chat is complete. *uucico* now returns to the *sys* file and executes the login chat. In our example, it would wait for the *login:* prompt, then send its user name (*neruda*), wait for the *password:* prompt, and send its password, *lorca*.

After completing authorization, the remote end is assumed to fire up its own *uucico*. The two will then enter the handshake phase described in the previous section.

Figure 12-1 shows the way the configuration files depend on each other.

What UUCP Needs to Know

Before you start writing the UUCP configuration files, you have to gather some information that UUCP needs to know.

First, you will have to figure out what serial device your modem is attached to. Usually, the (DOS) ports COM1 through COM4 map to the device special files */dev/cua0* through */dev/cua3*. Most distributions, such as Slackware, create a link */dev/modem* as a link to the appropriate *cua** device file, and configure *kermit*, *seyon*, etc. to use this generic file. In this case, you should use */dev/modem* in your UUCP configuration, too.

The reason for using a symbolic link is that all dial-out programs use so-called *lock files* to signal when a serial port is in use. The names of these lock files are a concatenation of the string *LCK..* and the device file name, for instance *LCK..cua1*. If programs use different names for the same device, they will fail to recognize each other's lock files. As a consequence, they will disrupt each other's session when started at the same time. This is not an unlikely event when you schedule your UUCP calls using a *crontab* entry.

For details of setting up your serial ports, please refer to Chapter 4, *Setting Up the Serial Hardware*.

Next, you must find out at what speed your modem and Linux will communicate. You have to set this speed to the maximum effective transfer rate you expect to get. The effective transfer rate may be much higher than the raw physical transfer rate your modem is capable of. For instance, many modems send and receive data at 2400 bps. Using compression protocols such as V.42bis, the actual transfer rate may climb up to 9600 bps.

Of course, if UUCP is to do anything, you will need the phone number of a system to call. Also, you will need a valid login ID and possibly a password for the remote machine.*

You will also have to know *exactly* how to log into the system. Do you have to press the return key before the login prompt appears? Does it display login: or user:? This is necessary for composing the *chat script*. If you don't know, or if the usual chat script fails, try to call the system with a terminal program like *kermit* or *minicom* and write down exactly what you have to do.

Site Naming

As with TCP/IP-based networking, your host has to have a name for UUCP networking. As long as you simply want to use UUCP for file transfers to or from sites you dial up directly, or on a local network, this name does not have to meet any standards.†

However, if you use UUCP for a mail or news link, you should think about having the name registered with the UUCP Mapping Project. The UUCP Mapping Project is described in Chapter 13, *Electronic Mail*. Even if you participate in a domain, you might consider having an official UUCP name for your site.

---

* If you're just going to try out UUCP, get the number of an archive site near you. Write down the login and password—they're public to make anonymous downloads possible. In most cases, they're something like **uucp/uucp** or **nuucp/uucp**.
† The only limitation is that it shouldn't be longer than seven characters, so as to not confuse UUCP implementations that run on an operating system that imposes a narrow limit on filenames. Names that are longer than seven characters are often truncated by UUCP. Some versions even limit the name to six characters.

Frequently, people choose their UUCP name to match the first component of their fully qualified domain name. Suppose your site's domain address is **swim.twobirds.com**; then your UUCP hostname would be **swim**. Think of UUCP sites as knowing each other on a first-name basis. Of course, you can also use a UUCP name completely unrelated to your fully qualified domain name.

However, make sure not to use the unqualified site name in mail addresses unless you have registered it as your official UUCP name.[*] At the very best, mail to an unregistered UUCP host will vanish in some big black bit bucket. If you use a name already held by some other site, this mail will be routed to that site and cause its postmaster no end of headaches.

By default, the UUCP suite uses the name set by *hostname* as the site's UUCP name. This name is commonly set in the */etc/rc.local* script. If your UUCP name is different from what you set your hostname to, you have to use the `hostname` option in the *config* file to tell *uucico* about your UUCP name. This is described below.

Taylor Configuration Files

We now return to the configuration files. Taylor UUCP gets its information from the following files:

config
: This is the main configuration file. You can define your site's UUCP name here.

sys This file describes all sites known to you. For each site, it specifies its name, what times to call it, which number to dial (if any), what type of device to use, and how to log on.

port
: Contains entries describing each port available, together with the line speed supported and the dialer to be used.

dial
: Describes dialers used to establish a telephone connection.

dialcode
: Contains expansions for symbolic dialcodes.

call
: Contains the login name and password to be used when calling a system. Rarely used.

---

[*] The UUCP Mapping Project registers all UUCP hostnames world-wide and makes sure they are unique. To register your UUCP name, ask the maintainers of the site that handles your mail; they will be able to help you with it.

passwd

> Contains login names and passwords systems may use when logging in. This file is used only when *uucico* does its own password checking.

Taylor configuration files are generally made up of lines containing keyword-value pairs. A hash sign introduces a comment that extends to the end of the line. To use a hash sign to mean itself, escape it with a backslash.

There are quite a number of options you can tune with these configuration files. We can't go into all the parameters here but will only cover the most important ones. Then you should be able to configure a modem-based UUCP link. Additional sections will describe the modifications necessary if you want to use UUCP over TCP/IP or over a direct serial line. A complete reference is given in the Texinfo documents that accompany the Taylor UUCP sources.

When you think you have configured your UUCP system completely, you can check your configuration using the *uuchk* tool (located in */usr/lib/uucp*). *uuchk* reads your configuration files and prints out a detailed report of the configuration values used for each system.

General Configuration Options—the config File

You won't generally use this file to describe much beside your UUCP hostname. By default, UUCP will use the name you set with the *hostname* command, but it is generally a good idea to set the UUCP name explicitly. Here is a sample *config* file:

```
# /usr/lib/uucp/config - UUCP main configuration file
hostname        vstout
```

A number of miscellaneous parameters can be set here too, such as the name of the spool directory or access rights for anonymous UUCP. The latter will be described in a later section.

How To Tell UUCP About Other Systems—the sys File

The *sys* file describes the systems your machine knows about. An entry is introduced by the **system** keyword; the subsequent lines up to the next **system** directive detail the parameters specific to that site. Commonly, a system entry will define parameters such as the telephone number and the login chat.

Parameters before the very first **system** line set default values used for all systems. Usually, you will set protocol paramters and the like in the defaults section.

Below, the most prominent fields are discussed in some detail.

System name

The `system` command names the remote system. You must specify the correct name of the remote system, not an alias you invented, because *uucico* will check it against what the remote system says it is called when you log on.[*]

Each system name can appear only once. If you want to use several sets of configurations for the same system (such as different telephone numbers *uucico* should try in turn), you can specify *alternates*. Alternates are described below.

Telephone number

If the remote system is to be reached over a telephone line, the `phone` field specifies the number the modem should dial. It may contain several tokens interpreted by *uucico*'s dialing procedure. An equal sign means to wait for a secondary dial tone, and a dash generates a one-second pause. For instance, some telephone installations will choke when you don't pause between dialing a special access code and the telephone number.[†]

Any embedded alphabetic string may be used to hide site-dependent information like area codes. Any such string is translated to a dialcode using the *dialcode* file. Suppose you have the following *dialcode* file:

```
# /usr/lib/uucp/dialcode - dialcode translation
Bogoham          024881
Coxton           035119
```

With these translations, you can use a phone number such as `Bogoham7732` in the *sys* file, which makes things probably a little more legible.

Port and speed

The `port` and `speed` options are used to select the device used for calling the remote system and the maximum speed to which the device should be set.[‡] A `system` entry may use either option alone or both options in conjunction. When looking up a suitable device in the *port* file, only those ports that have a matching port name and/or speed range are selected .

Generally, using the `speed` option only should suffice. If you have only one serial device defined in *port*, *uucico* will always pick the right one anyway, so you only have to give it the desired speed. If you have several modems attached to your systems, you still often don't want to name a particular port, because if *uucico* finds that there are several matches, it tries each device in turn until it finds an unused one.

---

[*] Older Version 2 UUCP's don't broadcast their name when being called; however, newer implementations often do, and so does Taylor UUCP.

[†] For instance, most companies' private installations require you to dial a 0 or 9 to get a line to the outside. I've been told this is called a *public exchange access code*.

[‡] The Baud rate of the tty must be at least as high as the maximum transfer speed.

The login chat

We already encountered the login chat script, which tells *uucico* how to log into the remote system. It consists of a list of tokens specifying strings expected and sent by the local *uucico* process. The intention is to make *uucico* wait until the remote machine sends a login prompt, then return the login name, wait for the remote system to send the password prompt, and send the password. Expect and send strings are given in alternation. *uucico* automatically appends a carriage return character (\r) to any send string. Thus, a simple chat script would look like this:

```
ogin: vstout ssword: catch22
```

You will notice that the expect fields don't contain the whole prompts. This is to make sure that the login succeeds even if the remote system broadcasts *Login:* instead of *login:*.

uucico also allows for some sort of conditional execution, for example in the case that the remote machine's *getty* needs to be reset before sending a prompt. For this, you can attach a sub-chat to an expect string, set off by a dash. The sub-chat is executed only if the main expect fails, i.e., a timeout occurs. One way to use this feature is to send a BREAK if the remote site doesn't display a login prompt. The following example gives a general-purpose chat script that should also work in case you have to hit return before the login appears. The empty first argument `""` tells UUCP to not wait for anything and continue with the next send string immediately.

```
"" \n\r\d\r\n\c ogin:-BREAK-ogin: vstout ssword: catch22
```

A couple of special strings and escape characters can occur in the chat script. The following is a partial list of characters legal in expect strings:

`"` The empty string. It tells *uucico* not to wait for anything, but proceed with the next send string immediately.

`\t` Tab character.

`\r` Carriage return character.

`\s` Space character. You need this to embed spaces in a chat string.

`\n` Newline character.

`\\` Backslash character.

On send strings, the following escape characters and strings are legal in addition to the above:

EOT

End of transmission character (^D).

BREAK
   Break character.

\c Suppress sending of carriage return at end of string.

\d Delay sending for 1 second.

\E Enable echo checking. This requires *uucico* to wait for the echo of everything it writes to be read back from the device before it can continue with the chat. It is primarily useful when used in modem chats (which we will encounter below). Echo checking is off by default.

\e Disable echo checking.

\K Same as BREAK.

\p Pause for fraction of a second.

Alternates

Sometimes it is desirable to have multiple entries for a single system, for instance if the system can be reached on different modem lines. With Taylor UUCP, you can do this by defining a so-called *alternate*.

An alternate entry retains all settings from the main system entry and specifies only those values that should be overridden in the default system entry or added to it. An alternate is offset from the system entry by a line containing the keyword `alternate`.

To use two phone numbers for **pablo**, you would modify its *sys* entry in the following way:

```
system      pablo
phone       123-456
... entries as above ...
alternate
phone       123-455
```

When calling **pablo**, *uucico* will first dial 123-456, and if this fails, it will try the alternate. The alternate entry retains all settings from the main system entry and overrides only the telephone number.

Restricting call times

Taylor UUCP provides a number of ways you may restrict the times when calls can be placed to a remote system. You might do this either because of limitations the remote host places on its services during business hours, or simply to avoid times with high call rates. Note that it is always possible to override call time restrictions by giving *uucico* the *–S* or *–f* option.

By default, Taylor UUCP will disallow connections at any time, so you *have* to use some sort of time specification in the *sys* file. If you don't care about call time restrictions, you can specify the `time` option with a value of `Any` in your *sys* file.

The simplest way to restrict call time is the `time` entry, which is followed by a string made up of a day and a time subfield. Day may be any of `Mo, Tu, We, Th, Fr, Sa, Su` combined, or `Any, Never,` or `Wk` for weekdays. The time consists of two 24-hour clock values, separated by a dash. They specify the range during which calls may be placed. The combination of these tokens is written without white space in between. Any number of day and time specifications may be grouped together with commas.

```
time          MoWe0300-0730,Fr1805-2000
```

This example allows calls on Mondays and Wednesdays from 3 a.m. to 7:30 a.m., and on Fridays between 6:05 p.m. and 10:00 p.m. When a time field spans midnight, say `Mo1830-0600`, it actually means Monday, between midnight and 6 a.m. and between 6:30 p.m. and midnight.

The special time strings `Any` and `Never` mean what they say: Calls may be placed at any or no time, respectively.

The `time` command takes an optional second argument that describes a retry time in minutes. When an attempt to establish a connection fails, *uucico* will not allow another attempt to dial up the remote host within a certain interval. For instance, when you specify a retry time of 5 minutes, *uucico* will refuse to call the remote system within 5 minutes after the last failure. By default, *uucico* uses an exponential backoff scheme, where the retry interval increases with each repeated failure.

The `timegrade` command allows you to attach a maximum spool grade to a schedule. For instance, assume you have the following `timegrade` commands in a `system` entry:

```
timegrade         N Wk1900-0700,SaSu
timegrade         C Any
```

This allows jobs with a spool grade of C or higher (usually mail is queued with grade B or C) to be transferred whenever a call is established, while news (usually queued with grade N) will be transferred only during the night and at weekends.

Just like `time`, the `timegrade` command takes a retry interval in minutes as an optional third argument.

However, a caveat about spool grades is in order here. First, the `timegrade` option applies only to what *your* systems sends; the remote system may still transfer anything it likes. You can use the `call-timegrade` option to explicitly request it to send only jobs above some given spool grade; but there's no guarantee it will obey this request.[*]

---

[*] If the remote system runs Talyor UUCP, it will obey.

Similarly, the `timegrade` field is not checked when a remote system calls in, so any jobs queued for the calling system will be sent. However, the remote system can explicitly request your *uucico* to restrict itself to a certain spool grade.

Available Devices—the port File

The *port* file tells *uucico* about the available ports. These may be modem ports, but other types such as direct serial lines and TCP sockets are supported as well.

Like the *sys* file, *port* consists of separate entries starting with the keyword `port` followed by the port name. This name may be used in the *sys* file's `port` statement. The name need not be unique; if there are several ports with the same name, *uucico* will try each in turn until it finds one that is not currently being used.

The `port` command should be followed immediately by the `type` statement, which indicates what type of port is described. Valid types are `modem`, `direct` for direct connections, and `tcp` for TCP sockets. If the `port` command is missing, the port type defaults to modem.

In this section, we cover only modem ports; TCP ports and direct lines are discussed in a later section.

For modem and direct ports, you have to specify the device for calling out using the `device` directive. Usually, this is the name of a device special file in the */dev* directory, like */dev/cua1.*[*]

In the case of a modem device, the port entry also determines what type of modem is connected to the port. Different types of modems have to be configured differently. Even modems that claim to be Hayes-compatible needn't be really compatible with each other. Therefore, you have to tell *uucico* how to initialize the modem and how to make it dial the desired number. Taylor UUCP keeps the descriptions of all dialers in a file named *dial*. To use any of these, you have to specify the dialer's name using the `dialer` command.

Sometimes, you will want to use a modem in different ways, depending on which system you call. For instance, some older modems don't understand when a high-speed modem attempts to connect at 14400 bps; they simply drop the line instead of negotiating a connect at 9600 bps, for instance. When you know site **drop** uses such a dumb modem, you have to set up your modem differently when calling them. For this, you need an additional port entry in the *port* file that specifies a different dialer. Now you can give the new port a different name, such as `serial1-slow`, and use the `port` directive in the **drop** system entry in *sys*.

---

* Some people use the *ttyS** devices instead, which are intended for dial-in only.

A better way is to distinguish the ports by the speeds they support. For instance, the two port entries for the above situation may look like this:

```
# NakWell modem; connect at high speed
port          serial1          # port name
type          modem            # modem port
device        /dev/cua1        # this is COM2
speed         38400            # supported speed
dialer        nakwell          # normal dialer
# NakWell modem; connect at low speed
port          serial1          # port name
type          modem            # modem port
device        /dev/cua1        # this is COM2
speed         9600             # supported speed
dialer        nakwell-slow     # don't attempt fast connect
```

The system entry for site **drop** would now give serial1 as port name, but request to use it at 9600 bps only. *uucico* will then automatically use the second port entry. All remaining sites that have a speed of 38400 bps in the system entry will be called using the first port entry.

How to Dial a Number—the dial File

The *dial* file describes the way various dialers are used. Traditionally, UUCP talks of dialers rather than modems, because in earlier times, it was usual practice to have one (expensive) automatic dialing device serve a whole bank of modems. Today, most modems have dialing support built in, so this distinction gets a little blurred.

Nevertheless, different dialers or modems may require a different configuration. You can describe each of them in the *dial* file. Entries in *dial* start with the `dialer` command that gives the dialer's name.

The most important entry besides `dialer` is the modem chat, specified by the `chat` command. Similar to the login chat, it consists of a sequence of strings *uucico* sends to the dialer and the responses it expects in return. It is commonly used to reset the modem to some known state and dial the number. The following sample `dialer` entry shows a typical modem chat for a Hayes-compatible modem:

```
# NakWell modem; connect at high speed
dialer        nakwell          # dialer name
chat          "" ATZ OK\r ATH1E0Q0 OK\r ATDT\T CONNECT
chat-fail     BUSY
chat-fail     ERROR
chat-fail     NO\sCARRIER
dtr-toggle    true
```

The modem chat begins with `""`, the empty expect string. uucico will therefore send the first command ATZ right away. ATZ is the Hayes command to reset the modem. It then waits until the modem has sent OK and sends the next command, which turns off local echo and the like. After the modem returns OK again, *uucico* sends the dialing command ATDT. The escape sequence \T in this string is replaced with the phone number taken from the system entry *sys* file. *uucico* then waits for the modem to return the string CONNECT, which signals that a connection with the remote modem has been established successfully.

Often, the modem fails to connect to the remote system, for instance, if the other system is talking to someone else and the line is busy. In this case, the modem will return some error message indicating the reason. Modem chats are not capable of detecting such messages; *uucico* will continue to wait for the expected string until it times out. The UUCP log file will therefore only show a bland "timed out in chat script" instead of the true reason.

However, Taylor UUCP allows you to tell *uucico* about these error messages using the `chat-fail` command as shown above. When *uucico* detects a chat-fail string while executing the modem chat, it aborts the call, and logs the error message in the UUCP log file.

The last command in the example shown above tells UUCP to toggle the DTR control line before starting the modem chat. Normally, the serial driver will raise DTR (*Data Terminal Ready*) when a process opens the device, to tell the attached modem that someone wants to talk to it. The `dtr-toggle` feature will in addition drop DTR, wait a moment, and raise it again. Many modems can be configured to react to a drop of DTR by going off-hook, entering command state, or resetting themselves.[*]

UUCP Over TCP

Absurd as it may sound, using UUCP to transfer data over TCP is not that bad an idea, especially when transferring large amounts of data such as Usenet news. On TCP-based links, news is generally exchanged using the NNTP protocol, where articles are requested and sent individually, without compression or any other optimization. Although adequate for large sites with several concurrent newsfeeds, this technique is very unfavorable for small sites that receive their news over a slow connection such as ISDN. These sites will usually want to combine the qualities of TCP with the advantages of sending news in large batches, which can be compressed and thus transferred with very low overhead. A standard way to transfer these batches is to use UUCP over TCP.

In *sys*, you would specify a system to be called via TCP in the following way:

```
system      gmu
address     news.groucho.edu
time        Any
port        tcp-conn
chat        ogin: vstout word: clouseau
```

---

[*] Some modems don't seem to like this and occasionally get hung.

The **address** command gives the IP address of the host or its fully qualified domain name. The corresponding *port* entry would read:

```
port            tcp-conn
type            tcp
service         540
```

The entry states that a TCP connection should be used when a *sys* entry references **tcp-conn**, and that *uucico* should attempt to connect to the TCP network port 540 on the remote host. This is the default port number of the UUCP service. Instead of the port number, you may also give a symbolic port name to the **service** command. The port number corresponding to this name will be looked up in */etc/services*. The common name for the UUCP service is **uucpd**.

Using a Direct Connection

Assume you use a direct line to connect your system **vstout** to **tiny**. Much like in the modem case, you have to write a system entry in the *sys* file. The **port** command identifies the serial port **tiny** is hooked up to.

```
system          tiny
time            Any
port            direct1
speed           38400
chat            ogin: cathcart word: catch22
```

In the *port* file, you have to describe the serial port for the direct connection. A **dialer** entry is not needed, because there's no need for dialing.

```
port            direct1
type            direct
speed           38400
device           /dev/ttyS1
```

The Do's and Don'ts of UUCP—Tuning Permissions

Command Execution

UUCP's task is to copy files from one system to another and to request execution of certain commands on remote hosts. Of course, you as an administrator would want to control what rights you grant other systems—allowing them to execute any command on your system is definitely not a good idea.

By default, the only commands Taylor UUCP allows other systems to execute on your machine are *rmail* and *rnews*, which are commonly used to exchange email and Usenet News over UUCP. The default search path used by *uuxqt* is a compile-time option, but should usually contain */bin*, */usr/bin*, and */usr/local/bin*. To change the set of commands for a particular system, you can use the commands keyword in the *sys* file. Similarly, the search path can be changed with the command-path statement. For instance, you may want to allow system **pablo** to execute the *rsmtp* command in addition to *rmail* and *rnews*:[*]

```
system        pablo
...
commands      rmail rnews rsmtp
```

File Transfers

Taylor UUCP also allows you to fine-tune file transfers in great detail. At one extreme, you can disable transfers to and from a particular system. Just set request to no, and the remote system will not be able to either retrieve files from your system or send it any files. Similarly, you can prohibit your users from transferring files to or from a system by setting transfer to no. By default, users on both the local and the remote system are allowed to upload and download files.

In addition, you can configure the directories to and from which files may be copied. Usually, you will want to restrict access from remote systems to a single directory hierarchy, but still allow your users to send files from their home directory. Commonly, remote users will be allowed to receive files only from the public UUCP directory */var/spool/uucppublic*. This is the traditional place to make files publicly available, very much like FTP servers on the Internet. It is commonly referred to using the tilde character.

Taylor UUCP provides four different commands to configure the directories for sending and receiving files. They are: local-send, which specifies the list of directories a user may ask UUCP to send files from; local-receive, which gives the list of directories a user may ask to receive files to; and remote-send and remote-receive, which do the analogous for requests from a foreign system. Consider the following example:

```
system          pablo
...
local-send      /home ~
local-receive   /home ~/receive
remote-send     ~ !~/incoming !~/receive
remote-receive  ~/incoming
```

The local-send command allows users on your host to send any files below */home* and from the public UUCP directory to **pablo**. The local-receive command allows them to receive files either to the world-writable *receive* directory in the *uucppublic*, or any world-writable directory below */home*. The remote-send directive allows **pablo** to request files from */var/spool/uucppublic*, except for files from the *incoming* and *receive* directories. This is signaled to *uucico* by preceding

---

[*] *rsmtp* is used to deliver mail with batched SMTP. This is described in the mail chapters.

the directory names with exclamation marks. Finally, the last line allows **pablo** to upload any files to **incoming**.

A major problem with file transfers using UUCP is that it will receive files only to directories that are world-writable. This may tempt some users to set up traps for other users, etc. However, there's no way to escape this problem except by disabling UUCP file transfers altogether.

Forwarding

UUCP provides a mechanism to have other systems execute file transfers on your behalf. For instance, this allows you to make **seci** retrieve a file from **uchile** for you and send it to your system. The following command would achieve this:

```
$ uucp -r seci!uchile!~/find-ls.gz ~/uchile.files.gz
```

This technique of passing a job through several systems is called *forwarding*. In the above example, the reason to use forwarding may be that **seci** has UUCP access to **uchile**, but your host doesn't. However, if you run a UUCP system, you would want to limit the forwarding service to a few hosts you trust not to run up a horrendous phone bill by making you download the latest X11R6 source release for them.

By default, Taylor UUCP disallows forwarding altogether. To enable forwarding for a particular system, you can use the `forward` command. This command specifies a list of sites the system may request you to forward jobs to and from. For instance, the UUCP administrator of **seci** would have to add the following lines to the *sys* file to allow **pablo** to request files from **uchile**:

```
####################
# pablo
system          pablo
...
forward         uchile
####################
# uchile
system          uchile
...
forward-to      pablo
```

The `forward-to` entry for **uchile** is necessary so that any files returned by it are actually passed on to **pablo**. Otherwise UUCP would drop them. This entry uses a variation of the `forward` command that permits **uchile** only to send files to **pablo** through **seci**, not the other way round.

To permit forwarding to any system, use the special keyword `ANY` (capital letters required).

Setting Up Your System for Dialing In

If you want to set up your site for dialing in, you have to permit logins on your serial port and customize some system files to provide UUCP accounts. This will be the topic of the current section.

Setting Up getty

If you want to use a serial line as a dial-in port, you have to enable a *getty* process on that port. However, some *getty* implementations aren't really suitable for this, because you usually want to use a serial port for dialing in and out. You therefore have to make sure to use a *getty* that is able to share the line with other programs like *uucico* or *minicom*. One program that does this is *uugetty* from the *getty_ps* package. Most Linux distributions have it; check for *uugetty* in your */sbin* directory. Another program I am aware of is Gert Doering's *mgetty*, which also supports reception of faxes. You can also obtain the latest versions of these from **sunsite.unc.edu** as either binary or source.

Explaining the differences in the way *uugetty* and *mgetty* handle logins is beyond the scope of this little section; for more information, refer to the Serial HOWTO by Greg Hankins, as well as the documentation that comes along with *getty_ps* and *mgetty*.

Serial HOWTO

Providing UUCP Accounts

Next, you have to set up user accounts that let remote sites log into your system and establish a UUCP connection. Generally, you will provide a separate login name to each system that polls you. When setting up an account for system **pablo**, you would probably give it the username **Upablo**.

For systems that dial in through the serial port, you usually have to add these accounts to the system password file */etc/passwd*. A good practice is to put all UUCP logins in a special group such as **uuguest**. The account's home directory should be set to the public spool directory */var/spool/uucppublic*; its login shell must be *uucico*.

If you have the shadow password suite installed, you can do this with the *useradd* command:

```
# useradd -d /var/spool/uucppublic -G uuguest -s /usr/lib/uucp/uucico Upablo
```

If you don't use the shadow password suite, you probably have to edit */etc/passwd* by hand, adding a line like the following, where 5000 and 150 are the numerical uid and gid assigned to user **Upablo** and group **uuguest**, respectively.

```
Upablo:x:5000:150:UUCP Account:/var/spool/uucppublic:/usr/lib/uucp/uucico
```

After installing the account, you have to activate it by setting its password with the *passwd* command.

To serve UUCP systems that connect to your site over TCP, you have to set up *inetd* to handle incoming connections on the uucp port. You do this by adding the following line to */etc/inetd.conf*:*

```
uucp   stream tcp   nowait root /usr/sbin/tcpd /usr/lib/uucp/uucico -l
```

The −*l* option makes *uucico* perform its own login authorization. It will prompt for a login name and a password just like the standard *login* program, but will rely on its private password database instead of */etc/passwd*. This private password file is named */usr/lib/uucp/passwd* and contains pairs of login names and passwords:

```
Upablo  IslaNegra
Ulorca  co'rdoba
```

Of course, this file must be owned by **uucp** and have permissions of 600.

If this database sounds like such a good idea that you would like to use it on normal serial logins, too, you will be disappointed to hear that this isn't possible at the moment without major contortions. First off, you need Taylor UUCP 1.05 for this, because it allows *getty* to pass the login name of the calling user to *uucico* using the −*u* option.† Then, you have to trick the *getty* you are using to invoke *uucico* instead of the usual */bin/login*. With *getty_ps*, you can do this by setting the LOGIN option in the configuration file. However, this disables interactive logins altogether. *mgetty*, on the other hand, has a nice feature that allows you to invoke different login commands based on the name the user provides. For instance, you can tell *mgetty* to use *uucico* for all users who provide a login name beginning with a capital U, but let everyone else be handled by the standard *login* command.

To protect your UUCP users from callers giving a false system name and snarfing all their mail, you should add `called-login` commands to each system entry in the *sys* file. This is described in the next section.

Protecting Yourself Against Swindlers

A major problem with UUCP is that the calling system can lie about its name; it announces its name to the called system after logging in, but the server doesn't have a way to check it. Thus, an attacker could log into his or her own UUCP account, pretend to be someone else, and pick up that other site's mail. This is particularly troublesome if you offer login via anonymous UUCP, where the password is made public.

Unless you know you can trust all sites that call your system to be honest, you *must* guard against this sort of impostor. The cure for this disease is to require

---

* Note that usually, *tcpd* has mode 700, so that you must invoke it as user **root**, not **uucp** as you would usually do.

† The −*u* option is present in 1.04, too, but is only a no-op.

each system to use a particular login name by specifying a `called-login` in *sys*. A sample system entry may look like this:

```
system          pablo
... usual options ...
called-login    Upablo
```

The upshot of this is that whenever a system logs in and pretends it is **pablo**, *uucico* will check whether it has logged in as **Upablo**. If it hasn't, the calling system will be turned down, and the connection is dropped. You should make it a habit to add the `called-login` command to every system entry you add to your *sys* file. It is important that you do this for *all* sytems, regardless of whether they will ever call your site or not. For those sites that never call you, you should probably set `called-login` to some totally bogus user name, such as **neverlogsin**.

Be Paranoid—Call Sequence Checks

Another way to fend off and detect impostors is to use call sequence checks. These help you protect against intruders that somehow manage to find out the password you log into your UUCP system with.

When using call sequence checks, both machines keep track of the number of connections established so far. It is incremented with each connection. After logging in, the caller sends its call sequence number, and the callee checks it against its own number. If they don't match, the connection attempt will be rejected. If the initial number is chosen at random, attackers will have a hard time guessing the correct call sequence number.

But call sequence checks do more for you than this: even if some very clever person should detect your call sequence number as well as your password, you will find this out. When the attacker calls your UUCP feed and steals your mail, this will increase the feeds call sequence number by one. The next time *you* call your feed and try to log in, the remote *uucico* will refuse you, because the numbers don't match anymore!

If you have enabled call sequence checks, you should check your log files regularly for error messages that hint at possible attacks. If your system rejects the call sequence number the calling system offers it, *uucico* will put a message into the log file saying something like "Out of sequence call rejected." If your system is rejected by its feed because the sequence numbers are out of sync, it will put a message in the log file saying "Handshake failed (RBADSEQ)."

To enable call sequence checks, you have to add following command to the system entry:

```
# enable call sequence checks
sequence        true
```

Also, you have to create the file containing the sequence number itself. Taylor UUCP keeps the sequence number in a file called *.Sequence* in the remote site's spool directory. It *must* be owned by **uucp** and must be mode 600 (i.e., readable and writeable only by **uucp**). It is best to initialize this file with an arbitrary, agreed-upon start value. Otherwise, an attacker might manage to guess the number by trying out all values smaller than, say, 60.

```
# cd /var/spool/uucp/pablo
# echo 94316 > .Sequence
# chmod 600 .Sequence
# chown uucp.uucp .Sequence
```

Of course, the remote site has to enable call sequence checks as well and start by using exactly the same sequence number as you.

Anonymous UUCP

If you want to provide anonymous UUCP access to your system, you first have to set up a special account for it as described above. A common practice is to give the anonymous account a login name and a password of **uucp**.

In addition, you have to set a few of the security options for unknown systems. For instance, you may want to prohibit them from executing any commands on your system. However, you cannot set these parameters in a *sys* file entry because the **system** command requires the system's name, which you don't have. Taylor UUCP solves this dilemma through the **unknown** command. **unknown** can be used in the *config* file to specify any command that can usually appear in a system entry:

```
unknown         remote-receive ~/incoming
unknown         remote-send ~/pub
unknown         max-remote-debug none
unknown         command-path /usr/lib/uucp/anon-bin
unknown         commands rmail
```

This will restrict unknown systems to downloading files from below the *pub* directory and uploading files to the *incoming* directory below */var/spool/uucppublic*. The next line will make *uucico* ignore any requests from the remote system to turn on debugging locally. The last two lines permit unknown systems to execute *rmail*, but the command path specified makes *uucico* look for the *rmail* command in a private directory named *anon-bin* only. This allows you to provide some special *rmail* that, for instance, forwards all mail to the superuser for examination. This allows anonymous users to reach the maintainer of the system, but prevents them at the same time from injecting any mail to other sites.

To enable anonymous UUCP, you must specify at least one **unknown** statement in *config*. Otherwise *uucico* will reject all unknown systems.

UUCP Low-level Protocols

To negotiate session control and file transfers with the remote end, *uucico* uses a set of standardized messages. This is often referred to as the high-level protocol. During the initialization phase and the hangup phase these are simply sent across as strings. However, during the real transfer phase, an additional low-level protocol is employed which is mostly transparent to the higher levels. This is to make error checks possible when using unreliable lines, for instance.

Protocol Overview

As UUCP is used over different types of connections, such as serial lines or TCP, or even X.25, specific low-level protocols are needed. In addition, several implementations of UUCP have introduced different protocols that do roughly the same thing.

Protocols can be divided into two categories: streaming and packet-oriented protocols. Protocols of the latter variety transfer a file as a whole, possibly computing a checksum over it. This is nearly free of any overhead but requires a reliable connection, because any error will cause the whole file to be retransmitted. These protocols are commonly used over TCP connections but are not suitable for use over telephone lines. Although modern modems do quite a good job at error correction, they are not perfect, nor is there any error detection between your computer and the modem.

On the other hand, packet protocols split up the file into several chunks of equal size. Each packet is sent and received separately, a checksum is computed, and an acknowledgment is returned to the sender. To make this more efficient, sliding-window protocols were invented, which allow for a limited number (a window) of outstanding acknowledgments at any time. This greatly reduces the amount of time *uucico* has to wait during a transmission. Still, the relatively large overhead compared to a streaming protocol makes packet protocols inefficient for use over TCP.

The width of the data path also makes a difference. Sometimes, sending 8-bit characters over a serial connection is impossible, for instance if the connection goes through a stupid terminal server that strips off the eight bit. When you transmit 8-bit characters over a 7-bit connection, they have to be quoted on transmission. Under worst-case assumptions, this doubles the amount of data to be transmitted, although compression done by the hardware may compensate for this. Lines that can transmit arbitrary 8-bit characters are usually called *8-bit clean*. This is the case for all TCP connections, as well as for most modem connections.

The following protocols are available with Taylor UUCP 1.04:

g   This is the most common protocol and should be understood by virtually all *uucico*'s. It does thorough error checking and is therefore well suited for noisy telephone links. *g* requires an 8-bit clean connection. It is a packet-oriented protocol which uses a sliding-window technique.

i   This is a bi-directional packet protocol, which can send and receive files at the same time. It requires a full-duplex connection and an 8-bit clean data path. It is currently understood only by Taylor UUCP.

t   This is a protocol intended for use over a TCP connection or other truly error-free networks. It uses packets of 1024 bytes and requires an 8-bit clean connection.

e   This should basically do the same as *t*. The main difference is that *e* is a streaming protocol.

f   This is intended for use with reliable X.25 connections. It is a streaming protocol and expects a 7-bit data path. 8-bit characters are quoted, which can make it very inefficient.

G   This is the System V Release 4 version of the *g* protocol. It is also understood by some other versions of UUCP.

a   This protocol is similiar to ZMODEM. It requires an 8-bit connection, but quotes certain control characters like XON and XOFF.

Tuning the Transmission Protocol

All protocols allow for some variation in packet sizes, timeouts, and the like. Usually, the defaults work well under standard circumstances, but may not be optimal for your situation. The *g* protocol, for instance, uses window sizes from 1 to 7, and packet sizes in powers of 2 ranging from 64 through 4096.[*] If your telephone line is usually so noisy that it drops more than 5 percent of all packets, you should probably lower the packet size and shrink the window. On the other hand, on very good telephone lines the protocol overhead of sending acknowledgments for every 128 bytes may prove wasteful, so you might increase the packet size to 512 or even 1024. Most binaries included in Linux distributions default to a window size of 7 and 128 byte packets.

Taylor UUCP provides a mechanism to suit your needs by tuning these parameters with the **protocol-parameter** command in the *sys* file. For instance, to set the *g* protocol's packet size to 512 when talking to **pablo**, you have to add:

```
system          pablo
...
protocol-parameter g  packet-size  512
```

---

[*] Most binaries included in Linux distributions default to a window size of 7 and 128-byte packets.

The tunable parameters and their names vary from protocol to protocol. For a complete list of them, refer to the documentation enclosed in the Taylor UUCP source.

Selecting Specific Protocols

Not every implementation of *uucico* speaks and understands each protocol, so during the initial handshake phase, both processes have to agree on a common protocol. The master *uucico* offers the slave a list of supported protocols by sending *Pprotlist*, from which the slave may pick one.

Based on the type of port used (modem, TCP, or direct), *uucico* will compose a default list of protocols. For modem and direct connections, this list usually comprises *i*, *a*, *g*, *G*, and *j*. For TCP connections, the list is *t*, *e*, *i*, *a*, *g*, *G*, *j*, and *f*. You can override this default list with the **protocols** command, which may be specified in a system entry as well as a port entry. For instance, you might edit the *port* file entry for your modem port like this:

```
port            serial1
...
protocols       igG
```

This will require any incoming or outgoing connection through this port to use *i*, *g*, or *G*. If the remote system does not support any of these, the conversation will fail.

Troubleshooting

This section describes what may go wrong with your UUCP connection and makes suggestions where to look for the error. However, I compiled these problems off the top of my head. There's much more that can go wrong.

In any case, enable debugging with *–xall*, and take a look at the output in *Debug* in the spool directory. It should help you to quickly recognize where the problem lies. Also, I have always found it helpful to turn on my modem's speaker when it doesn't connect. With Hayes-compatible modems, this is accomplished by adding *ATL1M1 OK* to the modem chat in the *dial* file.

The first check always should be whether all file permissions are set correctly. *uucico* should be setuid **uucp**, and all files in */usr/lib/uucp*, */var/spool/uucp*, and */var/spool/uucppublic* should be owned by **uucp**. There are also some hidden files* in the spool directory which must be owned by **uucp** as well.

***uucico* keeps saying "Wrong time to call"**: This probably means that in the system entry in *sys*, you didn't specify a **time** command that details when the remote

---

* That is, files whose names begin with a dot. Such files aren't normally displayed by the *ls* command.

system may be called, or you gave one which actually forbids calling at the current time. If no call schedule is given, *uucico* assumes the system can never be called.

uucico **complains that the site is already locked**: This means that *uucico* detects a lock file for the remote system in */var/spool/uucp*. The lock file may be from an earlier call to the system that crashed, or was killed. However, it's also likely that there's another *uucico* process sitting around that is trying to dial the remote system and has gotten stuck in a chat script, etc. If this *uucico* process doesn't succeed in connecting to the remote system, kill it with a hangup signal, and remove any lock files it left lying around.

I can connect to the remote site, but the chat script fails: Look at the text you receive from the remote site. If it's garbled, this might be a speed-related problem. Otherwise, confirm if it really agrees with what your chat script expects. Remember, the chat script starts with an expect string. If you receive the login prompt and send your name, but never get the password prompt, insert some delays before sending it, or even in between the letters. You might be too fast for your modem.

My modem does not dial: If your modem doesn't indicate that the DTR line has been raised when *uucico* calls out, you possibly haven't given the right device to *uucico*. If your modem recognizes DTR, check with a terminal program that you can write to it. If this works, turn on echoing with \E at the start of the modem chat. If it doesn't echo your commands during the modem chat, check if your line speed is too high or low for your modem. If you see the echo, check if you have disabled modem responses or set them to number codes. Verify that the chat script itself is correct. Remember that you have to write two backslashes to send one to the modem.

My modem tries to dial but doesn't get out: Insert a delay into the phone number. This is especially useful when dialing out from a company's internal telephone net. For people in Europe, who usually dial pulse-tone, try touch-tone. In some countries, postal services have been upgrading their nets recently. Touch-tone sometimes helps.

My log file says I have extremely high packet loss rates: This looks like a speed problem. Maybe the link between computer and modem is too slow (remember to adapt it to the highest effective rate possible). Or your hardware is too slow to service interrupts in time. With an NSC 16550A chipset on your serial port, 38 kbps work reasonably well; however, without FIFOs (like 16450 chips), 9600 bps is the limit. Also, make sure hardware handshake is enabled on the serial line.

Another likely cause is that hardware handshake isn't enabled on the port. Taylor UUCP 1.04 has no provisions for turning on RTS/CTS handshake. You have to enable this explicitly from *rc.serial* using the following command:

```
$ stty crtscts < /dev/cua3
```

I can log in, but handshake fails: Well, there can be a number of problems. The output in the log file should tell you a lot. Look at what protocols the remote site offers (it sends a string `Pprotlist` during the handshake). Maybe they don't have any in common (did you select any protocols in *sys* or *port?*).

If the remote system sends *RLCK*, there is a stale lockfile for you on the remote system. If it's not because you're already connected to the remote system on a different line, ask to have it removed.

If it sends *RBADSEQ*, the other site has conversation count checks enabled for you, but numbers didn't match. If it sends *RLOGIN*, you were not permitted to login under this ID.

Log Files

When compiling the UUCP suite to use Taylor-style logging, you have only three global log files, all of which reside in the spool directory. The main log file is named *Log* and contains all information about connections established and files transferred. A typical excerpt looks like this (after a little reformatting to make it fit the page):

```
uucico pablo - (1994-05-28 17:15:01.66 539) Calling system pablo (port cua3)
uucico pablo - (1994-05-28 17:15:39.25 539) Login successful
uucico pablo - (1994-05-28 17:15:39.90 539) Handshake successful
                (protocol 'g' packet size 1024 window 7)
uucico pablo postmaster (1994-05-28 17:15:43.65 539) Receiving D.pabloB04aj
uucico pablo postmaster (1994-05-28 17:15:46.51 539) Receiving X.pabloX04ai
uucico pablo postmaster (1994-05-28 17:15:48.91 539) Receiving D.pabloB04at
uucico pablo postmaster (1994-05-28 17:15:51.52 539) Receiving X.pabloX04as
uucico pablo postmaster (1994-05-28 17:15:54.01 539) Receiving D.pabloB04c2
uucico pablo postmaster (1994-05-28 17:15:57.17 539) Receiving X.pabloX04c1
uucico pablo - (1994-05-28 17:15:59.05 539) Protocol 'g' packets: sent 15,
                resent 0, received 32
uucico pablo - (1994-05-28 17:16:02.50 539) Call complete (26 seconds)
uuxqt pablo postmaster (1994-05-28 17:16:11.41 546) Executing X.pabloX04ai
                (rmail okir)
uuxqt pablo postmaster (1994-05-28 17:16:13.30 546) Executing X.pabloX04as
                (rmail okir)
uuxqt pablo postmaster (1994-05-28 17:16:13.51 546) Executing X.pabloX04c1
                (rmail okir)
```

The next important log file is *Stats*, which lists file transfer statistics. The section of *Stats* corresponding to the above transfer looks like this (again, the lines have been split to fit the page):

```
postmaster pablo (1994-05-28 17:15:44.78)
                received 1714 bytes in 1.802 seconds (951 bytes/sec)
postmaster pablo (1994-05-28 17:15:46.66)
                received 57 bytes in 0.634 seconds (89 bytes/sec)
postmaster pablo (1994-05-28 17:15:49.91)
                received 1898 bytes in 1.599 seconds (1186 bytes/sec)
```

```
postmaster pablo (1994-05-28 17:15:51.67)
                    received 65 bytes in 0.555 seconds (117 bytes/sec)
postmaster pablo (1994-05-28 17:15:55.71)
                    received 3217 bytes in 2.254 seconds (1427 bytes/sec)
postmaster pablo (1994-05-28 17:15:57.31)
                    received 65 bytes in 0.590 seconds (110 bytes/sec)
```

The third file is *Debug*. This is the place where debugging information is written. If you use debugging, you should make sure this file has a protection mode of 600. Depending on the debug mode you selected, it may contain the login and password you use to connect to the remote system.

Some UUCP binaries included in Linux distributions have been compiled to use HDB-style logging. HDB UUCP uses a whole bunch of log files stored below */var/spool/uucp/.Log*. This directory contains three more directories, named *uucico*, *uuxqt*, and *uux*. They contain the logging output generated by each of the corresponding commands, sorted into different files for each site. Thus, output from *uucico* when calling site **pablo** will go into *.Log/uucico/pablo*, while the subsequent *uuxqt* run will write to *.Log/uuxqt/pablo*. The lines written to the various log files are the same as with Taylor logging however.

When you enable debugging output with HDB-style logging compiled in, it will go to the *.Admin* directory below */var/spool/uucp*. During outgoing calls, debugging information will be sent to *.Admin/audit.local*, while the output from *uucico* when someone calls in will go to *.Admin/audit*.

CHAPTER THIRTEEN
ELECTRONIC MAIL

O ne of the most prominent uses of networking since the first networks were devised has been electronic mail. It started as a simple service that copied a file from one machine to another and appended it to the recipient's *mailbox* file. Basically, this is still what email is all about, although an ever growing net, with its complex routing requirements and its ever increasing load of messages, has made a more elaborate scheme necessary.

RFC 822

Various standards of mail exchange have been devised. Sites on the Internet adhere to one laid out in RFC 822, augmented by some RFCs that describe a machine-independent way of transferring special characters, and the like. Much thought has also been given recently to "multi-media mail," which deals with including pictures and sound in mail messages. Another standard, X.400, has been defined by CCITT.

Chapter 15

Quite a number of mail transport programs have been implemented for UNIX systems. One of the best known is the University of California at Berkeley's *sendmail*, which is used on a number of platforms. The original author was Eric Allman, who is now actively working on the *sendmail* team again. There are two Linux ports of *sendmail-5.56c* available. The *sendmail* version currently being developed is 8.6.5.

Chapter 14

The mail agent most commonly used with Linux is *smail-3.1.28*, written and copyrighted by Curt Landon Noll and Ronald S. Karr. This is the one included in most Linux distributions. We will refer to it simply as *smail*, although there are other versions of it which are entirely different and which we don't describe here.

Compared to *sendmail, smail* is rather young. For handling mail for a small site without complicated routing requirements, their capabilities are pretty close. For large sites, however, *sendmail* always wins, because its configuration scheme is much more flexible.

Both *smail* and *sendmail* support a set of configuration files that have to be customized. Apart from the information that is required to make the mail subsystem run (such as the local hostname), there are many more parameters that may be tuned. *sendmail*'s main configuration file is very hard to understand at first. It looks as if your cat has taken a nap on your keyboard with the shift key pressed. *smail* configuration files are more structured and easier to understand than *sendmail*'s, but don't give the user as much power in tuning the mailer's behavior. However, for small UUCP or Internet sites, the work required in setting up any of them is roughly the same.

In this chapter, we deal with what email is and what issues you as an administrator have to deal with. Chapter 14, *Getting smail Up and Running*, and Chapter 15, *Sendmail+IDA*, will give instructions on setting up *smail* and *sendmail* for the first time. The information provided there should suffice to get smaller sites operational, but there are many more options, and you can spend many happy hours in front of your computer configuring the fanciest features.

Toward the end of this chapter we briefly cover setting up *elm*, a very common mail user agent on many UNIXish systems, including Linux.

email HOWTO

For more information about issues specific to electronic mail on Linux, please refer to the Electronic Mail HOWTO by Vince Skahan, which is posted to *comp.os.linux.announce* regularly. The source distributions of *elm*, *smail*, and *sendmail* also contain very extensive documentation that should answer most of your questions on setting them up. If you are looking for information on email in general, a number of RFCs deal with this topic. They are listed in the bibliography at the end of the book.

What Is a Mail Message?

A mail message generally consists of a message body, which is the text of the message, and special data specifying recipients, transport medium, etc., very much like what you see when you look at a letter's envelope.

This administrative data falls into two categories. In the first category is any data that is specific to the transport medium, like the address of sender and recipient. It is therefore called the *envelope*. It may be transformed by the transport software as the message is passed along.

The second variety is any data necessary for handling the mail message, which is not particular to any transport mechanism, such as the message's subject line, a list of all recipients, and the date the message was sent. In many networks, it has become standard to prepend this data to the mail message, forming the so-called *mail header*. It is offset from the *mail body* by an empty line.[*]

---

[*] It is customary to append a *signature* or *.sig* to a mail message, usually containing information on the author, along with a joke or a motto. It is offset from the mail message by a line containing "– –" followed by a space.

RFC 822

Most mail transport software in the UNIX world uses a header format outlined in RFC 822. Its original purpose was to specify a standard for use on the ARPANET, but since it was designed to be independent from any environment, it has been easily adapted to other networks, including many UUCP-based networks.

RFC 822 is only the lowest common denominator however. More recent standards have been conceived to cope with growing needs such as data encryption, international character set support, and multi-media mail extensions (MIME).

In all these standards, the header consists of several lines, separated by newline characters. A line is made up of a field name, beginning in column one, and the field itself, offset by a colon and white space. The format and semantics of each field vary depending on the field name. A header field can be continued across a newline if the next line begins with a TAB. Fields can appear in any order.

A typical mail header may look like this:

```
From brewhq.swb.de!ora.com!andyo Wed Apr 13 00:17:03 1994
Return-Path: <brewhq.swb.de!ora.com!andyo>
Received: from brewhq.swb.de by monad.swb.de with uucp
        (Smail3.1.28.1 #6) id m0pqqlT-00023aB; Wed, 13 Apr 94 00:17 MET DST
Received: from ora.com (ruby.ora.com) by brewhq.swb.de with smtp
        (Smail3.1.28.1 #28.6) id <m0pqoQr-0008qhC>; Tue, 12 Apr 94 21:47 MEST
Received: by ruby.ora.com (8.6.8/8.6.4) id RAA26438; Tue, 12 Apr 94 15:56 -0400
Date: Tue, 12 Apr 1994 15:56:49 -0400
Message-Id: <199404121956.PAA07787@ruby>
From: andyo@ora.com (Andy Oram)
To: okir@monad.swb.de
Subject: Re: Your RPC section
```

Usually, all necessary header fields are generated by the mailer interface you use, like *elm*, *pine*, *mush*, or *mailx*. However, some are optional and may be added by the user. *elm*, for example, allows you to edit part of the message header. Others are added by the mail transport software. A list of common header fields and their meanings are given below:

From:
   This contains the sender's email address, and possibly the "real name." A complete zoo of formats is used here.

To:
   This is the recipient's email address.

Subject:
   Describes the content of the mail in a few words. At least that's what it *should* do.

Date:
   The date the mail was sent.

Reply-To:
> Specifies the address the sender wants the recipient's reply directed to. This may be useful if you have several accounts, but want to receive the bulk of mail only on the one you use most frequently. This field is optional.

Organization:
> The organization that owns the machine from which the mail originates. If your machine is owned by you privately, either leave this out, or insert "private" or some complete nonsense. This field is optional.

Message-ID:
> A string generated by mail transport on the originating system. It is unique to this message.

Received:
> Every site that processes your mail (including the machines of sender and recipient) inserts such a field into the header, giving its site name, a message ID, time and date it received the message, which site it is from, and which transport software was used. This is so that you can trace which route the message took, and can complain to the person responsible if something went wrong.

X-*anything:*
> No mail-related programs should complain about any header which starts with X-. It is used to implement additional features that have not yet made it into an RFC, or never will. This is used by the Linux Activists mailing list, for example, where the channel is selected by the X-Mn-Key: header field.

The one exception to this structure is the very first line. It starts with the keyword From, which is followed by a blank instead of a colon. To distinguish it from the ordinary From: field, it is frequently referred to as From_. It contains the route the message has taken in UUCP bang-path style (explained below), time and date it was received by the last machine that processed it, and an optional part specifying which host it was received from. Since this field is regenerated by every system that processes the message, it is somtimes subsumed under the envelope data.

The From_ field is there for backwards compatibility with some older mailers; it is not used very much anymore except by mail user interfaces that rely on it to mark the beginning of a message in the user's mailbox. To avoid potential trouble with lines in the message body that also begin with "From ", it has become standard procedure to escape any such occurrence by preceding it with a > character.

How Is Mail Delivered?

Generally, you will compose mail using a mailer interface like *mail* or *mailx*, or more sophisticated ones like *elm*, *mush*, or *pine*. These programs are called *mail user agents*, or MUAs. If you send a mail message, the interface program will in most cases hand it to another program for delivery. This is called the *mail transport agent*, or MTA. On some systems, there are different mail transport agents for local and remote delivery; on others, there is only one. The command for remote delivery is usually called *rmail*, the other is called *lmail* (if it exists).

Local delivery of mail is, of course, more than just appending the incoming message to the recipient's mailbox. Usually, the local MTA will understand aliasing (setting up local recipient addresses pointing to other addresses) and forwarding (redirecting a user's mail to some other destination). Also, messages that cannot be delivered must usually be *bounced*, returned to the sender along with some error message.

RFC 821

For remote delivery, the transport software used depends on the nature of the link. If the mail must be delivered over a network using TCP/IP, SMTP is commonly used. SMTP stands for *Simple Mail Transfer Protocol*. SMTP usually connects to the recipient's machine directly, negotiating the message transfer with the remote side's SMTP daemon.

In UUCP networks, mail will usually not be delivered directly, but rather be forwarded to the destination host by a number of intermediate systems. To send a message over a UUCP link, the sending MTA will usually execute *rmail* on the forwarding system using *uux*, and feed it the message on standard input.

Since this is done for each message separately, it may produce a considerable work load on a major mail hub, as well as clutter the UUCP spool queues with hundreds of small files taking up an unproportional amount of disk space.[*] Some MTAs therefore allow you to collect several messages for a remote system in a single batch file. The batch file contains the SMTP commands that the local host would normally issue if a direct SMTP connection was used. This is called BSMTP, or *batched* SMTP. The batch is then fed to the *rsmtp* or *bsmtp* program on the remote system, which will process the input as if a normal SMTP connection has occurred.

Email Addresses

For electronic mail, an address is made up of at least the name of a machine handling the person's mail and a user identification recognized by this system. This may be the recipient's login name, but may also be anything else. Other mail addressing schemes, like X.400, use a more general set of "attributes" which are used to look up the recipient's host in an X.500 directory server.

The way a machine name is interpreted, i.e., at which site your message will finally wind up, and how to combine this name with the recipient's username greatly depends on the network you are on.

---

[*] This is because disk space is usually allocated in blocks of 1024 bytes. So even a message of at most 400 bytes will eat a full kilobyte.

RFC 822

Internet sites adhere to the RFC 822 standard, which requires a notation of *user@host.domain*, where *host.domain* is the host's fully qualified domain name. The middle thing is called an "at" sign. Because this notation does not involve a route to the destination host but gives the (unique) hostname instead, it is called an *absolute* address.

In the original UUCP environment, the prevalent form was *path!host!user*, where *path* described a sequence of hosts the message had to travel before reaching the destination *host*. This construct is called the *bang path* notation, because an exclamation mark is loosely called a "bang." Today, many UUCP-based networks have adopted RFC 822 and understand this type of address.

Now, these two types of addressing don't mix too well. Assume an address of *hostA!user@hostB*. It is not clear whether the @ sign takes precedence over the path, or vice versa: do we have to send the message to *hostB*, which mails it to *hostA!user*, or should it be sent to *hostA*, which fowards it to *user@hostB*?

Addresses that mix different types of address operators are called *hybrid addresses*. Most notorious is the above example. It is usually resolved by giving the @ sign precedence over the path. In the above example, this means sending the message to *hostB* first.

However, there is a way to specify routes in RFC 822-conformant ways: *<@hostA,@hostB:user@hostC>* denotes the address of *user* on *hostC*, where *hostC* is to be reached through *hostA* and *hostB* (in that order). This type of address is frequently called a *route-addr address*.

Then, there is the % address operator: *user%hostB@hostA* will first be sent to *hostA*, which expands the rightmost (in this case, the only) percent sign to an @ sign. The address is now **user@hostB**, and the mailer will happily forward your message to *hostB*, which delivers it to *user*. This type of address is sometimes referred to as "Ye Olde ARPAnet Kludge," and its use is discouraged. Nevertheless, many mail transport agents nevertheless generate this type of address.

Other networks have still different means of addressing. DECnet-based networks, for example, use two colons as an address separator, yielding an address of *host::user*.[*] Lastly, the X.400 standard uses an entirely different scheme, describing a recipient by a set of attribute-value pairs, like country and organization.

On FidoNet, each user is identified by a code like **2:320/204.9**, consisting of four numbers denoting zone (2 is for Europe), net (320 being Paris and Banlieue), node (the local hub), and point (the individual user's PC). Fidonet addresses can be mapped to RFC 822; the above would be written as *Thomas.Quinot@p9.f2-04.n320.z2.fidonet.org*. Now didn't I say domain names were easy to remember?

---

[*] When trying to reach a DECnet address from an RFC 822 environment, you can use *"host::user"@relay*, where *relay* is the name of a known Internet-DECnet relay.

There are some implications to using these different types of addressing that will be described throughout the following sections. In an RFC 822 environment, however, you will rarely use anything other than absolute addresses such as *user@host.domain.*

How Does Mail Routing Work?

The process of directing a message to the recipient's host is called *routing*. Apart from finding a path from the sending site to the destination, it involves error checking as well as speed and cost optimization.

There is a big difference between the way a UUCP site handles routing and the way an Internet site does. On the Internet, the main job of directing data to the recipient host (once it is known by it's IP address) is done by the IP networking layer, while in the UUCP zone, the route has to be supplied by the user or generated by the mail transfer agent.

Mail Routing on the Internet

On the Internet, it depends entirely on the destination host whether any specific mail routing is performed at all. The default is to deliver the message to the destination host directly by looking up its IP address and leave the actual routing of the data to the IP transport layer.

Most sites will usually want to direct all inbound mail to a highly available mail server that is capable of handling all this traffic and have it distribute this mail locally. To announce this service, the site publishes a so-called MX record for their local domain in the DNS database. MX stands for *Mail Exchanger* and basically states that the server host is willing to act as a mail forwarder for all machines in this domain. MX records can also be used to handle traffic for hosts that are not connected to the Internet themselves, like UUCP networks, or company networks with hosts carrying confidential information.

MX records also have a *preference* associated with them. This is a positive integer. If several mail exchangers exist for one host, the mail transport agent will try to transfer the message to the exchanger with the lowest preference value, and only if this fails will it try a host with a higher value. If the local host is itself a mail exchanger for the destination address, it must not forward messages to MX hosts with a higher preference than its own; this is a safe way of avoiding mail loops.

Suppose that an organization, say Foobar, Inc., wants all their mail handled by their machine **mailhub**. They will then have MX records like this in the DNS database:

```
green.foobar.com.       IN  MX    5    mailhub.foobar.com.
```

This announces **mailhub.foobar.com** as a mail exchanger for **green.foobar.com** with a preference of 5. A host that wishes to deliver a message to *joe@green.foobar.com* will check DNS, and finds the MX record pointing at **mailhub**. If there's no MX with a preference smaller than 5, the message will be delivered to **mailhub**, which then dispatches it to **green**.

RFC 974

The above is really only a sketch of how MX records work. For more information on mail routing on the Internet, refer to RFC 974.

Mail Routing in the UUCP World

Mail routing on UUCP networks is much more complicated than on the Internet because the transport software does not perform any routing itself. In earlier times, all mail had to be addressed using bang paths. Bang paths specified a list of hosts through which to forward the message, separated by exclamation marks and followed by the user's name. To address a letter to Janet User on a machine named **moria**, you would have used the path *eek!swim!moria!janet*. Whis would have sent the mail from your host to **eek**, from there on to **swim**, and finally to **moria**.

The obvious drawback of this technique is that it requires you to remember much about the network topology, fast links, etc. Much worse than that, changes in the network topology—like links being deleted or hosts being removed—may cause messages to fail simply because you aren't aware of the change. And finally, in case you move to a different place, you will most likely have to update all these routes.

One thing, however, that made the use of source routing necessary was the presence of ambiguous hostnames. For instance, assume there are two sites named **moria**, one in the U.S. and one in France. Which site does *moria!janet* refer to now? This can be made clear by specifying what path to reach **moria** through.

The first step in disambiguating hostnames was the founding of the UUCP Mapping Project. It is located at Rutgers University and registers all official UUCP hostnames, along with information on their UUCP neighbors and their geographic location, making sure no hostname is used twice. The information gathered by the Mapping Project is published as the *Usenet Maps*, which are distributed regularly through Usenet.* A typical system entry in a map (after removing the comments) looks like this:

```
moria
        bert(DAILY/2),
        swim(WEEKLY)
```

This entry says that **moria** has a link to **bert**, which it calls twice a day, and **swim**, which it calls weekly. We will come back to the map file format in more detail below.

---

* Maps for sites registered with the UUCP Mapping Project are distributed through the newsgroup *comp.mail.maps*; other organizations may publish separate maps for their networks.

Using the connectivity information provided in the maps, you can automatically generate the full paths from your host to any destination site. This information is usually stored in the *paths* file, also called the *pathalias database*. Assume the maps state that you can reach **bert** through **ernie**; then a pathalias entry for **moria** generated from the map snippet above may look like this:

```
moria          ernie!bert!moria!%s
```

If you now give a destination address of *janet@moria.uucp*, your MTA will pick the route shown above and send the message to **ernie** with an envelope address of *bert!moria!janet*.

Building a *paths* file from the full Usenet maps is not a very good idea however. The information provided in them is usually rather distorted and occasionally out of date. Therefore, only a number of major hosts use the complete UUCP world maps to build their *paths* files. Most sites only maintain routing information for sites in their neighborhood and send any mail to sites they don't find in their databases to a smarter host with more complete routing information. This scheme is called *smart-host routing*. Hosts that have only one UUCP mail link (so-called *leaf sites*) don't do any routing of their own; they rely entirely on their smart host.

Mixing UUCP and RFC 822

The best cure against the problems of mail routing in UUCP networks so far is the adoption of the domain name system in UUCP networks. Of course, you can't query a name server over UUCP. Nevertheless, many UUCP sites have formed small domains that coordinate their routing internally. In the maps, these domains announce one or two hosts as their mail gateways so that there doesn't have to be a map entry for each host in the domain. The gateways handle all mail that flows into and out of the domain. The routing scheme inside the domain is completely invisible to the outside world.

This works very well with the smart-host routing scheme described above. Global routing information is maintained by the gateways only; minor hosts within a domain will get along with only a small hand written *paths* file that lists the routes inside their domain and the route to the mail hub. Even the mail gateways do not have to have routing information for every single UUCP host in the world anymore. Besides the complete routing information for the domain they serve, they only need to have routes to entire domains in their databases now. For instance, this pathalias entry will route all mail for sites in the **sub.org** domain to **smurf**:

```
.sub.org       swim!smurf!%s
```

Mail addressed to *claire@jones.sub.org* will be sent to **swim** with an envelope address of *smurf!jones!claire*.

The hierarchical organization of the domain name space allows mail servers to mix more specific routes with less specific ones. For instance, a system in France may have specific routes for subdomains of **fr**, but route any mail for hosts in the **us** domain toward some system in the U.S. In this way, domain-based routing (as this technique is called) greatly reduces the size of routing databases as well as the administrative overhead needed.

[] RFC 822

The main benefit of using domain names in a UUCP environment, however, is that compliance with RFC 822 permits easy gatewaying between UUCP networks and the Internet. Many UUCP domains nowadays have a link with an Internet gateway that acts as their smart host. Sending messages across the Internet is faster, and routing information is much more reliable because Internet hosts can use DNS instead of the Usenet Maps.

In order to be reachable from the Internet, UUCP-based domains usually have their Internet gateway announce an MX record for them (MX records were described above). For instance, assume that **moria** belongs to the **orcnet.org** domain. **gcc2.groucho.edu** acts as their Internet gateway. **moria** would therefore use **gcc2** as its smart host so that all mail for foreign domains is delivered across the Internet. On the other hand, **gcc2** would announce an MX record for ***.orcnet.org** and deliver all incoming mail for **orcnet** sites to **moria**. The asterisk in ***.orcnet.org** is a wildcard that matches all hosts in that domain that don't have any other record associated with them. This should normally be the case for UUCP-only domains.

The only remaining problem is that the UUCP transport programs can't deal with fully qualified domain names. Most UUCP suites were designed to cope with site names of up to eight characters, some even less, and using non-alphanumeric characters such as dots is completely out of the question for most.

Therefore, some mapping between RFC 822 names and UUCP hostnames is needed. The way this mapping is done is completely implementation-dependent. One common way of mapping FQDNs to UUCP names is to use the pathalias file:

```
moria.orcnet.org  ernie!bert!moria!%s
```

This will produce a pure UUCP-style bang path from an address that specifies a fully qualified domain name. Some mailers provide a special file for this; *sendmail*, for instance, uses the *uucpxtable*.

The reverse transformation (colloquially called domainizing) is sometimes required when sending mail from a UUCP network to the Internet. As long as the mail sender uses the fully qualified domain name in the destination address, this problem can be avoided by not removing the domain name from the envelope address when forwarding the message to the smart host. However, there are still some UUCP sites that are not part of any domain. They are usually domainized by appending the pseudo-domain **uucp**.

The pathalias database provides the main routing information in UUCP-based networks. A typical entry looks like this (site name and path are separated by TABs):

```
moria.orcnet.org    ernie!bert!moria!%s
moria               ernie!bert!moria!%s
```

This makes any message to **moria** be delivered via **ernie** and **bert**. Both **moria**'s fully qualified name and its UUCP name have to be given if the mailer does not have a separate way to map between these name spaces.

If you want to direct all messages to hosts inside some domain to its mail relay, you may also specify a path in the pathalias database, giving the domain name as target, preceded by a dot. For example, if all hosts in **sub.org** can be reached through **swim!smurf**, the pathalias entry might look like this:

```
.sub.org        swim!smurf!%s
```

Writing a pathalias file is acceptable only when you are running a site that does not have to do much routing. If you have to do routing for a large number of hosts, a better way is to use the *pathalias* command to create the file from map files. Maps can be maintained much easier, because you may simply add or remove a system by editing the system's map entry, and recreate the map file. Although the maps published by the Usenet Mapping Project aren't used for routing very much anymore, smaller UUCP networks may provide routing information in their own set of maps.

A map file mainly consists of a list of sites, listing the sites each system polls or is polled by. The system name begins in column one and is followed by a comma-separated list of links. The list may be continued across newlines if the next line begins with a tab. Each link consists of the name of the site followed by a cost given in brackets. The cost is an arithmetic expression made up of numbers and symbolic costs. Lines beginning with a hash sign are ignored.

As an example, consider **moria**, which polls **swim.twobirds.com** twice a day, and **bert.sesame.com** once per week. Moreover, the link to **bert** uses a slow 2400 bps modem. **moria** would publish the following maps entry:

```
moria.orcnet.org
        swim.twobirds.com(DAILY/2),
        bert.sesame.com(WEEKLY+LOW)
moria.orcnet.org = moria
```

The last line would make it known under its UUCP name, too. Note that it must be DAILY/2, because calling twice a day actually halves the cost for this link.

Using the information from such map files, *pathalias* is able to calculate optimal routes to any destination site listed in the paths file and produce a pathalias database from this which can then be used for routing to these sites.

pathalias provides a couple of other features like site-hiding (i.e., making sites accessible only through a gateway), etc. See the manual page for *pathalias* for details, as well as a complete list of link costs.

Comments in the map file generally contain additional information on the sites described in it. There is a rigid format in which to specify this information so that it can be retrieved from the maps. For instance, a program called *uuwho* uses a database created from the map files to display this information in a nicely formatted way.

When you register your site with an organization that distributes map files to its members, you generally have to fill out such a map entry.

Below is a sample map entry (in fact, it's the one for my site):

```
#N      monad, monad.swb.de, monad.swb.sub.org
#S      AT 486DX50; Linux 0.99
#O      private
#C      Olaf Kirch
#E      okir@monad.swb.de
#P      Kattreinstr. 38, D-64295 Darmstadt, FRG
#L      49 52 03 N / 08 38 40 E
#U      brewhq
#W      okir@monad.swb.de (Olaf Kirch); Sun Jul 25 16:59:32 MET DST 1993
#
monad   brewhq(DAILY/2)
# Domains
monad = monad.swb.de
monad = monad.swb.sub.org
```

The white space after the first two characters is a TAB. The meaning of most of the fields is pretty obvious; you will receive a detailed description from whichever domain you register with. The L field is the most fun to find out: it gives your geographical position in latitude/longitude and is used to draw the PostScript maps that show all sites for each country, as well as world-wide.[*]

Configuring elm

elm stands for "electronic mail" and is one of the more reasonably named UNIX tools. It provides a full-screen interface with a good help feature. We won't discuss here how to use *elm*, but only dwell on its configuration options.

Theoretically, you can run *elm* unconfigured, and everything works well—if you are lucky. But there are a few options that must be set, although they are only required on occasion.

When it starts, *elm* reads a set of configuration variables from the *elm.rc* file in */usr/lib/elm*. Then it will attempt to read the file *.elm/elmrc* in your home directory. You don't usually write this file yourself. It is created when you choose "save options" from *elm*'s options menu.

---

[*] They are posted regularly in *news.lists.ps-maps*. Beware. They're HUGE.

The set of options for the private *elmrc* file is also available in the global *elm.rc* file. Most settings in your private *elmrc* file override those of the global file.

Global elm Options

In the global *elm.rc* file, you must set the options that pertain to your host's name. For example, at the Virtual Brewery, the file for **vlager** would contain the following:

```
#
# The local hostname
hostname = vlager
#
# Domain name
hostdomain = .vbrew.com
#
# Fully qualified domain name
hostfullname = vlager.vbrew.com
```

These options set *elm*'s idea of the local hostname. Although this information is rarely used, you should set these options nevertheless. Note that these options only take effect when giving them in the global configuration file; when found in your private *elmrc*, they will be ignored.

National Character Sets

Recently, there have been proposals to amend the RFC 822 standard to support various types of messages, such as plain text, binary data, Postscript files, etc. The set of standards and RFCs covering these aspects are commonly referred to as MIME, or Multipurpose Internet Mail Extensions. Among other things, this also lets the recipient know if a character set other than standard ASCII has been used when writing the message, for example, using French accents or German umlauts. This is supported by *elm* to some extent.

The character set used by Linux internally to represent characters is usually referred to as ISO-8859-1, which is the name of the standard it conforms to. It is also known as Latin-1. Any message using characters from this character set should have the following line in its header:

```
Content-Type: text/plain; charset=iso-8859-1
```

The receiving system should recognize this field and take appropriate measures when displaying the message. The default for `text/plain` messages is a `charset` value of `us-ascii`.

To be able to display messages with character sets other than ASCII, *elm* must know how to print these characters. By default, when *elm* receives a message with a `charset` field other than `us-ascii` (or a content type other than `text/plain`, for that matter), it tries to display the message using a command called *metamail*.

Messages that require *metamail* to be displayed are shown with an *M* in the very first column in the overview screen.

Since Linux's native character set is ISO-8859-1, calling *metamail* is not necessary to display messages using this character set. If *elm* is told that the display understands ISO-8859-1, it will not use *metamail* but will display the message directly instead. This can be done by setting the following option in the global *elm.rc*:

```
displaycharset = iso-8859-1
```

Note that you should set this option even when you are never going to send or receive any messages that actually contain characters other than ASCII. This is because people who do send such messages usually configure their mailer to put the proper Content-Type: field into the mail header by default, whether or not they are sending ASCII-only messages.

However, setting this option in *elm.rc* is not enough. The problem is that when displaying the message with its built-in pager, *elm* calls a library function for each character to determine whether it is printable or not. By default, this function will only recognize ASCII characters as printable and display all other characters as ^?. You may overcome this by setting the environment variable LC_CTYPE to ISO-8859-1, which tells the library to accept Latin-1 characters as printable. Support for this and other features is available since *libc-4.5.8*.

When sending messages that contain special characters from ISO-8859-1, you should make sure to set two more variables in the *elm.rc* file:

```
charset = iso-8859-1
textencoding = 8bit
```

This makes *elm* report the character set as ISO-8859-1 in the mail header and send it as an 8-bit value (the default is to strip all characters to 7-bit).

Of course, any of these options can also be set in the private *elmrc* file instead of the global one.

CHAPTER FOURTEEN
GETTING SMAIL
UP AND RUNNING

Τhis chapter gives you a quick introduction to setting up *smail* and an overview of the functionality it provides. Although *smail* is largely compatible with *sendmail* in its behavior, its configuration files are completely different.

The main configuration file is */usr/lib/smail/config*. You always have to edit this file to reflect values specific to your site. If you are only a UUCP leaf site, you will have relatively little else to do, ever. Other files that configure routing and transport options may also be used; they will be dealt with briefly, too.

By default, *smail* processes and delivers all incoming mail immediately. If you have relatively high traffic, you may instead have *smail* collect all messages in the so-called *queue*, and process them at regular intervals only.

When handling mail within a TCP/IP network, *smail* is frequently run in daemon mode: at system boot time, it is invoked from *rc.inet2* and puts itself in the background where it waits for incoming TCP connections on the SMTP port (usually port 25). This is very beneficial whenever you expect to have a significant amount of traffic, because *smail* isn't started up separately for every incoming connection. The alternative would be to have *inetd* manage the SMTP port and have it spawn *smail* whenever there is a connection on this port.

smail has several flags that control its behavior; describing them in detail here wouldn't help you much. Fortunately, *smail* supports a number of standard modes of operation that are enabled when you invoke it by a special command name, like *rmail* or *smtpd*. Usually, these aliases are symbolic links to the *smail* binary itself. We will encounter most of them when discussing the various features of *smail*.

There are two links to *smail* that you should have under all circumstances: */usr/bin/rmail* and */usr/sbin/sendmail*.[*] When you compose and send a mail mes-

---

* This is the new standard location of *sendmail* according to the Linux File System Standard. Another common location is */usr/lib*.

sage with a user agent like *elm*, the message will be piped into *rmail* for delivery, with the recipient list given to it on the command line. The same happens with mail coming in via UUCP. Some versions of *elm*, however, invoke */usr/sbin/send-mail* instead of *rmail*, so you need both of them. For example, if you keep *smail* in */usr/local/bin*, type the following at the shell prompt:

```
# ln -s /usr/local/bin/smail /usr/bin/rmail
# ln -s /usr/local/bin/smail /usr/sbin/sendmail
```

smail(1)
smail(5)

If you want to dig further into the details of configuring *smail*, refer to the manual pages *smail(1)* and *smail(5)*. If they aren't included in your favorite Linux distribution, you can get them from the source to *smail*.

UUCP Setup

To use *smail* in a UUCP-only environment, the basic installation is simple. First, you must make sure you have the two symbolic links to *rmail* and *sendmail* mentioned above. If you expect to receive SMTP batches from other sites, you also have to make *rsmtp* a link to *smail*.

Vince Skahan's *smail* distribution includes sample configuration file. It is named *config.sample* and resides in */usr/lib/smail*. You have to copy it to *config* and edit it to reflect values specific to your site.

Assume your site is named **swim.twobirds.com** and is registered in the UUCP maps as **swim**. Your smart host is **ulysses**. Then your *config* file should look like this:

```
#
# Our domain names
visible_domain=two.birds:uucp
#
# Our name on outgoing mails
visible_name=swim.twobirds.com
#
# Use this as uucp-name as well
uucp_name=swim.twobirds.com
#
# Our smart host
smart_host=ulysses
```

The first statement tells *smail* about the domains your site belongs to. Insert their names here, separated by colons. If your sitename is registered in the UUCP maps, you should also add uucp. When being handed a mail message, *smail* determines your host's name using the *hostname* system call and checks the recipient's address against this hostname, tacking on all names from this list in turn. If the address matches any of these names or the unqualified hostname, the recipient is considered local, and *smail* attempts to deliver the message to a user or alias on the local host. Otherwise, the recipient is considered remote, and delivery to the destination host is attempted.

`visible_name` should contain a single, fully qualified domain name for your site that you want to use on outgoing mail. This name is used when generating the sender's address on all outgoing mail. You must make sure to use a name that *smail* recognizes as referring to the local host (i.e., the hostname with one of the domains listed in the `visible_domain` attribute). Otherwise, replies to your mail will bounce off your site.

The last statement sets the path used for smart-host routing (described in the last chapter). With this sample setup, *smail* will forward any mail for remote addresses to the smart host. The path specified in the `smart_path` attribute will be used as a route to the smart host. Since messages will be delivered via UUCP, the attribute must specify a system known to your UUCP software. Refer to Chapter 12, *Managing Taylor UUCP*, on making a site known to UUCP.

One option in the above file hasn't been explained yet; this is `uucp_name`. The reason to use the option is that by default, *smail* uses the value returned by *hostname* for UUCP-specific information such as the return path given in the `From_` header line. If your hostname is *not* registered with the UUCP Mapping Project, you should tell *smail* to use your fully qualified domain name instead.* This can be done by adding the `uucp_name` option to the *config* file.

Another file in */usr/lib/smail* is *paths.sample*. It is an example of what a *paths* file might look like. However, you will not need one unless you have mail links to more than one site. If you do, however, you will have to write one yourself or generate one from the Usenet maps. The *paths* file will be described later in this chapter.

Setup for a LAN

If you are running a site with two or more hosts connected by a LAN, you will have to designate one host to handle your UUCP connection to the outside world. Between the hosts on your LAN, you will probably want to exchange mail with SMTP over TCP/IP. Assume we're back at the Virtual Brewery again, and **vstout** is set up as the UUCP gateway.

In a networked environment, it is best to keep all user mailboxes on a single file system that is NFS-mounted on all other hosts. This allows users to move from machine to machine, without having to move their mail around (or even worse, check three or four machines for newly-arrived mail each morning). Therefore, you also want to make sender addresses independent from the machine the mail is written on. It is common practice to use the domain name all by itself in the

---

* The reason is this: Assume your hostname is **monad**, but it is not registered in the maps. However, there is a site in the maps called **monad**, so all mail to **monad!root**, even if sent from a direct UUCP neighbor of yours, will wind up on the other **monad**.

sender address, instead of a hostname. Janet User, for example, would specify *janet@vbrew.com* instead of *janet@vale.vbrew.com*. We explain below how to make the server recognize the domain name as a valid name for your site.

A different way of keeping all mailboxes on a central host is to use POP or IMAP. POP stands for *Post Office Protocol* and lets users access their mailboxes over a simple TCP/IP conection. IMAP, the *Interactive Mail Access Protocol*, is similar to POP, but more general. Clients and servers for IMAP and POP have been ported to Linux and are available from **sunsite.unc.edu** below */pub/Linux/system/Network*.

Writing the Configuration Files

The configuration for the Brewery works as follows. All hosts except the mail server itself (**vstout**) route all outgoing mail to the server using smart-host routing. **vstout** itself sends all outgoing mail to the real smart host that routes all of the Brewery's mail; this host is called **moria**.

The standard *config* file for all hosts other than **vstout** looks like this:

```
#
# Our domain:
visible_domain=vbrew.com
#
# What we name ourselves
visible_name=vbrew.com
#
# Smart-host routing: via SMTP to vstout
smart_path=vstout
smart_transport=smtp
```

This is very similar to what we used for a UUCP-only site. The main difference is that the transport used to send mail to the smart host is, of course, SMTP. The `visible_domain` attribute makes *smail* use the domain name instead of the local hostname on all outgoing mail.

On the UUCP mail gateway **vstout**, the *config* file looks a little different:

```
#
# Our hostnames:
hostnames=vbrew.com:vstout.vbrew.com:vstout
#
# What we name ourselves
visible_name=vbrew.com
#
# in the uucp world, we're known as vbrew.com
uucp_name=vbrew.com
#
# Smart transport: via uucp to moria
smart_path=moria
smart_transport=uux
#
```

```
# we're authoritative for our domain
auth_domains=vbrew.com
```

This *config* file uses a different scheme to tell *smail* what the local host is called. Instead of giving it a list of domains and letting it find the hostname with a system call, it specifies a list explicitly. The above list contains both the fully qualified and the unqualified hostname, and the domain name all by itself. This makes *smail* recognize *janet@vbrew.com* as a local address and deliver the message to *janet*.

The `auth_domains` variable names the domains for which **vstout** is considered to be authoritative. That is, if *smail* receives any mail addressed to **host.vbrew.com** where **host** does not name an existing local machine, it rejects the message and returns it to the sender. If this entry isn't present, any such message will be sent to the smart host, who will return it to **vstout** and so on. (Luckily, a feature called the *maximum hop count* allows a host to finally discard the message.)

Running smail

First, you have to decide whether to run *smail* as a separate daemon, or whether to have *inetd* manage the SMTP port and invoke *smail* only whenever an SMTP connection is requested from some client. Usually, you will prefer daemon operation on the mail server because it loads the machine far less than spawning *smail* over and over again for each single connection. As the mail server also delivers most incoming mail directly to the users, you will choose *inetd* operation on most other hosts.

Whatever mode of operation you choose for each individual host, you have to make sure you have the following entry in your */etc/services* file:

```
smtp            25/tcp          # Simple Mail Transfer Protocol
```

This defines the TCP port number that *smail* should use for SMTP conversations. Port number 25 is the standard defined by the Assigned Numbers RFC.

When run in daemon mode, *smail* puts itself in the background and waits for a connection to occur on the SMTP port. When a connection occurs, it forks and conducts an SMTP conversation with the peer process. The *smail* daemon is usually started by invoking it from the *rc.inet2* script using the following command:

```
/usr/local/bin/smail -bd -q15m
```

The *−bd* flag turns on daemon mode, and *−q15m* makes it process whatever messages have accumulated in the message queue every 15 minutes.

If you want to use *inetd* instead, your */etc/inetd.conf* file should contain a line like this:

```
smtp    stream  tcp nowait  root  /usr/sbin/smtpd smtpd
```

smtpd should be a symbolic link to the *smail* binary. Remember you have to make *inetd* re-read *inetd.conf* by sending it an HUP signal after making these changes.

Daemon mode and *inetd* mode are mutually exclusive. If you run *smail* in daemon mode, you should make sure to comment out any line in *inetd.conf* for the smtp service. Equivalently, when having *inetd* manage *smail*, make sure that *rc.inet2* does not start the *smail* daemon.

If Your Mail Doesn't Get Through

A number of features are available for troubleshooting installation problems. The first place to check are *smail*'s log files. They are kept in */var/spool/smail/log* and are named *logfile* and *paniclog*. The former lists all transactions, while the latter is only for error messages related to configuration errors and the like.

A typical entry in *logfile* looks like this:

```
04/24/94 07:12:04: [m0puwU8-00023UB] received
|             from: root
|          program: sendmail
|             size: 1468 bytes
04/24/94 07:12:04: [m0puwU8-00023UB] delivered
|              via: vstout.vbrew.com
|               to: root@vstout.vbrew.com
|          orig-to: root@vstout.vbrew.com
|           router: smart_host
|        transport: smtp
```

This shows that a message from **root** to *root@vstout.vbrew.com* has been properly delivered to host **vstout** over SMTP.

Messages *smail* cannot deliver generate a similar entry in the log file, but with an error message instead of the *delivered* part:

```
04/24/94 07:12:04: [m0puwU8-00023UB] received
|             from: root
|          program: sendmail
|             size: 1468 bytes
04/24/94 07:12:04: [m0puwU8-00023UB] root@vstout.vbrew.com ... deferred
   (ERR_148) transport smtp: connect: Connection refused
```

The above error is typical for a situation in which *smail* properly recognizes that the message should be delivered to **vstout** but is not able to connect to the SMTP service on **vstout**. If this happens, you either have a configuration problem, or TCP support is missing from your *smail* binaries.

This problem is not as uncommon as one might think. There have been precompiled *smail* binaries around, even in some Linux distributions, without support for TCP/IP networking. If this is the case for you, you have to compile *smail* yourself. Having installed *smail*, you can check if it has TCP networking support by telnetting to the SMTP port on your machine. This is what a successful connect to the SMTP server looks like:

```
$ telnet localhost smtp
Trying 127.0.0.1...
Connected to localhost.
Escape character is '^]'.
220 monad.swb.de Smail3.1.28.1 #6 ready at Sun, 23 Jan 94 19:26 MET
QUIT
221 monad.swb.de closing connection
```

If this test doesn't produce the SMTP banner (the line starting with the 220 code), first make sure that your configuration is *really* correct before you go through compiling *smail* yourself, which is described below.

If you encounter a problem with *smail* that you are unable to locate from the error message *smail* generates, you may want to turn on debugging messages. You can do this using the −*d* flag optionally followed by a number specifying the level of verbosity (you may not have any space between the flag and the numerical argument). *smail* will then print a report of its operation to the screen, which may give you more hints about what is going wrong.

If nothing else helps, you may want to invoke *smail* in Rogue mode by giving the −*bR* option on the command line. The manpage says on this option: "Enter the hostile domain of giant mail messages, and RFC standard scrolls. Attempt to make it down to protocol level 26 and back." Although this option won't solve your problems, it may provide you some comfort and consolation. ;-)

Compiling smail

If you know for sure that *smail* is lacking TCP network support, you have to get the source. It is probably included in your distribution if you got it via CD ROM; otherwise you can get it from the net via FTP.*

When compiling *smail*, you should start with the set of configuration files from Vince Skahan's *newspak* distribution. To compile in the TCP networking driver, you have to set the DRIVER_CONFIGURATION macro in the *conf/EDITME* file to either bsd-network or arpa-network. The former is suitable for LAN installations, but the Internet requires arpa-network. The difference between these two is that the arpa-network has a special driver for BIND service that is able to recognize MX records, which bsd-network doesn't.

---

* If you got *smail* with a Linux distribution from a vendor, you are entitled to the source code "for a nominal shipping charge," according to *smail*'s copying conditions.

Mail Delivery Modes

As noted above, *smail* is able to deliver messages immediately or queue them for later processing. If you choose to queue messages, *smail* will store away all mail in the *messages* directory below */var/spool/smail*. It will not process them until explicitly told to (this is also called "running the queue").

You can select one of three delivery modes by setting the `delivery_mode` attribute in the *config* file to either `foreground`, `background`, or `queued`. These select delivery in the foreground (immediate processing of incoming messages), in the background (message is delivered by a child of the receiving process, with the parent process exiting immediately after forking), and queued. Incoming mail will always be queued regardless of this option if the boolean variable `queue_only` is set in the *config* file.

If you turn on queuing, you have to make sure the queues are checked regularly, probably every 10 or 15 minutes. If you run *smail* in daemon mode, you have to add the option *–q10m* on the command line to process the queue every 10 minutes. Alternatively, you can invoke *runq* from *cron* at these intervals. *runq* should be a link to *smail*.

You can display the current mail queue by invoking *smail* with the *–bp* option. Equivalently, you can make *mailq* a link to *smail*, and invoke *mailq*:

```
$ mailq -v
m0pvB1r-00023UB  From: root   (in /var/spool/smail/input)
                 Date: Sun, 24 Apr 94 07:12 MET DST
                 Args: -oem -oMP sendmail root@vstout.vbrew.com
Log of transactions:
 Xdefer: <root@vstout.vbrew.com> reason: (ERR_148) transport smtp:
 connect: Connection refused
```

This shows a single message sitting in the message queue. The transaction log (which is only displayed if you give *mailq* the *–v* option) may give an additional reason why it is still waiting for delivery. If no attempt has been made yet to deliver the message, no transaction log will be displayed.

Even when you don't use queuing, *smail* will occasionally put messages into the queue when it finds that immediate delivery fails for a transient reason. For SMTP connections, this may be an unreachable host, but messages may also be deferred when the file system is found to be full. You should therefore put in a queue that is run every hour or so (using *runq*), or else any deferred message will stick around the queue forever.

Miscellaneous config Options

Here are a few of the more useful options you can set in the config file:

error_copy_postmaster
> If this boolean variable is set, any error will generate a message to the post-master. Usually, this is only done for errors that are due to a faulty configuration. The variable can be turned on by putting it in the *config* file, preceded by a plus (+).

max_hop_count
> If the hop count for a message (i.e., the number of hosts already traversed) equals or exceeds this number, attempts at remote delivery will result in an error message being returned to the sender. This is used to prevent messages from looping forever. The hop count is generally computed from the number of Received: fields in the mail header, but may also be set manually using the *−h* option on the command line.
>
> This variable defaults to 20.

postmaster
> The postmaster's address. If the address *Postmaster* cannot be resolved to a valid local address, then this is used as the last resort. The default is *root*.

Message Routing and Delivery

smail splits up mail delivery into three different tasks, the router, director, and transport modules.

The router module resolves all remote addresses, determining which host the message should be sent to next and which transport must be used. Depending on the nature of the link, different transports such as UUCP or SMTP may be used.

Local addresses are given to the director task, which resolves any forwarding or aliasing. For example, the address might be an alias or a mailing list, or the user might want to forward her mail to another address. If the resulting address is remote, it is handed to the router module for additional routing, otherwise it is assigned a transport for local delivery. By far the most common case will be delivery to a mailbox, but messages may also be piped into a command or appended to some arbitrary file.

The transport module is responsible for whatever method of delivery has been chosen. It tries to deliver the message, and in case of failure, either generates a bounce message or defers it for a later retry.

With *smail*, you have much freedom in configuring these tasks. For each of them, a number of drivers are available, from which you can choose those you need. You describe them to *smail* in a couple of files, namely *routers*, *directors*, and *transports*, located in */usr/lib/smail*. If these files do not exist, reasonable defaults are assumed that should be suitable for many sites that use either SMTP or UUCP for transport. If you want to change *smail*'s routing policy or modify a transport, you should get the sample files from the *smail* source distribution,[*] copy the sample files to */usr/lib/smail*, and modify them according to your needs.

Appendix B

Routing Messages

When given a message, *smail* first checks whether the destination is the local host or a remote site. If the target host address is one of the local hostnames configured in *config*, the message is handed to the director module. Otherwise, *smail* hands the destination address to a number of router drivers to find out which host to forward a message to. They can be described in the *routers* file; if this file does not exist, a set of default routers is used.

The destination host is passed to all routers in turn, and the router finding the most specific route is selected. Consider a message addressed to *joe@foo.bar.com*. One router might know a default route for all hosts in the **bar.com** domain, while another one has information for **foo.bar.com** itself. Since the latter is more specific, it is chosen over the former. If there are two routers that provide a "best match," the one coming first in the *routers* file is chosen.

This router now specifies the transport to be used, UUCP for instance, and generates a new destination address. The new address is passed to the transport along with the host to forward the message to. In the above example, *smail* might find out that **foo.bar.com** is to be reached via UUCP using the path *ernie!bert*. It will then generate a new target of *bert!foo.bar.com!user* and have the UUCP transport use this as the envelope address to be passed to **ernie**.

When using the default setup, the following routers are available:

- If the destination host address can be resolved using the *gethostbyname* or *gethostbyaddr* library call, the message will be delivered via SMTP. The only exception is that if the address is found to refer to the local host, it is handed to the director module, too.

  smail also recognizes dotted-quad IP addresses as legal hostnames, as long as they can be resolved through a *gethostbyaddr* call. For example, *scrooge@[149.76.12.4]* would be a valid, although highly unusual, mail address for **scrooge** on **quark.physics.groucho.edu**.

  If your machine is on the Internet, these routers are not what you are looking for because they don't support MX records. See below for what to do in this case.

---

[*] The default configuration files can be found in *samples/generic* below the source directory.

- If */usr/lib/smail/paths*, the pathalias database, exists, *smail* will try to look up the target host (minus any trailing **.uucp**) in this file. Mail to an address matched by this router will be delivered via UUCP using the path found in the database.

- The host address (minus any trailing **.uucp**) will be compared to the output of the *uuname* command to check if the target host is in fact a UUCP neighbor. If this is the case, the message will be delivered using the UUCP transport.

- If the address has not been matched by any of the above routers, it will be delivered to the smart host. The path to the smart host, as well as the transport to be used, are set in the *config* file.

These defaults work for many simple setups but fail if routing requirements get a little more complicated. If you are faced with any of the problems discussed below, you will have to install your own *routers* file to override the defaults. Some Linux distributions come with a set of configuration files that are tailored to work around these difficulties.

Appendix B

Probably the worst problems arise when your host lives in a dual universe with both dialup IP and UUCP links. You will then have hostnames in your *hosts* file that you only occasionally talk to through your SLIP link, so *smail* will attempt to deliver any mail for these hosts via SMTP. This is usually not what you want, because even if the SLIP link is activated regularly, SMTP is much slower than sending the mail over UUCP. With the default setup, there's no way of escaping *smail*.

You can avoid this problem by having *smail* check the *paths* file before querying the resolver and put all hosts you want to force UUCP delivery to into the *paths* file. If you don't want to send any messages over SMTP *ever*, you can also comment out the resolver-based routers altogether.

Another problem is that the default setup doesn't provide for true Internet mail routing, because the resolver-based router does not evaluate MX records. To enable full support for Internet mail routing, comment out the default router and uncomment the one that uses BIND instead. There are, however, *smail* binaries included in some Linux distributions that don't have BIND support compiled in. If you enable BIND but get a message in the *paniclog* file saying "router inet_hosts: driver bind not found," then you have to get the sources and recompile *smail* (see the section "Setup for a LAN" above).

Finally, it is generally not a good idea to use the *uuname* driver. For one thing, it will generate a configuration error when you don't have UUCP installed because no *uuname* command will be found. The second problem comes about when you have more sites listed in your UUCP *sys* file than you actually have mail links with. These may be sites that you only exchange news with or occasionally download files from via anonymous UUCP, but have no traffic with otherwise.

To work around the first problem, you can substitute a shell script for *uuname* which does a simple *exit 0*. The more general solution is, however, to edit the *routers* file and remove this driver altogether.

The paths Database

smail expects to find the pathalias database in the *paths* file below */usr/lib/smail*. This file is optional, so if you don't want to perform any pathalias routing at all, simply remove any existing *paths* file.

paths must be a sorted ASCII file containing entries that map destination site names to UUCP bang paths. The file has to be sorted because *smail* uses a binary search for looking up a site. Comments are not allowed in this file, and the site name must be separated from the path using a TAB. Pathalias databases are discussed in somewhat greater detail in Chapter 13, *Electronic Mail*.

If you generate this file by hand, you should make sure to include all legal names for a site. For example, if a site is known by both a plain UUCP name and a fully qualified domain name, you have to add an entry for each of them. The file can be sorted by piping it through the *sort* command.

If your site is only a leaf site, however, then no *paths* file should be necessary at all; just set up the smart-host attributes in your *config* file, and leave all routing to your mail feed.

Delivering Messages to Local Addresses

Most commonly, a local address is just a user's login name, in which case the message is delivered to the user's mailbox, */var/spool/mailuser-name*. Other cases include aliases and mailing list names, and mail forwarding by the user. In these cases, the local address expands to a new list of addresses, which may be either local or remote.

Apart from these "normal" addresses, *smail* can handle other types of local message destinations, like filenames and pipe commands. These are not addresses in their own right, so you can't send mail to, say, */etc/passwd@vbrew.com*; they are only valid if they have been taken from forwarding or alias files.

A *filename* is anything that begins with a slash (/) or a tilde (˜). The latter refers to the user's home directory and is possible only if the filename is taken from a *.forward* file or a forwarding entry in the mailbox (see below). When delivering to a file, *smail* appends the messages to the file, creating it if necessary.

A *pipe command* may be any UNIX command preceded by the pipe symbol (|). This causes *smail* to hand the command to the shell along with its arguments, but without the leading |. The message itself is fed to this command on standard input.

For example, to gate a mailing list into a local newsgroup, you might use a shell script named *gateit*, and set up a local alias which delivers all messages from this mailing list to the script using *"|gateit"*.

If the invocation contains white space, it has to be enclosed in double quotes. Due to the security issues involved, care is taken not to execute the command if the address has been obtained in a somewhat dubious way (for example, if the alias file from which the address was taken is writable by everyone).

Local Users

The most common case for a local address is to denote a user's mailbox. This mailbox is located in */var/spool/mail* and has the name of the user. It is owned by the user, with a group of **mail**, and has mode 660. If it does not exist, it is created by *smail*.

Note that although */var/spool/mail* is currently the standard place to put the mailbox files, some mail software may have different paths compiled in, for example */usr/spool/mail*. If delivery to users on your machine fails consistently, you should see if it helps to make this a symbolic link to */var/spool/mail*.

Two addresses are required by *smail*: **MAILER-DAEMON** and **postmaster**. When generating a bounce message for an undeliverable mail, a carbon copy is sent to the **postmaster** account for examination (in case this might be due to a configuration problem). The **MAILER-DAEMON** is used as the sender's address on the bounce message.

If these addresses do not name valid accounts on your system, *smail* implicitly maps **MAILER-DAEMON** to **postmaster**, and **postmaster** to **root**, respectively. You should usually override this by aliasing the **postmaster** account to whoever is responsible for maintaining the mail software.

Forwarding

A user may redirect her mail by having it forwarded to an alternative address using one of two methods supported by *smail*. One option is to put

```
Forward to recipient, ...
```

in the first line of her mailbox file. This will send all incoming mail to the specified list of recipients. Alternatively, she might create a *.forward* file in her home directory, which contains the comma-separated list of recipients. With this variety of forwarding, all lines of the file are read and interpreted.

Note that any type of address may be used. Thus, a practical example of a *.forward* file for vacations might be

```
janet, "|vacation"
```

The first address delivers the incoming message to *janet*'s mailbox nevertheless, while the *vacation* command returns a short notification to the sender.

Alias Files

smail is able to handle alias files compatible with those known by Berkeley's *sendmail*. Entries in the alias file can have the following form:

```
alias: recipients
```

recipients is a comma-separated list of addresses that will be substituted for the alias. The recipient list may be continued across newlines if the next line begins with a TAB.

A special feature allows *smail* to handle mailing lists from the alias file: if you specify :include:*filename* as recipient, *smail* will read the specified file and substitute its contents as a list of recipients.

The main aliases file is */usr/lib/aliases*. If you choose to make this file world-writable, *smail* wil not deliver any messages to shell commands given in this file. This is a sample *aliases* file:

```
# vbrew.com /usr/lib/aliases file
hostmaster: janet
postmaster: janet
usenet: phil
# The development mailing list.
development: joe, sue, mark, biff
        /var/mail/log/development
owner-development: joe
# Announcements of general interest are mailed to all
# of the staff
announce: :include: /usr/lib/smail/staff,
        /var/mail/log/announce
owner-announce: root
# gate the foobar mailing list to a local newsgroup
ppp-list: "|/usr/local/lib/gateit local.lists.ppp"
```

If an error occurs while delivering to an address generated from the *aliases* file, *smail* will attempt to send a copy of the error message to the "alias owner." For example, if delivery to *biff* fails when delivering a message to the *development* mailing list, a copy of the error message will be mailed to the sender, as well as to *postmaster* and *owner-development*. If the owner address does not exist, no additional error message will be generated.

When delivering to files or when invoking programs given in the *aliases* file, *smail* will become the **nobody** user to avoid security hassles. This can be a real nuisance, especially when delivering to files. In the file given above, for instance, the log files must be owned and writable by **nobody**, or delivery to them will fail.

Mailing Lists

Instead of using the *aliases* file, mailing lists may also be managed by means of files in the */usr/lib/smail/lists* directory. A mailing list named nag-bugs is described by the file *lists/nag-bugs*, which should contain the members' addresses separated by commas. The list may be given on multiple lines, with comments being introduced by a hash sign.

For each mailing list, a user (or alias) named **owner-***listname* should exist; any errors occurring when resolving an address are reported to this user. This address is also used as the sender's address on all outgoing messages in the Sender: header field.

UUCP-based Transports

A number of transports compiled into *smail* utilize the UUCP suite. In a UUCP environment, messages are usually passed on by invoking *rmail* on the next host, giving it the message on standard input and the envelope address on the command line. On your host, *rmail* should be a link to the *smail* command.

When handing a message to the UUCP transport, *smail* converts the target address to a UUCP bang path. For example, *user@host* will be transformed to *host!user*. Any occurrence of the % address operator is preserved, so *user%host@gateway* will become *gateway!user%host*. However, *smail* will never generate such addresses itself.

Alternatively, *smail* can send and receive BSMTP batches via UUCP. With BSMTP, one or more messages are wrapped up in a single batch that contains the commands the local mailer would issue if a real SMTP connection had been established. BSMTP is frequently used in store-and-forward (e.g., UUCP-based) networks to save disk space. The sample *transports* file in Appendix B, *Sample smail Configuration Files*, contains a transport dubbed bsmtp that generates partial BSMTP batches in a queue directory. They must be combined into the final batches later using a shell script that adds the appropriate HELO and QUIT commands.

smail(5)

To enable the bsmtp transport for specific UUCP links you have to use so-called *method* files. If you have only one UUCP link and use the smart-host router, you enable sending SMTP batches by setting the smart_transport configuration variable to bsmtp instead of uux.

To receive SMTP batches over UUCP, you must make sure that you have the unbatching command the remote site sends its batches to. If the remote site also uses *smail*, you need to make *rsmtp* a link to *smail*. If the remote site runs *sendmail*, you should additionally install a shell script named */usr/bin/bsmtp* that does a simple *exec rsmtp* (a symbolic link won't work).

SMTP-based Transports

smail currently supports an SMTP driver to deliver mail over TCP connections.[*] It is capable of delivering a message to any number of addresses on one single host, with the hostname being specified as either a fully qualified domain name that can be resolved by the networking software, or in dotted quad notation enclosed in square brackets. Generally, addresses resolved by any of the BIND, *gethostbyname*, or *gethostbyaddr* router drivers will be delivered to the SMTP transport.

The SMTP driver will attempt to connect to the remote host immediately through the smtp port as listed in */etc/services*. If it cannot be reached or the connection times out, delivery will be reattempted at a later time.

Delivery on the Internet requires that routes to the destination host be specified in the *route-addr* format described in Chapter 13, rather than as a UUCP bang path.[†] *smail* will therefore transform the address *user%host@gateway*, where **gateway** is reached via *host1!host2!host3*, into the source-route address *<@host2,@host3:user-%host@gateway>* which will be sent as the message's envelope address to *host1*. To enable these transformations (along with the built-in BIND driver), you have to edit the entry for the smtp driver in the *transports* file.

Appendix B

Hostname Qualification

Sometimes it is desirable to catch unqualified hostnames (i.e., those without a domain name) specified in sender or recipient addresses, for example, when gatewaying between two networks, where one requires fully qualified domain names. On an Internet-UUCP relay, unqualified hostnames should be mapped to the **uucp** domain by default. Address modifications other than these are questionable.

The */usr/lib/smail/qualify* file tells *smail* which domain names to tack onto which hostnames. Entries in the *qualify* file consist of a hostname beginning in column one, followed by the domain name. Lines containing a hash sign as the first non-white character are considered comments. Entries are searched in the order they appear in.

---

[*] The authors call this support "simple". For a future version of *smail*, they advertise a complete backend which will handle this more efficiently.

[†] However, the use of routes in the Internet is discouraged altogether. Fully qualified domain names should be used instead.

If no *qualify* file exists, no hostname qualification is performed at all.

A special hostname of * matches any hostname, thus enabling you to map all hosts not mentioned before into a default domain. It should be used only as the last entry.

At the Virtual Brewery, all hosts have been set up to use fully qualified domain names in the sender's addresses. Unqualified recipient addresses are considered to be in the **uucp** domain, so only a single entry in the *qualify* file is needed:

```
# /usr/lib/smail/qualify, last changed Feb 12, 1994 by janet
#
*              uucp
```

## CHAPTER FIFTEEN

SENDMAIL+IDA

Introduction to Sendmail+IDA

It's been said that you aren't a *real* UNIX system administrator until you've edited a *sendmail.cf* file. It's also been said that you're crazy if you've attempted to do so twice.

sendmail

sendmail is an incredibly powerful program. It's also incredibly difficult to learn and understand for most people. Any program whose definitive reference is 792 pages long quite justifiably scares most people off.

Sendmail+IDA is different. It removes the need to edit the always cryptic *sendmail.cf* file and allows the administrator to define the site-specific routing and addressing configuration through relatively easy to understand support files called *tables*. Switching to Sendmail+IDA can save you many hours of work and stress.

Compared to the other major mail transport agents, there is probably nothing that can't be done faster and simpler with Sendmail+IDA. Typical tasks that are required to run a normal UUCP or Internet site become simple to accomplish. Configurations that normally are extremely difficult are simple to create and maintain.

At this writing, the current version, *sendmail5.67b+IDA1.5*, is available via anonymous FTP from **vixen.cso.uiuc.edu**. It compiles without any patching required under Linux.

All the configuration files required to get Sendmail+IDA sources to compile, install, and run under Linux are included in *newspak-2.2.tar.gz* which is available via anonymous FTP on **sunsite.unc.edu** in the directory */pub/Linux/system/Mail*.

Overview of Configuration Files

Traditional *sendmail* is set up through a system configuration file (typically */etc/sendmail.cf* or */usr/lib/sendmail.cf*) that is not anything close to any language you've seen before. Editing the *sendmail.cf* file to provide customized behavior can be a humbling experience.

Sendmail+IDA makes such pain essentially a thing of the past by having all configuration options table-driven with rather easy to understand syntax. These options are configured by running *m4* (a macro processor) or *dbm* (a database processor) on a number of data files via Makefiles supplied with the sources.

The *sendmail.cf* file defines only the default behavior of the system. Virtually all special customization is done through a number of optional tables rather than by directly editing the *sendmail.cf* file. The following list describes the *sendmail* tables:

mailertable
Defines special behavior for remote hosts or domains

uucpxtable
Forces UUCP delivery of mail to hosts that are in DNS format

pathtable
Defines UUCP bang paths to remote hosts or domains

uucprelays
Short-circuits the pathalias path to well-known remote hosts

genericfrom
Converts internal addresses into generic ones visible to the outside world

xaliases
Converts generic addresses to/from valid internal ones

decnetxtable
Converts RFC 822 addresses to DECnet-style addresses

The sendmail.cf File

The *sendmail.cf* file for Sendmail+IDA is not edited directly, but is generated from an *m4* configuration file provided by the local system administrator. We will refer to this file as *sendmail.m4*.

This file contains a few definitions and otherwise merely points to the tables where the real work gets done. In general, it is only necessary to specify the following information:

- The pathnames and filenames used on the local system

- The name(s) the site is known by for email purposes

- Which default mailer (and perhaps smart relay host) is desired

A variety of parameters can be defined to establish the behavior of the local site or to override compiled-in configuration items. These configuration options are identified in the file *ida/cf/OPTIONS* in the source directory.

A *sendmail.m4* file for a minimal configuration (UUCP or SMTP with all non-local mail being relayed to a directly connected smart host) can be as short as 10 or 15 lines excluding comments.

An Example sendmail.m4 File

A *sendmail.m4* file for **vstout** at the Virtual Brewery is shown in Example 15-1. **vstout** uses SMTP to talk to all hosts on the Brewery's LAN and sends all mail for other destinations to **moria**, its Internet relay host, via UUCP.

Actually, most people don't name their configuration file *sendmail.m4*. Instead, they name it after their host—*vstout.m4* in this case. The name doesn't really matter as long as the output is called *sendmail.cf.*

Example 15-1: Sample Configuration File vstout.m4

```
dnl #----------------- SAMPLE SENDMAIL.M4 FILE -----------------
dnl # (the string 'dnl' is the m4 equivalent of commenting out a line)
dnl # you generally don't want to override LIBDIR from the compiled in paths
dnl #define(LIBDIR,/usr/local/lib/mail)dnl    # where all support files go
define(LOCAL_MAILER_DEF, mailers.linux)dnl    # mailer for local delivery
define(POSTMASTERBOUNCE)dnl                   # postmaster gets bounces
define(PSEUDODOMAINS, BITNET UUCP)dnl         # don't try DNS on these
dnl #-------------------------------------------   --------------------
dnl #
define(PSEUDONYMS, vstout.vbrew.com  vstout.UUCP vbrew.com)
dnl                                           # names we're known by
define(DEFAULT_HOST, vstout.vbrew.com)dnl     # our primary 'name' for mail
define(UUCPNAME, vstout)dnl                   # our uucp name
dnl #
dnl #-----------------------------------------------------------
dnl #
define(UUCPNODES, |uuname|sort|uniq)dnl       # our uucp neighbors
define(BANGIMPLIESUUCP)dnl                    # make certain that uucp
define(BANGONLYUUCP)dnl                       #  mail is treated correctly
define(RELAY_HOST, moria)dnl                  # our smart relay host
define(RELAY_MAILER, UUCP-A)dnl               # we reach moria via uucp
dnl #
dnl #-----------------------------------------------------------------
dnl #
dnl # the various dbm lookup tables
dnl #
define(ALIASES, LIBDIR/aliases)dnl            # system aliases
```

Example 15–1: Sample Configuration File vstout.m4 (continued)

```
define(DOMAINTABLE, LIBDIR/domaintable)dnl      # domainize hosts
define(PATHTABLE, LIBDIR/pathtable)dnl          # paths database
define(GENERICFROM, LIBDIR/generics)dnl         # generic from addresses
define(MAILERTABLE, LIBDIR/mailertable)dnl      # mailers per host or domain
define(UUCPXTABLE, LIBDIR/uucpxtable)dnl        # paths to hosts we feed
define(UUCPRELAYS, LIBDIR/uucprelays)dnl        # short-circuit paths
dnl #
dnl #----------------------------------------------------------------
dnl #
dnl # include the 'real' code that makes it all work
dnl # (provided with the source code)
dnl #
include(Sendmail.mc)dnl                         # REQUIRED ENTRY ! ! !
dnl #
dnl #----------- END OF SAMPLE SENDMAIL.M4 FILE -------
```

Typically Used sendmail.m4 Parameters

A few of the items in the *sendmail.m4* file are required all the time; others can be ignored if you can get away with defaults. The following sections describe each of the items from the *sendmail.m4* file in Example 15-1 in more detail.

Items that define paths

```
dnl #define(LIBDIR,/usr/local/lib/mail)dnl   # where all support files go
```

LIBDIR defines the directory where Sendmail+IDA expects to find configuration files, the various *dbm* tables, and special local definitions. In a typical binary distribution, this is compiled into the *sendmail* binary and does not need to be explicitly set in the *sendmail.m4* file.

The above line has a leading dnl, which means that this line is essentially a comment.

To change the location of the support files to a different location, remove the leading dnl from the above line, set the path to the desired location, and rebuild and reinstall the *sendmail.cf* file.

Defining the local mailer

```
define(LOCAL_MAILER_DEF, mailers.linux)dnl   # mailer for local delivery
```

Most operating systems provide a program to handle local mail delivery. Typical programs for many of the major variants of UNIX are already built into the *sendmail* binary.

In Linux, it is necessary to explicitly define the appropriate local mailer since a local delivery program is not necessarily present in the distribution you've installed. This is done by specifying LOCAL_MAILER_DEF in the *sendmail.m4* file.

For example, to have the commonly used *deliver* program provide this service, you would set LOCAL_MAILER_DEF to *mailers.linux*.[*]

The following file should then be installed as *mailers.linux* in the directory pointed to by LIBDIR. It explicitly defines the *deliver* program in the internal Mlocal mailer with the proper parameters so that *sendmail* will correctly deliver mail targeted for the local system. Unless you are a *sendmail* expert, you probably do not want to alter the following example.

```
# -- /usr/local/lib/mail/mailers.linux --
#      (local mailers for use on Linux )
Mlocal, P=/usr/bin/deliver, F=SlsmFDMP, S=10, R=25/10, A=deliver $u
Mprog,  P=/bin/sh,          F=lsDFMeuP,  S=10, R=10, A=sh -c $u
```

There is also a built-in default for *deliver* in the *Sendmail.mc* file that gets included into the *sendmail.cf* file. To specify it, you would not use the *mailers.linux* file, but would instead define the following in your *sendmail.m4* file:

```
dnl — (in sendmail.m4) —
define(LOCAL_MAILER_DEF, DELIVER)dnl      # mailer for local delivery
```

Unfortunately, *Sendmail.mc* assumes *deliver* is installed in */bin*, which is not the case with Slackware1.1.1 (which installs it in */usr/bin*). In this case you'd need to either fake it with a link or rebuild *deliver* from sources so that it resides in */bin*.

Dealing with bounced mail

```
define(POSTMASTERBOUNCE)dnl                  # postmaster gets bounces
```

Many sites find that it is important to ensure that mail is sent and received with close to a 100% success rate. While examining *syslogd* logs is helpful, the local mail administrator generally needs to see the headers on bounced mail in order to determine if the mail was undeliverable because of user error or a configuration error on one of the systems involved.

Defining POSTMASTERBOUNCE results in a copy of each bounced message being sent to the person defined as **Postmaster** for the system.

Unfortunately, setting this parameter also results in the *text* of the message being sent to the postmaster, which potentially has related privacy concerns for people using mail on the system.

Site postmasters should in general attempt to discipline themselves from reading mail not addressed to them (or do so via technical means such as shell scripts that delete the text of the bounced messages they receive).

---

[*] *deliver* was written by Chip Salzenberg (*chip%tct@ateng.com*). It is part of several Linux distributions and can be found in the usual anonymous FTP archives such as **ftp.uu.net**.

DNS-related items

```
define(PSEUDODOMAINS, BITNET UUCP)dnl        # don't try DNS on these
```

There are several well known networks that are commonly referenced in mail addresses for historical reasons but are not valid for DNS purposes. Defining PSEUDODOMAINS prevents needless DNS lookup attempts that will always fail.

Defining local system names

```
define(PSEUDONYMS, vstout.vbrew.com  vstout.UUCP vbrew.com)
dnl                                     # names we're known by
define(DEFAULT_HOST, vstout.vbrew.com)dnl   # our primary 'name' for mail
```

Frequently, systems wish to hide their true identity, serve as mail gateways, or receive and process mail addressed to "old" names by which they used to be known.

PSEUDONYMS specifies the list of all hostnames for which the local system will accept mail.

DEFAULT_HOST specifies the hostname that will appear in messages originating on the local host. It is important that this parameter be set to a valid value or all return mail will be undeliverable.

UUCP-related items

```
define(UUCPNAME, vstout)dnl                  # our uucp name
define(UUCPNODES, |uuname|sort|uniq)dnl      # our uucp neighbors
define(BANGIMPLIESUUCP)dnl                   # make certain that uucp
define(BANGONLYUUCP)dnl                      #  mail is treated correctly
```

Frequently, systems are known by one name for DNS purposes and another for UUCP purposes. UUCPNAME permits you to define a different hostname, which appears in the headers of outgoing UUCP mail.

UUCPNODES defines the commands that return a list of hostnames for the systems you are directly connected to via UUCP.

BANGIMPLIESUUCP and BANGONLYUUCP ensure that mail addressed with UUCP bang syntax is treated according to UUCP behavior rather than the more current DNS behavior used today on the Internet.

Relay systems and mailers

```
define(RELAY_HOST, moria)dnl                 # our smart relay host
define(RELAY_MAILER, UUCP-A)dnl              # we reach moria via UUCP
```

Many system administrators don't want to be bothered with the work needed to ensure that their system is able to reach all networks and systems on all networks worldwide. Instead they would rather relay all outgoing mail to another system that is known to be "smart."

RELAY_HOST defines the UUCP hostname of such a smart neighboring system.

RELAY_MAILER defines the mailer used to relay the messages there.

It is important to note that setting these parameters results in your outgoing mail being forwarded to this remote system, which will affect the load of that system. Be certain to get explicit agreement from the remote postmaster before you configure your system to use another system as a general-purpose relay host.

Configuration tables

```
define(ALIASES, LIBDIR/aliases)dnl          # system aliases
define(DOMAINTABLE, LIBDIR/domaintable)dnl   # domainize hosts
define(PATHTABLE, LIBDIR/pathtable)dnl       # paths database
define(GENERICFROM, LIBDIR/generics)dnl      # generic from addresses
define(MAILERTABLE, LIBDIR/mailertable)dnl   # mailers per host or domain
define(UUCPXTABLE, LIBDIR/uucpxtable)dnl     # paths to hosts we feed
define(UUCPRELAYS, LIBDIR/uucprelays)dnl     # short-circuit paths
```

With these macros, you can change the location where Sendmail+IDA looks for the various *dbm* tables that define the system's "real" behavior. It is generally wise to leave them in LIBDIR.

The master Sendmail.mc file

```
include(Sendmail.mc)dnl                     # REQUIRED ENTRY !!!
```

The authors of Sendmail+IDA provide the *Sendmail.mc* file which contains the true "guts" of what becomes the *sendmail.cf* file. Periodically, new versions are released to fix bugs or add functionality without requiring a full release and recompilation of *sendmail* from source. It is important *not* to edit this file.

So which entries are really required?

When not using any of the optional *dbm* tables, Sendmail+IDA delivers mail via the DEFAULT_MAILER (and possibly RELAY_HOST and RELAY_MAILER) defined in the *sendmail.m4* file used to generate *sendmail.cf*. It is easily possible to override this behavior through entries in the *domaintable* or *uucpxtable*.

A generic site that is on the Internet and speaks DNS, or one that is UUCP-only and forwards all mail via UUCP through a smart RELAY_HOST, probably does not need any specific table entries at all.

Virtually all systems should set the DEFAULT_HOST and PSEUDONYMS macros, which define the canonical site name and aliases it is known by, and DEFAULT_MAILER. If all you have is a relay host and relay mailer, you don't need to set these defaults since it works automatically.

UUCP hosts will probably need to set UUCPNAME to their official UUCP name. They will also probably need to set RELAY_MAILER and RELAY_HOST, which enable smart-host routing through a mail relay. The mail transport to be used is defined in RELAY_MAILER and should usually be *UUCP-A* for UUCP sites.

If your site is SMTP-only and talks DNS, you would change the DEFAULT_MAILER to TCP–A and probably delete the RELAY_MAILER and RELAY_HOST lines.

A Tour of Sendmail+IDA Tables

Sendmail+IDA provides a number of tables that allow you to override the default behavior of *sendmail* (specified in the *sendmail.m4* file) and define special behavior for unique situations, remote systems, and networks. These tables are post-processed with *dbm* using the Makefile provided with the distribution.

Most sites will need few, if any, of these tables. If your site does not require these tables, the easiest thing is probably to make them zero length files (with the *touch* command) and use the default Makefile in LIBDIR rather than editing the Makefile itself.

mailertable

The *mailertable* defines special treatment for specific hosts or domains based on the remote host or network name. It is frequently used on Internet sites to select an intermediate mail relay host or gateway to reach a remote network through, and to specify a particular protocol (UUCP or SMTP) to be used. UUCP sites will generally not need to use this file.

Order is important. *sendmail* reads the file top-down and processes the message according to the first rule it matches. So it is generally wise to place the most explicit rules at the top of the file and the more generic rules below.

Suppose you want to forward all mail for the computer science department at Groucho Marx University via UUCP to a relay host **ada**. To do so, you would have a *mailertable* entry that looked like the following:

```
# (in mailertable)
#
# forward all mail for the domain .cs.groucho.edu via UUCP to ada
UUCP-A,ada        .cs.groucho.edu
```

Suppose you want all mail to the larger **groucho.edu** domain to go to a different relay host **bighub** for address resolution and delivery. The expanded *mailertable* entries would look quite similar:

```
# (in mailertable)
#
# forward all mail for the domain cs.groucho.edu via UUCP to ada
UUCP-A,ada        .cs.groucho.edu
```

```
#
# forward all mail for the domain groucho.edu via UUCP to bighub
UUCP-A,bighub        .groucho.edu
```

As mentioned above, order is important. Reversing the order of the two rules shown above will result in all mail to **.cs.groucho.edu** going through the more generic **bighub** path instead of the explicit **ada** path that is really desired.

In the *mailertable* examples above, the *UUCP-A* mailer makes *sendmail* use UUCP delivery with domainized headers.

The comma between the mailer and remote system tells it to forward the message to **ada** for address resolution and delivery.

mailertable entries are of the following format:

```
mailer delimiter relayhost              host_or_domain
```

There are a number of possible mailers. The differences are generally in how they treat addresses. Typical mailers are *TCP-A* (TCP/IP with Internet-style addresses), *TCP-U* (TCP/IP with UUCP-style addresses), and *UUCP-A* (UUCP with Internet-style addresses).

The character that separates the mailer from the host portion on the left-hand-side of a *mailertable* line defines how the address is modified by the *mailertable*:

!   An exclamation point strips off the recipient hostname before forwarding to the mailer. This can be used when you essentially want to force mail into a misconfigured remote site.

,   A comma does not change the address in any way. The message is merely forwarded via the specified mailer to the specified relay host.

:   A colon removes the recipient hostname only if there are intermediate hosts between you and the destination. Thus, *foo!bar!joe* will have *foo* removed, while *xyzzy!janet* will remain unchanged.

The important thing is that *mailertable* only rewrites the envelope (to get the mail into the remote system). Rewriting anything other than the envelope is generally frowned upon due to the high probability of breaking the mail configuration.

uucpxtable

Usually, mail to hosts with fully qualified domain names is delivered via Internet-style (SMTP) delivery using DNS, or via the relay host. The *uucpxtable* forces delivery via UUCP routing by converting the domainized name into a UUCP-style, un-domainized remote hostname.

uucpxtable is frequently used when you're a mail forwarder for a site or domain, or when you wish to send mail via a direct and reliable UUCP link rather than have potentially multiple hops through the default mailer and any intermediate systems and networks.

UUCP sites that talk to UUCP neighbors who use domainized mail headers would use this file to force delivery of the mail through the direct UUCP point-to-point link between the two systems, rather than using the less direct route through the RELAY_MAILER and RELAY_HOST or through the DEFAULT_MAILER.

Internet sites who do not talk UUCP probably would not use the *uucpxtable*.

Suppose you provide mail forwarding service to a system called **sesame.com** in DNS, and **sesame** in the UUCP maps. You would need the following *uucpxtable* entry to force mail for their host to go through your direct UUCP connection:

```
#=============== /usr/local/lib/mail/uucpxtable ============
# Mail sent to joe@sesame.com is rewritten to sesame!joe and
# therefore delivered via UUCP
#
sesame            sesame.com
#
#-----------------------------------------------------------
```

pathtable

The *pathtable* is used to define explicit routing to remote hosts or networks. The *pathtable* file should be in pathalias-style syntax, sorted alphabetically. The two fields on each line must be separated by a real TAB, or else *dbm* might complain.

Most systems will not need any *pathtable* entries.

```
#=============== /usr/local/lib/mail/pathtable ================
#
# this is a pathalias-style paths file to let you kick mail to
# UUCP neighbors to the direct UUCP path so you don't have to
# go the long way through your smart host that takes other traffic
#
# you want real tabs on each line or m4 might complain
#
# route mail through one or more intermediate sites to a remote
# system using UUCP-style addressing.
#
sesame!ernie!%s          ernie
#
# forwarding to a system that is a UUCP neighbor of a reachable
# internet site.
#
swim!%s@gcc.groucho.edu    swim
#
# The following sends all mail for two networks through different
# gateways (see the leading '.' ?).
# In this example, "uugate" and "byte" are specific systems that serve
```

```
# as mail gateways to the .UUCP and .BITNET pseudo-domains respectively
#
%s@uugate.groucho.edu               .UUCP
byte!%s@mail.shift.com              .BITNET
#
#=================== end of pathtable ======================
```

domaintable

The *domaintable* is generally used to force certain behavior after a DNS lookup
has occurred. It permits the administrator to make shorthand names available for
commonly referenced systems or domains by replacing the shorthand name with
the proper one automatically. It can also be used to replace incorrect host or
domain names with the "correct" information.

Most sites will not need any *domaintable* entries.

The following example shows how to replace an incorrect address, which people
are attempting to mail to, with the correct address:

```
#============== /usr/local/lib/mail/domaintable =================
#
#
brokenhost.correct.domain           brokenhost.wrong.domain
#
#
#=================== end of domaintable ========================
```

aliases

Aliases permit a number of things to happen:

- They provide a shorthand or well known name for mail to be addressed to in
  order to go to one or more persons.

- They invoke a program with the mail message as the input to the program.

- They send mail to a file.

All systems require aliases for **Postmaster** and **MAILER-DAEMON** to be RFC-
compliant.

Always be extremely aware of security when defining aliases that invoke programs
or write to programs since *sendmail* generally runs setuid **root**.

Changes to the *aliases* file do not take effect until the command

```
# /usr/lib/sendmail -bi
```

is executed to build the required *dbm* tables. This can also be done by executing
the *newaliases* command, usually from *cron*.

Details concerning mail aliases may be found in the *aliases(5)* manual page. A sample *aliases* file is shown in Example 15-2.

Example 15–2: Sample aliases File

```
#-------------------- /usr/local/lib/mail/aliases ------------------
#
# demonstrate commonly seen types of aliases
#
usenet:         janet                    # alias for a person
admin:          joe,janet                # alias for several people
newspak-users:  :include:/usr/lib/lists/newspak
                                         # read recipients from a file
changefeed:     | /usr/local/lib/gup     # alias that invokes a program
complaints:     /var/log/complaints      # alias that writes mail to a file
#
# The following two aliases must be present to be RFC-compliant.
# It is important to have them resolve to 'a person' who reads mail routinely.
#
postmaster:     root                     # required entry
MAILER-DAEMON:  postmaster               # required entry
#
#------------------------------------------------------------------
```

Rarely Used Tables

The following tables are available but are rather infrequently used. Consult the documentation that comes with the Sendmail+IDA source for details.

uucprelays
> The *uucprelays* file is used to "short-circuit" the UUCP path to especially well known sites rather than using a multi-hop or unreliable path generated by processing the UUCP maps with *pathalias*.

genericfrom and *xaliases*
> The *genericfrom* file hides local usernames and addresses from the outside world by automatically converting local usernames to generic sender addresses that do not match internal usernames.
>
> The associated *xalparse* utility automates the generation of the *genericfrom* and *aliases* files so that both incoming and outgoing username translations occur from a master *xaliases* file.

decnetxtable
> The *decnetxtable* rewrites domainized addresses into DECnet-style addresses, much like the *domaintable* can be used to rewrite undomainized addresses into domainized SMTP-style addresses.

Installing sendmail

In this section, we'll take a look at how to install a typical binary distribution of Sendmail+IDA, and walk through what needs to be done to make it localized and functional.

The current binary distribution of Sendmail+IDA for Linux can be obtained from **sunsite.unc.edu** in */pub/Linux/system/Mail*. Even if you have an earlier version of *sendmail*, I strongly recommend you go to the *sendmail5.67b+IDA1.5* version since all required Linux-specific patches are now in the vanilla sources. Also, several significant security holes have been plugged that were in versions prior to about December 1, 1993.

If you are building *sendmail* from the sources, you should follow the instructions in the *READMEs* included in the source distribution. The current Sendmail+IDA source is available from **vixen.cso.uiuc.edu**. To build Sendmail+IDA on Linux, you also need the Linux specific configuration files from *newspak-2.2.tar.gz*, which is available on **sunsite.unc.edu** in the */pub/Linux/system/Mail* directory.

If you have previously installed *smail* or another mail delivery agent, you'll probably want to remove (or rename) all the files from *smail* to be safe.

Extracting the Binary Distribution

First, you have to unpack the archive file in some safe location:

```
$ gunzip -c sendmail5.65b+IDA1.5+mailx5.3b.tgz | tar xvf -
```

If you have a "modern" *tar*, for example from a recent Slackware Distribution, you can probably just do a *tar -zxvf filename.tgz* and get the same results.

Unpacking the archive creates the directory *sendmail5.65b+IDA1.5+mailx5.3b*. In this directory, you'll find a complete installation of Sendmail+IDA plus a binary of the *mailx* user agent. All file paths below this directory reflect the location where the files should be installed, so it's safe to work up a *tar* command to move them over:

```
# cd sendmail5.65b+IDA1.5+mailx5.3b
# tar cf - . | (cd /; tar xvvpoof -)
```

Building sendmail.cf

To build a *sendmail.cf* file customized for your site, you have to write a *sendmail.m4* file and process it with *m4*. In */usr/local/lib/mail/CF*, you'll find a sample file called *sample.m4*. Copy it to another name—the convention is to use *yourhostname.m4*—and edit it to reflect the situation of your site.

The sample file is set up for a UUCP-only site that has domainized headers and talks to a smart host. Sites like this only need to edit a few items.

In the current section, I will only give a short overview of the macros you have to change. For a complete description of what they do, please refer to the earlier discussion of *sendmail.m4*.

LOCAL_MAILER_DEF
> Define the file that defines the mailers for local mail delivery. See the section "Defining the Local Mailer" above for what goes in here.

PSEUDONYMS
> Define all the names your local host is known by.

DEFAULT_HOST
> Put in your fully qualified domain name. This name will appear as your hostname in all outgoing mail.

UUCPNAME
> Put in your unqualified hostname.

RELAY_HOST and RELAY_MAILER
> If you talk UUCP to a smart host, set RELAY_HOST to the UUCP name of your "smart relay" UUCP neighbor. Use the *UUCP-A* mailer if you want domainized headers.

DEFAULT_MAILER
> If you are on the Internet and talk DNS, you should set this to TCP-A. This tells sendmail to use the *TCP-A* mailer, which delivers mail via SMTP using normal RFC-style addressing for the envelope. Internet sites probably do not need to define RELAY_HOST or RELAY_MAILER.

To create the *sendmail.cf* file, execute the command:

```
# make yourhostname.cf
```

This processes the *yourhostname.m4* file and creates *yourhostname.cf* from it.

Next, you should test whether the configuration file you've created does what you expect it to do. This is explained in the following two sections.

Once you're happy with its behavior, copy it into place with the command:

```
# cp yourhostname.cf /etc/sendmail.cf
```

At this point, your *sendmail* system is ready for action. Put the following line in the appropriate startup file (generally */etc/rc.inet2*). You can also execute it by hand to have the process start up now:

```
# /usr/lib/sendmail -bd -q1h
```

Testing the sendmail.cf File

To put *sendmail* into test mode, you invoke it with the *–bt* flag. The default configuration file is the *sendmail.cf* file that is installed on the system. You can test an alternate file by using the *–Cfilename* option.

In the following examples, we test *vstout.cf*, the configuration file generated from the *sendmail.m4* file shown in Example 15-1.

```
# /usr/lib/sendmail -bt -Cvstout.cf
ADDRESS TEST MODE
Enter <ruleset> <address>
[Note: No initial ruleset 3 call]
>
```

The following tests ensure that *sendmail* is able to deliver all mail to users on your system. In all cases the result of the test should be the same and point to the local system name with the LOCAL mailer.

First test how mail to a local user would be delivered:

```
# /usr/lib/sendmail -bt -Cvstout.cf
ADDRESS TEST MODE
Enter <ruleset> <address>
[Note: No initial ruleset 3 call]
> 3,0 me
rewrite: ruleset  3    input: me
rewrite: ruleset  7    input: me
rewrite: ruleset  9    input: me
rewrite: ruleset  9 returns: < me >
rewrite: ruleset  7 returns: < > , me
rewrite: ruleset  3 returns: < > , me
rewrite: ruleset  0    input: < > , me
rewrite: ruleset  8    input: < > , me
rewrite: ruleset 20    input: < > , me
rewrite: ruleset 20 returns: < > , @ vstout . vbrew . com , me
rewrite: ruleset  8 returns: < > , @ vstout . vbrew . com , me
rewrite: ruleset 26    input: < > , @ vstout . vbrew . com , me
rewrite: ruleset 26 returns: $# LOCAL $@ vstout . vbrew . com $: me
rewrite: ruleset  0 returns: $# LOCAL $@ vstout . vbrew . com $: me
```

The output shows how *sendmail* processes the address internally. It is handed to various rulesets which analyze it, invoke other rulesets in turn, and break it up into its components.

In our example, we passed the address *me* to rulesets 3 and 0 (this is the meaning of the *3,0* entered before the address). The last line shows the parsed address as returned by ruleset 0, containing the mailer the message would be delivered by and the host and user name given to the mailer.

Next, test mail to a user on your system with UUCP syntax.

```
# /usr/lib/sendmail -bt -Cvstout.cf
ADDRESS TEST MODE
Enter <ruleset> <address>
[Note: No initial ruleset 3 call]
> 3,0 vstout!me
rewrite: ruleset  3    input: vstout ! me
[...]
rewrite: ruleset  0 returns: $# LOCAL $@ vstout . vbrew . com  $: me
>
```

Next, test mail addressed to a user on your system with Internet syntax to your fully qualified hostname:

```
# /usr/lib/sendmail -bt -Cvstout.cf
ADDRESS TEST MODE
Enter <ruleset> <address>
[Note: No initial ruleset 3 call]
> 3,0 me@vstout.vbrew.com
rewrite: ruleset  3    input: me @ vstout . vbrew . com
[...]
rewrite: ruleset  0 returns: $# LOCAL $@ vstout . vbrew . com $: me
>
```

You should repeat the above two tests with each of the names you specified in the PSEUDONYMS and DEFAULT_NAME parameters in your *sendmail.m4* file.

Lastly, test that you can mail to your relay host:

```
# /usr/lib/sendmail -bt -Cvstout.cf
ADDRESS TEST MODE
Enter <ruleset> <address>
[Note: No initial ruleset 3 call]
> 3,0 fred@moria.com
rewrite: ruleset  3    input: fred @ moria . com
rewrite: ruleset  7    input: fred @ moria . com
rewrite: ruleset  9    input: fred @ moria . com
rewrite: ruleset  9 returns: < fred > @ moria . com
rewrite: ruleset  7 returns: < @ moria . com > , fred
rewrite: ruleset  3 returns: < @ moria . com > , fred
rewrite: ruleset  0    input: < @ moria . com > , fred
rewrite: ruleset  8    input: < @ moria . com > , fred
rewrite: ruleset  8 returns: < @ moria . com > , fred
rewrite: ruleset 29    input: < @ moria . com > , fred
rewrite: ruleset 29 returns: < @ moria . com > , fred
rewrite: ruleset 26    input: < @ moria . com > , fred
rewrite: ruleset 25    input: < @ moria . com > , fred
rewrite: ruleset 25 returns: < @ moria . com > , fred
rewrite: ruleset  4    input: < @ moria . com > , fred
rewrite: ruleset  4 returns: fred @ moria . com
```

```
rewrite: ruleset 26 returns: < @ moria . com > , fred
rewrite: ruleset  0 returns: $# UUCP-A $@ moria $: < @ moria . com > , fred
>
```

Integration Testing sendmail.cf and the Tables

At this point, you've verified that mail will have the desired default behavior and that you'll be able to both send and receive validly addressed mail. To complete the installation, it may be necessary to create the appropriate *dbm* tables to get the desired final results.

After creating the table(s) that are required for your site, you must process them through *dbm* by typing *make* in the directory containing the tables.

If you are UUCP-only, you do *not* need to create any of the tables mentioned in the *README.linux* file. You'll just have to touch the files so that the Makefile works.

If you're UUCP-only and you talk to sites in addition to your smart host, you'll need to add *uucpxtable* entries for each (or mail to them will also go through the smart host) and run *dbm* against the revised *uucpxtable*.

First, you need to make certain that mail through your RELAY_HOST is sent to them via the RELAY_MAILER:

```
# /usr/lib/sendmail -bt -Cvstout.cf
ADDRESS TEST MODE
Enter <ruleset> <address>
[Note: No initial ruleset 3 call]
> 3,0 fred@sesame.com
rewrite: ruleset  3   input: fred @ sesame . com
rewrite: ruleset  7   input: fred @ sesame . com
rewrite: ruleset  9   input: fred @ sesame . com
rewrite: ruleset  9 returns: < fred > @ sesame . com
rewrite: ruleset  7 returns: < @ sesame . com > , fred
rewrite: ruleset  3 returns: < @ sesame . com > , fred
rewrite: ruleset  0   input: < @ sesame . com > , fred
rewrite: ruleset  0   input: < @ sesame . com > , fred
rewrite: ruleset  8 returns: < @ sesame . com > , fred
rewrite: ruleset 29   input: < @ sesame . com > , fred
rewrite: ruleset 29 returns: < @ sesame . com > , fred
rewrite: ruleset 26   input: < @ sesame . com > , fred
rewrite: ruleset 25   input: < @ sesame . com > , fred
rewrite: ruleset 25 returns: < @ sesame . com > , fred
rewrite: ruleset  4   input: < @ sesame . com > , fred
rewrite: ruleset  4 returns: fred @ sesame . com
rewrite: ruleset 26 returns: < @ sesame . com > , fred
rewrite: ruleset  0 returns: $# UUCP-A $@ moria $: < @ sesame . com > , fred
>
```

If you have UUCP neighbors other than your `RELAY_HOST`, you need to ensure that mail to them has the proper behavior. Mail addressed with UUCP-style syntax to a host you talk UUCP with should go directly to them (unless you explicitly prevent it with a *domaintable* entry). Assume host **swim** is a direct UUCP neighbor of yours. Then feeding *swim!fred* to *sendmail* should produce the following result:

```
# /usr/lib/sendmail -bt -Cvstout.cf
ADDRESS TEST MODE
Enter <ruleset> <address>
[Note: No initial ruleset 3 call]
> 3,0 swim!fred
rewrite: ruleset  3   input: swim ! fred
[...lines omitted...]
rewrite: ruleset  0 returns: $# UUCP $@ swim $: < > , fred
>
```

If you have *uucpxtable* entries to force UUCP delivery to certain UUCP neighbors who send their mail with Internet-style domainized headers, that also needs to be tested:

```
# /usr/lib/sendmail -bt -Cvstout.cf
ADDRESS TEST MODE
Enter <ruleset> <address>
[Note: No initial ruleset 3 call]
> 3,0 dude@swim.2birds.com
rewrite: ruleset  3   input: dude @ swim . 2birds . com
[...lines omitted...]
rewrite: ruleset  0 returns: $# UUCP $@ swim . 2birds $: < > , dude
>
```

Administrivia and Stupid Mail Tricks

Now that we've discussed the theory of configuring, installing, and testing a Sendmail+IDA system, let's take a few moments to look into things that *do* happen routinely in the life of a mail administrator.

Remote systems sometimes break. Modems or phone lines fail. DNS definitions are set incorrectly due to human error. Networks go down unexpectedly. In such cases, mail administrators need to know how to react quickly, effectively, and *safely* to keep mail flowing through alternate routes until the remote systems or service providers can restore normal services.

The rest of this chapter is intended to provide you with the solutions to the most frequently encountered electronic mail emergencies.

Forwarding Mail to a Relay Host

To forward mail for a particular host or domain to a designated relay system, you generally use the *mailertable*. For example, to forward mail for **backwood.org** to their UUCP gateway system **backdoor**, put the following entry into *mailertable*:

```
UUCP-A,backdoor    backwood.org
```

Forcing Mail into Misconfigured Remote Sites

Internet hosts frequently have trouble getting mail into misconfigured remote sites. There are several variants of this problem, but the general symptom is that mail is bounced by the remote system or never gets there at all.

These problems can put the local system administrator in a bad position because your users generally don't care that you don't personally administer every system worldwide (or know how to get the remote administrator to fix the problem). They just know that their mail didn't get through to the desired recipient on the other end and that you're a likely person to complain to.

A remote site's configuration is their problem, not yours. In all cases, be certain to *not* break your site in order to communicate with a misconfigured remote site. If you can't get in touch with the postmaster at the remote site to get them to fix their configuration in a timely manner, you have two options:

- It is generally possible to force mail into the remote system successfully, although since the remote system is misconfigured, replies on the remote end might not work, but then that's the remote administrator's problem.

  You can fix the bad headers in the envelope on your outgoing messages only by using a *domaintable* entry for their host/domain that results in the invalid information being corrected in mail originating from your site:

  ```
  braindead.correct.domain.com       braindead.wrong.domain.com
  ```

- Frequently, misconfigured sites bounce mail back to the sending system and effectively say "that mail isn't for this site" because they do not have their PSEUDONYMNS or equivalent set properly in their configuration. It is possible to totally strip off all hostname and domain information from the envelope of messages going from your site to them.

  The **!** in the following *mailertable* delivers mail to their remote site making it appear to their *sendmail* as if it had originated locally on their system. Note that this changes only the envelope address, so the proper return address will still show up in the message.

  ```
  TCP!braindead.correct.domain.com   braindead.wrong.domain.com
  ```

Regardless, even if you get mail into their system, there is no guarantee that they can reply to your message (they're broken, remember) but then their users are yelling at their administrators rather than your users yelling at you.

Forcing Mail to Be Transferred via UUCP

In an ideal world (from the Internet perspective), all hosts have records in the Domain Name Service and will send mail with fully qualified domain names.

If you happen to talk via UUCP to such a site, you can force mail to go through the point-to-point UUCP connection rather than through your default mailer by essentially "un-domainizing" the remote site's hostname through the *uucpxtable*.

To force UUCP delivery to **sesame.com**, you would put the following in your *uucpxtable*:

```
# un-domainize sesame.com to force UUCP delivery
sesame      sesame.com
```

The result is that sendmail will then determine (via UUCPNODES in the *sendmail.m4* file) that you are directly connected to the remote system and will queue the mail for delivery with UUCP.

Preventing Mail from Being Delivered via UUCP

The opposite condition also occurs. Frequently, systems may have a number of direct UUCP connections that are used infrequently or that are not as reliable and always available as the default mailer or relay host.

For example, in the Seattle area there are a number of systems that exchange the various Linux distributions via anonymous UUCP when the distributions are released. These systems talk UUCP only when necessary, so it is generally faster and more reliable to send mail through multiple, very reliable hops and common (and always available) relay hosts.

It is easy to prevent UUCP delivery of mail to a host that you are directly connected to. If the remote system has a fully qualified domain name, you can add an entry like this to the *domaintable*:

```
# prevent mail delivery via UUCP to a neighbor
snorkel.com      snorkel
```

This will replace any occurrence of the UUCP name with the FQDN, and thus prevent a match by the UUCPNODES line in the *sendmail.m4* file. The result is generally that mail will go via the RELAY_MAILER and RELAY_HOST (or DEFAULT_ MAILER).

Running the sendmail Queue on Demand

To process queued messages immediately, merely type */usr/lib/runq*. This invokes *sendmail* with the appropriate options to cause it to run through the queue of pending jobs immediately rather than waiting for the next scheduled run.

Reporting Mail Statistics

Many site administrators (and the persons they work for) are interested in the volume of mail passing to, from, and through the local site. There are a number of ways to quantify mail traffic:

- *sendmail* comes with a utility called *mailstats* that reads a file called */usr/local/lib/mail/sendmail.st* and reports the number of messages and number of bytes transferred by each of the mailers used in the *sendmail.cf* file. This file must be created by the local administrator manually for *sendmail* logging to occur. The running totals are cleared by removing and recreating the *sendmail.st* file. One way is to do the following:

    ```
    # cp /dev/null /usr/lib/local/mail/sendmail.st
    ```

- Probably the best way to do quality reporting regarding who uses mail and how much volume passes to, from, and through the local system is to turn on mail debugging with *syslogd*. Generally, this means running the */etc/syslogd* daemon from your system startup file (which you should be doing anyway), and adding a line to */etc/syslog.conf* that looks something like the following:

    ```
    mail.debug                    /var/log/syslog.mail
    ```

    If you use `mail.debug` and get medium to high mail volume, the syslog output can get quite large. Output files from *syslogd* generally need to be rotated or purged on a routine basis from *crond*.

    There are a number of commonly available utilities that can summarize the output of mail logging from *syslogd*. One of the more well known utilities is *syslog-stat.pl*, a *perl* script that is distributed with the Sendmail+IDA sources.

Mixing and Matching Binary Distributions

There is no true standard configuration of electronic mail transport and delivery agents, and there is no "one true directory structure."

Accordingly, it is necessary to ensure that all the various pieces of the system (Usenet news, mail, TCP/IP) agree on the location of the local mail delivery program (*lmail*, *deliver*, etc.), remote mail delivery program (*rmail*), and the mail transport program (*sendmail* or *smail*). Such assumptions are not generally documented, although use of the *strings* command can help determine what files and directories are expected. The following are some problems we've seen in the past with some of the commonly available Linux binary distributions and sources.

- Some versions of the NET-2 distribution of TCP/IP have services defined for a program called *umail* rather than *sendmail.*

- Various ports of *elm* and *mailx* look for a delivery agent of */usr/bin/smail* rather than *sendmail.*

- Sendmail+IDA has a built-in local mailer for *deliver*, but expects it to be located in */bin* rather than the more typical Linux location of */usr/bin.*

Rather than go through the trouble of building all the mail clients from sources, we generally fake it with the appropriate soft links.

Where to Get More Information

email HOWTO
sendmail

For more information on *sendmail,* see the Linux Electronic Mail HOWTO posted regularly to *comp.answers.* It is also available via anonymous FTP on **rtfm.mit.edu.** However, the definitive place is in the Sendmail+IDA sources. Look in the directory *ida/cf,* below the source directory, for the files *DBM-GUIDE, OPTIONS,* and *Sendmail.mc.*

## CHAPTER SIXTEEN

NETNEWS

Usenet History

The idea of network news was born in 1979 when two graduate students, Tom Truscott and Jim Ellis, thought of using UUCP to connect machines for the purpose of information exchange among UNIX users. They set up a small network of three machines in North Carolina.

Initially, traffic was handled by a number of shell scripts (later rewritten in C), but they were never released to the public. They were quickly replaced by "A" News, the first public release of news software.

A News was not designed to handle more than a few articles per group and day. When the volume continued to grow, it was rewritten by Mark Horton and Matt Glickman, who called it the "B" release (a.k.a. B News). The first public release of B News was version 2.1 in 1982. It was expanded continuously, with several new features added. Its current version is B News 2.11. It is slowly becoming obsolete, its last official maintainer having switched to INN.

Another rewrite was done and released in 1987 by Geoff Collyer and Henry Spencer; this is release "C," or C News. Since its release, there have been a number of patches to C News, the most prominent being the C News Performance Release. On sites that carry a large number of groups, the overhead involved in frequently invoking *relaynews*, which is responsible for dispatching incoming articles to other hosts, is significant. The Performance Release adds an option to *relaynews* that allows it to run in *daemon mode*, in which the program puts itself in the background. The Performance Release is the C News version currently included in most Linux releases.

All news releases up to C were primarily targeted for UUCP networks, although they could be used in other environments as well. Efficient news transfer over networks like TCP/IP or DECNet required a new scheme. So in 1986, the *Network News Transfer Protocol* (NNTP) was introduced. It is based on network connections and specifies a number of commands to interactively transfer and retrieve articles.

There are a number of NNTP-based applications available from the Net. One of them is the *nntpd* package by Brian Barber and Phil Lapsley, which you can use to provide newsreading service to a number of hosts inside a local network. *nntpd* was designed to complement news packages such as B News or C News to give them NNTP features.

A different NNTP package is INN, or *Internet News*. It is not merely a front end, but a news system in its own right. It comprises a sophisticated news relay daemon that can maintain several concurrent NNTP links efficiently, and is therefore the news server of choice for many Internet sites.

What is Usenet, Anyway?

Zen

One of the most astounding facts about Usenet is that it isn't part of any organization, nor does it have any sort of centralized network management authority. In fact, it's part of Usenet lore that except for a technical description, you cannot define *what* it is; you can only say what it isn't.

At the risk of sounding stupid, one might define Usenet as a collaboration of separate sites who exchange Usenet news. To be a Usenet site, all you have to do is find another Usenet site and strike an agreement with its owners and maintainers to exchange news with you. Providing another site with news is also called *feeding* it, whence another common axiom of Usenet philosophy originates: "Get a feed, and you're on it."

RFC 822

The basic unit of Usenet news is the article. This is a message a user writes and "posts" to the net. In order to enable news systems to deal with it, it is prepended with administrative information, the so-called article header. It is very similar to the mail header format laid down in the Internet mail standard RFC 822, in that it consists of several lines of text, each beginning with a field name terminated by a colon, which is followed by the field's value.[*]

Articles are submitted to one or more *newsgroups*. One may consider a newsgroup a forum for articles relating to a common topic. All newsgroups are organized in a hierarchy, with each group's name indicating its place in the hierarchy. This often makes it easy to see what a group is all about. For example, anybody can see from the newsgroup name that *comp.os.linux.announce* is used for announcements concerning a computer operating system named Linux.

---

[*] The format of Usenet news messages is specified in RFC 1036, "Standard for interchange of USENET messages."

These articles are then exchanged between all Usenet sites that are willing to carry news from this group. When two sites agree to exchange news, they are free to exchange whatever newsgroups they like to, and may even add their own local news hierarchies. For example, **groucho.edu** might have a news link to **barn-yard.edu**, which is a major news feed, and several links to minor sites which it feeds news. Now, Barnyard College might receive all Usenet groups, while GMU only wants to carry a few major hierarchies like *sci, comp, rec,* etc. Some of the downstream sites, say a UUCP site called **brewhq**, will want to carry even fewer groups, because they don't have the network or hardware resources. On the other hand, **brewhq** might want to receive newsgroups from the *fj* hierarchy, which GMU doesn't carry. It therefore maintains another link with **gargleblaster.com**, who carries all *fj* groups, and feeds them to **brewhq**. The news flow is shown in Figure 16-1.

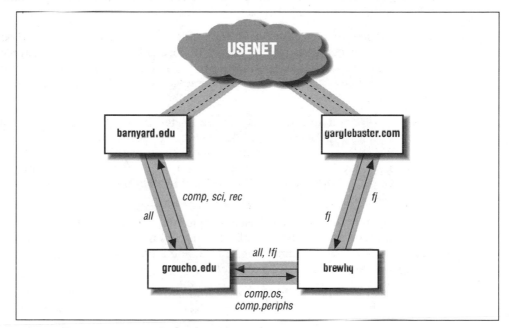

Figure 16–1. Usenet news flow through Groucho Marx University

The labels on the arrows originating from **brewhq** may require some explanation, though. By default, it wants all locally generated news to be sent to **groucho.edu**. However, as **groucho.edu** does not carry the *fj* groups, there's no point in sending it any messages from those groups. Therefore, the feed from **brewhq** to GMU is labelled *all,!fj,* meaning that all groups except those below *fj* are sent to it.

How Does Usenet Handle News?

Today, Usenet has grown to enormous proportions. Sites that carry the whole of Netnews usually transfer something like a paltry sixty megabytes a day.* Of course, this requires much more than pushing around files. So let's take a look at the way most UNIX systems handle Usenet news.

News is distributed through the net by various transports. The historical medium used to be UUCP, but today the main traffic is carried by Internet sites. The routing algorithm used is called *flooding*: Each site maintains a number of links (*news feeds*) to other sites. Any article generated or received by the local news system is forwarded to them, unless it has already been at that site, in which case it is discarded. A site may find out about all other sites the article has already traversed by looking at the `Path:` header field. This header contains a list of all systems the article has been forwarded by in bang path notation.

To distinguish articles and recognize duplicates, Usenet articles have to carry a message ID (specified in the `Message-Id:` header field), which combines the posting site's name and a serial number into `<serial@site>`. For each article processed, the news system logs this ID into a *history* file against which all newly arrived articles are checked.

The flow between any two sites may be limited by two criteria. For one, an article is assigned a distribution (in the `Distribution:` header field) which may be used to confine it to a certain group of sites. On the other hand, the newsgroups exchanged may be limited by both the sending or receiving system. The set of newsgroups and distributions allowed for transmission to a site are usually kept in the *sys* file.

The sheer number of articles usually requires that improvements be made to the above scheme. On UUCP networks, the natural thing to do is collect articles over a period of time and combine them into a single file, which is compressed and sent to the remote site. This is called *batching*.

An alternative technique is the *ihave/sendme* protocol that prevents duplicate articles from being transferred in the first place, thus saving net bandwidth. Instead of putting all articles in batch files and sending them along, only the message IDs of articles are combined into a giant "ihave" message and sent to the remote site. The remote site reads this message, compares it to its history file, and returns the list of articles it wants in a "sendme" message. Only these articles are then sent.

Of course, ihave/sendme only makes sense if it involves two big sites that receive news from several independent feeds each, and who poll each other often enough for an efficient flow of news.

---

* Wait a moment: 60 Megs at 9600 bps, that's 60 million by 1200, that is... mutter, mutter,... Hey! That's 34 hours!

RFC 977

Sites that are on the Internet generally rely on TCP/IP-based software that uses the Network News Transfer Protocol, NNTP. It transfers news between feeds and provides Usenet access to single users on remote hosts.

NNTP knows three different ways to transfer news. One is a real-time version of ihave/sendme, also referred to as *pushing* news. The second technique is called *pulling* news, in which the client requests a list of articles in a given newsgroup or hierarchy that have arrived at the server's site after a specified date, and chooses those it cannot find in its history file. The third mode is for interactive newsreading and allows you or your newsreader to retrieve articles from specified newgroups, as well as post articles with incomplete header information.

At each site, news is kept in a directory hierarchy below */var/spool/news*, each article in a separate file, and each newsgroup in a separate directory. The directory name is made up of the newsgroup name, with the components being the path components. Thus, *comp.os.linux.misc* articles are kept in */var/spool/news/comp/os/linux/misc*. The articles in a newsgroup are assigned numbers in the order they arrive. This number serves as the file's name. The range of numbers of articles currently online is kept in a file called *active*, which at the same time serves as a list of newsgroups known at your site.

Since disk space is a finite resource,[*] one has to start throwing away articles after some time. This is called *expiring*. Usually, articles from certain groups and hierarchies are expired at a fixed number of days after they arrive. This may be overridden by the poster by specifying a date of expiration in the Expires: field of the article header.

---

* Some people claim that Usenet is a conspiracy by modem and hard disk vendors.

CHAPTER SEVENTEEN

C NEWS

O ne of the most popular software packages for Netnews is C News. It was designed for sites that carry news over UUCP links. This chapter will discuss the central concepts of C News and basic installation and maintenance tasks.

C News stores its configuration files in */usr/lib/news*, and most of its binaries in the */usr/lib/news/bin* directory. Articles are kept below */var/spool/news*. You should make sure that virtually all files in these directories are owned by user **news**, group **news**. Most problems arise from files being inaccessible to C News. Make it a rule for you to become user **news** using *su* before you touch anything in there. The only exception is *setnewsids*, which is used to set the real user ID of some news programs. It must be owned by **root** and must have the setuid bit set.

In this chapter, we describe all C News configuration files in detail and show you what you have to do to keep your site running.

Delivering News

Articles can be fed to C News in several ways. When a local user posts an article, the newsreader usually hands it to the *inews* command, which completes the header information. News from remote sites, be it a single article or a whole batch, is given to the *rnews* command, which stores it in the */var/spool/news/in.coming* directory, from where it will be picked up at a later time by *newsrun*. With any of these two techniques, however, the article will eventually be handed to the *relaynews* command.

For each article, the *relaynews* command first checks if the article has already been seen at the local site by looking up the message ID in the *history* file. Duplicate articles will be dropped. Then, *relaynews* looks at the Newsgroups: header line to find out if the local site requests articles from any of these groups. If it does, and the newsgroup is listed in the *active* file, *relaynews* tries to store the article in the corresponding directory in the news spool area. If this directory does not exist, it is created. The article's message ID will then be logged to the *history* file. Otherwise, *relaynews* drops the article.

If *relaynews* fails to store an incoming article because a group it has been posted to is not listed in your *active* file, the article will be moved to the *junk* group.[*] *relaynews* will also check for stale or misdated articles and reject them. Incoming batches that fail for any other reason are moved to */var/spool/news/in.coming/bad*, and an error message is logged.

After this, the article will be relayed to all other sites that request news from these groups using the transport specified for each particular site. To make sure it isn't sent to a site that has already seen it, each destination site is checked against the article's Path: header field, which contains the list of sites the article has traversed so far, written in bang-path style. Only if the destination site's name does not appear in this list will the article be sent to it.

C News is commonly used to relay news between UUCP sites, although it is also possible to use it in an NNTP environment. To deliver news to a remote UUCP site—either in single articles or whole batches—*uux* is used to execute the *rnews* command on the remote site and feed the article or batch to it on standard input.

When batching is enabled for a given site, C News does not send any incoming article immediately, but appends its path name to a file, usually called *out.going/site/togo*. Periodically, a batcher program is executed from a *crontab* entry,[†] which puts the articles in one or more files, optionally compresses them, and sends them to *rnews* at the remote site.

Figure 17-1 shows the news flow through *relaynews*. Articles may be relayed to the local site (denoted by ME), to some site named **ponderosa** via email, and a site named **moria**, for which batching is enabled.

Installation

To install C News, un-*tar* the files into their proper places if you haven't already done so, and edit the configuration files listed below. They are all located in */usr/lib/news*. Their formats will be described in the following sections.

---

* There may be a difference between the groups that exist at your site, and those that your site is willing to receive. For example, the subscription list may specify *comp.all*, which means all newsgroups below the *comp* hierarchy, but at your site, a number of *comp* groups are not listed in *active*. Articles posted to those groups will be moved to *junk*.
† Note that this should be the *crontab* of **news**, in order to not mangle file permissions.

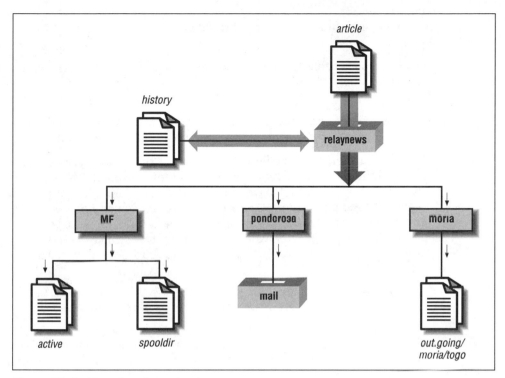

Figure 17–1. News flow through relaynews

sys You probably have to modify the ME line that describes your system, although using all/all is always a safe bet. You also have to add a line for each site you feed news to.

If you are a leaf site, you only need a line that sends all locally generated articles to your feed. Assume your feed is *moria*, then your *sys* file should look like this:

```
ME:all/all::
moria/moria.orcnet.org:all/all,!local:f:
```

organization

Your organization's name, for example, "Virtual Brewery, Inc." On your home machine, enter "private site," or anything else you like. Most people will not call your site properly configured if you haven't customized this file.

newsgroups

A list of all newsgroups, with a one-line description of each one's purpose. These descriptions are frequently used by your newsreader when displaying the list of all groups you are subscribed to.

mailname

> Your site's mail name, e.g., **vbrew.com**.

whoami

> Your site's name for news purposes. Quite often, the UUCP site name is used, for example, **vbrew**.

explist

> You should probably edit this file to reflect your preferred expiry times for some special newsgroups. Disk space may play an important role in it.

To create an initial hierarchy of newsgroups, obtain an *active* and a *newsgroups* file from the site that feeds you, and install them in */usr/lib/news*, making sure they are owned by **news** and have a mode of 644. Remove all *to.** groups from the active file, and add *to.my-site* and *to.feed-site*, as well as *junk* and *control*. The *to.** groups are normally used for exchanging ihave/sendme messages, but you should create them regardless of whether you plan to use ihave/sendme or not. Next, replace all article numbers in the second and third field of *active* using the following commands:

```
# cp active active.old
# sed 's/ [0-9]* [0-9]* / 0000000000 00001 /' active.old > active
# rm active.old
```

The second command is an invocation of *sed*, one of my favorite UNIX commands. This invocation replaces two strings of digits with a string of zeroes and the string 000001, respectively.

Finally, create the news spool directory and the subdirectories used for incoming and outgoing news:

```
# cd /var/spool
# mkdir news news/in.coming news/out.going
# chown -R news.news news
# chmod -R 755 news
```

If you're using a later release of C News, you may also have to create the *out.master* directory in the news spool directory.

If you're using newsreaders from a different distribution than the C News you have running, you may find that some expect the news spool in */usr/spool/news* rather than */var/spool/news*. If your newsreader doesn't seem to find any articles, create a symbolic link from */usr/spool/news* to */var/spool/news*.

Now, you are ready to receive news. Note that you don't have to create any directories other than those shown above, because each time C News receives an article from a group for which there's no spool directory, it will create it.

In particular, this happens to *all* groups an article has been cross-posted to. So, after a while, you will find your news spool cluttered with directories for newsgroups you have never subscribed to, like *alt.lang.teco*. You may prevent this by either removing all unwanted groups from *active*, or by regularly running a shell script which removes all empty directories below */var/spool/news* (except *out.going* and *in.coming*, of course).

Chapter 14
Chapter 15

C News needs a user to send error messages and status reports to. By default, this is **usenet**. If you use the default, you have to set up an alias for it which forwards all of its mail to one or more responsible persons. You may also override this behavior by setting the environment variable NEWSMASTER to the appropriate name. You have to do so in **news**'s *crontab* file, as well as every time you invoke an administrative tool manually, so installing an alias is probably easier.

While you're hacking */etc/passwd*, make sure that every user has her real name in the pw_gecos field of the password file (this is the fourth field). It is a question of Usenet netiquette that the sender's real name appears in the From: field of the article. Of course, you will want to do so anyway when you use mail.

The sys File

The *sys* file, located in */usr/lib/news*, controls which hierarchies you receive and forward to other sites. Although there are maintenance tools named *addfeed* and *delfeed*, I think it's better to maintain this file by hand.

The *sys* file contains entries for each site you forward news to, as well as a description of the groups you will accept. An entry looks like this:

```
site[/exclusions]:grouplist[/distlist][:flags[:cmds]]
```

Entries may be continued across newlines using a backslash (\). A hash sign (#) denotes a comment.

site

> This is the name of the site the entry applies to. One usually chooses the site's UUCP name for this. There has to be an entry for your site in the *sys* file too, or you will not receive any articles yourself.
>
> The special site name ME denotes your site. The ME entry defines all groups you are willing to store locally. Articles that aren't matched by the ME line will go to the *junk* group.
>
> Since C News checks *site* against the site names in the Path: header field, you have to make sure they really match. Some sites use their fully qualified domain name in this field, or an alias like news.*site.domain*. To prevent any articles from being returned to these sites, you have to add these to the exclusion list, separated by commas.
>
> For the entry applying to site **moria**, for instance, the *site* field would contain moria/moria.orcnet.org.

grouplist

> This is a comma-separated subscription list of groups and hierarchies for this particular site. A hierarchy may be specified by giving the hierarchy's prefix (such as *comp.os* for all groups whose names start with this prefix), optionally followed by the keyword *all* (e.g., *comp.os.all*).
>
> A hierarchy or group is excluded from forwarding by preceding it with an exclamation mark. If a newsgroup is checked against the list, the longest match applies. For example, if *grouplist* contains this list:
>
> ```
> !comp,comp.os.linux,comp.folklore.computers
> ```
>
> no groups from the *comp* hierarchy except *comp.folklore.computers* and all groups below *comp.os.linux* will be fed to that site.
>
> If the site requests to be forwarded all news you receive yourself, enter `all` as *grouplist*.

distlist

> This value is offset from the *grouplist* by a slash and contains a list of distributions to be forwarded. Again, you may exclude certain distributions by preceding them with an exclamation mark. All distributions are denoted by `all`. Omitting *distlist* implies a list of `all`.
>
> For example, you may use a distribution list of `all,!local` to prevent news for local use only from being sent to remote sites.
>
> There are usually at least two distributions: `world`, which is often the default distribution used when none is specified by the user, and `local`. There may be other distributions that apply to a certain region, state, country, etc. Finally, there are two distributions used by C News only; these are `sendme` and `ihave`, and are used for the sendme/ihave protocol.
>
> The use of distributions is a subject of debate. For one, some newsreaders create bogus distributions by simply using the top-level hierarchy, for example, *comp* when posting to *comp.os.linux*. Distributions that apply to regions are often questionable, too, because news may travel outside of your region when sent across the Internet.[*] Distributions applying to an organization, however, are very meaningful; for example, to prevent confidential information from leaving the company network. This purpose, however, is generally served better by creating a separate newsgroup or hierarchy.

---

[*] It is not uncommon for an article posted in say, Hamburg, to go to Frankfurt via **reston.ans.net** in the Netherlands, or even via some site in the U.S.

flags

This option describes certain parameters for the feed. It may be empty, or a combination of the following:

F   This flag enables batching.

f   This is almost identical to the F flag, but allows C News to calculate the size of outgoing batches more precisely.

I   This flag makes C News produce an article list suitable for use by ihave/sendme. Additional modifications to the *sys* and the *batchparms* file are required to enable ihave/sendme.

n   This creates batch files for active NNTP transfer clients like *nntpxmit* (see Chapter 18, *A Description of NNTP*). The batch files contain the article's filename along with its message ID.

L   This tells C News to transmit only articles posted at your site. This flag may be followed by a decimal number *n*, which makes C News transfer articles posted only within *n* hops from your site. C News determines the number of hops from the Path: field.

u   This tells C News to batch only articles from unmoderated groups.

m   This tells C News to batch only articles from moderated groups.

You may use at most one of F, f, I, or n.

cmds

This field contains a command to be executed for each article unless batching is enabled. The article will be fed to the command on standard input. This should only be used for very small feeds; otherwise the load on both systems will be too high.

The default command is

```
uux - -r -z remote-system!rnews
```

This invokes *rnews* on the remote system, feeding it the article on standard input.

The default search path for commands given in this field is */bin:/usr/bin:- /usr/lib/news/bin/batch*. The latter directory contains a number of shell scripts whose names start with *via*; they are briefly described later in this chapter.

If batching is enabled using either of the F or f, I or n flags, C News expects to find a filename in this field rather than a command. If the filename does not begin with a slash (/), it is assumed to be relative to */var/spool/news/out.going*. If the field is empty, it defaults to *remote-system/togo*.

When setting up C News, you will most probably have to write your own *sys* file. To help you with it, here is a sample file for **vbrew.com**, from which you may copy what you need.

```
# We take whatever they give us.
ME:all/all::
# We send everything we receive to moria, except for local and
# brewery-related articles. We use batching.
moria/moria.orcnet.org:all,!to,to.moria/all,!local,!brewery:f:
# We mail comp.risks to jack@ponderosa.uucp
ponderosa:comp.risks/all::rmail jack@ponderosa.uucp
# swim gets a minor feed
swim/swim.twobirds.com:comp.os.linux,rec.humor.oracle/all,!local:f:
# Log mail map articles for later processing
usenet-maps:comp.mail.maps/all:F:/var/spool/uumaps/work/batch
```

The active File

The *active* file is located in */usr/lib/news* and lists all groups known at your site and the articles currently online. You will rarely have to touch it, but we explain it nevertheless for sake of completeness. Entries take the following form:

```
newsgroup high low perm
```

newsgroup is the group's name. *low* and *high* are the lowest and highest numbers of articles currently available. If none are available at the moment, *low* is equal to *high*+1.

At least, that's what the *low* field is meant to do. However, for efficiency, C News doesn't update this field. This wouldn't be such a big loss if there weren't some newsreaders that depend on it. For instance, *trn* checks this field to see if it can purge any articles from its thread database. To update the *low* field, you therefore have to run the *updatemin* command regularly (or, in earlier versions of C News, the *upact* script).

perm is a parameter detailing the access users are granted to the group. It takes one of the following values:

y   Users are allowed to post to this group.

n   Users are not allowed to post to this group. However, the group may still be read.

x   This group has been disabled locally. This happens sometimes when news admininistrators (or their superiors) take offense to articles posted to certain groups.

Articles received for this group are not stored locally, although they are forwarded to the sites that request them.

m   This denotes a moderated group. When a user tries to post to this group, an intelligent newsreader will notify her of this and send the article to the moderator instead. The moderator's address is taken from the *moderators* file in */usr/lib/news*.

`=real-group`
This marks *newsgroup* as being a local alias for another group, namely *real-group*. All articles posted to *newsgroup* will be redirected to it.

In C News, you will generally not have to access this file directly. Groups can be added or deleted locally using *addgroup* and *delgroup* (see the section "Maintenance Tools and Tasks" below). A `newgroup` control message adds a group for the whole of Usenet, while a `rmgroup` message deletes a group. *Never send such a message yourself!* For instructions on how to create a newsgroup, read the monthly postings in *news.announce.newusers*.

A file closely related to *active* is *active.times*. Whenever a group is created, C News logs a message to this file containing the name of the group created, the date of creation, whether it was done by a `newgroup` control message or locally, and who did it. This is for the convenience of newsreaders who may notify the user of any recently created groups. It is also used by the NEWGROUPS command of NNTP.

Article Batching

News batches follow a particular format which is the same for B News, C News, and INN. Each article is preceded by a line like this:

```
#! rnews count
```

count is the number of bytes in the article. When batch compression is used, the resulting file is compressed as a whole and preceded by another line, indicated by the message to be used for unpacking. The standard compression tool is *compress*, which is marked by

```
#! cunbatch
```

Sometimes, when having to send batches via mail software that removes the eighth bit from all data, a compressed batch may be protected using what is called *c7-encoding*; these batches will be marked by *c7unbatch*.

When a batch is fed to *rnews* on the remote site, it checks for these markers and processes the batch appropriately. Some sites also use other compression tools, like *gzip*, and precede their gzipped files with *zunbatch* instead. C News does not recognize non-standard headers like these; you have to modify the source to support them.

In C News, article batching is performed by */usr/lib/news/bin/batch/sendbatches*, which takes a list of articles from the *site/togo* file, and puts them into several newsbatches. It should be executed once per hour or even more frequently, depending on the volume of traffic. Its operation is controlled by the *batchparms* file in */usr/lib/news*. This file describes the maximum batch size allowed for each site, the batching and optional compression program to be used, and the transport for delivering it to the remote site. You may specify batching parameters on a per-site basis, as well as a set of default parameters for sites not explicitly mentioned.

To perform batching for a specific site, use the following command:

```
# su news -c "/usr/lib/news/bin/batch/sendbatches site"
```

When invoked without arguments, *sendbatches* handles all batch queues. The interpretation of "all" depends on the presence of a default entry in *batchparms*. If one is found, all directories in */var/spool/news/out.going* are checked; otherwise, it cycles through all entries in *batchparms*. Note that *sendbatches*, when scanning the *out.going* directory, takes only those directories that contain no dots or at signs (@) as sitenames.

When installing C News, you will most likely find a *batchparms* file in your distribution which contains a reasonable default entry, so there's a good chance that you won't have to touch the file. Just in case, we describe its format. Each line consists of six fields, separated by spaces or tabs:

```
site size max batcher muncher transport
```

`site` is the name of the site the entry applies to. The *togo* file for this site must reside in *out.going/togo* below the news spool. A site name of `/default/` denotes the default entry.

`size` is the maximum size of article batches created (before compression). For single articles larger than this, C News makes an exception and puts them in a single batch by themselves.

`max` is the maximum number of batches created and scheduled for transfer before batching stalls for this particular site. This is useful in case the remote site should be down for a long time, because it prevents C News from cluttering your UUCP spool directories with zillions of newsbatches.

C News determines the number of queued batches using the *queulen* script in */usr/lib/news/bin*. Vince Skahan's *newspak* release should contain a script for BNU-compatible UUCPs. If you use a different flavor of spool directories, for example, Taylor UUCP, you might have to write your own.[*]

---

[*] If you don't care about the number of spool files (because you're the only person using your computer, and you don't write articles by the megabyte), you may replace the script's contents by a simple *exit 0* statement.

The *batcher* field contains the command used for producing a batch from the list of articles in the *togo* file. For regular feeds, this is usually *batcher*. For other purposes, alternative batchers may be provided. For instance, the ihave/sendme protocol requires the article list to be turned into ihave or sendme control messages, which are posted to the newsgroup *to.site*. This is performed by *batchih* and *batchsm*.

The *muncher* field specifies the command used for compression. Usually, this is *compcun*, a script that produces a compressed batch.* Alternatively, you might provide a muncher that uses *gzip*, say *gzipcun* (to be clear: you have to write it yourself). You have to make sure that *uncompress* on the remote site is patched to recognize files compressed with *gzip*.

If the remote site does not have an *uncompress* command, you may specify *nocomp*, which does not do any compression.

The last field, *transport*, describes the transport to be used. A number of standard commands for different transports are available whose names begin with *via*. *sendbatches* passes them the destination sitename on the command line. If the *batchparms* entry is not /default/, it derives the sitename from the *site* field by stripping it of anything after and including the first dot or slash. If the *batchparms* entry is /default/, the directory names in *out.going* are used.

There are two commands that use *uux* to execute *rnews* on the remote system; *viauux* and *viauuxz*. The latter sets the *−z* flag for (older versions of) *uux* to keep it from returning success messages for each article delivered. Another command, *viamail*, sends article batches to the user **rnews** on the remote system via mail. Of course, this requires that the remote system somehow feeds all mail for **rnews** to their local news system. For a complete list of these transports, refer to the *newsbatch* manual page.

All commands from the last three fields must be located in either *out.going/site* or */usr/lib/news/bin/batch*. Most of them are scripts, so that you can easily tailor new tools for your personal needs. They are invoked as a pipe. The list of articles is fed to the batcher on standard input, which produces the batch on standard output. This is piped into the muncher, and so on.

A sample file is given below.

```
# batchparms file for the brewery
# site        | size    |max    |batcher  |muncher    |transport
#-------------+---------+-------+---------+-----------+-----------
/default/       100000  22       batcher   compcun     viauux
swim             10000  10       batcher   nocomp      viauux
```

---

* As shipped with C News, *compcun* uses *compress* with the 12-bit option, since this is the least common denominator for most sites. You may produce a copy of it, say *compcun16*, where you use 16-bit compression. The improvement is not too impressive, though.

Expiring News

In B News, expiring used to be performed by a program called *expire*, which took a list of newsgroups as arguments, along with a time specification after which articles had to be expired. To have different hierarchies expire at different times, you had to write a script that invoked *expire* for each of them separately. C News offers a more convenient solution to this. In a file called *explist*, you may specify newsgroups and expiration intervals. A command called *doexpire* is usually run once a day from *cron*, and processes all groups according to this list.

Occasionally, you may want to retain articles from certain groups even after they have been expired; for example, you might want to keep programs posted to *comp.sources.unix*. This is called *archiving*. *explist* permits you to mark groups for archiving.

An entry in *explist* looks like this:

```
grouplist perm times archive
```

grouplist is a comma-separated list of newsgroups to which the entry applies. Hierarchies may be specified by giving the group name prefix, optionally appended with `all`. For example, for an entry applying to all groups below *comp.os*, you might either enter `comp.os` or `comp.os.all`.

When expiring news from a group, the name is checked against all entries in *explist* in the order given. The first matching entry applies. For example, to throw away the majority of *comp* after four days, except for *comp.os.linux.announce*, which you want to keep for a week, you simply have an entry for the latter, which specifies a seven-day expiration period, followed by that for *comp*, which specifies four days.

The `perm` field details if the entry applies to moderated, unmoderated, or any groups. It may take the values `m`, `u`, or `x`, which denote moderated, unmoderated, or any type.

The third field, `times`, usually contains only a single number. This is the number of days after which articles will be expired if they haven't been assigned an artificial expiration date in an `Expires:` field in the article header. Note that this is the number of days counting from its *arrival* at your site, not the date of posting.

The `times` field may, however, be more complex than that. It may be a combination of up to three numbers separated from one another by a dash. The first denotes the number of days that have to pass before the article is considered a candidate for expiration. It is rarely useful to use a value other than zero. The second field is the above-mentioned default number of days after which it will be expired. The third is the number of days after which an article will be expired unconditionally, regardless of whether it has an `Expires:` field or not. If only the middle number is given, the other two take default values. These may be specified using the special entry `/bounds/`, which is described below.

The fourth field, *archive*, denotes whether the newsgroup is to be archived and where. If no archiving is intended, a dash should be used. Otherwise, you either use a full pathname (pointing to a directory) or an at-sign (@). The at-sign denotes the default archive directory, which must then be given to *doexpire* by using the −*a* flag on the command line. An archive directory should be owned by **news**. When *doexpire* archives an article from say, *comp.sources.unix*, it stores it in the directory *comp/sources/unix* below the archive directory, creating it if necessary. The archive directory itself, however, will not be created.

There are two special entries in your *explist* file that *doexpire* relies on. Instead of a list of newsgroups, they have the keywords /bounds/ and /expired/. The /bounds/ entry contains the default values for the three values of the *times* field described above.

The /expired/ field determines how long C News will hold on to lines in the *history* file. This is needed because C News will not remove a line from the history file once the corresponding article(s) have been expired, but will hold on to it in case a duplicate should arrive after this date. If you are fed by only one site, you can keep this value small. Otherwise, a couple of weeks is advisable on UUCP networks, depending on the delays you experience with articles from these sites.

A sample *explist* file with rather tight expiry intervals is reproduced below:

```
# keep history lines for two weeks. Nobody gets more than three months
/expired/                       x      14      -
/bounds/                        x      0-1-90  -
# groups we want to keep longer than the rest
comp.os.linux.announce          m      10      -
comp.os.linux                   x      5       -
alt.folklore.computers          u      10      -
rec.humor.oracle                m      10      -
soc.feminism                    m      10      -
# Archive *.sources groups
comp.sources,alt.sources        x      5       @
# defaults for tech groups
comp,sci                        x      7       -
# enough for a long weekend
misc,talk                       x      4       -
# throw away junk quickly
junk                            x      1       -
# control messages are of scant interest, too
control                         x      1       -
# catch-all entry for the rest of it
all                             x      2       -
```

Expiring presents several potential problems. One is that your newsreader might rely on the third field of the active file, which contains the number of the lowest article online. When expiring articles, C News does not update this field. If you need (or want) to have this field represent the real situation, you need to run a program called *updatemin* after each run of *doexpire*. (In older versions of C News, this was done by a script called *upact*.)

C News does not expire by scanning the newsgroup's directory, but simply checks the *history* file if the article is due for expiration.[*] If your history file somehow gets out of sync, articles may be around on your disk forever, because C News has literally forgotten them.[†] You can repair this by using the *addmissing* script in */usr/lib/news/bin/maint*, which will add missing articles to the *history* file, or *mkhistory*, which rebuilds the entire file from scratch. Don't forget to become **news** before invoking it, or else you will wind up with a *history* file unreadable by C News.

Miscellaneous Files

There are a number of files that control the behavior of C News but are not essential to its functioning. All of them reside in */usr/lib/news*. We will describe them briefly.

newsgroups
> This is a companion file of *active* which contains a list of each newsgroup name along with a one-line description of its main topic. This file is automatically updated when C News receives a **checknews** control message.

localgroups
> If you have a number of local groups that you don't want C News to complain about every time you receive a **checknews** message, put their names and descriptions in this file, just like they would appear in *newsgroups*.

mailpaths
> This file contains the moderator's address for each moderated group. Each line contains the group name followed by the moderator's email address (offset by a tab).

RFC 822
> Two special entries are provided as default: **backbone** and **internet**. Both provide, in bang-path notation, the path to the nearest backbone site and the site that understands RFC 822-style addresses (*user@host*). The default entries are

```
internet                backbone
```

> You will not have to change the **internet** entry if you have *smail* or *sendmail* installed, because they understand RFC 822-addressing.

---

[*] The article's date of arrival is kept in the middle field of the history line, given in seconds since January 1, 1970.
[†] I don't know *why* this happens, but for me, it does from time to time.

The **backbone** entry is used whenever a user posts to a moderated group whose moderator is not listed explicitly. If the newsgroup's name is *alt.sewer*, and the **backbone** entry contains *path!%s*, C News will mail the article to *path!alt-sewer*, hoping that the backbone machine is able to forward the article. To find out which path to use, ask the news-admin at the site that feeds you. As a last resort, you can also use *uunet.uu.net!%s*.

distributions

This file is not really a C News file, but it is used by some newsreaders and *nntpd*. It contains the list of distributions recognized by your site and a description of their (intended) effects. For example, Virtual Brewery has the following file:

```
world        everywhere in the world
local        Only local to this site
nl           Netherlands only
mugnet       MUGNET only
fr           France only
de           Germany only
brewery      Virtual Brewery only
```

log This file contains a log of all C News activities. It is culled regularly by running *newsdaily*; copies of the old log files are kept in *log.o, log.oo*, etc.

errlog

This is a log of all error messages created by C News. These do not include articles junked due to wrong group, etc. This file is mailed to the newsmaster (**usenet** by default) automatically by *newsdaily* if it is found to be non-empty.

errlog is cleared by *newsdaily*. Old copies are kept in *errlog.o* and companions.

batchlog

This logs all runs of *sendbatches*. It is usually of scant interest only. It is also attended by *newsdaily*.

watchtime

This is an empty file created each time *newswatch* is run.

Control Messages

The Usenet news protocol knows a special category of articles which evoke certain responses or actions by the news system. These are called *control* messages. They are recognized by the presence of a Control: field in the article header, which contains the name of the control operation to be performed. There are several types of them, all of which are handled by shell scripts located in */usr/lib/news/ctl*.

Most of these will perform their action automatically at the time the article is processed by C News without notifying the newsmaster. By default, only check-groups messages will be handed to the newsmaster, but you may change this by editing the scripts.

The cancel Message

The most widely known message is cancel, with which a user can cancel an article sent by her earlier. This effectively removes the article from the spool directories, if it exists. The cancel message is forwarded to all sites that receive news from the groups affected, regardless of whether the article has been seen already or not. This is to take into account the possibility that the original article has been delayed over the cancellation message. Some news systems allow users to cancel other person's messages; this is of course a definite no-no.

newgroup and rmgroup

Two messages dealing with creation or removal of newsgroups are the newgroup and rmgroup message. Newsgroups below the "usual" hierarchies may be created only after a discussion and voting has been held among Usenet readers. The rules applying to the *alt* hierarchy allow for something close to anarchy. For more information, see the regular postings in *news.announce.newusers* and *news.announce.newgroups*. Never send a newgroup or rmgroup message yourself unless you definitely know that you are allowed to.

The checkgroups Message

checkgroups messages are sent by news administrators to make all sites within a network synchronize their *active* files with the realities of Usenet. For example, commercial Internet service providers might send out such a message to their customers' sites. Once a month, the "official" checkgroups message for the major hierarchies is posted to *comp.announce.newgroups* by its moderator. However, it is posted as an ordinary article, not as a control message. To perform the check-groups operation, save this article to a file, say */tmp/check*, remove everything up to the beginning of the control message itself, and feed it to the checkgroups script using the following command:

```
# su news -c "/usr/lib/news/bin/ctl/checkgroups" < /tmp/check
```

This will update your *newsgroups* file, adding the groups listed in *localgroups*. The old *newsgroups* file will be moved to *newsgroups.bac*. Note that posting the message locally will rarely work, because *inews* refuses to accept that large an article.

If C News finds mismatches between the checkgroups list and the *active* file, it will produce a list of commands that would bring your site up to date and mail it to the news administrator.

The output typically looks like this:

```
From news Sun Jan 30 16:18:11 1994
Date: Sun, 30 Jan 94 16:18 MET
From: news (News Subsystem)
To: usenet
Subject: Problems with your active file
The following newsgroups are not valid and should be removed.
        alt.ascii-art
        bionet.molbio.gene-org
        comp.windows.x.intrisics
        de.answers
You can do this by executing the commands:
        /usr/lib/news/bin/maint/delgroup alt.ascii-art
        /usr/lib/news/bin/maint/delgroup bionet.molbio.gene-org
        /usr/lib/news/bin/maint/delgroup comp.windows.x.intrisics
        /usr/lib/news/bin/maint/delgroup de.answers
The following newsgroups were missing.
        comp.binaries.cbm
        comp.databases.rdb
        comp.os.geos
        comp.os.qnx
        comp.unix.user-friendly
        misc.legal.moderated
        news.newsites
        soc.culture.scientists
        talk.politics.crypto
        talk.politics.tibet
```

When you receive a message like this from your news system, don't believe it blindly. Depending on who sent the checkgroups message, it may lack a few groups or even entire hierarchies; so you should be careful about removing any groups. If you find groups are listed as missing that you want to carry at your site, you have to add them using the *addgroup* script. Save the list of missing groups to a file and feed it to the following little script:

```
#!/bin/sh
cd /usr/lib/news
while read group; do
    if grep -si "^$group[[:space:]].*moderated" newsgroup; then
        mod=m
    else
        mod=y
    fi
    /usr/lib/news/bin/maint/addgroup $group $mod
done
```

sendsys, version, and senduuname

Finally, there are three messages that can be used to find out about the network's topology. These are `sendsys`, `version`, and `senduuname`. They cause C News to return to the sender the *sys* file, a software version string, and the output of *uuname*, respectively. C News is very laconic about `version` messages; it returns a simple, unadorned "C."

Again, you should *never* issue such a message unless you have made sure that it cannot leave your (regional) network. Replies to `sendsys` messages can quickly bring down a UUCP network.[*]

C News in an NFS Environment

A simple way to distribute news within a local network is to keep all news on a central host and export the relevant directories via NFS so that newsreaders may scan the articles directly. The advantage of this method over NNTP is that the overhead involved in retrieving and threading articles is significantly lower. NNTP, on the other hand, wins in a heterogeneous network where equipment varies widely among hosts, or where users don't have equivalent accounts on the server machine.

When using NFS, articles posted on a local host have to be forwarded to the central machine, because accessing adminstrative files might otherwise expose the system to race-conditions that leave the files inconsistent. Also, you might want to protect your news spool area by exporting it read-only, which requires forwarding to the central machine, too.

C News handles this transparently. When you post an article, your newsreader usually invokes *inews* to inject the article into the news system. This command runs a number of checks on the article, completes the header, and checks the file *server* in */usr/lib/news*. If this file exists and contains a hostname different from the local host's name, *inews* is invoked on that server host via *rsh*. Since the *inews* script uses a number of binary commands and support files from C News, you have to either have C News installed locally, or mount the news software from the server.

For the *rsh* invocation to work properly, each user must have an equivalent account on the server system, i.e., one to which she can log in without being asked for a password.

Make sure that the hostname given in *server* literally matches the output of the *hostname* command on the server machine, or else C News will loop forever when trying to deliver the article.

---

[*] I wouldn't try this on the Internet, either.

Maintenance Tools and Tasks

Despite the complexity of C News, a news administrator's life can be fairly easy because C News provides you with a wide variety of maintenance tools. Some of these are intended to be run regularly from *cron*, like *newsdaily*. Using these scripts greatly reduces daily care and feeding requirements of your C News installation.

Unless stated otherwise, these commands are located in */usr/lib/news/bin/maint*. Note that you must become user **news** before invoking these commands. Running them as superuser may render these files inaccessible to C News.

newsdaily
> The name already says it: runs this once a day. It is an important script that helps you keep log files small, retaining copies of each from the last three runs. It also tries to sense any anomalies, like stale batches in the incoming and outgoing directories, postings to unkown or moderated newsgroups, etc. Resulting error messages will be mailed to the newsmaster.

newswatch
> This is a script that should be run regularly to look for anomalies in the news system, once an hour or so. It is intended to detect problems that will have immediate effect on the operability of your news system, and mail a trouble report to the newsmaster. Things checked include stale lock files that don't get removed, unattended input batches, and disk space shortage.

addgroup
> Adds a group to your site locally. The proper invocation is
>
>   addgroup groupname y|n|m|=realgroup
>
> The second argument has the same meaning as the flag in the *active* file, meaning that anyone may post to the group (y), that no one may post (n), that it is moderated (m), or that it is an alias for another group (=realgroup).
>
> You might also want to use *addgroup* when the first articles in a newly created group arrive earlier than the newgroup control message that is intended to create it.

delgroup
> Allows you to delete a group locally. Invoke it as
>
>   delgroup groupname
>
> You still have to delete the articles that remain in the newsgroup's spool directory. Alternatively, you might leave it to the natural course of events (a.k.a. *expire*) to make them go away.

addmissing
> Adds missing articles to the *history* file. Run this script when there are articles that seem to hang around forever.

newsboot
> This script should be run at system boot time. It removes any lock files left over when news processes were killed at shutdown, and closes and executes any batches left over from NNTP connections that were terminated when shutting down the system.

newsrunning
> This resides in */usr/lib/news/bin/input* and may be used to disable unbatching of incoming news, for instance during work hours. You may turn off unbatching by invoking

```
/usr/lib/news/bin/input/newsrunning off
```

> It is turned on by using on instead of off.

CHAPTER EIGHTEEN
A DESCRIPTION
OF NNTP

RFC 977

D ue to the different network transport used, NNTP provides for a vastly different approach to news exchange from C news. NNTP stands for
Network News Transfer Protocol. It is not a particular software package,
but an Internet Standard. It is based on a stream-oriented connection—usually
over TCP—between a client anywhere in the network and a server on a host that
keeps Netnews on disk storage. The stream connection allows the client and
server to interactively negotiate article transfer with nearly no turnaround delay,
thus keeping the number of duplicate articles low. Together with the Internet's
high transfer rates, this adds up to a news transport that surpasses the original
UUCP networks by far. While some years ago it was not uncommon for an article
to take two weeks or more before it arrived in the last corner of Usenet, this is
now often less than two days; on the Internet itself, it is even within the range of
minutes.

Various commands allow clients to retrieve, send, and post articles. The difference
between sending and posting is that the latter may involve articles with incomplete
header information.[*] Article retrieval may be used by news transfer clients as well
as newsreaders. This makes NNTP an excellent tool for providing news access to
many clients on a local network without going through the contortions that are
necessary when using NFS.

NNTP also provides for an active and a passive way of news transfer, colloquially
called "pushing" and "pulling." Pushing is basically the same as the C news
ihave/sendme protocol. The client offers an article to the server through the
"*IHAVE <msgid>*" command, and the server returns a response code that indicates
whether it already has the article or if it wants it. If so, the client sends the article,
terminated by a single dot on a separate line.

Pushing news has the single disadvantage that it places a heavy load on the server
system, since it has to search its history database for every single article.

---

* When posting an article over NNTP, the server always adds at least one header field,
which is Nntp-Posting-Host:. It contains the client's hostname.

The opposite technique is pulling news, in which the client requests a list of all (available) articles from a group that have arrived after a specified date. This query is performed by the NEWNEWS command. From the returned list of message IDs, the client selects those articles it does not yet have, using the ARTICLE command for each of them in turn.

The problem with pulling news is that it needs tight control by the server over which groups and distributions it allows a client to request. For example, it has to make sure that no confidential material from newsgroups local to the site are sent to unauthorized clients.

There are also a number of convenience commands for newsreaders that permit them to retrieve the article header and body separately, or even single header lines from a range of articles. This lets you keep all news on a central host, with all users on the (presumably local) network using NNTP-based client programs for reading and posting. This is an alternative to exporting the news directories via NFS, as described in Chapter 17, *C News*.

An overall problem of NNTP is that it allows a knowledgeable person to insert articles into the news stream with false sender specification. This is called *news faking*.[*] An extension to NNTP allows you to require user authentication for certain commands.

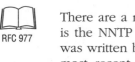

RFC 977

There are a number of NNTP packages available. One of the more widely known is the NNTP daemon, also known as the *reference implementation*. Originally, it was written by Stan Barber and Phil Lapsley to illustrate the details of RFC 977. Its most recent version is *nntpd-1.5.11*, which will be described below. You may either get the source and compile it yourself, or use the *nntpd* from Fred van Kempen's *net-std* binary package. No ready-to-go binaries of *nntpd* are provided, because of various site-specific values that must be compiled in.

The *nntpd* package consists of a server and two clients for pulling and pushing news, respectively, as well as an *inews* replacement. They live in a B News environment, but with a little tweaking, they will be happy with C News, too. However, if you plan to use NNTP for more than offering newsreaders access to your news server, the reference implementation is not really an option. We will therefore discuss only the NNTP daemon contained in the *nntpd* package and leave out the client programs.

There is also a package called *InterNet News*, or INN, that was written by Rich Salz. It provides both NNTP and UUCP-based news transport, and is more suitable for large news hubs. When it comes to news transport over NNTP, it is definitely better than *nntpd*. INN is currently at version *inn-1.4sec*. There is a kit for building INN on a Linux machine from Arjan de Vet; it is available from **sunsite.unc.edu** in the *system/Mail* directory. If you want to set up INN, please refer to the documentation that comes with the source, as well as the INN FAQ posted regularly to *news.software.b*.

---

[*] The same problem exists with SMTP, the Simple Mail Transfer Protocol.

Installing the NNTP Server

The NNTP server is called *nntpd*, and may be compiled in two ways, depending on the expected load on the news system. There are no compiled versions available, because of some site-specific defaults that are hard-coded into the executable. All configuration is done through macros defined in *common/conf.h*.

nntpd may be configured as either a standalone server that is started at system boot time from *rc.inet2*, or a daemon managed by *inetd*. In the latter case, you have to have the following entry in */etc/inetd.conf*:

```
nntp    stream tcp nowait    news    /usr/etc/in.nntpd    nntpd
```

If you configure *nntpd* as standalone, make sure that any such line in *inetd.conf* is commented out. In either case, you have to make sure the following line appears in */etc/services*:

```
nntp    119/tcp    readnews untp    # Network News Transfer Protocol
```

To temporarily store any incoming articles, *nntpd* also needs a *.tmp* directory in your news spool. You should create it using the following commands:

```
# mkdir /var/spool/news/.tmp
# chown news.news /var/spool/news/.tmp
```

Restricting NNTP Access

Access to NNTP resources is governed by the file *nntp_access* in */usr/lib/news*. Lines in this file describe the access rights granted to foreign hosts. Each line has the following format:

```
site    read|xfer|both|no    post|no    [!exceptgroups]
```

If a client connects to the NNTP port, *nntpd* attempts to obtain the host's fully qualified domain name from its IP address by reverse lookup. The client's hostname and IP address are checked against the *site* field of each entry in the order in which they appear in the file. Matches may be either partial or exact. If an entry matches exactly, it applies; if the match is partial, it only applies if there is no other match following it that is at least as good. *site* may be specified in one of the following ways:

Hostname
> This is a fully qualified domain name of a host. If this matches the client's canonical hostname literally, the entry applies, and all following entries are ignored.

IP address
> This is an IP address in dotted quad notation. If the client's IP address matches this, the entry applies, and all following entries are ignored.

Domain name
> This is a domain name, specified as *.*domain*. If the client's hostname matches the domain name, the entry matches.

Network name
> This is the name of a network as specified in */etc/networks*. If the network number of the client's IP address matches the network number associated with the network name, the entry matches.

Default
> The string default matches any client.

Entries with a more general site specification should be specified earlier, because any matches by these will be overridden by later, more exact matches.

The second and third fields describe the access rights granted to the client. The second details the permissions to retrieve news by pulling (**read**), and transmit news by pushing (**xfer**). A value of **both** enables both; **no** denies access altogether. The third field grants the client the right to post articles, i.e., deliver articles with incomplete header information, which is completed by the news software. If the second field contains **no**, the third field is ignored.

The fourth field is optional and contains a comma-separated list of groups the client is denied access to.

This is a sample *nntp_access* file:

```
#
# by default, anyone may transfer news, but not read or post
default                 xfer            no
#
# public.vbrew.com offers public access via modem, we allow
# them to read and post to any but the local.* groups
public.vbrew.com        read            post        !local
#
# all other hosts at the brewery may read and post
*.vbrew.com             read            post
```

NNTP Authorization

When capitalizing the access tokens like **xfer** or **read** in the *nntp_acces* file, *nntpd* requires the authorization from the client for the respective operations. For instance, when specifying a permission of **Xfer** or **XFER**, *nntpd* will not let the client transfer articles to your site unless it passes authorization.

The authorization procedure is implemented by means of a new NNTP command named AUTHINFO. Using this command, the client transmits a username and a password to the NNTP server. *nntpd* will validate them by checking them against the */etc/passwd* database and verify that the user belongs to the **nntp** group.

The current implementation of NNTP authorization is only experimental and has therefore not been implemented very portably. The result of this is that it works only with plain-style password databases; shadow passwords will not be recognized.

nntpd Interaction with C News

When receiving an article, *nntpd* has to deliver it to the news subsystem. Depending on whether it was received as a result of an IHAVE or POST command, the article is handed to *rnews* or *inews*, respectively. Instead of invoking *rnews*, you may also configure it (at compile time) to batch the incoming articles and move the resulting batches to */var/spool/news/in.coming*, where they are left for *relaynews* to pick them up at the next queue run.

To be able to properly perform the ihave/sendme protocol, *nntpd* has to be able to access the *history* file. At compile time, you therefore have to make sure the path is set correctly. You should also make sure that C news and *nntpd* agree on the format of your history file. C news uses *dbm* hashing functions to access it; however, there are quite a number of different and slightly incompatible implementations of the *dbm* library. If C news has been linked with a different *dbm* library than you have in your standard *libc*, you have to link *nntpd* with this library, too.

A typical symptom of *nntpd* and C news disagreeing on the database format are error messages in the system log that *nntpd* could not open it properly, or duplicate articles received via NNTP. A good test is to pick an article from your spool area, telnet to the nntp port, and offer it to *nntpd* as shown in the example below. Of course, you have to replace *<msg@id>* with the message-ID of the article you want to feed to *nntpd* again.

```
$ telnet localhost nntp
Trying 127.0.0.1...
Connected to localhost
Escape characters is '^ ]'.
201 vstout NNTP[auth] server version 1.5.11t (16 November 1991) ready at
Sun Feb 6 16:02:32 1194 (no posting)
IHAVE <msg@id>
435 Got it.
QUIT
```

This conversation shows the proper reaction of *nntpd*; the message "Got it" tells you that it already has this article. If you get a message of "*335 Ok*" instead, the lookup in the history file failed for some reason. Terminate the conversation by typing Ctrl-D. You can check what has gone wrong by checking the system log; *nntpd* logs all kinds of messages to the daemon facility of *syslog*. An incompatible *dbm* library usually manifests itself in a message complaining that *dbminit* failed.

CHAPTER NINETEEN
NEWSREADER
CONFIGURATION

A newsreader is a program that users invoke to view, store, and create news articles. Several newsreaders have been ported to Linux. Below, I will describe the basic setup for the three most popular ones, namely *tin*, *trn*, and *nn*.

One of the most effective newsreaders is

```
$ find /var/spool/news -name '[0-9]*' -exec cat {} \; | more
```

This is the way UNIX die-hards read their news.

Most newsreaders, however, are much more sophisticated. They usually offer a full-screen interface with separate levels for displaying all groups the user has subscribed to, an overview of all articles in each group, and individual articles.

At the newsgroup level, most newsreaders display a list of articles, showing their subject lines and authors. In big groups, it is difficult for the user to keep track of articles relating to each other, although it is possible to identify responses to earlier articles.

A response usually repeats the original article's subject, prepending it with "Re:". Additionally, the message ID of the article it is a direct follow-up to may be given in the References: header line. Sorting articles by these two criteria generates small clusters (in fact, trees) of articles, which are called *threads*. One of the tasks in writing a newsreader is devising an efficient scheme of threading, because the time required for this is proportional to the square of the number of articles.

Here, we will not go into how the user interfaces are built. All newsreaders currently available for Linux have a good help function, so you ought to get along.

In the following sections, we will deal only with administrative tasks. Most of these relate to the creation of threads databases and accounting.

tin Configuration

The most versatile newsreader with respect to threading is *tin*. It was written by Iain Lea and is loosely modeled on an older newsreader named *tass* (written by Rich Skrenta). It does its threading when the user enters the newsgroup, and it is pretty fast unless you're doing this via NNTP.

On a 486DX50, it takes roughly 30 seconds to thread 1000 articles when reading directly from disk. Over NNTP to a loaded news server, this would be somewhere over 5 minutes.[*] You may improve this time by regularly updating your index file with the *−u* option, or by invoking *tin* with the *−U* option.

Usually, *tin* dumps its threading databases in the user's home directory below *.tin/index*. This may be costly in terms of resources, however, so you should keep a single copy of them in a central location. This may be achieved by making *tin* setuid to **news**, for example, or some entirely unprivileged account.[†] *tin* will then keep all thread databases below */var/spool/news/.index*. For any file access or shell escape, it will reset its effective uid to the real uid of the user who invoked it.[‡]

A better solution is to install the *tind* indexing daemon that regularly updates the index files. This daemon, however, is not included in any release of Linux, so you have to compile it yourself. If you are running a LAN with a central news server, you may even run *tind* on the server and have all clients retrieve the index files via NNTP. This requires an extension to NNTP. Patches for *nntpd* that implement this extension are included in the *tin* source.

The version of *tin* included in some Linux distributions has no NNTP support compiled in, but most do have it now. When invoked as *rtin* or with the *−r* option, *tin* tries to connect to the NNTP server specified in the file */etc/nntpserver* or in the NNTPSERVER environment variable. The *nntpserver* file simply contains the server's name on a single line.

trn Configuration

trn is the successor to an older newsreader too, namely *rn* (which means *read news*). The "t" in its name stands for "threaded." It was written by Wayne Davidson.

Unlike *tin*, *trn* has no provision for generating its threading database at run-time. Instead, it uses those prepared by a program called *mthreads* that has to be invoked regularly from *cron* to update the index files.

---

* Things improve drastically if the NNTP server does the threading itself and lets the client retrieve the threads databases; INN-1.4 does this, for instance.
† However, do *not* use **nobody** for this. As a rule, no files or commands whatsoever should be associated with this user.
‡ This is the reason why you will get ugly error messages when invoking it as superuser. But then, you shouldn't do routine work as **root** anyway.

Not running *mthreads*, however, doesn't mean you cannot access new articles, it only means you will have all those "Novell buys out Linux!!" articles scattered across your article selection menu, instead of a single thread you may easily skip.

To turn on threading for particular newsgroups, *mthreads* is invoked with the list of newsgroups on the command line. The list is made up in exactly the same fashion as the one in the *sys* file:

```
$ mthreads comp,rec,!rec.games.go
```

This command will enable threading for all of *comp* and *rec*, except for *rec.games.go* (people who play Go don't need fancy threads). After that, you simply invoke it without any option at all to make it thread any newly arrived articles. Threading of all groups found in your *active* file can be turned on by invoking *mthreads* with a group list of *all*.

If you're receiving news during the night, you will customarily run *mthreads* once in the morning, but you can also to do so more frequently if needed. Sites that have very heavy traffic may want to run *mthreads* in daemon mode. When it is started at boot time using the *–d* option, it puts itself in the background, wakes up every 10 minutes to check if there are any newly-arrived articles, and threads them. To run *mthreads* in daemon mode, put the following line in your *rc.news* script:

```
/usr/local/bin/rn/mthreads -dcav
```

The *–a* option makes *mthreads* automatically turn on threading for new groups as they are created; *–v* enables verbose log messages to the *mthreads* log file *mt.log* in the directory where you have *trn* installed.

Chapter 17

Old articles no longer available must be removed from the index files regularly. By default, only articles whose number is below the low water mark will be removed.* Articles above this number who have been expired nevertheless (because the oldest article has been assigned a long expiry date by an Expires: header field) may be removed by giving *mthreads* the *–e* option to force an "enhanced" expiry run. When *mthreads* is running in daemon mode, the *–e* option makes it put in such an enhanced expiry run once a day, shortly after midnight.

nn Configuration

nn, written by Kim F. Storm, claims to be a newsreader whose ultimate goal is not to read news. Its name stands for "No News," and its motto is "No news is good news. *nn* is better."

To achieve this ambitious goal, *nn* comes with a large assortment of maintenance tools that not only allow generation of threads, but also extensive checks on the

---

* Note that C news doesn't update this low water mark automatically; you have to run *updatemin* to do so.

consistency of these databases, accounting, gathering of usage statistics, and access restrictions. There is also an administration program called *nnadmin*, which allows you to perform these tasks interactively. It is very intuitive, so we will not dwell on these aspects and only deal with the generation of the index files.

The *nn* threads database manager is called *nnmaster*. It is usually run as a daemon, started from the *rc.news* or *rc.inet2* script. It is invoked as

```
/usr/local/lib/nn/nnmaster -l -r -C
```

This enables threading for all newsgroups present in your *active* file.

Equivalently, you may invoke *nnmaster* periodically from *cron*, giving it a list of groups to act upon. This list is very similar to the subscription list in the *sys* file, except that it uses blanks instead of commas. Instead of the fake group name `all`, an empty argument of `""` should be used to denote all groups. A sample invocation is

```
# /usr/local/lib/nn/nnmaster !rec.games.go rec comp
```

Note that the order is significant. The leftmost group specification that matches always wins. Thus, if we had put `!rec.games.go` after `rec`, all articles from this group would have been threaded nevertheless.

nn offers several methods to remove expired articles from its databases. The first is to update the database by scanning the news group directories and discarding the entries whose corresponding article is no longer available. This is the default operation obtained by invoking *nnmaster* with the *−E* option. It is reasonably fast unless you're doing this via NNTP.

Method 2 behaves exactly like a default expiry run of *mthreads*, in that it only removes those entries that refer to articles whose number is below the low water mark in the *active* file. It may be enabled using the *−e* option.

Finally, a third strategy is to discard the entire database and recollect all articles. This may be done by giving *−E3* to *nnmaster*.

The list of groups to be expired is given by the *−F* option in the same fashion as above. However, if you have *nnmaster* running as daemon, you must kill it (using *−k*) before expiry can take place, and restart it with the original options afterwards. Thus the proper command to run expire on all groups using method 1 is:

```
# nnmaster -kF ""
# nnmaster -lrC
```

There are many more flags that may be used to fine-tune the behavior of *nn*. If you are concerned about removing bad articles or digestifying article digests, read the *nnmaster* manual page.

nnmaster relies on a file named *GROUPS*, which is located in */usr/local/lib/nn*. If it does not exist initially, it is created. For each newsgroup, it contains a line that begins with the group's name, optionally followed by a time stamp and flags. You may edit these flags to enable certain behavior for the group in question, but you may not change the order in which the groups appear.[*] The flags allowed and their effects are detailed in the *nnmaster* manual page, too.

---

[*] This is because their order has to agree with that of the entries in the (binary) *MASTER* file.

APPENDIX A

A Null Printer Cable for PLIP

To make a null printer cable for use with a PLIP connection, you need two 25-pin connectors (called DB-25) and some 11-conductor cable. The cable must be at most 15 meters long.

If you look at the connector, you should be able to read tiny numbers at the base of each pin, from 1 for the pin top left (if you hold the broader side up) to 25 for the pin bottom right. For the null printer cable, you have to connect the following pins of both connectors with each other:

D0	2	–	15	ERROR
D1	3	–	13	SLCT
D2	4	–	12	PAPOUT
D3	5	–	10	ACK
D4	6	–	11	BUSY
GROUND	25	–	25	GROUND
ERROR	15	–	2	D0
SLCT	13	–	3	D1
PAPOUT	12	–	4	D2
ACK	10	–	5	D3
BUSY	11	–	6	D4

All remaining pins remain unconnected. If the cable is shielded, the shield should be connected to the DB-25's metallic shell on one end only.

SAMPLE SMAIL CONFIGURATION FILES

smail(8)

 his section shows sample configuration files for a UUCP leaf site on a local area network. They are based on the sample files included in the source distribution of *smail-3.1.28*. Although I make a feeble attempt to explain how these files work, you are advised to read the very fine *smail(8)* manual page, which discusses these files in great length. Once you've understood the basic idea behind *smail* configuration, it's worthwhile reading. It's easy!

The first file shown is the *routers* file, which describes a set of routers to *smail*. When *smail* has to deliver a message to a given address, it hands the address to all routers in turn until one of them matches it. Matching here means that the router finds the destination host in its database, be it the *paths* file, */etc/hosts*, or whatever routing mechanism the router interfaces to.

Entries in *smail* configuration files always begin with a unique name identifying the router, transport, or director. They are followed by a list of attributes that define its behavior. This list consists of a set of global attributes, such as the *driver* used, and private attributes that are only understood by that particular driver. Attributes are separated by commas, while the sets of global and private attributes are separated from each other using a semicolon.

To make these fine distinctions clear, assume you want to maintain two separate *pathalias* files; one containing the routing information for your domain, and a second containing global routing information, probably generated from the UUCP maps. With *smail*, you can now specify two routers in the *routers* file, both of which use the `pathalias` driver. This driver looks up hostnames in a pathalias database. It expects to be given the name of the file in a private attribute:

```
#
# pathalias database for intra-domain routing
domain_paths:
        driver=pathalias,       # look up host in a paths file
        transport=uux;          # if matched, deliver over UUCP
        file=paths/domain,      # file is /usr/lib/smail/paths/domain
        proto=lsearch,          # file is unsorted (linear search)
        optional,               # ignore if the file does not exist
        required=vbrew.com,     # look up only *.vbrew.com hosts
```

```
#
# pathalias database for routing to hosts outside our domain
world_paths:
        driver=pathalias,       # look up host in a paths file
        transport=uux;          # if matched, deliver over UUCP
        file=paths/world,       # file is /usr/lib/smail/paths/world
        proto=bsearch,          # file is sorted with sort(1)
        optional,               # ignore if the file does not exist
        -required,              # no required domains
        domain=uucp,            # strip ending ".uucp" before searching
```

The second global attribute given in each of the two *routers* entries above defines the transport that should be used when the router matches the address. In our case, the message will be delivered using the *uux* transport. Transports are defined in the *transports* file, which is explained below.

You can fine-tune which transport a message will be delivered by if you specify a method file instead of the `transports` attribute. Method files provide a mapping from target hostnames to transports. We won't deal with them here.

The following *routers* file defines routers for a local area network that query the resolver library. On an Internet host, however, you would want to use a router that handles MX records. You should therefore uncomment the alternative inet_bind router that uses *smail*'s built-in BIND driver.

In an environment that mixes UUCP and TCP/IP, you may encounter the problem that you have hosts in your */etc/hosts* file that you have only occasional SLIP or PPP contact with. Usually, you would still want to send any mail for them over UUCP. To prevent the `inet_hosts` driver from matching these hosts, you have to put them into the *paths/force* file. This is another pathalias-style database and is consulted before *smail* queries the resolver.

```
# A sample /usr/lib/smail/routers file
#
# force - force UUCP delivery to certain hosts, even when
#         they are in our /etc/hosts
force:
        driver=pathalias,       # look up host in a paths file
        transport=uux;          # if matched, deliver over UUCP
        file=paths/force,       # file is /usr/lib/smail/paths/force
        optional,               # ignore if the file does not exist
        proto=lsearch,          # file is unsorted (linear search)
        -required,              # no required domains
        domain=uucp,            # strip ending ".uucp" before searching
# inet_addrs - match domain literals containing literal
#         IP addresses, such as in janet@[172.16.2.1]
inet_addrs:
        driver=gethostbyaddr,   # driver to match IP domain literals
        transport=smtp;         # deliver using SMTP over TCP/IP
        fail_if_error,          # fail if address is malformed
        check_for_local,        # deliver directly if host is ourself
```

```
    # inet_hosts - match hostnames with gethostbyname(3N)
    #        Comment this out if you wish to use the BIND version instead.
    inet_hosts:
            driver=gethostbyname,       # match hosts with the library function
            transport=smtp;             # use default SMTP
            -required,                  # no required domains
            -domain,                    # no defined domain suffixes
            -only_local_domain,         # don't restrict to defined domains
    # inet_hosts - alternate version using BIND to access the DNS
    #inet_hosts:
    #       driver=bind,                # use built-in BIND driver
    #       transport=smtp;             # use TCP/IP SMTP for delivery
    #
    #       defnames,                   # use standard domain searching
    #       defer_no_connect,           # try again if the nameserver is down
    #       -local_mx_okay,             # fail (don't pass through) an MX
    #                                   # to the local host
    #
    # pathalias database for intra-domain routing
    domain_paths:
            driver=pathalias,           # look up host in a paths file
            transport=uux;              # if matched, deliver over UUCP
            file=paths/domain,          # file is /usr/lib/smail/paths/domain
            proto=lsearch,              # file is unsorted (linear search)
            optional,                   # ignore if the file does not exist
            required=vbrew.com,         # look up only *.vbrew.com hosts
    #
    # pathalias database for routing to hosts outside our domain
    world_paths:
            driver=pathalias,           # look up host in a paths file
            transport=uux;              # if matched, deliver over UUCP
            file=paths/world,           # file is /usr/lib/smail/paths/world
            proto=bsearch,              # file is sorted with sort(1)
            optional,                   # ignore if the file does not exist
            -required,                  # no required domains
            domain=uucp,                # strip ending ".uucp" before searching
    # smart_host - a partically specified smarthost director
    #       If the smart_path attribute is not defined in
    #       /usr/lib/smail/config, this router is ignored.
    #       The transport attribute is overridden by the global
    #       smart_transport variable
    smart_host:
            driver=smarthost,           # special-case driver
            transport=uux;              # by default deliver over UUCP
            -path,                      # use smart_path config file variable
```

The handling of mail for local addresses is configured in the *directors* file. It is made up just like the *routers* file, with a list of entries that each define a director. Directors do *not* deliver a message, they merely perform all the redirection that is possible, for instance, through aliases, mail forwarding, and the like.

When delivering mail to a local address, such as *janet*, *smail* passes the username to all directors in turn. If a director matches, it either specifies a transport the message should be delivered by (for instance, to the user's mailbox file) or generates a new address (for instance, after evaluating an alias).

Because of the security issues involved, directors usually do a lot of checking for whether the files they use may be compromised or not. Addresses obtained in a somewhat dubious way (for instance, from a world-writable *aliases* file) are flagged as unsecure. Some transport drivers will turn down such addresses, for instance, the transport that delivers a message to a file.

Apart from this, *smail* also *associates a user* with each address. Any write or read operations are performed as the user. For delivery to **janet**'s mailbox, the address is of course associated with **janet**. Other addresses, such as those obtained from the *aliases* file, have other users associated with them, for instance, the **nobody** user.

For details of these features, please refer to the *smail(8)* manpage.

```
# A sample /usr/lib/smail/directors file
# aliasinclude - expand ":include:filename" addresses produced
#        by alias files
aliasinclude:
        driver=aliasinclude,     # use this special-case driver
        nobody;                  # access file as nobody user if unsecure
        copysecure,              # get permissions from alias director
        copyowners,              # get owners from alias director
# forwardinclude - expand ":include:filename" addrs produced
#        by forward files
forwardinclude:
        driver=forwardinclude,   # use this special-case driver
        nobody;                  # access file as nobody user if unsecure
        checkpath,               # check path accessibility
        copysecure,              # get perms from forwarding director
        copyowners,              # get owners from forwarding director
# aliases - search for alias expansions stored in a database
aliases:
        driver=aliasfile,        # general-purpose aliasing director
        -nobody,                 # all addresses are associated
                                 # with nobody by default anyway
        sender_okay,             # don't remove sender from expansions
        owner=owner-$user;       # problems go to an owner address
        file=/usr/lib/aliases,   # default: sendmail compatible
        modemask=002,            # should not be globally writable
        optional,                # ignore if file does not exist
        proto=lsearch,           # unsorted ASCII file
# dotforward - expand .forward files in user home directories
dotforward:
        driver=forwardfile,      # general-purpose forwarding director
        owner=real-$user,        # problems go to the user's mailbox
        nobody,                  # use nobody user, if unsecure
```

```
        sender_okay;                # sender never removed from expansion
        file=~/.forward,            # .forward file in home directories
        checkowner,                 # the user can own this file
        owners=root,                # or root can own the file
        modemask=002,               # it should not be globally writable
        caution=0-10:uucp:daemon,   # don't run things as root or daemons
        # be extra careful of remotely accessible home directories
        unsecure="~ftp:~uucp:~nuucp:/tmp:/usr/tmp",
# forwardto - expand a "Forward to " line at the top of
#       the user's mailbox file
forwardto:
        driver=forwardfile,
        owner=Postmaster,           # errors go to Postmaster
        nobody,                     # use nobody user, if unsecure
        sender_okay;                # don't remove sender from expansion
        file=/var/spool/mail/${lc:user}, # location of user's mailbox
        forwardto,                  # enable "Forward to " check
        checkowner,                 # the user can own this file
        owners=root,                # or root can own the file
        modemask=0002,              # under System V, group mail can write
        caution=0-10:uucp:daemon,   # don't run things as root or daemons
# user - match users on the local host with delivery to their mailboxes
user:   driver=user;                # driver to match usernames
        transport=local,            # local transport goes to mailboxes
# real_user - match usernames when prefixed with the string "real-"
real_user:
        driver=user;                # driver to match usernames
        transport=local,            # local transport goes to mailboxes
        prefix="real-",             # for example, match real-root
# lists - expand mailing lists stored below /usr/lib/smail/lists
lists:  driver=forwardfile,
        caution,                    # flag all addresses with caution
        nobody,                     # and then associate the nobody user
        sender_okay,                # do NOT remove the sender
        owner=owner-$user;          # the list owner
        # map the name of the mailing list to lower case
        file=lists/${lc:user},
```

After successfully routing or directing a message, *smail* hands the message to the transport specified by the router or director that matches the address. These transports are defined in the *transports* file. Again, a transport is defined by a set of global and private options.

The most important option defined by each entry is the driver that handles the transport, for instance the `pipe` driver, which invokes the command specified in the `cmd` attribute. Apart from this, there are a number of global attributes a transport may use that perform various transformations on the message header and possibly the message body. The `return_path` attribute, for instance, makes the transport insert a `Return_Path` field in the message header. The `unix_from_hack` attribute makes it precede every occurrence of the word `From` at the beginning of a line with a > character.

```
# A sample /usr/lib/smail/transports file
# local - deliver mail to local users
local:  driver=appendfile,         # append message to a file
        return_path,               # include a Return-Path: field
        from,                      # supply a From_ envelope line
        unix_from_hack,            # insert > before From in body
        local;                     # use local forms for delivery
        file=/var/spool/mail/${lc:user}, # location of mailbox files
        group=mail,                # group to own file for System V
        mode=0660,                 # group mail can access
        suffix="\n",               # append an extra newline
# pipe - deliver mail to shell commands
pipe:   driver=pipe,               # pipe message to another program
        return_path,               # include a Return-Path: field
        from,                      # supply a From_ envelope line
        unix_from_hack,            # insert > before From in body
        local;                     # use local forms for delivery
        cmd="/bin/sh -c $user",    # send address to the Bourne Shell
        parent_env,                # environment info from parent addr
        pipe_as_user,              # use user-id associated with address
        ignore_status,             # ignore a non-zero exit status
        ignore_write_errors,       # ignore write errors, i.e., broken pipe
        umask=0022,                # umask for child process
        -log_output,               # do not log stdout/stderr
# file - deliver mail to files
file:   driver=appendfile,
        return_path,               # include a Return-Path: field
        from,                      # supply a From_ envelope line
        unix_from_hack,            # insert > before From in body
        local;                     # use local forms for delivery
        file=$user,                # file is taken from address
        append_as_user,            # use user-id associated with address
        expand_user,               # expand ~ and $ within address
        suffix="\n",               # append an extra newline
        mode=0600,                 # set permissions to 600
# uux - deliver to the rmail program on a remote UUCP site
uux:    driver=pipe,
        uucp,                      # use UUCP-style addressing forms
        from,                      # supply a From_ envelope line
        max_addrs=5,               # at most 5 addresses per invocation
        max_chars=200;             # at most 200 chars of addresses
        cmd="/usr/bin/uux - -r -a$sender -g$grade $host!rmail $(($user)$)",
        pipe_as_sender,            # have uucp logs contain caller
        log_output,                # save error output for bounce messages
#       defer_child_errors,        # retry if uux returns an error
# demand - deliver to a remote rmail program, polling immediately
demand: driver=pipe,
        uucp,                      # use UUCP-style addressing forms
        from,                      # supply a From_ envelope line
        max_addrs=5,               # at most 5 addresses per invocation
        max_chars=200;             # at most 200 chars of addresses
        cmd="/usr/bin/uux - -a$sender -g$grade $host!rmail $(($user)$)",
```

```
        pipe_as_sender,            # have uucp logs contain caller
        log_output,                # save error output for bounce messages
#       defer_child_errors,        # retry if uux returns an error
# hbsmtp - half-baked BSMTP. The output files must
#       be processed regularly and sent out via UUCP.
hbsmtp: driver=appendfile,
        inet,                      # use RFC 822-addressing
        hbsmtp,                    # batched SMTP w/o HELO and QUIT
        -max_addrs, -max_chars;    # no limit on number of addresses
        file="/var/spool/smail/hbsmtp/$host",
        user=root,                 # file is owned by root
        mode=0600,                 # only read-/writeable by root.
# smtp - deliver using SMTP over TCP/IP
smtp:   driver=tcpsmtp,
        inet,
        -max_addrs, -max_chars;    # no limit on number of addresses
        short_timeout=5m,              # timeout for short operations
        long_timeout=2h,               # timeout for longer SMTP operations
        service=smtp,                  # connect to this service port
# For internet use: uncomment the below 4 lines
#       use_bind,                      # resolve MX and multiple A records
#       defnames,                      # use standard domain searching
#       defer_no_connect,              # try again if the nameserver is down
#       -local_mx_okay,                # fail an MX to the local host
```

COPYRIGHT AND LICENSING INFORMATION

In this appendix, we reprint the GNU General Public License (the *GPL* or *copyleft*), under which Linux is licensed. It is reproduced here to clear up some of the confusion about Linux's copyright status—Linux is *not* shareware, and it is *not* in the public domain. The bulk of the Linux kernel is Copyright © 1993 by Linus Torvalds, and other software and parts of the kernel are copyrighted by their authors. Thus, Linux *is* copyrighted; however, you may redistribute it under the terms of the GPL.

Many networking utilities and daemons used in Linux were ported from the Berkeley Software Distribution of UNIX. The copyright agreement by which the University of Berkeley makes this software available to the public is different from the GNU public license that covers the kernel and the Free Software Foundation. In this appendix, we print the source code copyright and redistribution information that appears on BSD source files.

Complete copyright information for this book is given first. It is a continuation of information contained on the copyright page at the beginning of this book.

Linux Network Administrator's Guide— Copyright Information

Copyright © 1993-1995 Olaf Kirch
Kattreinstr. 38, 64295 Darmstadt, Germany
okir@monad.swb.de

UNIX is a trademark of Univel.
Linux is not a trademark, and has no connection to UNIX or Univel.

The version of the *Linux Network Administrator's Guide* that has been distributed through the Linux Documentation Project may be reproduced under the conditions described here.

The O'Reilly & Associates, Inc. edition of this book cannot be photocopied or otherwise reproduced.

The Linux Network Administrator's Guide may be reproduced and distributed in whole or in part, subject to the following conditions:

1.   The copyright notice above and this permission notice must be preserved complete on all complete or partial copies.

2.   Any translation or derivative work of *The Linux Network Administrator's Guide* must be approved by the author in writing before distribution.

3.   If you distribute *The Linux Network Administrator's Guide* in part, instructions for obtaining the complete version of *The Linux Network Administrator's Guide* must be included, and a means for obtaining a complete version provided.

4.   Small portions may be reproduced as illustrations for reviews or **quotes** in other works without this permission notice if proper citation is given.

5.   The GNU General Public License referenced below may be reproduced under the conditions given within it.

6.   Several sections of this document are held under separate copyright. When these sections are covered by a different copyright, the seperate copyright is noted. **If you distribute The Linux Network Administrator's Guide in part, and that part is, in whole, covered under a seperate, noted copyright, the conditions of that copyright apply.**

Exceptions to these rules may be granted for academic purposes: Write to Olaf Kirch at the above address, or email *okir@monad.swb.de*, and ask. These restrictions are here to protect us as authors, not to restrict you as educators and learners.

All source code in *The Linux Network Administrator's Guide* is placed under the GNU General Public License. This appendix contains a copy of the GNU "GPL."

The author is not liable for any damages, direct or indirect, resulting from the use of information provided in this document.

GNU GENERAL PUBLIC LICENSE Version 2, June 1991

Copyright © 1989, 1991 Free Software Foundation, Inc. 675 Mass Ave, Cambridge, MA 02139, USA. Everyone is permitted to copy and distribute verbatim copies of this license document, but changing it is not allowed.

Preamble

The licenses for most software are designed to take away your freedom to share and change it. By contrast, the GNU General Public License is intended to guarantee your freedom to share and change free software—to make sure the software is free for all its users. This General Public License applies to most of the Free Software Foundation's software and to any other program whose authors commit to using it. (Some other Free Software Foundation software is covered by the GNU Library General Public License instead.) You can apply it to your programs, too.

When we speak of free software, we are referring to freedom, not price. Our General Public Licenses are designed to make sure that you have the freedom to distribute copies of free software (and charge for this service if you wish), that you receive source code or can get it if you want it, that you can change the software or use pieces of it in new free programs; and that you know you can do these things.

To protect your rights, we need to make restrictions that forbid anyone to deny you these rights or to ask you to surrender the rights. These restrictions translate to certain responsibilities for you if you distribute copies of the software, or if you modify it.

For example, if you distribute copies of such a program, whether gratis or for a fee, you must give the recipients all the rights that you have. You must make sure that they, too, receive or can get the source code. And you must show them these terms so they know their rights.

We protect your rights with two steps: (1) copyright the software, and (2) offer you this license which gives you legal permission to copy, distribute and/or modify the software.

Also, for each author's protection and ours, we want to make certain that everyone understands that there is no warranty for this free software. If the software is modified by someone else and passed on, we want its recipients to know that what they have is not the original, so that any problems introduced by others will not reflect on the original authors' reputations.

Finally, any free program is threatened constantly by software patents. We wish to avoid the danger that redistributors of a free program will individually obtain patent licenses, in effect making the program proprietary. To prevent this, we have made it clear that any patent must be licensed for everyone's free use or not licensed at all.

The precise terms and conditions for copying, distribution and modification follow.

Terms and Conditions for Copying, Distribution, and Modification

1. This License applies to any program or other work which contains a notice placed by the copyright holder saying it may be distributed under the terms of this General Public License. The "Program", below, refers to any such program or work, and a "work based on the Program" means either the Program or any derivative work under copyright law: that is to say, a work containing the Program or a portion of it, either verbatim or with modifications and/or translated into another language. (Hereinafter, translation is included without limitation in the term "modification".) Each licensee is addressed as "you".

   Activities other than copying, distribution and modification are not covered by this License; they are outside its scope. The act of running the Program is not restricted, and the output from the Program is covered only if its contents constitute a work based on the Program (independent of having been made by running the Program). Whether that is true depends on what the Program does.

2. You may copy and distribute verbatim copies of the Program's source code as you receive it, in any medium, provided that you conspicuously and appropriately publish on each copy an appropriate copyright notice and disclaimer of warranty; keep intact all the notices that refer to this License and to the absence of any warranty; and give any other recipients of the Program a copy of this License along with the Program.

   You may charge a fee for the physical act of transferring a copy, and you may at your option offer warranty protection in exchange for a fee.

3. You may modify your copy or copies of the Program or any portion of it, thus forming a work based on the Program, and copy and distribute such modifications or work under the terms of Section 1 above, provided that you also meet all of these conditions:

   a. You must cause the modified files to carry prominent notices stating that you changed the files and the date of any change.

   b. You must cause any work that you distribute or publish, that in whole or in part contains or is derived from the Program or any part thereof, to be licensed as a whole at no charge to all third parties under the terms of this License.

   c. If the modified program normally reads commands interactively when run, you must cause it, when started running for such interactive use in the most ordinary way, to print or display an announcement including an appropriate copyright notice and a notice that there is no warranty (or else, saying that you provide a warranty) and that users may redistribute the program under these conditions, and telling the user how to view a copy of this License. (Exception: if the Program itself is interactive but does not normally print such an announcement, your work based on the Program is not required to print an announcement.)

These requirements apply to the modified work as a whole. If identifiable sections of that work are not derived from the Program, and can be reasonably considered independent and separate works in themselves, then this License, and its terms, do not apply to those sections when you distribute them as separate works. But when you distribute the same sections as part of a whole which is a work based on the Program, the distribution of the whole must be on the terms of this License, whose permissions for other licensees extend to the entire whole, and thus to each and every part regardless of who wrote it.

Thus, it is not the intent of this section to claim rights or contest your rights to work written entirely by you; rather, the intent is to exercise the right to control the distribution of derivative or collective works based on the Program.

In addition, mere aggregation of another work not based on the Program with the Program (or with a work based on the Program) on a volume of a storage or distribution medium does not bring the other work under the scope of this License.

4. You may copy and distribute the Program (or a work based on it, under Section 2) in object code or executable form under the terms of Sections 1 and 2 above provided that you also do one of the following:

    a. Accompany it with the complete corresponding machine-readable source code, which must be distributed under the terms of Sections 1 and 2 above on a medium customarily used for software interchange; or,

    b. Accompany it with a written offer, valid for at least three years, to give any third party, for a charge no more than your cost of physically performing source distribution, a complete machine-readable copy of the corresponding source code, to be distributed under the terms of Sections 1 and 2 above on a medium customarily used for software interchange; or,

    c. Accompany it with the information you received as to the offer to distribute corresponding source code. (This alternative is allowed only for noncommercial distribution and only if you received the program in object code or executable form with such an offer, in accord with Subsection b above.)

The source code for a work means the preferred form of the work for making modifications to it. For an executable work, complete source code means all the source code for all modules it contains, plus any associated interface definition files, plus the scripts used to control compilation and installation of the executable. However, as a special exception, the source code distributed need not include anything that is normally distributed (in either source or binary form) with the major components (compiler, kernel, and so on) of the operating system on which the executable runs, unless that component itself accompanies the executable.

If distribution of executable or object code is made by offering access to copy from a designated place, then offering equivalent access to copy the source code from the same place counts as distribution of the source code, even though third parties are not compelled to copy the source along with the object code.

5.   You may not copy, modify, sublicense, or distribute the Program except as expressly provided under this License. Any attempt otherwise to copy, modify, sublicense or distribute the Program is void, and will automatically terminate your rights under this License. However, parties who have received copies, or rights, from you under this License will not have their licenses terminated so long as such parties remain in full compliance.

6.   You are not required to accept this License, since you have not signed it. However, nothing else grants you permission to modify or distribute the Program or its derivative works. These actions are prohibited by law if you do not accept this License. Therefore, by modifying or distributing the Program (or any work based on the Program), you indicate your acceptance of this License to do so, and all its terms and conditions for copying, distributing or modifying the Program or works based on it.

7.   Each time you redistribute the Program (or any work based on the Program), the recipient automatically receives a license from the original licensor to copy, distribute or modify the Program subject to these terms and conditions. You may not impose any further restrictions on the recipients' exercise of the rights granted herein. You are not responsible for enforcing compliance by third parties to this License.

8.   If, as a consequence of a court judgment or allegation of patent infringement or for any other reason (not limited to patent issues), conditions are imposed on you (whether by court order, agreement or otherwise) that contradict the conditions of this License, they do not excuse you from the conditions of this License. If you cannot distribute so as to satisfy simultaneously your obligations under this License and any other pertinent obligations, then as a consequence you may not distribute the Program at all. For example, if a patent license would not permit royalty-free redistribution of the Program by all those who receive copies directly or indirectly through you, then the only way you could satisfy both it and this License would be to refrain entirely from distribution of the Program.

If any portion of this section is held invalid or unenforceable under any particular circumstance, the balance of the section is intended to apply and the section as a whole is intended to apply in other circumstances.

It is not the purpose of this section to induce you to infringe any patents or other property right claims or to contest validity of any such claims; this section has the sole purpose of protecting the integrity of the free software distribution system, which is implemented by public license practices. Many people have made generous contributions to the wide range of software distributed through that system in reliance on consistent application of that system; it is up to the author/donor to decide if he or she is willing to distribute software through any other system and a licensee cannot impose that choice.

This section is intended to make thoroughly clear what is believed to be a consequence of the rest of this License.

9. If the distribution and/or use of the Program is restricted in certain countries either by patents or by copyrighted interfaces, the original copyright holder who places the Program under this License may add an explicit geographical distribution limitation excluding those countries, so that distribution is permitted only in or among countries not thus excluded. In such case, this License incorporates the limitation as if written in the body of this License.

10. The Free Software Foundation may publish revised and/or new versions of the General Public License from time to time. Such new versions will be similar in spirit to the present version, but may differ in detail to address new problems or concerns.

   Each version is given a distinguishing version number. If the Program specifies a version number of this License which applies to it and "any later version", you have the option of following the terms and conditions either of that version or of any later version published by the Free Software Foundation. If the Program does not specify a version number of this License, you may choose any version ever published by the Free Software Foundation.

11. If you wish to incorporate parts of the Program into other free programs whose distribution conditions are different, write to the author to ask for permission. For software which is copyrighted by the Free Software Foundation, write to the Free Software Foundation; we sometimes make exceptions for this. Our decision will be guided by the two goals of preserving the free status of all derivatives of our free software and of promoting the sharing and reuse of software generally.

12. NO WARRANTY

   BECAUSE THE PROGRAM IS LICENSED FREE OF CHARGE, THERE IS NO WARRANTY FOR THE PROGRAM, TO THE EXTENT PERMITTED BY APPLICABLE LAW. EXCEPT WHEN OTHERWISE STATED IN WRITING THE COPYRIGHT HOLDERS AND/OR OTHER PARTIES PROVIDE THE PROGRAM "AS IS" WITHOUT WARRANTY OF ANY KIND, EITHER EXPRESSED OR IMPLIED, INCLUDING, BUT NOT LIMITED TO, THE IMPLIED WARRANTIES OF MERCHANTABILITY AND FITNESS FOR A PARTICULAR PURPOSE. THE ENTIRE RISK AS TO THE QUALITY AND PERFORMANCE OF THE PROGRAM IS

WITH YOU. SHOULD THE PROGRAM PROVE DEFECTIVE, YOU ASSUME THE COST OF ALL NECESSARY SERVICING, REPAIR OR CORRECTION.

13. IN NO EVENT UNLESS REQUIRED BY APPLICABLE LAW OR AGREED TO IN WRITING WILL ANY COPYRIGHT HOLDER, OR ANY OTHER PARTY WHO MAY MODIFY AND/OR REDISTRIBUTE THE PROGRAM AS PERMITTED ABOVE, BE LIABLE TO YOU FOR DAMAGES, INCLUDING ANY GENERAL, SPECIAL, INCIDENTAL OR CONSEQUENTIAL DAMAGES ARISING OUT OF THE USE OR INABILITY TO USE THE PROGRAM (INCLUDING BUT NOT LIMITED TO LOSS OF DATA OR DATA BEING RENDERED INACCURATE OR LOSSES SUSTAINED BY YOU OR THIRD PARTIES OR A FAILURE OF THE PROGRAM TO OPERATE WITH ANY OTHER PROGRAMS), EVEN IF SUCH HOLDER OR OTHER PARTY HAS BEEN ADVISED OF THE POSSIBILITY OF SUCH DAMAGES.

END OF TERMS AND CONDITIONS

Appendix: How to Apply These Terms to Your New Programs

If you develop a new program, and you want it to be of the greatest possible use to the public, the best way to achieve this is to make it free software which everyone can redistribute and change under these terms.

To do so, attach the following notices to the program. It is safest to attach them to the start of each source file to most effectively convey the exclusion of warranty; and each file should have at least the "copyright" line and a pointer to where the full notice is found.

> `<one line to give the program's name and a brief idea of what it does.>` Copyright © 19yy `<name of author>`

This program is free software; you can redistribute it and/or modify it under the terms of the GNU General Public License as published by the Free Software Foundation; either version 2 of the License, or (at your option) any later version.

This program is distributed in the hope that it will be useful, but WITHOUT ANY WARRANTY; without even the implied warranty of MERCHANTABILITY or FITNESS FOR A PARTICULAR PURPOSE. See the GNU General Public License for more details.

You should have received a copy of the GNU General Public License along with this program; if not, write to the Free Software Foundation, Inc., 675 Mass Ave, Cambridge, MA 02139, USA.

Also add information on how to contact you by electronic and paper mail.

If the program is interactive, make it output a short notice like this when it starts in an interactive mode:

```
Gnomovision version 69, Copyright (C) 19yy name of author
Gnomovision comes with ABSOLUTELY NO WARRANTY; for details type `show w'.
This is free software, and you are welcome to redistribute it
under certain conditions; type `show c' for details.
```

The hypothetical commands "show w" and "show c" should show the appropriate parts of the General Public License. Of course, the commands you use may be called something other than "show w" and "show c"; they could even be mouse-clicks or menu items—whatever suits your program.

You should also get your employer (if you work as a programmer) or your school, if any, to sign a "copyright disclaimer" for the program, if necessary. Here is a sample; alter the names·

Yoyodyne, Inc., hereby disclaims all copyright interest in the program 'Gnomovision' (which makes passes at compilers) written by James Hacker.

<signature of Ty Coon>, 1 April 1989 Ty Coon, President of Vice

This General Public License does not permit incorporating your program into proprietary programs. If your program is a subroutine library, you may consider it more useful to permit linking proprietary applications with the library. If this is what you want to do, use the GNU Library General Public License instead of this License.

The Berkeley Software Distribution Copyright

Redistribution and use in source and binary forms, with or without modification, are permitted provided that the following conditions are met:

1. Redistributions of source code must retain the above copyright notice, this list of conditions and the following disclaimer.

2. Redistributions in binary form must reproduce the above copyright notice, this list of conditions and the following disclaimer in the documentation and/or other materials provided with the distribution.

3. All advertising materials mentioning features or use of this software must display the following acknowledgement:

    This product includes software developed by the University of California, Berkeley and its contributors.

4. Neither the name of the University nor the names of its contributors may be used to endorse or promote products derived from this software without specific prior written permission.

THIS SOFTWARE IS PROVIDED BY THE REGENTS AND CONTRIBUTORS "AS IS" AND ANY EXPRESS OR IMPLIED WARRANTIES, INCLUDING, BUT NOT LIMITED TO, THE IMPLIED WARRANTIES OF MERCHANTABILITY AND FITNESS FOR A PARTICULAR PURPOSE ARE DISCLAIMED. IN NO EVENT SHALL THE REGENTS OR CONTRIBUTORS BE LIABLE FOR ANY DIRECT, INDIRECT, INCIDENTAL, SPECIAL, EXEMPLARY, OR CONSEQUENTIAL DAMAGES (INCLUDING, BUT NOT LIMITED TO, PROCUREMENT OF SUBSTITUTE GOODS OR SERVICES; LOSS OF USE, DATA, OR PROFITS; OR BUSINESS INTERRUPTION) HOWEVER CAUSED AND ON ANY THEORY OF LIABILITY, WHETHER IN CONTRACT, STRICT LIABILITY, OR TORT (INCLUDING NEGLIGENCE OR OTHERWISE) ARISING IN ANY WAY OUT OF THE USE OF THIS SOFTWARE, EVEN IF ADVISED OF THE POSSIBILITY OF SUCH DAMAGE.

SAGE:
THE SYSTEM ADMINISTRATORS GUILD

If you are not getting everything you need from posting to *comp.os.linux.** groups and reading documentation, maybe it's time to consider joining SAGE, the System Administrators Guild, sponsored by Usenix. The main goal of SAGE is to advance system administration as a profession. SAGE brings together system and network administrators to foster professional and technical development, share problems and solutions, and communicate with users, management, and vendors on system administration topics.

Current SAGE initiatives include:

- Co-sponsoring with USENIX the highly successful, annual System Administration (LISA) Conferences.

- Publishing "Job Descriptions for System Administrators," edited by Tina Darmohray, the first in a series of very practical booklets and resource guides covering system administration issues and techniques.

- Creating an archive site, **ftp.sage.usenix.org**, for papers from the System Administration Conferences and sysadmin-related documentation.

- Establishing working groups in areas important to system administrators, such as jobs, publications, policies, electronic information distribution, education, vendors, and standards.

To learn more about the USENIX Association and its Special Technical Group, SAGE, contact the USENIX Association office at 510-528-8649 in the U.S. or by email to *office@usenix.org*. To receive information electronically, finger *info@usenix.org*. Annual membership in SAGE is just $25 (you must also be a member of USENIX). Members enjoy free subscriptions to *;login:* and Computing Systems, a refereed technical quarterly; discounts on conference and symposia registration; and savings on purchases of publications and other services.

GLOSSARY

An enormous difficulty in networking is to remember what all the abbreviations and terms one encounters really mean. Here's a list of those used frequently throughout the guide, along with a short explanation.

ACU
> Automatic Call Unit. A modem.

ARP
> Address Resolution Protocol. Used to map IP addresses to Ethernet addresses.

ARPA
> Advanced Research Project Agency, later DARPA. Founder of the Internet.

ARPANET
> The ancestor of today's Internet; an experimental network funded by the U.S. Defense Advanced Research Project Agency (DARPA).

Assigned Numbers
> The title of an RFC published regularly that lists the publicly allocated numbers used for various things in TCP/IP networking. For example, it contains the list of all port numbers of well-known services like *rlogin*, *telnet*, etc. The most recent release of this document is RFC 1340.

bang path
> In UUCP networks, a special notation for the path from one UUCP site to another. The name derives from the use of exclamation marks ("bangs") to separate the hostnames. Example: *foo!bar!ernie!bert* denotes a path to host **bert**, traveling (in this order) through **foo**, **bar**, and **ernie**.

BBS
> Bulletin Board System. A dial-up mailbox system.

BGP

Border Gateway Protocol. A protocol for exchanging routing information between autonomous systems.

BIND

The Berkeley Internet Name Domain server. An implementation of a DNS server.

BNU

Basic Networking Utilities. This is the most common UUCP variety at the moment. It is also known as HoneyDanBer UUCP. This name is derived from the authors' names: P. Honeyman, D.A. Novitz, and B.E. Redman.

broadcast network

A network that allows one station to address a datagram to all other stations on the network simultaneously.

BSD

Berkeley Software Distribution. A UNIX flavor.

canonical hostname

A host's primary name within the Domain Name System. This is the host's only name that has an A record associated with it, and which is returned when performing a reverse lookup.

CCITT

Comiteé Consultatif International de Télégraphique et Téléphonique. An International organization of telephone services, etc.

CSLIP

Compressed Serial Line IP. A protocol for exchanging IP packets over a serial line, using header compression of most TCP/IP datagrams.

DNS

Domain Name System. This is a distributed database used on the Internet for mapping of hostnames to IP addresses.

EGP

External Gateway Protocol. A protocol for exchanging routing information between autonomous systems.

Ethernet

> In colloquial terms, the name of a sort of network equipment. Technically, Ethernet is part of a set of standards set forth by the IEEE. The Ethernet hardware uses a single piece of cable, frequently co-ax cable, to connect a number of hosts, and allows transfer rates of up to 10 Mbps. The Ethernet protocol defines the manner in which hosts may communicate over this cable.[*]

FQDN

> Fully Qualified Domain Name. A hostname with a domain name tacked onto it so that it is a valid index into the Domain Name database.

FTP

> File Transfer Protocol. The protocol one of the best-known file transfer service is based on and named after.

FYI

> "For Your Information." Series of documents with informal information on Internet topics.

GMU

> Groucho Marx University. Fictitious university used as an example throughout this book.

GNU

> "GNU's not Unix"—this recursive acronym is the name of a project by the Free Software Association to provide a coherent set of UNIX-tools that may be used and copied free of charge. All GNU software is covered by a special copyright notice called the GNU General Public License (GPL), or Copyleft. The GPL is reproduced in Appendix C, *Copyright and Licensing Information*.

HoneyDanBer

> The name of a UUCP variety. See also BNU.

host

> Generally, a network node: something that is able to receive and transmit network messages. This will usually be a computer, but you can also think of X terminals, or smart printers.

---

[*] As an aside, the Ethernet protocol commonly used by TCP/IP is *not* exactly the same as IEEE 802.3. Ethernet frames have a type field where IEEE 802.3 frames have a length field.

ICMP
> Internet Control Message Protocol. A networking protocol used by IP to return error information to the sending host, etc.

IEEE
> Institute of Electrical and Electronics Engineers. Another standards organization. From a UNIX user's point of view, their most important achievements are probably the POSIX standards, which define aspects of UNIX systems ranging from system call interfaces and semantics to administration tools. Apart from this, the IEEE developed the specifications for Ethernet, Token Ring, and Token Bus networks. A widely-used standard for binary representation of real numbers is also due to the IEEE.

IETF
> Internet Engineering Task Force.

internet
> A computer network formed of a collection of individual smaller networks.

Internet
> A particular world-wide internet.

IP
> Internet Protocol. A networking protocol.

ISO
> International Standards Organization.

ISDN
> Integrated Services Digital Network. New telecommunications technology using digital instead of analogue circuitry.

LAN
> Local Area Network. A small computer network.

MX
> Mail Exchanger. A DNS resource record type used for marking a host as a mail gateway for a domain.

network, packet-switched
> A variety of networks that provide instantaneous forwarding of data by breaking all data up in small packets, which are tramsported to their destination individually. Packet-switched networks rely on permanent or semi-permanent connections.

network, store-and-forward

This is pretty much the opposite of a packet-switched network. These networks transfer data as entire files and don't use permanent connections. Instead, hosts connect to each other only at certain intervals and transfer all data at once. This requires that data be stored intermediately until a connection is established.

NFS

Network File System. A standard networking protocol and software suite for accessing data on remote disks transparently.

NIS

Network Information System. An RPC-based application that allows the sharing of configuration files such as the password file between several hosts. See also the entry under YP.

NNTP

Network News Transfer Protocol. Used to transfer news over TCP network connections.

octet

On the Internet, the technical term referring to a quantity of eight bits. It is used rather than *byte*, because there are machines on the Internet that have byte sizes other than eight bits.

OSI

Open Systems Interconnection. An ISO standard on network software.

path

Often used in UUCP networks as a synonym for *route*. Also see *bang path*.

PLIP

Parallel Line IP. A protocol for exchanging IP packets over a parallel line such as a printer port.

port, TCP or UDP

Ports are TCP's and UDP's abstraction of a service endpoint. Before a process can provide or access some networking service, it must claim (bind) a port. Together with the hosts' IP addresses, ports uniquely identify the two peers of a TCP connection.

portmapper

The portmapper is the mediator between the program numbers used by RPC as an identification of individual RPC servers, and the TCP and UDP port numbers those services are listening to.

PPP

The point-to-point protocol. PPP is a flexible and fast link-layer protocol used to send various network protocols such as IP or IPX across a point-to-point connection. Apart from being used on serial (modem) links, PPP can also be employed as the link-level protocol on top of ISDN.

RARP

Reverse Address Resolution Protocol. It permits hosts to find out their IP address at boot time.

resolver

This is a library responsible for mapping hostnames to IP addresses and vice versa.

resource record

This is the basic unit of information in the DNS database, commonly abbreviated as RR. Each record has a certain type and class associated with it, for instance, a record mapping a hostname to an IP address has a type of A (for address) and a class of IN (for the Internet Protocol).

reverse lookup

The act of looking up a host's name based on a given IP address. Within DNS, this is done by looking up the host's IP address in the **in-addr.arpa** domain.

RFC

Request For Comments. Series of documents describing Internet standards.

RIP

Routing Information Protocol. This is a routing protocol used to dynamically adjust routes inside a (small) network.

route

The sequence of hosts that a piece of information has to travel through from the originating host to the destination host. Finding an appropriate route is also called *routing*.

routing daemon

In larger networks, network topology changes are hard to adapt to manually, so facilities are used to distribute current routing information to the network's member hosts. This is called dynamic routing; the routing information is exchanged by *routing daemons* running on central hosts in the network. The protocols they employ are called *routing protocols*.

RPC

Remote Procedure Call. Protocol for executing procdures inside a process on a remote host.

RR

Short for *resource record*.

RS-232

This is a very common standard for serial interfaces.

RTS/CTS

A colloquial name for the hardware handshake performed by two devices communicating over RS-232. The name derives from the two circuits involved, RTS ("Ready To Send") and CTS ("Clear To Send").

RTM Internet Worm

A virus-like program that used several flaws in VMS and BSD 4.3 Unix to spread through the Internet. Several "mistakes" in the program caused it to multiply without bound, and so effectively bringing down large parts of the Internet. RTM is the author's initials (Robert T. Morris), which he left in the program.

site

An agglomeration of hosts which, to the outside, behave almost like a single network node. For example, when speaking from an Internet point of view, one would call Groucho Marx University a site, regardless of the complexity of its interior network.

SLIP

Serial Line IP. This is a protocol for exchanging IP packets over a serial line. See also *CSLIP*.

SMTP

Simple Mail Transfer Protocol. Used for mail transport over TCP connections, but also for mail batches transported over UUCP links (batched SMTP).

SOA
> Start of Authority. A DNS resource record type.

System V
> A UNIX flavor.

TCP
> Transmission Control Protocol. A networking protocol.

TCP/IP
> Sloppy description of the Internet protocol suite as a whole.

UDP
> User Datagram Protocol. A networking protocol.

UUCP
> Unix to Unix Copy. A suite of network transport commands for dial-up networks.

Version 2 UUCP
> An aging UUCP variety.

virtual beer
> Every Linuxer's favorite drink. The first mention of virtual beer I remember was in the release notes of the Linux 0.98.X kernel, where Linus listed the "Oxford Beer Trolls" in his credits section for sending along some virtual beer.

well-known services
> This term is frequently used to refer to common networking services such as *telnet* and *rlogin*. In a more technical sense, it describes all services that have been assigned an official port number in the Assigned Numbers RFC.

YP
> Yellow Pages. An older name for NIS which is no longer used, because Yellow Pages is a trademark of British Telecom. Nevertheless, most NIS utilities have retained names with a prefix of *yp*.

BIBLIOGRAPHY

Related Books

[Computer Networks] Tanenbaum, Andrew S. *Computer Networks*. Prentice Hall
   International. 1989.

> This book gives you a very good insight into general networking issues. Using the OSI
> Reference Model, it explains the design issues of each layer, and the algorithms that
> may be used to achieve these. At each layer, the implementations of several networks,
> among them the ARPAnet, are compared to each other. The only drawback this book
> has is the abundance of abbreviations, which sometimes makes it hard to follow what
> the author says. But this is probably inherent to networking.

[Connecting] Estrada, Susan. *Connecting to the Internet: An O'Reilly Buyer's Guide*.
   O'Reilly & Associates. 1993.

> This contains practical advice for choosing an Internet provider and a type of Internet
> feed. It helps you decide the type of service you need and evaluate the different costs
> cited by different vendors. The book includes an international list of Internet providers.

[DNS] Albitz, Paul, and Liu, Cricket. *DNS and BIND*. O'Reilly & Associates. 1992.

> This book is useful for all who have to manage DNS name service. It explains all fea-
> tures of DNS in great detail and give examples that make even those BIND options
> plausible that appear outright weird at first sight. I found it fun to read, and really
> learned a lot from it.

[Expect] Libes, Don. *Exploring Expect: A Tcl-based Toolkit for Automating Interactive Programs*. O'Reilly & Associates. 1995.

[Installation] Welsh, Matt. *Installation and Getting Started Guide*. Linux Documentation Project.

> This books helps you to get a Linux distribution running on your system. It covers all
> installation tasks, from the basics of creating your filesystems up to initial system
> administration tasks.

[Internetworking] Comer, Douglas R. *Internetworking with TCP/IP, Volume 1: Principles, Protocols, and Architecture*. Prentice Hall International. 1991.

[Linux—Unleashing] Strobel, Stefan, and Uhl, Thomas. *Linux—Unleashing the Workstation in Your PC*. Springer-Verlag. 1994.

Also available in German, this book is an introduction to the packages available for Linux, and a guide to its installation and configuration.

[Managing UUCP] O'Reilly, Tim, and Todino, Grace. *Managing UUCP and Usenet, 10th ed.* O'Reilly & Associates. 1992.

This is the standard book on UUCP networking. It covers Version 2 UUCP as well as BNU. It helps you to set up your UUCP node from the start, giving practical tips and solutions for many problems, like testing the connection, or writing good chat scripts. It also deals with more exotic topics, like how to set up a travelling UUCP node, or the subtleties present in different flavors of UUCP. The second part of the book deals with Usenet and Netnews software. It explains the configuration of both B News (version 2.11) and C News, and introduces you to netnews maintenance tasks.

[NFS and NIS] Stern, Hal. *Managing NFS and NIS*. O'Reilly & Associates. 1992.

This is a companion book to Craig Hunt's TCP/IP book. It covers the use of NIS, the Network Information System, and NFS, the Network File System, in extenso, including the configuration of an automounter, and PC/NFS.

[NIS+] Ramsey, Rick. *All about Administering NIS+*. Prentice Hall. 1993.

[Running Linux] Welsh, Matt. *Running Linux*. O'Reilly & Associates. 1995.

Another, more comprehensive book that covers the same ground as the same author's *Installation and Getting Started Guide*, but with additional information about free software tools that are provided with Linux distributions.

[sendmail] Costales, Bryan, with Eric Allman and Neil Rickert. *sendmail*. O'Reilly & Associates. 1993.

A complete book about installing this package, serving both as guide and reference.

[TCP/IP] Hunt, Craig. *TCP/IP Network Administration*. O'Reilly & Associates. 1992.

If the Linux Network Administrators' Guide is not enough for you, get this book. It deals with everything from obtaining an IP address to troubleshooting your network to security issues. Its focus is on setting up TCP/IP, that is, interface configuration, the setup of routing, and name resolution. It includes a detailed description of the facilities offered by the routing daemons *routed* and *gated*, which supply dynamic routing.

It also describes the configuration of application programs and network daemons, such as *inetd*, the *r* commands, NIS, and NFS. The appendix has a detailed reference of *gated*, and *named*, and a description of Berkeley's *sendmail* configuration.

[UNIX Network Programming] Stevens, Richard W. *UNIX Network Programming*. Prentice Hall International. 1990.

This is probably *the* most widely used book on TCP/IP network programming, which, at the same time, tells you a lot about the nuts and bolts of the Internet Protocols.[*]

[UNIX Security] Garfinkel, Simson, and Spafford, Gene. *Practical UNIX Security*. O'Reilly & Associates. 1992.

This is a must-have for everyone who manages a system with network access, and for others as well. The book discusses all issues relevant to computer security, ranging from the basic security features UNIX offers to physical security. Although you should strive to secure all parts of your system, the discussion of networks and security is the most interesting part of the book in our context. Apart from basic security policies that concern the Berkeley services (*telnet*, *rlogin*, etc.), NFS, and NIS, it also deals with enhanced security features like MIT's Kerberos, Sun's Secure RPC, and the use of fire-walls to shield your network from attacks from the Internet.

[Whole Internet] Krol, Ed. *The Whole Internet User's Guide & Catalog, 2nd Ed.* O'Reilly & Associates. 1994.

A guide to all the services on the Internet, including full instructions on using them plus a listing of popular sites.

[Zen] Kehoe, Brendan P. *Zen and the Art of the Internet.*

"Zen" was probably *the* first Internet Guides, introducing the novice user to the various trades, services and the folklore of the Internet. Being a 100-page tome, it covers topics ranging from email to Usenet news to the Internet Worm. It is available via anonymous FTP from many FTP servers, and may be freely distributed and printed. A printed copy is also available from Prentice Hall.

HOWTOs

The following is an excerpt of the HOWTO-INDEX, version 2.0 (17 March 1994), written by Matt Welsh.

What are Linux HOWTOs? Linux HOWTOs are short online documents which describe in detail a certain aspect of configuring or using the Linux system. For example, there is the Installation HOWTO, which gives instructions on installing Linux, and the Mail HOWTO, which describes how to set up and configure mail under Linux. Other examples include the NET-2-HOWTO (previously the NET-2-FAQ) and the Printing HOWTO. Information in HOWTOs is generally more detailed and in-depth than what can be squeezed into the Linux FAQ. For this reason, the Linux FAQ is being rewritten. A large amount of the information

---

[*] Note that Stevens has just written a new TCP/IP, called *TCP/IP Illustrated, Volume 1, The Protocols*, published by Addison Wesley. I didn't have the time to look at it, though.

contained therein will be relegated to various HOWTO documents. The FAQ will be a shorter list of frequently asked questions about Linux, covering small specific topics. Most of the "useful" information in the FAQ will now be covered in the HOWTOs.

HOWTOs are comprehensive documents—much like an FAQ but generally not in question-and-answer format. However, many HOWTOs contain an FAQ section at the end. For example, the NET-2-FAQ has been renamed to the NET-2-HOWTO, because it wasn't in question-and-answer format. However, you will see the NET-2-HOWTO named as the NET-2-FAQ in many places. The two docs are one and the same.

HOWTOs can be retrieved via anonymous FTP from the following sites, as well as the many mirror sites, which are listed in the Linux META-FAQ (see below).

```
sunsite.unc.edu:/pub/Linux/docs/HOWTO
tsx-11.mit.edu:/pub/linux/docs/HOWTO
```

The Index, printed below, lists the currently available HOWTOs. HOWTOs are also posted regularly to the newsgroups *comp.os.linux* and *comp.os.linux.announce*. In addition, a number of the HOWTOs will be crossposted to *news.answers*. Therefore, you can find the Linux HOWTOs on the *news.answers* archive site **rtfm.mit.edu**.

The following Linux HOWTOs are currently available.

Linux Busmouse HOWTO, by Battersby, Mike. Information on bus mouse compatibility with Linux.

Linux CDROM HOWTO, by Tranter, Jeff. Information on CD-ROM drive compatibility for Linux.

Linux Distribution HOWTO, by Welsh, Matt. A list of mail order distributions and other commercial services.

Linux DOSEMU HOWTO, by Deisher, Michael E. HOWTO about the Linux MS-DOS Emulator, DOSEMU.

Linux Ethernet HOWTO, by Gortmaker, Paul. Information on Ethernet hardware compatibility for Linux.

Linux Ftape HOWTO, by maintainer, Linux ftape-HOWTO. Information on ftape drive compatibility with Linux.

Linux Hardware Compatibility HOWTO, by Carp, Ed. A near-extensive list of hardware known to work with Linux.

Linux HOWTO Index, by Welsh, Matt. Index of HOWTO documents about Linux.

Linux Installation HOWTO, by Welsh, Matt. How to obtain and install the Linux software.

Linux JE-HOWTO, by Yamazaki, Yasuhiro. Information on JE, a set of Japanese language extensions for Linux.

Linux Keystroke HOWTO, by Fortuna, Zenon. How to bind macro actions to keystrokes under Linux.

Linux MGR HOWTO, by Broman, Vincent. Information on the MGR graphics interface for Linux.

Linux Electronic Mail HOWTO, by Skahan, Vince. Information on Linux-based mail servers and clients.

Linux NET-2 HOWTO, by Dawson, Terry. How to configure TCP/IP networking, SLIP, PLIP, and PPP under Linux.

Linux News HOWTO, by Skahan, Vince. Information on Usenet news server and client software for Linux.

The Linux NIS(YP)/NIS+/NYS HOWTO, by Dell'Amico, Andrea, DSouza, Mitchum, and Embsen, Erwin. Introduction and installation information for NIS packages.

Linux PCI-HOWTO, by Will, Michael. Information on PCI-architecture compatibility with Linux.

Linux Printing HOWTO, by Taylor, Grant. HOWTO on printing software for Linux.

Linux SCSI HOWTO, by Eckhardt, Drew. Information on SCSI driver compatibility with Linux.

Linux Serial HOWTO, by Hankins, Greg. Information on use of serial devices and communications software.

Linux Sound HOWTO, by Tranter, Jeff. Sound hardware and software for the Linux operating system.

Linux Term HOWTO, by Reynolds, Bill. HOWTO use the "term" communications package on Linux systems.

Linux Tips HOWTO, by Reed, Vince. HOWTO on miscellaneous tips and tricks for Linux.

Linux UUCP HOWTO, by Skahan, Vince. Information on UUCP software for Linux.

XFree86 HOWTO, by Geyer, Helmut. HOWTO on installation of XFree86.

RFCs

RFC 1597. *Address Allocation for Private Internets*. Rekhter, Y., and Watson, T.J., et al.

> This RFC lists the IP network numbers private organizations can use internally without having to register these network numbers with the Internet Assigned Numbers Authority (IANA). The document also discusses the advatanges and disadvantages of using these numbers.

RFC 1340. *Assigned Numbers*. Postel, J., and Reynolds, J.

> The Assigned Numbers RFC defines the meaning of numbers used in various protocols, such as the port numbers standard TCP and UDP servers are known to listen on, and the protocol numbers used in the IP datagram header.

RFC 1144. *Compressing TCP/IP headers for low-speed serial links*. Jacobson, V.

> This document describes the algorithm used to compress TCP/IP headers in CSLIP and PPP. Very worthwhile reading!

RFC 1033. *Domain Administrators Operations Guide*. Lottor, M.

> Together with its companion RFCs, RFC 1034 and RFC 1035, this is the definitive source on DNS, the Domain Name System.

RFC 1034. *Domain Names—Concepts and Facilities*. Mockapetris, P. V.

> A companion to RFC 1033.

RFC 1035. *Domain names—Implementation and Specification*. Mockapetris, P. V.

> A companion to RFC 1033.

RFC 974. *Mail Routing and the Domain System*. Partridge, C.

> This RFC describes mail routing on the Internet. Read this for the full story about MX records.

RFC 1548. *The Point-to-Point Protocol (PPP)*. Simpson, W. A.

> The standard for the PPP method of transporting datagrams over point-to-point links.

RFC 977. *Network News Transfer Protocol*. Kantor, B., and Lapsley, P.

> The definition of NNTP, the common news transport used on the Internet.

RFC 1094. *NFS: Network File System Protocol specification*. Nowicki, B.

> The formal specification of the NFS and mount protocols (version 2).

RFC 1055. *Nonstandard for Transmission of IP Datagrams over Serial Lines: SLIP*. Romkey, J. L.

> Describes SLIP, the Serial Line Internet Protocol.

RFC 1057. *RPC: Remote Procedure Call Protocol Specification: Version 2*. Sun Microsystems, Inc.

RFC 1058. *Routing Information Protocol*. Hedrick, C. L.

> Describes RIP, which is used to exchange dynamic routing information within LANs and MANs.

RFC 1535. *A Security Problem and Proposed Correction with Widely Deployed DNS Software*. Gavron, E.

> This RFC discusses a security problem with the default search list used by older versions of the BIND resolver library.

RFC 821. *Simple Mail Transfer Protocol*. Postel, J. B.

> Defines SMTP, the mail transport protocol over TCP/IP.

RFC 1036. *Standard for the Interchange of USENET messages*. Adams, R., and Horton, M. R.

> This RFC describes the format of Usenet News messages, and how they are exchanged on the Internet as well as on UUCP networks. A revision of this RFC is expected to be released in the near future.

RFC 822. *Standard for the Format of ARPA Internet text messages*. Crocker, D.

> This is the definitive source of wisdom regarding, well, RFC-conformant mail. Everyone knows it, few have really read it.

RFC 968. *Twas the Night Before Start-up*. Cerf, V.

> Who says the heroes of networking remain unsung?

INDEX

About the Author

Olaf Kirch has a degree in Mathematics from Technische Universitaet Darmstadt. He presently works as a UNIX programmer for a company producing a CAD system. A Linux fan for a couple of years now, he is amazed at the pace at which its development continues to progress.

For relaxation, Olaf likes painting, drawing, and reading (anything from nineteenth-century poetry to detective novels and Japanese manga). He likes to spend time outdoors whenever possible. He doesn't have a driver's license (never had one), so he goes about most of his daily routine by bicycle. When he gets away from his keyboard for more than a few days, he likes to go mountain-walking.

Colophon

Our look is the result of reader comments, our own experimentation, and feedback from distribution channels. Distinctive covers complement our distinctive approach to technical topics, breathing personality and life into potentially dry subjects.

Edie Freedman designed the cover of *Linux Network Administrator's Guide*. The cover image is adapted from a 19th-century engraving from *Marvels of the New West: A Vivid Portrayal of the Stupendous Marvels in the Vast Wonderland West of the Missouri River*, by William Thayer (The Henry Bill Publishing Co., Norwich, CT, 1888).

Thayer gives the following history of this graphic: "This illustration is not a fancy sketch. It is the photograph of a stockman, taken when he was mounted and ready to start for his ranch a few score of mile away. Wearing 'half an acre of hat' to protect his face from the hot sun, with a scarf about his neck for a like purpose, and his apparel well adapted to his business, his appearance is so changed that an introduction to his own wife may be quite necessary. He may be a millionaire, though he looks like a shack. He may be proud as Lucifer, but necessity arrays him in a homely dress; and he appears humble. Seated upon a Mexican saddle, which cost a hundred dollars, if it is a good one, and drawing upon the reins of a bridle that cost twenty-five or fifty more, if it is worthy of an aspiring stockman, he put spurs to his horse, and is off in a jiffy. Grass does not grow under his horse's feet. The animal is trained to the saddle, and the stockman is trained to him, and the two are so trained together, that they fly over the plain as if they were one thing, as much as the parts of a whole. It is a lonely ride to his ranch, forty, fifty, sixty, perhaps a hundred miles away; but his head is full of business and his heart of contentment—about the happiest looking man, though he may be the homeliest, to be found within cattledom. If he happens to pass a prairie post-office, the unique affair serves to remind him that humans do live in the 'silent and solemn country' through which he is passing."

The cover layout was produced with Quark XPress 3.3 and Adobe Photoshop 2.5 software, using the ITC Garamond Condensed font.

Jennifer Niederst and Edie Freedman designed the interior layouts. Chapter opening graphics are from the Dover Pictorial Archive and *Marvels of the New West*. Interior fonts are Adobe ITC Garamond and Adobe Courier. Text was prepared in SGML using the DocBook 2.1 DTD. The print version of this book was created by translating the SGML source into a set of gtroff macros using a filter developed at ORA by Norman Walsh. Steve Talbott designed and wrote the underlying macro set on the basis of the GNU gtroff -gs macros; Lenny Muellner adapted them to SGML and implemented the book design. The GNU groff text formatter version 1.08 was used to generate PostScript output.

The illustrations that appear in the book were created in Aldus Freehand 4.0 by Chris Reilley.

More Titles from O'Reilly

Linux

Linux in a Nutshell

*By Jessica P. Hekman &
the Staff of O'Reilly & Associates
1st Edition January 1997
438 pages, ISBN 1-56592-167-4*

Linux in a Nutshell covers the core
commands available on common Linux
distributions. This isn't a scaled-down quick
reference of common commands, but a
complete reference containing all user,
programming, administration, and networking commands.
Also documents a wide range of GNU tools.

Linux Multimedia Guide

*By Jeff Tranter
1st Edition September 1996
386 pages, ISBN 1 56592-219-0*

Linux is increasingly popular among
computer enthusiasts of all types, and one
of the applications where it is flourishing
is multimedia. This book tells you how to
program such popular devices as sound
cards, CD-ROMs, and joysticks. It also
describes the best free software packages that support manipulation
of graphics, audio, and video and offers guidance on fitting the
pieces together.

Running Linux, 2nd Edition

*By Matt Welsh & Lar Kaufman
2nd Edition August 1996
650 pages, ISBN 1-56592-151-8*

Linux is the most exciting development
today in the UNIX world—and some would
say in the world of the PC-compatible.
A complete, UNIX-compatible operating
system developed by volunteers on the
Internet, Linux is distributed freely in
electronic form and for low cost from many vendors. This
second edition of *Running Linux* covers everything you need to
understand, install, and start using your Linux system, including a
comprehensive installation tutorial, complete information on system
maintenance, tools for document development and programming,
and guidelines for network and web site administration.

Linux Device Drivers

*By Alessandro Rubini
1st Edition February 1998
432 pages, ISBN 1-56592-292-1*

This practical guide is for anyone who
wants to support computer peripherals
under the Linux operating system or who
wants to develop new hardware and run it
under Linux. It shows step-by-step how to
write a driver for character devices, block
devices, and network interfaces, illustrated with examples you
can compile and run. Focuses on portability.

Learning the bash Shell, 2nd Edition

*By Cameron Newham &
Bill Rosenblatt
2nd Edition January 1998
336 pages, ISBN 1-56592-347-2*

This second edition covers all of the
features of *bash* Version 2.0, while still
applying to *bash* Version 1.x. It includes
one-dimensional arrays, parameter
expansion, more pattern-matching
operations, new commands, security improvements, additions
to ReadLine, improved configuration and installation, and an
additional programming aid, the *bash* shell debugger.

Using Samba

*By Peter Kelly, Perry Donham &
David Collier-Brown
1st Edition July 1999 (est.)
300 pages (est.), Includes CD-ROM
ISBN 1-56592-449-5*

Samba turns a UNIX or Linux system into a
file and print server for Microsoft Windows
network clients. This complete guide to
Samba administration covers basic 2.0
configuration, security, logging, and troubleshooting. Whether
you're playing on one note or a full three-octave range, this book
will help you maintain an efficient and secure server. Includes a
CD-ROM of sources and ready-to-install binaries.

O'REILLY®

TO ORDER: **800-998-9938** • **order@oreilly.com** • **http://www.oreilly.com/**

OUR PRODUCTS ARE AVAILABLE AT A BOOKSTORE OR SOFTWARE STORE NEAR YOU.

FOR INFORMATION: **800-998-9938** • **707-829-0515** • **info@oreilly.com**

UNIX Basics

Learning the UNIX Operating System, 4th Edition

By Jerry Peek, Grace Todino & John Strang
4th Edition December 1997
106 pages, ISBN 1-56592-390-1

If you are new to UNIX, this concise introduction will tell you just what you need to get started and no more. The new fourth edition covers the Linux operating system and is an ideal primer for someone just starting with UNIX or Linux, as well as for Mac and PC users who encounter a UNIX system on the Internet. This classic book, still the most effective introduction to UNIX in print, now includes a quick-reference card.

Learning GNU Emacs, 2nd Edition

By Debra Cameron, Bill Rosenblatt & Eric Raymond
2nd Edition September 1996
560 pages, ISBN 1-56592-152-6

Learning GNU Emacs is an introduction to Version 19.30 of the GNU Emacs editor, one of the most widely used and powerful editors available under UNIX. It provides a solid introduction to basic editing, a look at several important "editing modes" (special Emacs features for editing specific types of documents, including email, Usenet News, and the World Wide Web), and a brief introduction to customization and Emacs LISP programming. The book is aimed at new Emacs users, whether or not they are programmers. Includes quick-reference card.

Volume 3M: X Window System User's Guide, Motif Edition, 2nd Edition

By Valerie Quercia & Tim O'Reilly
2nd Edition January 1993
956 pages, ISBN 1-56592-015-5

The *X Window System User's Guide, Motif Edition* orients the new user to window system concepts and provides detailed tutorials for many client programs, including the xtermterminal emulator and the twm, uwm, and mwm window managers. Later chapters explain how to customize the X environment. Revised for Motif 1.2 and X11 Release 5.

Learning the Korn Shell

By Bill Rosenblatt
1st Edition June 1993
360 pages, ISBN 1-56592-054-6

A thorough introduction to the Korn shell, both as a user interface and as a programming language. This book provides a clear explanation of the Korn shell's features, including *ksh* string operations, co-processes, signals and signal handling, and command-line interpretation. *Learning the Korn Shell* also includes real-life programming examples and a Korn shell debugger (*kshdb*).

Using csh and tcsh

By Paul DuBois
1st Edition August 1995
242 pages, ISBN 1-56592-132-1

Using csh and tcsh describes from the beginning how to use these shells interactively to get your work done faster with less typing. You'll learn how to make your prompt tell you where you are (no more pwd); use what you've typed before (history); type long command lines with few keystrokes (command and filename completion); remind yourself of filenames when in the middle of typing a command; and edit a botched command without retyping it.

Learning the vi Editor, 6th Edition

By Linda Lamb & Arnold Robbins
6th Edition October 1998
348 pages, ISBN 1-56592-426-6

This completely updated guide to editing with vi, the editor available on nearly every UNIX system, now covers four popular vi clones and includes command summaries for easy reference. It starts with the basics, followed by more advanced editing tools, such as ex commands, global search and replacement, and a new feature, multi-screen editing.

O'REILLY®

TO ORDER: **800-998-9938** • **order@oreilly.com** • **http://www.oreilly.com/**
OUR PRODUCTS ARE AVAILABLE AT A BOOKSTORE OR SOFTWARE STORE NEAR YOU.
FOR INFORMATION: **800-998-9938** • **707-829-0515** • **info@oreilly.com**

How to stay in touch with O'Reilly

1. Visit Our Award-Winning Web Site

http://www.oreilly.com/

★ "Top 100 Sites on the Web" —*PC Magazine*
★ "Top 5% Web sites" —*Point Communications*
★ "3-Star site" —*The McKinley Group*

Our web site contains a library of comprehensive product information (including book excerpts and tables of contents), downloadable software, background articles, interviews with technology leaders, links to relevant sites, book cover art, and more. File us in your Bookmarks or Hotlist!

2. Join Our Email Mailing Lists

New Product Releases

To receive automatic email with brief descriptions of all new O'Reilly products as they are released, send email to: **listproc@online.oreilly.com**
Put the following information in the first line of your message (*not* in the Subject field):
subscribe oreilly-news

O'Reilly Events

If you'd also like us to send information about trade show events, special promotions, and other O'Reilly events, send email to:
listproc@online.oreilly.com
Put the following information in the first line of your message (*not* in the Subject field):
subscribe oreilly-events

3. Get Examples from Our Books via FTP

There are two ways to access an archive of example files from our books:

Regular FTP

- ftp to:
  ftp.oreilly.com
  (login: anonymous
  password: your email address)
- Point your web browser to:
  ftp://ftp.oreilly.com/

FTPMAIL

- Send an email message to:
  ftpmail@online.oreilly.com
  (Write "help" in the message body)

4. Contact Us via Email

order@oreilly.com
To place a book or software order online. Good for North American and international customers.

subscriptions@oreilly.com
To place an order for any of our newsletters or periodicals.

books@oreilly.com
General questions about any of our books.

software@oreilly.com
For general questions and product information about our software. Check out O'Reilly Software Online at **http://software.oreilly.com/** for software and technical support information. Registered O'Reilly software users send your questions to: **website-support@oreilly.com**

cs@oreilly.com
For answers to problems regarding your order or our products.

booktech@oreilly.com
For book content technical questions or corrections.

proposals@oreilly.com
To submit new book or software proposals to our editors and product managers.

international@oreilly.com
For information about our international distributors or translation queries. For a list of our distributors outside of North America check out:
http://www.oreilly.com/www/order/country.html

O'Reilly & Associates, Inc.
101 Morris Street, Sebastopol, CA 95472 USA
TEL   707-829-0515 or 800-998-9938
          (6am to 5pm PST)
FAX   707-829-0104

O'REILLY®

Titles from O'Reilly

WEB
Advanced Perl Programming
Apache: The Definitive Guide,
   2nd Edition
ASP in a Nutshell
Building Your Own Web Conferences
Building Your Own Website™
CGI Programming with Perl
Designing with JavaScript
Dynamic HTML:
   The Definitive Reference
Frontier: The Definitive Guide
HTML: The Definitive Guide,
   3rd Edition
Information Architecture
   for the World Wide Web
JavaScript Pocket Reference
JavaScript: The Definitive Guide,
   3rd Edition
Learning VB Script
Photoshop for the Web
WebMaster in a Nutshell
WebMaster in a Nutshell,
   Deluxe Edition
Web Design in a Nutshell
Web Navigation:
   Designing the User Experience
Web Performance Tuning
Web Security & Commerce
Writing Apache Modules

PERL
Learning Perl, 2nd Edition
Learning Perl for Win32 Systems
Learning Perl/TK
Mastering Algorithms with Perl
Mastering Regular Expressions
Perl5 Pocket Reference, 2nd Edition
Perl Cookbook
Perl in a Nutshell
Perl Resource Kit—UNIX Edition
Perl Resource Kit—Win32 Edition
Perl/TK Pocket Reference
Programming Perl, 2nd Edition
Web Client Programming with Perl

GRAPHICS & MULTIMEDIA
Director in a Nutshell
Encyclopedia of Graphics
   File Formats, 2nd Edition
Lingo in a Nutshell
Photoshop in a Nutshell
QuarkXPress in a Nutshell

USING THE INTERNET
AOL in a Nutshell
Internet in a Nutshell
Smileys
The Whole Internet for Windows95
The Whole Internet:
   The Next Generation
The Whole Internet
   User's Guide & Catalog

JAVA SERIES
Database Programming with
   JDBC and Java
Developing Java Beans
Exploring Java, 2nd Edition
Java AWT Reference
Java Cryptography
Java Distributed Computing
Java Examples in a Nutshell
Java Foundation Classes in a Nutshell
Java Fundamental Classes Reference
Java in a Nutshell, 2nd Edition
Java in a Nutshell, Deluxe Edition
Java I/O
Java Language Reference, 2nd Edition
Java Media Players
Java Native Methods
Java Network Programming
Java Security
Java Servlet Programming
Java Swing
Java Threads
Java Virtual Machine

UNIX
Exploring Expect
GNU Emacs Pocket Reference
Learning GNU Emacs, 2nd Edition
Learning the bash Shell, 2nd Edition
Learning the Korn Shell
Learning the UNIX Operating System,
   4th Edition
Learning the vi Editor, 6th Edition
Linux in a Nutshell
Linux Multimedia Guide
Running Linux, 2nd Edition
SCO UNIX in a Nutshell
sed & awk, 2nd Edition
Tcl/Tk in a Nutshell
Tcl/Tk Pocket Reference
Tcl/Tk Tools
The UNIX CD Bookshelf
UNIX in a Nutshell, System V Edition
UNIX Power Tools, 2nd Edition
Using csh & tcsh
Using Samba
vi Editor Pocket Reference
What You Need To Know:
   When You Can't Find Your
   UNIX System Administrator
Writing GNU Emacs Extensions

SONGLINE GUIDES
NetLaw   NetResearch
NetLearning   NetSuccess
NetLessons   NetTravel

SOFTWARE
Building Your Own WebSite™
Building Your Own Web Conference
WebBoard™ 3.0
WebSite Professional™ 2.0
PolyForm™

SYSTEM ADMINISTRATION
Building Internet Firewalls
Computer Security Basics
Cracking DES
DNS and BIND, 3rd Edition
DNS on WindowsNT
Essential System Administration
Essential WindowsNT
   System Administration
Getting Connected:
   The Internet at 56K and Up
Linux Network Administrator's Guide
Managing IP Networks with
   Cisco Routers
Managing Mailing Lists
Managing NFS and NIS
Managing the WindowsNT Registry
Managing Usenet
MCSE: The Core Exams in a Nutshell
MCSE: The Electives in a Nutshell
Networking Personal Computers
   with TCP/IP
Oracle Performance Tuning,
   2nd Edition
Practical UNIX & Internet Security,
   2nd Edition
PGP: Pretty Good Privacy
Protecting Networks with SATAN
sendmail, 2nd Edition
sendmail Desktop Reference
System Performance Tuning
TCP/IP Network Administration,
   2nd Edition
termcap & terminfo
The Networking CD Bookshelf
Using & Managing PPP
Virtual Private Networks
WindowsNT Backup & Restore
WindowsNT Desktop Reference
WindowsNT Event Logging
WindowsNT in a Nutshell
WindowsNT Server 4.0 for
   Netware Administrators
WindowsNT SNMP
WindowsNT TCP/IP Administration
WindowsNT User Administration
Zero Administration for Windows

X WINDOW
Vol. 1: Xlib Programming Manual
Vol. 2: Xlib Reference Manual
Vol. 3M: X Window System
   User's Guide, Motif Edition
Vol. 4M: X Toolkit Intrinsics
   Programming Manual,
   Motif Edition
Vol. 5: X Toolkit Intrinsics
   Reference Manual
Vol. 6A: Motif Programming Manual
Vol. 6B: Motif Reference Manual
Vol. 8 : X Window System
   Administrator's Guide

PROGRAMMING
Access Database Design and
   Programming
Advanced Oracle PL/SQL
   Programming with Packages
Applying RCS and SCCS
BE Developer's Guide
BE Advanced Topics
C++: The Core Language
Checking C Programs with lint
Developing Windows Error Messages
Developing Visual Basic Add-ins
Guide to Writing DCE Applications
High Performance Computing,
   2nd Edition
Inside the Windows 95 File System
Inside the Windows 95 Registry
lex & yacc, 2nd Edition
Linux Device Drivers
Managing Projects with make
Oracle8 Design Tips
Oracle Built-in Packages
Oracle Design
Oracle PL/SQL Programming,
   2nd Edition
Oracle Scripts
Oracle Security
Palm Programming:
   The Developer's Guide
Porting UNIX Software
POSIX Programmer's Guide
POSIX.4: Programming
   for the Real World
Power Programming with RPC
Practical C Programming, 3rd Edition
Practical C++ Programming
Programming Python
Programming with curses
Programming with GNU Software
Pthreads Programming
Python Pocket Reference
Software Portability with imake,
   2nd Edition
UML in a Nutshell
Understanding DCE
UNIX Systems Programming for SVR4
VB/VBA in a Nutshell: The Languages
Win32 Multithreaded Programming
Windows NT File System Internals
Year 2000 in a Nutshell

USING WINDOWS
Excel97 Annoyances
Office97 Annoyances
Outlook Annoyances
Windows Annoyances
Windows98 Annoyances
Windows95 in a Nutshell
Windows98 in a Nutshell
Word97 Annoyances

OTHER TITLES
PalmPilot: The Ultimate Guide

O'REILLY®

TO ORDER: **800-998-9938** • **order@oreilly.com** • **http://www.oreilly.com/**
OUR PRODUCTS ARE AVAILABLE AT A BOOKSTORE OR SOFTWARE STORE NEAR YOU.
FOR INFORMATION: **800-998-9938** • **707-829-0515** • **info@oreilly.com**

International Distributors

UK, EUROPE, MIDDLE EAST AND AFRICA (EXCEPT FRANCE, GERMANY, AUSTRIA, SWITZERLAND, LUXEMBOURG, LIECHTENSTEIN, AND EASTERN EUROPE)

INQUIRIES
O'Reilly UK Limited
4 Castle Street
Farnham
Surrey, GU9 7HS
United Kingdom
Telephone: 44-1252-711776
Fax: 44-1252-734211
Email: josette@oreilly.com

ORDERS
Wiley Distribution Services Ltd.
1 Oldlands Way
Bognor Regis
West Sussex PO22 9SA
United Kingdom
Telephone: 44-1243-779777
Fax: 44-1243-820250
Email: cs-books@wiley.co.uk

FRANCE

ORDERS
GEODIF
61, Bd Saint-Germain
75240 Paris Cedex 05, France
Tel: 33-1-44-41-46-16 (French books)
Tel: 33-1-44-41-11-87 (English books)
Fax: 33-1-44-41-11-44
Email: distribution@eyrolles.com

INQUIRIES
Éditions O'Reilly
18 rue Séguier
75006 Paris, France
Tel: 33-1-40-51-52-30
Fax: 33-1-40-51-52-31
Email: france@editions-oreilly.fr

GERMANY, SWITZERLAND, AUSTRIA, EASTERN EUROPE, LUXEMBOURG, AND LIECHTENSTEIN

INQUIRIES & ORDERS
O'Reilly Verlag
Balthasarstr. 81
D-50670 Köln
Germany
Telephone: 49-221-973160-91
Fax: 49-221-973160-8
Email: anfragen@oreilly.de (inquiries)
Email: order@oreilly.de (orders)

CANADA (FRENCH LANGUAGE BOOKS)
Les Éditions Flammarion ltée
375, Avenue Laurier Ouest
Montréal (Québec) H2V 2K3
Tel: 00-1-514-277-8807
Fax: 00-1-514-278-2085
Email: info@flammarion.qc.ca

HONG KONG
City Discount Subscription Service, Ltd.
Unit D, 3rd Floor, Yan's Tower
27 Wong Chuk Hang Road
Aberdeen, Hong Kong
Tel: 852-2580-3539
Fax: 852-2580-6463
Email: citydis@ppn.com.hk

KOREA
Hanbit Media, Inc.
Sonyoung Bldg. 202
Yeksam-dong 736-36
Kangnam-ku
Seoul, Korea
Tel: 822-554-9610
Fax: 822-556-0363
Email: hant93@chollian.dacom.co.kr

PHILIPPINES
Mutual Books, Inc.
429-D Shaw Boulevard
Mandaluyong City, Metro
Manila, Philippines
Tel: 632-725-7538
Fax: 632-721-3056
Email: mbikikog@mnl.sequel.net

TAIWAN
O'Reilly Taiwan
No. 3, Lane 131
Hang-Chow South Road
Section 1, Taipei, Taiwan
Tel: 886-2-23968990
Fax: 886-2-23968916
Email: benh@oreilly.com

CHINA
O'Reilly Beijing
Room 2410
160, FuXingMenNeiDaJie
XiCheng District
Beijing, China PR 100031
Tel: 86-10-86631006
Fax: 86-10-86631007
Email: frederic@oreilly.com

INDIA
Computer Bookshop (India) Pvt. Ltd.
190 Dr. D.N. Road, Fort
Bombay 400 001 India
Tel: 91-22-207-0989
Fax: 91-22-262-3551
Email: cbsbom@giasbm01.vsnl.net.in

JAPAN
O'Reilly Japan, Inc.
Kiyoshige Building 2F
12-Bancho, Sanei-cho
Shinjuku-ku
Tokyo 160-0008 Japan
Tel: 81-3-3356-5227
Fax: 81-3-3356-5261
Email: japan@oreilly.com

ALL OTHER ASIAN COUNTRIES
O'Reilly & Associates, Inc.
101 Morris Street
Sebastopol, CA 95472 USA
Tel: 707-829-0515
Fax: 707-829-0104
Email: order@oreilly.com

AUSTRALIA
WoodsLane Pty., Ltd.
7/5 Vuko Place
Warriewood NSW 2102
Australia
Tel: 61-2-9970-5111
Fax: 61-2-9970-5002
Email: info@woodslane.com.au

NEW ZEALAND
Woodslane New Zealand, Ltd.
21 Cooks Street (P.O. Box 575)
Waganui, New Zealand
Tel: 64-6-347-6543
Fax: 64-6-345-4840
Email: info@woodslane.com.au

LATIN AMERICA
McGraw-Hill Interamericana
Editores, S.A. de C.V.
Cedro No. 512
Col. Atlampa
06450, Mexico, D.F.
Tel: 52-5-547-6777
Fax: 52-5-547-3336
Email: mcgraw-hill@infosel.net.mx

O'REILLY®